Pelican Books
Imperial China

Raymond Dawson is a Fellow of Wadham College, Oxford,
where, as an undergraduate, he read *Literae Humaniores*
and then Chinese. In 1952 he was appointed to the Spalding
Lectureship at Durham University. There he built up a
large museum collection, which led to the foundation of
the Gulbenkian Museum of Oriental Art in 1961. His
previous publications include *The Legacy of China, The
Chinese Chameleon, an Analysis of European Conceptions
of Chinese Civilization* and *An Introduction to Classical
Chinese.* He has also written two volumes of *New
Statesman* crossword puzzles, which he began composing
under the pseudonym of 'Set-square' to supplement his
student grant and which he has continued ever since.
Raymond Dawson is married and has three children. They
live at Garsington.

The History of Human Society

General Editor: J. H. Plumb

Raymond Dawson

Imperial China

Penguin Books
*by arrangement with
Hutchinson of London*

Penguin Books Ltd, Harmondsworth,
Middlesex, England
Penguin Books, 625 Madison Avenue, New York,
New York 10022, U.S.A.
Penguin Books Australia Ltd, Ringwood,
Victoria, Australia
Penguin Books Canada Ltd, 41 Steelcase Road West,
Markham, Ontario, Canada
Penguin Books (N.Z.) Ltd, 182–190 Wairau Road,
Auckland 10, New Zealand

First published by Hutchinson & Co. Ltd 1972
Published in Pelican Books 1976

Copyright © Raymond Dawson, 1972
Introduction © J. H. Plumb, 1972

Made and printed in Great Britain by
Hazell Watson & Viney Ltd, Aylesbury, Bucks
Set in Linotype Juliana

Contents

List of Illustrations

List of Maps

Preface

Dr Plumb's invitation to contribute to the *History of Human Society* came at a time when I was about to extend and bring up to date my reading on some of the periods of Chinese history covered by this book; so, although I have always been very well aware of the difficulties involved in attempting to compress the history of Imperial China into the space of a single volume, I felt that it would be wrong to refuse to collaborate in this valuable series, especially since it is extremely difficult to persuade scholars to abandon their special research interests and write on broader themes.

My task is not quite as formidable as it might have been, since the first imperial period, that of the Ch'in and Han Dynasties, will be described in the forthcoming volume on Classical China. The end of the Han will provide a convenient climax to that volume, since that dynasty represents the culmination of the development of Chinese society in its purest form. After its collapse the Buddhist religion spread rapidly and other foreign influences poured into the country, so that the new civilization which emerged in later imperial times was very different from the old Classical model of antiquity.

After the downfall of the Han nearly four centuries elapsed before the founding of the T'ang, which was the next of the great and viable dynasties. In the interim China had been under one rule for only a short period at the end of the third century until it was reunited in 589 by the Sui, the T'ang's short-lived predecessor; so in terms of lasting achievement this age is in most respects of minor importance in the history of human society as compared with the great dynasties that follow. I have therefore started my book with a comparatively short chapter recounting the history of China prior to the Sui Dynasty, including some account of the period which will eventually be covered by the volume on Classical China. This brief chapter is designed to give the reader such outline of the earlier history as is essential to an understanding of the twelve centuries of imperial Chinese history which form the main subject of the work. The final volume of this trilogy will be entitled *China and the West*, and will take up the story of the decline of traditional Chinese civilization in the nineteenth century and its transformation under the impact of the European powers and America. I therefore take leave of the reader in 1793, at Ch'ien-lung's summer palace, at the moment when the octogenarian emperor, the last monarch to preside over imperial China in the days of its greatness, is entertaining the Macartney Embassy, which is trying to secure better trading conditions for British merchants in China.

I should like to have been able to avoid using a single chrono-logical narrative, and instead to have dealt with the political, economic, social, cultural and other major aspects of Chinese history each in turn; but the long time-span covered by this book and the great changes in the shape and character of China during its imperial period render such an approach impossible. To understand the development of human society in China one has to attempt to interrelate the various forces, personal and political, economic and social, military and technological, which go to shape the course of history. This unfortunately means that such matters as art and literature, which are the adornments of a civilization rather than its flesh and bones, must take a secondary place; and, in any case, a serious attempt to deal with these topics would demand additional volumes rather than mere para-graphs. Nevertheless, in order to do more justice to these sub-jects than can conveniently be fitted into the book's narrative, I have tried to construct the illustrations section so that it does not merely throw light on certain items in the book, but rather pre-sents a kind of potted survey of Chinese culture.

For various pieces of help in connection with these illustrations I wish to thank Jonathan Clarke, S. Howard Hansford, Joseph Needham, Keith Pratt, Mary Tregear, and Roderick Whitfield. I am indebted to Patrick Cavendish for reading the book and per-suading me that it was worth publishing, and to my wife for various kinds of assistance. I am also profoundly grateful for the detailed researches of other scholars and sad that lack of space has prevented me from doing full justice to their work. I am sorry that I cannot acknowledge the heavy debt I owe to them without the apparatus of footnotes which is inappropriate to a series of this kind.

There are so many ways of writing general histories that it is difficult to strike the right balance. I have given more attention to the activities of emperors than may suit some contemporary tastes. This is partly because I wanted to pay some attention to the different characteristics of the reigns of important sovereigns in order to avoid the tendency of one-volume histories to generalize about whole dynasties, partly because I believe that the occupants of the dragon throne did play an important part in Chinese history, and partly because the general reader can reasonably expect to be told something about the lives of those rulers who have especially captured the imaginations of the Chinese people.

Throughout the writing of this volume I have been aware that Chinese history is so rich and complex and the sources so uneven in quality that it would be impossible for me, or indeed for anyone else, to produce a book which would satisfy specialist historians of China. On completing the book I am even more conscious that to distil from the lives of millions and the events of centuries something which can be read in a few hours is to get no nearer to a thorough understanding of China than a momentary glance can take in the complex personality of an individual human being. On the other hand I have been encouraged to persevere with the writing of such a book by the hope and belief that even a superficial knowledge of the other great civilizations not only has great intrinsic interest, but also gives the reader points of comparison which sharpen his awareness of the character of his own civilization, and at the same time fosters that deepened sense of our common humanity, which is the most hopeful guarantee of the future of our race on this planet.

RAYMOND DAWSON

Introduction

By J. H. Plumb

1

Over the last fifty to a hundred years man's belief that the historical process proved that he was acquiring a greater mastery over nature has received a brutal buffeting. In his early youth H. G. Wells, a man of vast creative energy, of rich delight in the human spirit, and of all-pervading optimism, viewed the future with confidence; science, born of reason, was to be humanity's panacea. When, in the years of his maturity, he came to write his *Outline of History*, his vision was darker, although still sustained with hope. World War I, with its senseless and stupid slaughter of millions of men, brought the sickening realization that man was capable of provoking human catastrophes on a global scale. The loss of human liberty, the degradations and brutalities imposed by fascism and communism during the 1920s and 1930s, followed in 1939 by the renewed world struggle, these events finally shattered Wells's eupeptic vision, and in sad and disillusioned old age he wrote *Mind at the End of its Tether*. His hope of mankind had almost vanished. Almost but not quite: for Wells's lifetime witnessed what, as a young writer, he had prophesied – technical invention not only on a prodigious scale but in those realms of human activity that affected the very core of society. And this extraordinary capacity of man to probe the complexities of nature and to invent machinery capable of exploiting his knowledge remained for Wells the only basis for hope, no matter how slender that might be.

If the belief of a man of Wells's passionate and intelligent humanism could be so battered and undermined, it is not surprising that lesser men were unable to withstand the climate of despair that engulfed the Western World between the two world wars. The disillusion of these years is apparent in painting, in music, in literature – everywhere in the Western World we are brought up sharply by an expression of anguish, by the flight from social and historical reality into a frightened, self-absorbed world of personal feeling and expression. Intellectual life, outside science, has pursued much the same course as artistic life, although it has shown greater ingenuity and a tougher-minded quality. Theology, philosophy and sociology have tended to reduce themselves to technical problems of exceptional professional complexity, but of small social importance. Their practitioners have largely ceased to instruct and enliven, let alone sustain the confidence of ordinary men and women.

In this atmosphere of cultural decay and of professional retreat, history and its philosophy have suffered. As in so many intellectual disciplines its professional workers have resolutely narrowed the focus of their interests to even more specialized fields of inquiry. The majority of historians have withdrawn from general culture, in order to maintain, at a high intellectual level, an academic discipline. They have left the meaning and purpose of history to trained philosophers and spent their leisure hours tearing to shreds the scholarship of anyone foolish enough to attempt to give the story of mankind a meaning and a purpose: writers as diverse as H. G. Wells and Arnold Toynbee have been butchered with consummate skill. The blunders of scholarship and the errors of interpretation have counted everything; intention nothing. Few academic historians, secure in the cultivation of their minute gardens, have felt any humility towards those who would tame the wilderness. In consequence, an atmosphere of anarchic confusion pervades the attitude of Western man to his past.

A hundred years ago, in the first flood of archaeological discovery, scholars possessed great confidence: the history of mankind seemed to most to point to an obvious law of human progress. The past was but a stepping-stone to the future. First adumbrated by the philosophers of the late Renaissance – Bodin in France and Bacon in England – the idea of progress became an article of common faith during the Enlightenment. And progress came to mean not only the technical progress that had preoccupied Bacon but also moral progress. By the nineteenth century the history of man demonstrated for many an improvement in the very nature of man himself as well as in his tools and weapons. Such optimism, such faith in man's capacity for rational behaviour, was shaken both by discoveries in science and in history as well as by events. By the middle of the twentieth century man's irrational drives appeared to be stronger than his intellectual capacities. Freud and Marx laid bare the hollow hypocrisy of so-called rational behaviour either in individuals or in society. Also, the rise and fall of civilizations, laid bare by the spade, seemed to point to a cynical pattern in human destiny which made nonsense of any idea of continuous progress; and this naturally attracted the prophets of Western doom. Yet more persuasive still, and, perhaps, more destructive of confidence in human destiny, was the utter loss of all sense of human control brought about by global wars and violent revolutions. Only those men or societies who felt life was going their way, the revolutionaries and, above all, the Marxists, believed any longer in the laws of historical progress. For the rest, retrogression seemed as tenable a thesis as progress.

This disillusion in the West suited academic historians. It relieved them of their most difficult problems. If they happened to be religious they were content to leave the ultimate meaning of history to God; if they were rationalists they took refuge either in the need for more historical knowledge or in the philosophic difficulties of a subject that by its very nature was devoid of the same objective treatment that gave such authority to scientific inquiry. In the main they concentrated upon their professional work. And this was an exceptionally important and necessary task. What the common reader rarely recognizes is the inadequacy of the factual material that was at the command of an historian one hundred years ago or even fifty years ago. Scarcely any archives were open to him; most repositories of records were unsorted and uncatalogued; almost every generalization about a man or an event or an historical process was three-quarters guesswork, if not more. Laboriously, millions of facts have been brought to light, ordered and rendered coherent within their own context. Specialization has proliferated like a cancer, making detail livid, but blurring the outlines of the story of mankind, and rendering it almost impossible for a professional historian to venture with confidence beyond his immediate province. And that can be very tiny – the Arkansas and Missouri Railway Strike of

1921; the place-names of Rutland; seventeenth-century Rouen; the oral history of the Barotse; the philosophy of Hincmar of Rheims. And so it becomes ever more difficult for the professional historian to reach across to ordinary intelligent men and women or make his subject a part of human culture. The historical landscape is blurred by the ceaseless activity of its millions of professional ants. Of course, attempts at synthesis have to be made. The need to train young professional historians, or the need to impart some knowledge of history to students of other disciplines, has brought about competent digests of lengthy periods that summarize both facts and analysis. Occasionally such books have been written with such skill and wisdom that they have become a part of the West's cultural heritage. A few historians, driven by money or fame or creative need, have tried to share their knowledge and understanding of the past with the public at large.

But the gap between professional knowledge and history for the masses gets steadily wider; professional history becomes more accurate, more profound, whilst public history remains tentative and shallow.

This series is an attempt to reverse this process. Each volume will be written by a professional historian of the highest technical competence; but these books will not exist *in vacuo*, for the series is designed to have a unity and a purpose. But, perhaps, first it is best to say what it is not.

It is not a work of reference: there are no potted biographies of the Pharaohs, the Emperors of China or the Popes; no date lists of battles; no brief histories of painting, literature, music. Nor is this series a Universal History. All events that were critical in the history of mankind may not necessarily find a place. Some will; some will not. Works of reference, more or less factually accurate, exist in plenty and need not be repeated. It is not my intention to add yet another large compilation to what exists. Nor is this a 'philosophic' history. It does not pretend to reveal a recurring pattern in history that will unveil its purpose. Fundamentally philosophy, except in the use of language, is as irrelevant to history as it is to science. And lastly this series will not cover all human societies. There will be two volumes devoted to Russia, none to Germany. There will be histories of China and Japan but not of Indonesia. The Jews have a volume to themselves, the Parsees do not. And so on. Yet the series is called *The History of Human Society* for very good reasons. This history has a theme and a position in time.

The theme is the most obvious and the most neglected; obvious because everyone is aware of it from the solitary villagers of Easter Island to the teeming cities of the Western World; neglected because it has been fashionable for professional and Western historians to concern themselves either with detailed professional history that cannot have a broad theme or with the spiritual and metaphysical aspects of man's destiny that are not his proper province. What, therefore, is the theme of *The History of Human Society*? It is this : that the condition of man now is superior to what it was. That two great revolutions – the neolithic and the industrial – have enabled men to establish vast societies of exceptional complexity in which the material well-being of generations of mankind has made remarkable advances; that the second, and most important, revolution has been achieved by the Western World; that we are witnessing its most intensive phase now, one in which ancient patterns of living are crumbling before the demands of industrial society; that life in the suburbs of London, Lagos, Djakarta, Rio de Janeiro and Vladivostok will soon have more in common than they have in difference; that this, therefore, is a moment to take stock, to unfold how this came about, to evoke the societies of the past whilst we are still close enough to many of them to feel intuitively the compulsion and needs of their pattern of living. I, however, hope, in these introductions, which it is my intention to write for each book, to provide a sense of unity. The authors themselves will not be so concerned with the overriding theme. Their aim will be to reconstruct the societies on which they are experts. They will lay bare the structure of their societies – their economic basis, their social organizations, their aspirations, their cultures, their religions and their conflicts. At the same time they will give a sense of what it was like to have lived in them. Each book will be an authoritative statement in its own right, and independent of the rest of the series. Yet each, set alongside the rest, will give a sense of how human society has changed and grown from the time man hunted and gathered his food to this nuclear and electronic age. This could only have been achieved by the most careful selection of authors. They needed, of course, to be established scholars of distinction, possessing the ability to write attractively for the general reader. They needed also to be wise, to possess steady, unflickering compassion for the strange necessities of men; to be quick in understanding, slow in judgement, and to have in them some of that relish for life, as fierce and as instinctive as an animal's, that has upheld ordinary men and women in the worst of times. The authors of these books are heart-wise historians with sensible, level heads.

The range and variety of human societies is almost as great as the range and variety of human temperaments, and the selection for this series is in some ways as personal as an anthology. A Chinese, a Russian, an Indian or an African would select a different series; but we are Western men writing for Western men. The westernization of the world by industrial technology is one of the main themes of the series. Each society selected has been in the main stream of this development or belongs to that vast primitive ocean whence all history is derived. Some societies are neglected because they would only illustrate in a duller way societies which appear in the series; some because their history is not well enough known to a sufficient depth of scholarship to be synthesized in this way; some because they are too insignificant.

There are, of course, very important social forces – feudalism, technological change or religion, for example – which have moulded a variety of human societies at the same time. Much can be learnt from the comparative study of their influence. I have, however, rejected this approach, once recorded history is reached. My reason for rejecting this method is because human beings experience these forces in communities, and it is the experience of men in society with which this series is primarily concerned.

Lastly, it need hardly be said that society is not always synonymous with the State. At times, as with the Jews, it lacks even territorial stability; yet the Jews provide a fascinating study of symbiotic social groupings, and to have left them out would be unthinkable, for they represent, in its best-known form, a wide human experience – a social group embedded in an alien society.

As well as a theme, which is the growth of man's control over his environment, this series may also fulfil a need. That is to restore a little confidence in man's capacity not only to endure the frequent catastrophes of human existence but also in his intellectual abilities. That many of his habits, both of mind and heart, are bestial, needs scarcely to be said. His continuing capacity for evil need not be stressed. His greed remains almost as strong as it was when he first shuffled on the ground. And yet the miracles created by his cunning are so much a part of our daily lives that we take their wonder for granted. Man's ingenuity – based securely on his capacity to reason – has won astonishing victories over the physical world – and in an amazingly brief span of time. Such triumphs, so frequently overlooked and even more frequently belittled, should breed a cautious optimism. Sooner or later, painfully perhaps and slowly, the same intellectual skill may be directed to the more difficult and intransigent problems of human living – man's social and personal relations – not only directed, but perhaps accepted, as the proper way of ordering human life. The story of man's progress over the centuries, studded with pitfalls and streaked with disaster as it is, ought to strengthen both hope and will.

Yet a note of warning must be sounded. The history of human society, when viewed in detail, is far more often darkened with tragedy than it is lightened with hope. As these books will show, life for the nameless millions of mankind who have already lived and died has been wretched, short, hungry and brutal. Few societies have secured peace; none stability for more than a few centuries; prosperity, until very recent times, was the lucky chance of a small minority. Consolations of gratified desire, the soothing narcotic of ritual, and the hope of future blessedness have often eased but rarely obliterated the misery which has been the lot of all but a handful of men since the beginning of history. At long last that handful is growing to a significant proportion in a few favoured societies. But throughout human history most men have derived pitifully little from their existence. A belief in human progress is not incompatible with a sharp realization of the tragedy not only of the lives of individual men but also of epochs, cultures and societies. Loss and defeat, too, are themes of this series, as well as progress and hope.

2

If one turns to a poem by Po Chü-i, or reads a biography by Ssu-ma Ch'ien, or contemplates a painting by Tung Ch'i-ch'ang, there are no serious difficulties in communication between the civilizations of China and of Europe; although in translation subtleties of tone and language may be lost and the painting at first glance seem in a strange idiom, the underlying emotions are those of our common experience. Nor do we find much difficulty intellectually with Confucius or even Mo Tzu, weirdly elliptical though he may be at times, for again their insights into social man would apply with equal pertinence to the West. And yet when we contemplate the whole panorama of Imperial China's past, its history is so very different from our own and the experience, the culture, the attitude to life of its myriad peoples subtly and strangely different from Europe's. There seem to be two separate worlds and civilizations cut apart by the great barriers of mountain and desert. This is a mirage, for Europe's life was changed time and time again by developments in China itself in ways that none realized. Mainly this was technological – printing, gunpowder, compasses, paper and much else, but each full of explosive consequences for Europe; more so, oddly enough, than for China itself, for many of the technological achievements of the Chinese people did not become the violent social catalysts that they did when transferred to Europe. One example must suffice : developments in hydraulics and in improved varieties of rice did indeed have a most dramatic effect in raising China's population which, in turn, led to economic diversity and to social and political complexities, but they did not help to change the fundamental nature of Chinese society in the way that gunpowder, printing and the compass helped to change Europe's. This was partly due to the odd nature of European society – its fragmentation, its aggressive ideologies and its economic imbalance that prevented it acquiring the stability that is so marked a feature of Chinese society, from the Han to the Ch'ing.*

The stability of Chinese civilization is perhaps the most fascinating of its qualities to the European historian whose working life is spent dealing with revolution, social conflict, nationalist wars and constant cultural change and at times destruction. Almost as amazing as the stability of China are the power and influence which scholars, artists and literati exercised not only in Chinese society, but also in Chinese government. In no civilization have intellectuals played so powerful a role.

One of the reasons, however, for both the stability of Chinese civilization and the influence of the mandarin-scholar often escapes notice – the nature of Chinese writing. And again, perhaps, this can best be illustrated if we compare the effect of printing on the civilization of China with its influence on Europe. After all, printing was invented in China in the T'ang period many centuries before Gutenberg, but its influence on Chinese society was far, far less than might have been expected. Printing not only makes knowledge more accurate as well as preserving it against loss, but also may permit a wide dissemination of learning : an edition of a hundred volumes can be printed in a fraction of the time that it would take to inscribe them by hand and, of course, at a fraction of the cost. Once printing was established in the West it created conditions for a possible cultural explosion; simply because the Western alphabet is easy to learn the alphabet prints an easy systematization of language and knowledge in alphabetical dictionaries, encyclopaedias, gazetteers. Any reasonably intelligent and dedicated man or woman can, once he has mastered the elements of reading, attack with confidence almost any branch of knowledge that is printed in his language. Hence, once printing had been established in the West there was the possibility of *cultural seepage* : a literate weaver or carpenter could read – not only the Bible or political tracts but also books that could improve his ability as a craftsman or businessman. Printing in the West not only intensified the possibilities of

---

*See my introduction to Donald Dudley, *Roman Society*, in this series.

ideological clashes between contending social groups, but also encouraged upward social mobility : the self-taught man is a common phenomenon in the West, rare in China, and furthermore the cost of teaching children was within the means of ambitious parents of very modest means in the West, rarely so in China. In order to cope with the printed language in China at a very, very modest level, one needs to master at least 4000 characters; without alphabetical dictionaries it is less easy to build rapidly on basic knowledge and to become so literate as to be able to master the classics of religion or government. This, in China, required years of study and hard work. Hence, although China invented printing, its social dynamic, although modest by Europe's experiences, was, nevertheless, important, for it enabled China to create a much larger scholarly class than would have been possible in a purely scribal society, one large enough to handle the administrative problems of the vast extension of Chinese power. Nevertheless the nature of its writing inhibited rapid cultural seepage and the scholarly arts were largely the monopoly of the mandarins and the scholar-gentry from which they came. Literacy was never – in a sense – so marketable in China as it became in the West and in consequence it was more socially confined – with profound social consequences. Literacy in China was always, before and after print, a far greater achievement for these Chinese than it had been for a Roman or a Greek, let alone for a European of modern times. In consequence even sophisticated and highly specialized social groups were dependent on the literate scholar to a degree that was unusual in Western society – armies and navies, for example, or commercial activity above the local or primitive level. The social importance, therefore, of the scholar was profound. For so complex a society as China was even by Han times, the scholars were essential, indeed crucial, for commerce as well as government; so crucial and so numerous that they were able to impose on government and society many of their attitudes to life and destiny. Naturally, in spite of frequent conflicts in ideas they were able to impose, too, a consistency of thought and style which no other society has ever achieved. Also, in spite of occasional outbursts of persecution and repression, there was a liberality in Chinese thought towards religious and philosophical matters that was exceptional rather than usual in Europe until very modern times.

The intellectual and cultural stability of China was also aided by the nature of Confucianism with its strong emphasis on social and secular virtues, and its denial of the apocalyptic vision, a philosophy of life which fitted the urbane scholar-gentry like a glove and also had the advantage of idealizing their life-style at the expense of all other social groups. And as ever in human affairs, fortune also aided the stability of Chinese civilization. Invasions of devastating power overtook China time and time again yet China never, despite the impact of a foreign religion like Buddhism, suffered the cultural change that Europe experienced through the fall of Rome and the rise of Christianity which created that duality of culture – pagan and Christian – which raised such profound questions about the nature of human destiny within an historical context in Europe. China's past stretched unbroken to the beginning of time. Of course, China experienced massive political upheavals as well as invasion and domination, but all were neatly and safely accommodated in the elastic political theory of the mandarinate – the concept of the Mandate of Heaven, by which a highly generalized deity granted its favour to the successful and withdrew it from the defeated, a philosophy so accommodating that its attractions to conquerors must have been self-obvious. And of course again it should be remembered that no conquerors could in the long run rule China without the mandarinate. Their arms might take them to China, only the mandarinate could keep them there. And it is the mandarinate with its philosophy that could absorb catastrophe so easily into a timeless destiny that lies at the heart of the stability of Chinese society. And of course the sense of timelessness was aided by the deeply conservative nature of the scholar-gentry in literature, painting and in the decorative arts so that a poem written in the T'ang and read by a Ming scholar seemed not very archaic either in feeling or in expression.

And this gives Imperial China much of its unique quality, as Dawson demonstrates over and over again in this perceptive book, a quality which derives from both the continuity of Chinese civilization and the unique dominance of an intellectual and literary class in politics, administration and economic welfare, a dominance that has been matched in no other civilization. And yet it would be folly to regard Chinese society and culture as linked in the matrix of history, unchangeable and unchanging.

Much of the early history of Imperial China, particularly of the brilliant T'ang, is one of growth and expansion: it was during this dynasty that China really absorbed the South which was so totally different from the wind-swept, pine-clad North of its regions: the new crops, the rich exploitable soil, enabled population and wealth to grow hand in hand, thereby stimulating the prosperity of all China, enabling vast irrigation works and canals to be undertaken and so again improve the quality and the prosperity of Chinese life. So multitudinous a population, so complex a government, created problems of administration and of finance of an order never faced by any Western government until very recent times – calling for ingenuity, invention and technological innovation from printing to paper-money. And the South, as Edward Schafer has shown in his remarkable book *The Vermilion Bird*, changed the imagery of literature as fundamentally as the mechanics of the economy. Nor did China remain unchanging and inert with the collapse of the T'ang: by the time of the Sung – in the eleventh and twelfth centuries – the Chinese were exporting to the Philippines and to India. And it is as well to remind ourselves that Chinese junks had reached East Africa before the European caravel. Nor was China a closed society: it was much more open to ideas, much more tolerant of religious diversity than Europe became until the nineteenth century: one has only to recall that groups of Jews, Christians and Muslims were to be found in sixteenth-century China and for most of its history, Buddhism – a totally foreign religion – existed in reasonable harmony both with Confucianism and Taoism – and what periods of persecution it suffered were due to economic and political reasons rather than religious. China, as Dawson emphasizes, was a vital, growing and developing society right up to the time of its involvement with Europe, but change and growth were slower, less cataclysmic and rarely involved the superstructure of society or the fundamental principles upon which it was based. The European by the very nature of his historical experience sees growth and change in dramatic terms – renaissances and revolutions, discovery and reformation; whereas, seemingly changeless, China grew, as it were, underwater, out of sight, advancing in wealth and prosperity but also in social control, so that eighteenth-century China – less creative maybe than the T'ang, the Sung or even the Ming – enjoyed a standard of civilization reached by no other iron-age Empire. One has only to read the dispatches of Macartney, who journeyed to Peking in 1790, to grasp this. He was amazed by the prosperity, the cleanliness and quality of life of the Chinese people, even though he himself came from the most affluent and prosperous of all European countries – Britain. And, of course, the standard of living of the mandarinate could only be matched by the richest European aristocrats. Like all European aristocrats, he responded at once to the delights of the eye that Chinese art and architecture offered him. A certain uniformity of taste – that strikes like a chord in music – is typical of tightly bound aristocracies, whether European or Chinese: fortunately, too, Europe had been dominated by aristocratic taste for centuries and in the eighteenth developed an elegance and on occasion an economy that resonated with the Chinese culture; sufficiently so to make appreciation of the Chinese come easily in the decorative arts. Understanding of Chinese literature and of philosophy came later; literature in any widespread sense only in this century: depending as most of us do on translation, only a fragment of the literary riches of China is available to us: a pity for no other civilization possesses such a store of lyric poetry of such haunting beauty. Indeed, in artistic achievement Imperial China has few if any equals: and we still know its objects better than its thoughts and words.

Only very recently have we learned, through the works of Dr Joseph Needham, of an almost equally great achievement in Chinese science and technology. Here the accomplishments were remarkable and yet they never acted so catalytically as Western inventions: indeed Chinese inventions transplanted to the West, such as gunpowder, printing and the compass, along with a host of others, never had the dramatic effect on their own society that they had on Europe. China, surreptitiously as it were, changed the Western world whilst it only slowly changed itself. And again, technological advance led to pure science or even to a scientific élite consciously searching for universal principles that would explain nature and the way it worked. The reasons why China did not develop either science, a scientific attitude or even industry (as against mass crafts) are exceedingly complex and indeed have rarely been explored.

Certainly the complexities of literacy with its too time-consuming method of learning combined with the deep involvement of many of its literary élite in administration and government with its natural commitment to tradition played its part, but so too did the success of Chinese society. True, there were great famines and ghastly and bloody wars during the upheavals which followed the fall of a dynasty, but neither disasters were long-lasting in their effects on a predominantly peasant and craft society. And the remarkable feature of Chinese society that struck all writers from Marco Polo to Lord Macartney was its orderliness, its affluence amongst the rich and the comparative prosperity of its poor. Imperial Chinese society worked, as few societies have, bringing peace and modest subsistence to millions. Indeed it is a sobering thought for Western man to realize that Chinese society has embraced probably the majority of human beings who have so far existed : and if that is a slight exaggeration, certainly no other society can compare with it in extent or duration. It would seem to argue for the merits of the intellectual in government and for a society based on the principles of social immobility centred in tradition. So long as one keeps one's eyes on the mandarin and the prosperous gentry from which they came, that attitude might seen justifiable – few social élites have created so urbane, so sophisticated, so sensitive a culture, or one in which the relations between the aspirations of the individual and the needs of society have been kept so delicately in balance.

But always in the background there are the masses, shadowy, scarcely known, much less known in many ways than in the West, possessing a counter culture that can only be dimly perceived, but indicative of tribulation, suffering and frustration. They need to be remembered, for it is easy to succumb to the sophisticated charms of mandarin culture, so nostalgic in whatever it touches – poetry, painting, even the decorative arts. And yet the whole force of Chinese philosophy, religion and social custom was used to maintain not only order and obedience, but also subservience and the acceptance of poverty. Millions were made to be content with little, and still are, but in the end this may prove more helpful for humanity's capacity for survival than the appetite for acquisition which was fostered in the West, not only amongst the rich, acquisitive entrepreneurs, whether aristocratic, mercantile or industrial, but also amongst its peasantry and its industrial working classes.

Western man knows far too little of Chinese experience, whether of Imperial or modern times; the lessons of its history are still obscure and the greatness of its achievement, except in art and literature, little appreciated; and comparison between Chinese and Western experience and analysis of the similarities and differences in intellectual and social structure scarcely begun. But at least there can be less excuse now that we have this fine book of Dawson's with its panoramic view of Chinese history and society stretching well over a thousand years.

I

China before the Sui Dynasty

1

It would be inappropriate in this volume to go back to the origins of Chinese civilization or to deal with the period for which our knowledge is based mainly upon archaeological evidence, but at the time when the shadowy past begins to emerge into the light of recorded and datable historical events – in the eighth century B.C. – the home of Chinese civilization was a loose confederation of states in the valleys of the Yellow River and its two tributaries, the Wei and the Fen. These states nominally acknowledged the leadership of the Chou king, whose domains were in the area of the modern city of Loyang. They were linked together by close ties of kinship between the ruling families and the belief that they owed their origin to the establishment of fiefs by the founders of the Chou Dynasty, who in the eleventh century B.C. had conquered an earlier dynasty known as the Shang, which was famous above all for the magnificent bronze sacrificial vessels produced by its craftsmen. They regarded themselves as culturally superior to the surrounding 'barbarian' peoples, for they had been blessed with geographical and climatic conditions favourable to the development of agriculture, which distinguished them from the tribes dwelling in mountain and forest, who had to get their living primarily from hunting and fishing. An agricultural way of life implies the storage of grain from one season to the next, which necessitates the growth of defended settlements to protect these stores from marauders. Thus walled cities develop, and re-sources are accumulated which eventually enable the people to evolve a culture much more sophisticated than that demanded by the mere needs of subsistence.

The Wei valley provided a strong military base, being sur-rounded by high mountains except to the east, where a narrow outlet along the Yellow River valley was easily defended but also provided the opportunity to sally forth and attack neighbouring states. The Chou people had come originally from this valley, and so did the Ch'in, who unified China in 221 B.C. and established the first great imperial dynasty. This happened after centuries of bitter struggle among the ancient Yellow River states and others farther south in the Yangtze area, which had gradually become more closely involved with their northern neighbours. During these centuries the old feudalistic bases of society had been challenged, yielding to systems of government in which there was scope for people to be employed because of their ability rather than because of their kinship ties or noble ancestry. The military arts also became less of an aristocratic pursuit when iron was used for weapons as well as the much more costly bronze from which the swords and daggers of the Shang and early Chou nobles had been made. The big social changes taking place raised important questions about the nature of government and the duties of men in society, so the fifth and fourth centuries B.C. were famous as a period of contention between rival philosophies, which were mainly concerned with such issues. Among the so-called 'hundred schools' which flourished at that time the one inspired by Confucius was destined to have a profound formative influence on Chinese civilization.

Both Confucius and his most famous disciple Mencius spent their lives trying to persuade rulers to behave more humanely towards their subjects, thus founding the powerful tradition that rulers and officials were 'father and mother' of the people in their charge. In fact, in the opinion of Mencius, if rulers did not win the approval of the populace by their kingly behaviour, they forfeited the 'Mandate of Heaven', which was the basic justification of their power; so, according to the Confucian tradition, rebellion against an evil ruler was permissible. The Confucians were also strong advocates of the promotion of men on account of their ability, and so established the principle of the career open to talent which even in antiquity gave birth to a system of appointing civil servants through competitive examination. This was also the age of the two great Taoist classics, *Chuang-tzu* and *Tao Te Ching*, which, by contrast with Confucian teachings, regarded ethical judgements as arbitrary, rebelled against the artificiality of society, and sought a return to the Way of Nature, which for the genuine adept meant recourse to mystical practices. The philosophy of Legalism, on the other hand, rejected the Confucian appeal to morality and sense of duty on the ground that a state could only be governed effectively by a harsh system of law which applied to all equally.

The Legalists provided the ideology behind the Ch'in Dynasty, which was too ruthless to survive and after a mere fifteen years was replaced by the Han. The Ch'in founder's chief legacies to China were his standardization of the script, which was also simplified into something very similar to modern writing; the completion of the Great Wall, which incorporated earlier stretches built by the feudal states, to form a 1400-mile-long barrier segregating the Chinese from the northern nomads; and the execrated 'burning of the books', the purpose of which was to remove from private hands and keep only in the imperial library all works except the historical records of Ch'in and books on certain practical subjects. The loss to Chinese learning became even more serious when the imperial library was burnt down at the fall of the dynasty.

In extent of territory and methods of administration the Han Dynasty was to establish patterns which were followed by the later great imperial dynasties. The empire's domains were expanded, especially under Wu Ti ('Martial Emperor'),* who reigned from 141 to 87 B.C., to take in a great deal of present-day South China, and in the north much territory beyond the Great Wall was incorporated, together with the huge expanse of the Tarim basin in Central Asia. The latter area, which in later times was controlled by the Chinese during only a few periods of military strength, opened up the profitable transcontinental trade routes, which carried silk in large quantities as far as Rome.

The second important development of this period was the establishment of Confucianism as the dominant philosophy of the state. Once the Han Dynasty had consolidated itself, scholars

---

* Since Chinese names are notoriously difficult to remember, I have often supplied a translation of imperial titles.

attempted to restore the old literature which had largely been destroyed under the Ch'in. Some works could be pieced together from the memories of learned old men who had known them by heart, and in other cases hidden manuscripts came to light. The task of reconstituting these texts and interpreting them for their contemporaries provided much work for the erudite, especially since the old books were obscure because of the change in the form of the written characters; and this activity developed into a tradition of textual criticism which has been one of the most important preoccupations of Chinese scholarship. Prominent among the works restored in this way was a group of ancient books known as the Five Classics, allegedly composed or edited by Confucius; and gradually works associated with the Confucian tradition began to occupy a dominant position, although the type of Confucianism which emerged contained many other ingredients apart from the humane moralizings of the sage. The Han scholars began to venerate Confucius as a model prototype of themselves, and virtually to adopt him as a kind of patron saint, so the books he had used and taught from naturally came to be regarded as the ideal educational curriculum. Under the Martial Emperor professorships in the Five Classics were founded, a university was formed, and examinations were held for entry into the civil service, a method of recruitment which was not used in Europe until nearly two thousand years later. Later in the Han period sacrifices to Confucius began to be regularly conducted at all government schools. The great respect for learning engendered by the drive to restore the ancient books, together with the idea of choosing officials steeped in Confucian literature, survived as fundamental characteristics of Chinese civilization.

Another great scholarly tradition started in the Han period was the writing of dynastic histories. This again reflected the intense interest of the Chinese people in the past, which they saw as a model for present and future conduct. In the time of the Martial Emperor there lived the father of Chinese history, Ssu-ma Ch'ien, whose *Historical Records* was one of the most remarkable books ever written. It was a complete history of China down to his own times, composed with the utmost conscientiousness in preserving without significant modification what he regarded as the most reliable sources as well as with consummate literary skill in making his own necessary contribution. The work was arranged in a most sophisticated way, so that, apart from the 'basic annals', there is a large biographical section and also a collection of essays on the history of various matters appertaining to government, such as ritual, the calendar, and economic affairs. Another great historian, Pan Ku, who lived in the first century A.D., produced a history of the Former Han Dynasty, which followed the general pattern laid down by Ssu-ma Ch'ien, but added more of the valuable topical essays. This became the prototype of the dynastic histories, which in later times were composed by teams of scholars under official auspices, using material collected day by day during the course of the previous dynasty.

The Han empire had grown too rapidly out of a system of small states for it to develop the techniques of administration to give it a chance of surviving indefinitely. Maps of the period are misleading because they give no impression of the degree of control exercised by the Han within the precisely defined frontiers which are shown. The south of the country was still the haunt of non-Han tribes, the predecessors of the minority peoples of today who, despite much persecution over the centuries, have still maintained their separate identity. In large areas Chinese culture was very thinly spread, being restricted to small groups of settlers forced to colonize the country or to the partly sinicized ruling families of the tribes. The unification of China was still only a matter of political power, and there was no question yet of the permeation throughout its frontiers of a common culture. It would not be difficult for the empire to fall apart again.

A further menace to the integrity of Han China were the barbarians beyond the frontier, especially the Hsiung-nu (or Huns) to the north, who were powerful and united during the early part of the Han Dynasty. Indeed, it was necessary for the Chinese to keep them happy by sending them tribute. It was not until after 60 B.C., when the Hsiung-nu began to wage fratricidal wars, that it was possible for the Chinese to bring the southernmost branch of them within their own tributary system. The ultimate aim of Han policy was to absorb these barbarians and treat them as Chinese, so they were taught to live in settled communities and practise agriculture. They were also used to man the frontiers; but, as the Romans also discovered, it was dangerous to absorb too many barbarians, for in times of imperial weakness they might not prove reliable.

At the same time a seemingly inevitable process of economic decline began to operate. As also happened in later dynasties the lot of the peasants deteriorated: the growth of population stimulated by earlier success and prosperity left them with less land to cultivate than their forebears. Great estates also grew up and employed an increasing proportion of the peasant population as tenants, so that the rest had to pay higher taxes. Inevitably state revenue began to decline. The Former Han finally collapsed early in the first century A.D. and, after a brief interregnum, the Later Han attempted to restore former glories; but although it was possible for this dynasty to build up sufficient strength to get South China firmly back under control and even to re-conquer the Central Asian domains and hold them for a time at the end of the century, the revival was short-lived. The large private estates had survived as an intolerable financial burden, and the government no longer had the strength to build up an efficient bureaucracy based on merit, which could act to control the abuses of the great landowners. Serious rebellions broke out and it was impossible for the government to contain them. The old system of drafting peasants for military service had collapsed, and had been replaced by the use of professional forces. These had tended to become the private armies of the powerful generals, who were at the same time members of the rich landowning class which had been dominating the state. The country was falling apart, and for the last thirty years before its demise in A.D. 220, the Han Dynasty survived in name only.

The anarchy of the closing years of the Han eventually resolved into a pattern of virtually independent warlord régimes. In the north the most powerful military leader, Ts'ao Ts'ao, eventually succeeded in conquering and unifying the whole of North China, but he died in A.D. 220 before he had achieved the obvious next step of founding a new dynasty. In the same year the Han emperor, now no more than a puppet, ceded the throne to Ts'ao Ts'ao's son, but the broad stream of the Yangtze and the high mountains which barred off the Szechwan basin prevented the new dynasty, which was called the Wei, from incorporating the south and south-west into the empire. Instead separate régimes, also nurturing imperial ambitions, established themselves in these areas. In the south-west Liu Pei, claiming descent from the Han royal family, founded a new Han dynasty, sometimes called the Shu Han, since Shu was the name of the ancient state which had occupied this region in pre-imperial times. In the area around the lower Yangtze and to the south of that river Sun Ch'üan established a kingdom with the ancient regional name of Wu, its capital being the city which is now Nanking.

Many tales were told about the exploits of such heroes as Ts'ao Ts'ao and Chu-ko Liang, a clever strategist who figured prominently in the history of the Shu Han kingdom, so the period of the Three Kingdoms came to be regarded as an exciting and romantic age. The events of the time inspired a cycle of legends which were eventually worked up into a famous novel called *Romance of the Three Kingdoms*, which reached its final form in the fourteenth century; and one of the chief figures of the period was later canonized as the God of War. It was an age darkened by civil war, with each of the Three Kingdoms attempting to build up its strength so as to conquer the others, but not even being able to control the powerful landlords within its own frontiers. Officials were appointed through a subjective grading of their character and ability rather than by examination, and this method was an open invitation to corruption on the part of those functionaries charged with making recommendations. At the same time in remote districts families were able to usurp and make hereditary the administration of their locality, and the central government was powerless to intervene. But the political system did not develop into a genuinely feudal one, with independent barons having hereditary power over their regions: on the contrary, the powerful families exercised their power through control of the bureaucratic apparatus, which still survived from Han times.

In these circumstances the Ts'ao family's tenure of the throne was very shaky, and in A.D. 265 it was replaced by a successful military family called Ssu-ma, whose dynasty was entitled the Chin. Two years previously a Wei general had brought off the conquest of Shu Han, and in A.D. 280 Wu fell and the empire was reunited. The Chin founder made an attempt to curb the power of the great families and clearly acquired some prestige abroad, for he received embassies and tribute from countries of the Far West, such as Ferghana, and also received emissaries from states in what in modern times has been called Indo-China. After his death in A.D. 290 the dynasty was ruined by the Ssu-ma princes who, as virtually independent military governors, destroyed the country by warring against each other with the huge armies which were at their command. The central government collapsed, the impoverished peasants took to banditry, famine was rife, and the time was ripe for a newcomer to restore unity and lay claim to the Mandate of Heaven. This time the internecine folly laid open the way for barbarian intrusion, and in A.D. 304 a completely sinicized Hsiung-nu called Liu Yüan proclaimed himself King of Han and conquered the greater part of North China. Liu claimed descent from the Han imperial family, and thus the Han emperors' policy of making political matches with Hsiung-nu women had borne fruit in a Hsiung-nu claimant to the imperial throne. In A.D. 311 and 316 the great cities of Loyang and Changan were captured, events which have been compared in significance with the Gothic sack of Rome in A.D. 410, but the complete conquest of China was beyond his capacity. Indeed until A.D. 439, when North China was reunited under the Northern Wei Dynasty, this area was a cockpit for various contending barbarian régimes, and because of the number of separate states which had existence during this time, it is known as the period of the Sixteen Kingdoms.

The only part of the Chin empire that remained to a Ssu-ma was the former territory of Wu, where Ssu-ma Jui had been established as military governor. Here he was joined by many refugees from the north, and in A.D. 317 he inaugurated the Eastern Chin Dynasty, which was to survive for another century as the sole repository of the hopes for a restoration of Han greatness. Unfortunately it suffered throughout its duration from the same lack of strong centralized power. Nevertheless this was an important period in the colonization and development of South China, for as a result of the southward migration following the disasters in the north, the number of Chinese resident south of the Yangtze increased five-fold during the next century and a half. During this period an entirely new kind of civilization began to develop. Quite apart from the growing influence of Buddhism which, as we shall see later, was also bringing big changes to North China, the climate, scenery, and agriculture were so different from those of the northern homelands, that eventually they would nurture a softer, more effete way of life among people who had turned their backs on the cold North Chinese winters and the constant fear of barbarian invasions. But the perennial weakness of the central government was for the present a real obstacle to prosperity. The Eastern Chin Dynasty was snuffed out in A.D. 420, and none of the four short-lived dynasties which filled the interval between this time and the reunification of China by the Sui in A.D. 589 was able to improve on this position. Indeed it was the northern amalgam of Chinese and barbarian culture which eventually made the reunification possible.

In the early fourth century, at the time when Liu Yüan first established a barbarian régime in North China, there were already many people of foreign origin living in the country. This was due not only to the policy of settling barbarians within the frontier, but also to the Chinese warlords' dependence on large numbers of foreign mercenaries to fight their battles for them. Contemporary sources say that half the population of the Changan area at the end of the third century consisted of foreigners. The fragmentation and instability of political control during the Sixteen Kingdoms period were basically due to the very deep rifts in North Chinese society: these included not merely the divisions between barbarian and Chinese, but also the antipathy between the barbarians who favoured sinicization and those who remained true to their own traditions, as well as the conflict between the different barbarian peoples – Hsiung-nu, Tibetans and others – who had poured in to fill the vacuum left by the failure of the Chinese to establish a strong régime in the north.

It was not until A.D. 439 that one of the tribal states came out on top. This was the Northern Wei state, which had been established by a people known as the T'o-pa, who had moved into northern Shansi and, after adopting this dynastic name in A.D.

386, had gradually spread until they had eliminated all the other northern Chinese régimes. Once North China was under one rule again, the Northern Wei increasingly adapted themselves to Chinese culture and methods of administration, and by the end of the fifth century they had even moved their capital from the frontier town of Tatung to Loyang, an ancient Chinese seat of government, and had made Chinese the only court language, adopted Chinese dress and surnames, and encouraged inter-marriage with the Chinese people. Soon the dynasty was destroyed as the result of a wave of reaction against the excessive adoption of Chinese customs. From A.D. 535 North China was split in half again and it was not until A.D. 577 that it was reunited under the Northern Chou Dynasty, which only survived another four years before being replaced by the Sui.

2

In spite of the bitter conflicts and submission to barbarian rule that disfigured Chinese history from the third to the sixth centuries, the Middle Kingdom suffered no Dark Age comparable with that experienced by Europe. The intellectual traditions of the past were maintained, and indeed, to the lasting enrichment of Chinese culture, Confucianism and Taoism were joined by Buddhism to form the so-called 'three doctrines' which henceforward dominated Chinese religious and philosophical thought. At the same time the age did not lack its great poets and painters, and in science and technology the Chinese forged far ahead of Europe and achieved a position of superiority which they were to retain until the sixteenth century.

It is sometimes said that Confucianism was discredited by the failure and decline of the Han Dynasty, but although it is true that the depressing nature of the times did encourage a movement away from the this-worldliness of Confucianism towards the consolations of Taoist escapism, it must be remembered that the only pattern for the successful government of the Chinese empire was the Confucian Han one, so that anyone who wished to commend himself as the rightful heir to the Han empire must follow the correct Confucian precedents. Thus the Wei kingdom reopened the national university and attempted to reinstitute examinations in the Five Classics, while the conduct of court business continued to have a Confucian flavour, with policies being supported by the citation of hallowed examples from the Golden Age of antiquity. But even in Han times an important ingredient of the successful recipe for running an empire had been supplied by the Legalist tradition, which particularly appealed to men of practical ability who dealt with administrative, technological, and military problems at the grass roots level, where Confucian ethical appeals and sanctions must often have seemed high-minded and irrelevant.

Moreover the two systems of thought were not always in conflict with each other. Chinese law, for example, was extremely harsh, reflecting the Legalist belief in the supreme political importance of a rigorous penal code. On the other hand, the traditional Confucian belief was that adherence to the Rites was sufficient to preserve the social order, and that a universal system of law was unnecessary. But at least there was agreement between the two about how the masses should be treated, for the Confucians did not believe that their code of honour was within the scope of 'the small people'. This attitude was reflected in the existence of different penalties for gentlemen and ordinary people: a well-known example of this which survived throughout imperial Chinese history was that graduates were exempt from corporal punishment. One of the main Legalist devices for ensuring that the law was obeyed was the harsh principle of mutual responsibility, which meant that the whole family could suffer for the crime of one person. Despite the humanity of the sage's own teaching, Confucianism could even tolerate this principle because it stressed the closeness of family ties. So although Legalism had ceased to have separate identity as a philosophical school, its ideas were still very influential, and we shall see that in later Chinese history the state runs on a mixture of Confucianism and Legalism, with a swing towards Legalist absolutism in harsh times, and in easier periods a tendency towards the milder Confucian beliefs in government by men of merit.

Buddhism was also to make a big impact on Chinese political

life in spite of the fact that its founder was one who had rejected the world. The Buddha was an Indian prince of the sixth century B.C. who, unable to bear the contrast between the pampered luxury in which he lived and the suffering outside, left his palace and became a religious mendicant, and eventually attained a state of enlightenment (Buddha means 'the Enlightened One'). The core of his beliefs is expressed in the Four Noble Truths: that life is suffering, that suffering is caused by desire, that suffering can be ended by getting rid of desire, and that the way to do this is to practise the Noble Eightfold Path. This comprises the Buddhist rules for right living, which are concerned not only with moral conduct, but also with mental discipline and achieving the right intellectual insights. The final goal is to attain a condition known as Nirvana, which involves breaking the endless chain of existence through the ending of all desires. Buddhist doctrine was not written down for several centuries, and consequently many different sects evolved out of the various traditions concerning his teaching, and an enormous quantity of sacred texts was produced.

When Buddhism first came to China is still uncertain. According to the tradition, the religion was first introduced after the Emperor Ming, who reigned from A.D. 58 to 75, had seen a golden deity in a dream, and in response to his ministers' advice, had dispatched envoys to the west in search of more information about the sage and his teachings. But there is evidence that it already existed in the Middle Kingdom at that time. It came in along the trade routes from the oasis communities of Central Asia, and obviously the breakthrough must have occurred early in the first century B.C., when China held a strong position in that area because of the conquests of the Martial Emperor, so that many merchants, envoys, hostages and other people from those parts naturally found themselves in the Chinese capital at Changan, bringing their religion with them. During the Later Han era Loyang was an important centre of the faith, but by the end of the dynasty, although many Chinese had had some contact with Buddhism not only in their own country but through service in Central Asia, it was still very largely a foreign religion practised only by foreigners.

Since Buddhism bore certain superficial resemblances to Taoism, the Chinese, who were accustomed to thinking of their own country as the sole centre of civilization, at first regarded it as a branch of that religion: the story was told that Lao Tzu, the reputed founder of Taoism, had travelled to the west to reform the barbarians, and what he had taught there had been an inferior version of Taoism suited to the barbarians' intelligence, which had developed into Buddhism. Similarly in later times Christian missionaries were to regard the ancient religion of China as a debased form of Christianity.

The assimilation of Buddhism into China provides an interesting example of how the cross-fertilization of cultures works. Since the religion was introduced under the aegis of Taoism, this determined the nature of the Buddhist material initially propagated in the Middle Kingdom. Translations were not only selective in accordance with the interest of readers, but also misleading because of the impossibility of accurately conveying the unfamiliar terminology. Key terms had to be rendered by means of Chinese equivalents which would carry for the reader all kinds of inappropriate associations supplied from his own cultural background. Moreover translation could only be the uncertain product of collaborative efforts, for no Chinese is thought to have known any Sanskrit before the late fourth century A.D. The languages and literatures were also profoundly different, the uninflected Chinese, written in characters, contrasting strongly with the polysyllabic, highly inflected and alphabetical Indian language. Chinese literature was more earthbound, Chinese philosophy less speculative, Chinese concepts of space and time more finite, and Chinese aspirations more worldly than their Indian equivalents, so no genuine understanding could be reached until after much blind groping in the initial stages.

Deliberate mistranslation was also sometimes employed in order to make the material acceptable to the Chinese tradition, for there were several points at which the Confucian way of life was firmly opposed to Buddhism. For example, the Chinese creed placed great emphasis on the family, but the Buddhist ideal was to renounce all family ties as the historical Buddha himself had done. Fortunately apologists for the foreign religion were able to point to worthies mentioned in the Confucian Classics who had behaved in an un-Confucian manner; and even those who went in for celibacy had their heroic prototypes, although this was really the worst of all sins, since it meant that there would be no descendants to make the family offerings. Withdrawal from the world could also be condoned, for it was a treasured Confucian principle that the good minister should retire when good order did not prevail in the state. So not only did the Taoists play their part in securing the acceptance of Buddhism, but even valid Confucian arguments were used to secure its toleration; and a good example of compromise were the prayers frequently offered up by Buddhist monks and nuns for their departed ancestors.

Another obstacle to the acceptance of Buddhism was that, although in India the faith had evolved with time and ramified into sects in different parts of the country, the Chinese could not see this development, but were confronted with a confused mass of scriptures and doctrines, which sometimes flatly contradicted each other. The impossibility of reconciling all these conflicting teachings led to the development of sects in China, and the haphazard way in which religious writings came into the country and were translated was an impetus to the great pilgrimages made by devout Chinese monks, whose main aim was not, as with Christian pilgrims, to visit holy places, but to collect scriptures in order to obtain more of the truth. This bewildering confrontation with different varieties of Buddhism is very reminiscent of the impact of conflicting sects of Protestant Christianity on the puzzled Chinese during the nineteenth century.

Buddhism fared very differently in the north and south of China. In the north in the state of Wei during the Three Kingdoms period, the religion made little progress. Some translation work went on, but it made no impact on the general philosophical and literary scene. However, the renewal of contacts with the Buddhist lands of Central Asia which came during the Chin Dynasty was reflected in increased religious activity. For the first time we hear of Buddhist travellers from China going to these western regions in search of scriptures, while the new influx of preachers and texts led to a fresh outburst of translation activity, and the religion began to make some headway with the great families, including the ruling Ssu-mas. But soon these Buddhistic

Chinese gentry families were swept south as the barbarians established themselves in the north, where the foreign religion eventually functioned almost as a state church in the non-Chinese kingdoms there.

The chief pioneer of this development was a certain Fo-t'u-teng, a monk of Central Asian origin, who arrived in North China just at the time when Loyang was sacked. He gained the confidence of Shih Lo, who was ruler of the Hsiung-nu Later Chao Dynasty from A.D. 319 to 333, and served him not only as court chaplain but also as political adviser, much impressing his master with his magical powers and in particular his ability to predict the outcome of military operations, bring down rain, and relieve sickness. Indeed some of the feats recorded in his biography are quite remarkable : he only had to say a spell over his begging bowl to cause blue lotus flowers to spring up therefrom, while he also had the grotesque ability to produce his intestines through a hole in his chest. This kind of thing went down very well with Shih Lo, an illiterate who had started out in life as a slave, so this versatile monk achieved an astonishingly rapid spread of the doctrine. Shih Lo had most of his sons brought up in a Buddhist temple, and many hundreds of temples and monasteries were built at Fo-t'u-teng's instigation. Other monks in North China also made it their deliberate policy to obtain whatever support and protection they could by acting as political advisers so that they could freely propagate their faith. What helped to make the northern non-Chinese states receptive to Buddhism was the very thing which made the religion difficult for the Confucian to swallow – its foreignness. Indeed this was a positive attraction to rulers who feared that they might be drawn into the Chinese cultural spider's-web by becoming too dependent on the political expertise of Confucian-style Chinese intellectuals. And not only was the religion foreign, but so also were many of the monks, whose appeal was that they possessed no ties of loyalty to family or faction and could give whole-hearted service to the ruler himself.

The tradition of the adviser monk was continued when the T'o-pa Wei Dynasty imposed some stability on North China : a celebrated monk called Fa-kuo acted as imperial adviser and also exercised administrative control over the monastic community throughout the dynasty's domains. Unfortunately such close contact with temporal power offended against the Buddhist precept that monks should not make obeisance to rulers, being cut off from the world and therefore not subject to earthly kings. The only solution to this problem was to convert the ruler into a being which a Buddhist monk could appropriately reverence, so the emperor was duly made into a Tathagata, so that in future it was *qua* Tathagata that the emperor received his adviser's respects.

At times when Buddhism was favoured by the non-Chinese rulers in the north, the religion was lavishly patronized. Splendid temples were built, and large gifts of land and treasure were handed over to the church. In return there were regular prayers for the prosperity of the ruling house. Among the grandest monuments to Buddhism were the huge figures carved out of the cliff-face at Yünkang, near Tatung, the capital of the Northern Wei Dynasty. This project was conceived as a means of showing repentance for an earlier persecution of the faith and as a splendid example of imperial patronage. In the eyes of devout Buddhists such enormous figures would serve as concrete symbols of the permanence of the religion by contrast with the destructible images fashioned in wood and metal which had not survived the persecution. Artistically the work owed much to influences from Central Asia and India, for at this time the Northern Wei rulers were in close touch with the Central Asian kingdoms. Some of these sent tribute to their court, which might have included images to serve as models for these sculptures. But the colossal scale makes them artistically inferior to the best Gandharan work. The project was carried out during the reign of the Emperor Hsiao-wen (A.D. 471–99). After the capital was removed to Loyang, a site for Buddhist sculpture was found at Lungmen, only about ten miles from the city, where the River Yi flows between two cliffs well suited to the purpose. Work continued there until at least the middle of the eighth century, with a further peak of activity in the second half of the seventh century under the patronage of the Empress Wu, by which time the deities were being depicted in a less awe-inspiring and more lifelike guise.

By the end of the Northern Wei Dynasty the religion had taken root so firmly that there were two million monks and thirty thousand temples in North China. A debased form of Buddhism, which offered easy access to a paradise known as the Pure Land in return for simple faith in Amitabha, the Buddha who presided over it, was peddled in the villages, and the monasteries had become a serious drain on the economy. Already the rapid growth of the faith had led to one persecution. In A.D. 446, as a result of Confucian and Taoist machinations, the emperor decided that the monks throughout the entire realm should be executed, and stupas, scriptures and paintings destroyed. Although many monks went into hiding, taking sutras and images with them, there was much destruction of life and religious property. A similar persecution, also stimulated by an alliance of convenience between Confucianism and Taoism, took place in A.D. 574–8, but in the long run it was ineffective because Buddhism was now so deeply rooted.

A distinctive feature of Northern Buddhism was that, as a result of closer contacts with Central Asia, it was easier to pursue the search for a deeper understanding of the religion and to work for better translations. A disciple of Fo-t'u-teng called Tao-an (A.D. 312–85) was the first to show an enlightened understanding of the problems, and his work was followed up by the greatest of missionary translators, Kumarajiva, who came from Kucha in the Tarim basin. During the last decade of his life (he died in A.D. 413) he headed an enormous translation team composed of several hundreds of monks, working as doctrinal experts, editors, sub-editors, copyists and in various other capacities, a most sophisticated project which achieved a remarkably high output both in quality and quantity.

In South China it was with the influx of northern families early in the fourth century that the history of a distinctive type of Buddhism started. Those émigrés from the north who wished to escape from the difficulties of the times and live in retirement found a suitable retreat in the monasteries, and saw in the doctrines of Buddhism a new justification for the practice of keeping away from the bustle of the world in troubled times. Moreover, since power was monopolized by the great land-owning families, there were few opportunities for the scholarly in politics or at court, so it was the monasteries which became the centres of learning and culture. Thus many of the influential monks of this period were men who had had their early education in the Confucian Classics and had also been touched by the revival of interest in Taoism before they had come into contact with Buddhism. Even after entering the ranks of the religious they continued to take part in the scholarly pursuits of cultured laymen, such as literary composition, calligraphy, the study of antiquities and even the exposition of the Confucian or Taoist Classics. For their part many cultured laymen also became interested in the Buddhist philosophy and actively patronized the religion : they would visit monasteries, converse with learned monks, help in the translation of the scriptures, paint murals in temples and monasteries, and conform with the Buddhist rules for laymen. The achievement of the many distinguished monks who were learned both in traditional Chinese culture and in Buddhism made the foreign religion increasingly acceptable to the Chinese, and within a century it had become an integral part of the intellectual and cultural life of South China.

During this same period remarkable scientific and technological achievements were beginning to make an impact on life in China. Later the new techniques which the Chinese had pioneered would travel beyond the frontiers of the Middle Kingdom and transform the history of the world. The four inventions which should be given pride of place because of their effect on mankind at large are paper, printing, gunpowder and the magnetic compass. A.D. 105 was the traditional date for the invention of paper, which was made from tree bark, hemp, old rags and fishing nets, but archaeological discoveries show that it was in use long before this. It was not until the eighth century that the secret of this uniquely cheap writing material found its way across to Western Asia and thence to Europe. This discovery, together with the invention of printing, which will be described in detail in a later chapter although the foundations were already being laid during this period, made possible a world in which learning was widely disseminated instead of being merely the privilege of a few. Magnetism was known to no other people in the ancient world apart from the Chinese, but as early as the Han Dynasty diviners were already making use of a kind of primitive compass. In that period it was only employed for such purposes as the choice of propitious sites for buildings or tombs, and its use in navigation did not come until possibly as late as the tenth century. When the discovery reached Europe, it provided an essential tool in European exploration and colonization. Chemistry had also made much progress, and many pieces of bronze apparatus dating from the Han period have survived. A strong stimulus to such developments was the preoccupation of Taoists with the quest for an elixir of immortality, which encouraged experimentation with all kinds of chemical substances. These researches led to major contributions to the advancement of medical knowledge, and the richness of the Chinese *materia medica* at an early stage in their history is only now beginning to be appreciated in the West. But the really earth-shaking result of these alchemical activities was the discovery of gunpowder. At first it was merely used in fireworks and it was not until the tenth century that it came into military use. Only in the hands of the Europeans did it have devastating effects, enabling them to dominate the world they had explored by means of the magnetic compass.

Just as important for its effect on warfare was the development of the foot-stirrup, the earliest evidence of which appears on tomb-figurines dating from about A.D. 300 : by welding the rider to his steed it enhanced the efficiency of the cavalryman and guaranteed his supremacy in warfare for several hundred years, culminating in the Mongol domination of most of the Euro-Asian land-mass in the fourteenth century. The Chinese also led the world in making the horse more efficient in its civil capacity, as a draught-animal, by developing improvements in equine harness. In ancient times they employed a form of breast-strap harness which was much superior to the harness used in antiquity in the Old World, and even used the modern type of collar harness as early as the fifth century A.D., about three hundred years before it was available in Europe.

A wide range of other inventions may be mentioned only briefly, since a mere list gives a good impression of the variety of technological achievement during this period. The huge supply of manpower available was no obstacle to the appearance of such a labour-saving device as the humble wheelbarrow in the third century A.D., a thousand years before it arrived on the European scene. Turning to something of larger significance, iron and steel technology was already far advanced by this time, for many cast-iron tools and weapons dating from the great Iron Age of about four hundred B.C. have been excavated, although it was to be another eighteen centuries after this before cast-iron was known and used in Europe. Another important use of iron which probably originated during this period, although the earliest evidence is from the Sui Dynasty, is in the construction of iron-chain suspension bridges to replace some of the old bamboo cable suspension bridges, which were commonly used to cross ravines in south-west China; and another engineering triumph of the Sui period which ought to be mentioned at this point is the oldest segmental arch bridge, which is still standing at Chaohsien in Hopei province. In the iron industry a key development had been the use of piston bellows operated by water-power, which dated from the first century A.D., and was the earliest application of water-power to industry in China; but with their great need to control waterways for irrigation purposes and flood prevention, the Chinese had been especially efficient in hydraulic engineering from very early times, and canal and irrigation systems had already been established during the Chou period.

Other inventions improved the quality and beauty of the material things by which they were surrounded in their everyday lives. The domestication of the silkworm and the development of the silk industry over three thousand years ago provided not only a fine material for clothing but also something for writing and painting on, as well as ensuring the Chinese a long lead over Europeans in the development of textile machinery. From an even earlier period the Chinese had been proficient in the technique of carving the very hard and beautiful stone known to us as jade, which they prized greatly and used for ritual objects as well as for a variety of secular purposes. Chinese potters were perfecting the art of making pure white porcelain, more than a thousand years before the secret of its manufacture was discovered in Europe. Lacquer-work was also far advanced, and beautifully decorated bowls, dishes, toilet-boxes and trays were already being made in the Chou period, principally in the Changsha area, where the earliest example of painting on silk has also been excavated.

Although all these various techniques which we owe to China have done so much to mould and change our world that they are bound to have the biggest impact on our imagination, it should not be forgotten that the Chinese also made their mark in more purely scientific matters. In astronomy they recorded eclipses and other celestial phenomena in remote antiquity and were the most accurate observers of such occurrences anywhere in the world before the Renaissance. In mathematics they had many achievements to their credit, and it has been estimated that between 250 B.C. and A.D. 1250 China exported more mathematical ideas than she imported. Indeed the intellectual climate in China during the early centuries A.D. was much more congenial to the development of scientific thought than was the atmosphere in Europe until recent centuries. The growth of science was not inhibited by religious dogma, and indeed the two great native systems of thought, Confucianism and Taoism, were in some ways positively helpful. Confucianism was particularly concerned with the improvement of things in this world and with the alleviation of the economic lot of mankind, so the local official was always expected to show an interest in technological improvements which might contribute to this; and the Chinese type of bureaucratic state was geared to the patronage of large-scale technological projects, such as were undertaken in the realm of hydraulic engineering. Taoism, too, as we have seen, did encourage an inquiring approach to nature and the development of experimental techniques in dealing with natural substances. Nevertheless, in spite of the big lead which the Chinese had over the Europeans, we shall see in what follows that Chinese society lacked the element which could fuse all these ideas and techniques together and use them to usher in the modern world of scientific and technological achievement. Indeed Chinese society went on its way relatively unruffled by discoveries which were to change the course of European history beyond all recognition.

2

The Sui and the T'ang Dynasties

1

Since the Sui Dynasty succeeded in unifying China for the first time for nearly three centuries, it is worth recounting its history in some detail. The Sui emperors' achievement did require great political acumen as well as harshness, but little credit has generally been given by the Chinese to this epoch-making dynasty; and the second of the two sovereigns, Yang Ti ('Emblazoned Emperor'), has been popularly known as the archvillain among Chinese rulers, a prize not easy to win since there are several very strong contenders. When a new dynasty was established, the official historians who had been assigned the task of writing up the history of the previous dynasty were bound to justify their own emperor's usurpation by depicting the last, deposed ruler of that dynasty in an unfavourable light. Unfortunately for the reputation of the Sui, the whole dynasty had lasted for less than forty years and had been acted out within the memory of the T'ang historians. Almost the whole of it therefore took on the character of the régimes of the traditional 'bad last emperors', whose prototypes were the tyrants Chieh and Chou, whose forfeiture of the Mandate of Heaven had led to the downfall of the Hsia and Shang Dynasties in remote antiquity so that they had been much reviled by Confucian philosophers. Only the very early years of the reign of the founder, Wen Ti ('Cultured Emperor'), are painted in brighter colours. The deterioration from early virtue and from the great achievement of reunification to a situation in which all claim to the Mandate of Heaven could be considered lost was a very abrupt decline which needed explaining away in terms of the evil and hubris of the Sui rulers. Nevertheless their rule, although marred by the bloody intrigue endemic at the Chinese court, showed that they had the energy and foresight to do what was basically necessary for the founding of a strong and lasting state.

The events leading to the establishment of this important dynasty nicely illustrate both the role of chance in human affairs and the bitter conflicts which determined whose hand controlled the destinies of medieval China. Yang Chien, the future Cultured Emperor, suddenly emerged from a bunch of front-runners any one of whom might have won the race for political power. Yang had been born in a Buddhist temple in A.D. 541, and his up-bringing had been much more Buddhist than Confucian. In his twenties he had made rapid progress in official life and in 566 had married a woman from a powerful non-Chinese noble family, named Tu-hu, a devout Buddhist and a strong-minded woman who was to exert a formidable influence upon her husband. The sequence of events which led to Yang Chien's sudden rise to power began with the death in 578 of the energetic Yü-wen Yung, who had reigned for seventeen years as the Martial Emperor of the Northern Chou Dynasty and had just succeeded in reuniting the whole of North China by the conquest of the state of Ch'i during the previous year. Unfortunately his son and heir Hsüan Ti was a capricious youth who squandered all his father's hard-won successes, and it fell to Yang Chien to stop the rot. This came about because Yang happened to be the new emperor's father-in-law, which relationship put him at the centre of intrigue and also of danger. The lascivious young sovereign soon decided to do away with Yang's daughter in order to replace her as empress with a new favourite stolen from an imperial prince, whose chagrin at this loss had driven him to rebellion and death. The deposed empress's mother, the redoubtable lady Tu-hu, successfully pleaded for her life, but thereafter the future of the whole Yang family was under a cloud and Yang himself was given a posting which was tantamount to exile. Then in June 580 Hsüan Ti died, leaving on the throne his infant son, to whom he had nominally abdicated a year previously. Yang was now persuaded by his friends to seize the regency, an office for which he was a natural candidate, being the emperor's grandfather, but which he accepted with reluctance, his wife remarking that the job was like 'riding a tiger'. Soon his fears were realized. Although he promptly took the very necessary step of summoning Hsüan Ti's five brothers to the capital, half the empire was soon in open rebellion, and he narrowly escaped assassination at the hands of two of the summoned princes, who were forthwith executed. However, by the end of the year all the rebels had been crushed, and early in the following year Yang Chien was able to inaugurate a new dynasty. Soon the remaining members of the Yü-wen royal family, including the little ex-emperor, had been liquidated.

This sudden rise to power was reflected in Yang Chien's subsequent conduct as emperor. His early career had proved him an excellent administrator, but all his experience in the forty years before he ascended the throne had not prepared him for the supreme position; and a fear that others might rise as swiftly as he had done made him unduly suspicious of his subordinates and unwilling to delegate authority. He also felt insecure because he had attained power so rapidly that he could not be sure that he had not acted before his predecessors had properly forfeited the Mandate of Heaven and that the unseen powers might not punish him for his hubris. These feelings were intensified because he was of a superstitious nature as a result of his un-Confucian upbringing. His sense of insecurity sometimes manifested itself in uncontrollable rages leading to violent despotic action, while the victims of his suspicious nature even included his own sons, with disastrous consequences to the dynasty. He lived an extremely frugal life, again perhaps to avoid incurring the hostility of fate, and was reputedly the only monogamist among Chinese emperors, his wife sternly forbidding him any extra-marital consolations. 'My wife is the Son of Heaven and allows me no freedom,' he declared when she encompassed the death of the only girl upon whom he had been tempted to bestow his affections.

It is often a sense of insecurity that spurs a man on to take energetic action. The first few years of the Cultured Emperor's reign would be vital. At the same time as he was ruthlessly exterminating members of the deposed dynasty (who could be thought justly punished for having betrayed the Mandate of Heaven), he had to give early evidence of the inauguration of a reign which would justify his own assumption of the Mandate. To mark the beginning of a new régime it was the custom to show that a clean sweep was being made by such measures as the declaration of an amnesty, the introduction of a new calendar, and the drafting of a new legal code. The latter was a necessary initial undertaking since the fundamental principle of the Legalist philosophy which had permeated Chinese society was that the task of government was to guide people by rewards and punishments, while the concept of rulers as primarily lawgivers and punishers also figures prominently in the ancient Chinese classic known as the *Book of History*. Hence a thorough revision of the legal code was undertaken in 583, the result being a marginally milder and much simplified version of the previous system.

Another hallowed task of government, which had been urged strongly by the Confucian philosopher Mencius, was provision of the people's livelihood, while the lesson of history was that peasant starvation was the prelude to the fall of dynasties. There was a twofold problem: firstly to ensure the production of a sufficient quantity of grain; and secondly to see that it became available to the people as and when it was wanted.

Previous régimes had attempted to solve the first problem, which had faced rulers throughout medieval times as a result of the widespread chaos, depopulation and abandonment of land during the troubled times at the end of the Han and the unstable period of disunion. To ensure production of sufficient grain, and inhibit the growth of large estates, systems of land-redistribution had been introduced. The Sui devised its own scheme, but it was not very effective because amounts of land allocated varied enormously according to rank and also because the population was so unevenly spread that in the highly populated areas peasants could not hope to get more than a fraction of their proper allotment.

It was the second problem, that of distribution, which the Sui tackled with new energy. In North China the harvest was unreliable because of the danger of flood or drought, so it was vitally important not only to have granaries of sufficient capacity to store grain from the years of good harvest to help out during the lean years, but also to have a satisfactory means of transporting grain to disaster areas. Even in times of good harvest huge quantities of grain had to be conveyed to the capital to feed the swelling urban population, which already amounted to about a million people. In the third year of the Cultured Emperor's reign, the granaries at Changan being empty, corvée labour was assigned the task of transporting grain to solve the immediate problem, and various other steps were taken towards a long-term solution. Granaries were established at key points in the Yellow River valley and on the River Wei, while exemption from military service was granted those capable of transporting grain over the difficult rapids at Sanmen, a point on the Yellow River about a hundred miles east of the confluence with the River Wei, where there is now an important hydro-electric station constructed by the People's Republic. Furthermore, since the Wei was treacherous for navigation because of sandbanks, the Cultured Emperor built the Canal for Enlarging Communications to provide a safe link between the Yellow River and the capital. Two years later he gave instructions for the establishment in all prefectures of 'ever-normal granaries', which were so called because their purpose was to keep prices steady by storing sufficient grain from good harvests to allow for distribution in lean years. However, the beneficial effect of these energetic measures was reduced by a series of disastrous years during which the area around the capital suffered from drought, while other districts were repeatedly flooded. In 594 drought in Kuanchung was so serious that the whole court moved to Loyang, where the emperor had established another capital, his escort being ordered to assist the streams of refugees who poured along the same route in search of food. This journey of the whole court from Changan to Loyang was to be repeated many times during the succeeding dynasty.

Wen Ti also made energetic efforts to improve the economy by adopting new measures to deter tax evasion and also to prevent avoidance of the corvée, a practice which was reported to be especially rife in the area of the former Northern Ch'i state. At the same time it was vital to ensure the security of the northern frontier and, to this end, a large number of military colonies were established in the area north of the Great Wall.

In addition to providing for the material well-being and security of the state, the Cultured Emperor had to show concern for the spiritual interests of his subjects if he were to be deemed truly worthy of the title of Son of Heaven. At a time when Buddhism was gaining ground rapidly, his own devotion to that faith was a great asset, but in the early years Confucianism had a more important role to play since it constituted the only corpus of belief and practice which could secure the legitimization of a dynasty. At the beginning the emperor performed the appropriate time-honoured ritual of filially conferring posthumous imperial titles on his father and mother and establishing an imperial ancestral temple and he soon instituted a commission under the chairmanship of the President of the Board of Rites (the head of an important government department) to ensure that the court functioned in accordance with the hallowed rules of propriety. He inculcated Confucian virtues by granting tax exemption to sons noted for their filial piety and to other paragons of the Confucian virtues, and by establishing schools of Confucian studies throughout the country, and a national college at the capital. The purpose of these institutions was also to train future officials and so relieve the ruler from dependence on the powerful families who monopolized public office. A small-scale beginning to the system of recruitment for the civil service by competitive examination was made. This system, which had its precursor in the Former Han Dynasty, was to grow into one of the most remarkable contributions made by the Chinese to world civilization. The climax of the emperor's performance of the traditional ritual was attained in 595 with the great sacrifice at the sacred mountain of T'ai-shan, a solemn ceremony which the Son of Heaven could only undertake after much hesitation and preparation when he already had a fine record of achievements to report to Heaven. Even then, with characteristic fear of hubris he shrank from the ultimate solemnity of a sacrifice at the summit, contenting himself with a lesser observance at the foot of the mountain. Nevertheless he had gained all the propaganda advantage of a splendid progress through the most populous parts of China to take part in this ceremony which was to set the final seal on his high destiny, while his reluctance to go through the full rite would also win him credit for a seemly modesty.

This grand occasion did not take place until after the Sui conquest of South China and the reunification of the country, but before dealing with this topic it would be more convenient to see what use the Sui founder made of the other major religions, both of which had been persecuted under the previous dynasty. Though his preference was for Buddhism, he shrewdly supported Taoism as well. He patronized the cult of Lao Tzu, the deified founder of the Taoist religion and reputed author of the *Tao Te Ching* ('The Way and Its Power'), which had widely appealed to intellectuals during the period of disunion. He also established a Taoist institute, which was to serve not only as a centre for the study of such subjects as astrology and geomancy, in which the Taoists were particularly interested, but also as the organ for control of the Taoist clergy. But the religious policy which was dearest to the ruler's own heart and most welcome to the people was the revival of Buddhism, especially in view of its long persecution under the previous dynasty. Nevertheless, like Taoism, it was kept firmly under state control so that the church did not grow so large as to become the menace to the state it had previously been. Thus the Cultured Emperor had the wisdom to patronize all of the three religions. His Buddhism too was of a conveniently unsectarian and therefore unexceptionable type, although he did show some leaning towards the T'ien T'ai faith, an inclination which was likely to commend him to the part of the Chinese world which remained to be conquered, since the strongholds of this popular sect were in the south. He was also represented as a great and good Buddhist king after the pattern of Asoka, as a munificent patron of the religion, and as a fulfilment of the Buddha's own prophecy that at a time when the *dharma* was in decay a great sovereign would appear in China.

This was an important part of the ideological preparation for the attempted reunification of China by the conquest of the south, but when Wen Ti eventually decided to make a move he gave notice of his intentions in the Confucian language appropriate to the situation. His edict justifying his projected conquest, of which 300,000 copies were distributed in the area south of the Yangtze, accused the Ch'en régime in South China of a long list of vices abhorred by Confucian moralists. He also wrote to the Ch'en ruler listing the crimes which made it his duty to relieve him of the throne. The actual campaign in 589 did not last long, and although the southern aristocrats attempted a rising a year later, it was crushed by the same ruthless general who had been responsible for the initial conquest. The population of the area south of the Yangtze was small, for it amounted to not more than about a ninth of the total figure of nearly fifty millions, so the territory was not strong enough to withstand a well prepared military expedition supported by an efficient commissariat. Moreover the inhabitants of Ch'en had been granted a ten-year tax remission and were not likely to make great efforts on behalf of their former masters.

When Confucianism had done its work of justifying the usurpation and the unification, the Cultured Emperor became disillusioned with it, and in 601 even went so far as to issue an edict for the abolition of the Confucian schools. For the remaining few years of his reign he concentrated on making Buddhism the common faith for an empire owing allegiance to himself as a model and divinely appointed Buddhist ruler. He established reliquary pagodas throughout the country to serve as permanent symbols of the dynasty's devotion to Buddhism, again closely following the example of King Asoka. When the shrines were inaugurated, miracles duly occurred, and an imperial commission was set up to publish a compilation of such auspicious happenings.

But the Cultured Emperor's end was near, and it was indeed remarkable that he had survived so long. Only two out of the two dozen or so emperors who had reigned over the northern dynasties during the previous two hundred years had even been fortunate enough to attain the age of forty, which he had already reached at the time of his usurpation. The irony of his position was that the more firmly he established the dynasty, the more strongly he might fear his own sons' ambition. It is not surprising that he was of a suspicious and cruel disposition. Among the nomadic Turco-Mongol traditions, with which the northern Chinese were familiar, was one which did not permit a ruler to continue beyond a fate-appointed time, while another enjoined parricide as an almost religious duty. Although the Chinese respect for filial piety was in direct contrast with the nomadic mores, it was not unknown for princes to connive at the deaths of their imperial fathers, so by 603 the ageing emperor had had all his sons disgraced and deprived of their rank one after the other, except for the favourite Yang Kuang, who seems by then to have been determined to succeed his father at the earliest opportunity. The following year Wen Ti fell ill and died, possibly murdered on the orders of Yang Kuang, who succeeded him as Yang Ti ('Emblazoned Emperor').

Yang Kuang, the second son of the Cultured Emperor, was only twelve when the dynasty was founded, but his father had immediately introduced him to affairs of state by giving him a post which carried the general responsibility for the defence of the northern frontier, under the guidance of trusted advisers. Later he took part in the campaign to conquer the Ch'en and, at the age of twenty-two, he became viceroy of the south with the task of smoothly integrating the recently subdued areas into the Sui empire. Like all his brothers he had had a Buddhist upbringing, and so both inclination and high policy prompted him to use his patronage of this religion as a means of reassuring the southerners and reconciling them to Sui rule. One of his first acts was to receive the 'Bodhisattva vows' for lay Buddhists, and he became a well-known patron of temples and shrines. At the same time, like his father, he saw the wisdom of drawing on what Confucianism and Taoism had to offer, and of showing himself as a patron of southern culture in general, which climate, natural environment and freedom from barbarian conquest had conspired to make very different from that of the north. He was obviously a very able administrator and with his experience of two key areas of the country, the northern frontier, which must always be guarded against barbarian invasion, and the recently conquered south which needed tactful handling, he was gaining the kind of experience which marked him out as a potential successor to the throne. But since he was only his father's second son, his very eminence and distinction was a source of danger to him, unless he could succeed in bringing about the disgrace of his elder brother. His intrigues finally succeeded in the year 600, when his brother the crown prince was degraded and reduced to the status of a commoner, while he himself was proclaimed crown prince. There is no means of being sure about the circumstances in which he succeeded. The fullest accounts of the old emperor's death say that, as he lay dying, the princess of the Ch'en ruling house who had become his favourite after the death of the redoubtable Empress Tu-hu complained that Yang Kuang had improperly accosted her, and that the dying emperor wished therefore to restore his eldest son to the position of crown prince, but Yang Kuang intercepted the message summoning the eldest son, and shortly afterwards it was reported that the emperor had died.

Whether Yang Kuang hastened his father's end or not, he was quick to make his own hold on the throne secure. His elder brother Yang Yung and Yung's sons were soon put to death and another brother was killed the following year. Yet another brother was in prison throughout Yang Kuang's reign. Nor did Yang Kuang's own eldest son survive long to nurture possible ambitions of prematurely succeeding his father on the throne. He died in 606, and the second son also soon fell into disgrace.

Yang Kuang was a pleasure-loving man who contrasted strongly with the strict father, whom he despised as an uncouth northerner. He favoured southerners rather than the north-westerners who had surrounded his father, restoring Confucian education and the examination system to give scope for new men. These came not only from the south, but also from the north-east, the home of Confucius, where there was still a strong Confucian tradition. In contrast with the timid Wen Ti, Yang Kuang was a vain man who likened himself to the great Emperor Wu of the Han Dynasty. He soon plunged into energetic measures aimed at making the Sui empire great, and it was not long before grandiose schemes began to place a burden on the state's resources in wealth and manpower. A splendid second capital was built at Loyang, which was a more conveniently situated central site, more easily supplied with grain, and closer to his power base in the south, where he planned a third capital at Yangchow. West of the city he constructed a palace with great parks and gardens, stocked with flora and fauna from all over the empire, embodying the royal love of luxury which Confucian moralists decried. Many people had to be uprooted to form a population for this great new city.

The Emblazoned Emperor had built the new Loyang to strengthen his own positon, but his next scheme had a vital influence on the course of Chinese history. We have seen how much attention his father had paid to the problem of water transport from the Yellow River valley to Changan, to ensure delivery of the grain tribute and food for the capital. Now it was necessary for a similar link to be forged with the prosperous and increasingly productive south. Making some use of already existing canals, Yang Ti established a waterway which linked the important centres of Loyang and Yangchow. This was constructed in 605. In 610 the waterway was extended to reach Hangchow. In the meantime a further canal had been excavated linking the Loyang area to the area of modern Peking in the north-east, which was especially important in assisting communications with the northern frontier. All this labour imposed a heavy burden on the people, but at least the great cost in lives and wealth had some justification in political terms, for the problem of linking the key areas of a large empire is of vital importance for its survival and growing prosperity. The Roman method was to build fast straight roads, but the Chinese utilized the very flat terrain and numerous lakes and rivers of the eastern part of the country to construct canals. These could incidentally provide water for irrigation channels, which were essential for the development of rice cultivation. To store the grain carried along these canals, the emperor added to the system established by his father two enormous granary complexes, one six miles and one three miles in circumference, which, like the canals, were to prove valuable assets to the succeeding dynasty.

Once Loyang and Yangchow were linked the emperor made a splendid progress in his imperial barge escorted by a specially constructed flotilla of dragon-boats, thus symbolizing the union of the long-separated north and south. This journey left its mark on the popular imagination for years to come, but another immense undertaking long remembered with bitterness was the rebuilding of the Great Wall, on which work commenced in 607. The sources report that, of the million labourers conscripted for the work, over half died. If this is true, such reckless disregard for human life cannot even be condoned because the Wall contributed to the security and prosperity of future generations. If frontier armies were unreliable or if political power at the centre was too weak to control the outlying area of the country, no defensive system, however strong, could protect the Chinese state.

The more imaginative and less inhumane way of dealing with frontier problems was to establish agricultural military colonies, and such colonies were in fact established by the emperor in the western frontier regions in 609, for in the early part of his reign he had been particularly successful in reopening and developing trade and diplomatic relations in this area, pushing further towards Central Asia than any emperor since Han times. Tunhwang and Hami were among the important trading-posts which came under Chinese control, and the territory of the T'u-yü-hun in northern Tibet was annexed after a military campaign. Many representatives of western border states came to court, and many acknowledged the emperor's suzerainty when he went on a tour of the region in 609. But trouble elsewhere soon weakened his hold on this area. In the north the T'u-ch'üeh or Turks were most formidable opponents. They had been a powerful menace to the Ch'i and Chou dynasties, from which they had exacted heavy tribute, but the Sui had succeeded in reducing their effectiveness by sowing dissension among their leaders, so that a definite division between eastern and western Turks began to emerge. Unfortunately in 607 it became clear that the eastern Turks were in league with the King of Koguryo, a vassal state situated in what is at present Liaotung and North Korea. Throughout most of the reign of the Cultured Emperor peaceful relations had prevailed and Koguryo had sent tribute. But the king's refusal to come to heel after the Emblazoned Emperor had found out about his connection with the Turks left the Sui sovereign no alternative but to embark on a series of difficult punitive campaigns against his vassal. The first campaign resulted in heavy losses for the Chinese forces, and the third (in 614) was interrupted by a serious rebellion in the heart of the empire which threatened Loyang itself and, although this was ultimately unsuccessful, it sparked off a series of revolts which led to the downfall of the dynasty. As the Sui history says, nine-tenths of the empire became bandits. Despite the confusion, the Emblazoned Emperor undertook a journey to the far north in 615 to inspect the Great Wall, but he was surprised by a force of eastern Turks and besieged for a whole month in a city called Yenmen, which was south of the Wall. Nothing could have more clearly demonstrated to the emperor that his costly work on this fortification had not been very fruitful.

After suffering this great blow to his prestige, Yang Ti lost heart. With one last show of extravagance he ordered a new imperial flotilla to replace the one which had been destroyed in the recent uprisings, and then sailed off in a final blaze of splendour for his beloved Yangchow, where he watched helplessly the struggle between rival contenders for his throne until he was murdered in 618.

Thus by a too hasty attempt to build the great empire of his dreams the Emblazoned Emperor had paid the price of vanity by pulling it in ruins about him. Nevertheless some of his achievements would live on and bring great benefit to his successors, leaving him only the odium of the tyrant who had made them possible. If he had succeeded in founding a great dynasty, he would have fared better at the hands of history; but for the ruin of a dynasty the emperor must be largely responsible in the eyes of those who regard the emperor's vice or virtue as one of the fundamental forces of history. The good achievements are swallowed up in the blackness of what followed: he was a patron of literature and was responsible for the rehabilitation of the Confucian educational system which had been scrapped by his father towards the end of his reign, but his cultural achievements were outshone by the glories of the T'ang. To later generations he became for the scholar-bureaucrat a prime example of an evil rule to be quoted as a monitory precedent, while the common people alternately shuddered at his cruelty and vicariously shared in his sensuality as recounted by the story-tellers. To sum up such a man's qualities in terms of good and evil is futile, especially when the history of his reign was written by usurpers, and we do not know how much they distorted the truth. All we know is that in the days before modern machinery, enduring human achievements cost much human suffering. Just as the harshness of the Ch'in had paved the way for the solid accomplishments of the Han, so the equally short-lived Sui had laid the foundation of T'ang greatness.

2

By harsh means the Sui had shown that it was possible for the Han territories to be united under one rule again, and now it was for the T'ang to profit from their predecessors' experience and build a lasting empire. This dynasty is reputedly one of the golden ages of Chinese civilization, for new heights were reached in literature and in the arts and crafts; but the epoch also had its darker side. We meet men who appeal to us for their humanity and virtue, but for one Po Chü-i, whose poems bear witness to his sadness at the lot of the poor, there were a hundred harsh officials, and for one saintly Hsüan-tsang, who travelled to the Far West in search of Buddhist scriptures, there were a thousand monks who combined ignorance of their creed with a facility for extorting money from the peasants. For the great majority of the Chinese people the problems of eking out a living and of satisfying or evading the demands of the tax-collector were overwhelming, while at court no emperor could feel truly secure until all his possible rivals had been butchered. Indeed during the second half of the dynasty, after the rebellion of An Lu-shan had made strong central control impossible, the sovereigns' thrones were at the mercy of the eunuchs, who, like freedmen at the court of the Roman emperors, had risen from their base estate to wield enormous power; while their lives and deaths were in the hands of Taoist alchemists, who proffered immortality drugs to men whose true need was not to prolong the natural tenure of life, but to introduce a stable political system which would prevent their normal span being cut short by the sword.

The first half of the dynasty is dominated by the reigns of three of China's most famous rulers, each of whom made a distinctive impact on the course of events, and had an influence far more powerful than might be credited by those who think that history is mainly shaped by blind economic forces rather than by percipient individuals. The first of these three was Li Shih-min, posthumously known as T'ai-tsung ('Grand Ancestor'), who as a very young man had played a leading part in putting his father on the throne as the first T'ang emperor in 618 and who reigned himself from 626 to 649. The feeble and sickly successor of this powerful monarch was soon dominated by one of his concubines, who exercised supreme power until her death in 705, for the last fifteen years being the only woman in Chinese history who ever occupied the dragon throne in name as well as in reality. Finally came Hsüan-tsung ('Mysterious Ancestor'), who put an end to the squalid period which ensued after the downfall of the Empress Wu, and reigned for forty-four years until the An Lu-shan rebellion brought about his abdication.

The brief reign of Li Shih-min's father, Li Yüan, known to history as Kao-tsu ('High Progenitor'), was mainly occupied with the task of consolidating the dynasty. Li Yüan had been an important official engaged on the dual task of suppressing local revolts and warding off Turkish invasion in the last years of the Sui; and it was understandable that, coming from a northern family which had much intermarried with 'barbarians', he should have eventually thrown in his lot with the Turks, who then helped to place him on the throne in Changan. The ambitious son, Shih-min, is said to have been responsible for urging his father to rebel, but since he was only eighteen at the time, it must be suspected that his role was exaggerated in the pages of history by men inclined to project his later achievement back into adolescent ambition. By contrast the High Progenitor has been depicted in history as a weak and vacillating figure, but reluctance to take on a job with such insecurity of tenure as the Chinese throne, dismissal from which would not mean a long and happy retirement cherishing the thought of his subjects' gratitude, must be rated as ordinary prudence. The Sui founder, too, had shrunk from claiming to be worthy of the Mandate of Heaven.

It was not until 624 that the internecine struggles came to an end. They had raged continuously since the rebellions which foreshadowed the collapse of the Sui Dynasty. Li Shih-min was constantly in the saddle during this period, while his father had to tackle the pressing problems facing the new administration. The tasks of keeping the empire united and of making it prosperous and secure were formidable. During the long years of disunion, the grand families had exerted a powerful independence which they would be reluctant to give up; and it would be difficult, if not impossible, to introduce measures which strongly conflicted with their interests, since these families provided the officials whose task was to enforce the law. It was the peasants who had to bear the burden of the running of the state by their contribution of taxes and corvée labour, and one of the fundamental tasks of administration was to ensure that they were prosperous enough to pay their due and were not forced into tax evasion. The key to the whole problem was the ownership of land. The traditional doctrine was that 'Under the broad heavens, all lands belong to the king', as the ancient Classic, the *Book of Songs*, had put it; and the T'ang government again tried to go back to this first principle, although the private possession and sale of land had been a fact of life for centuries. They adopted a system of 'land equalization' which was very similar to one which had been introduced by the Northern Wei and preserved in modified form by the later northern dynasties including the Sui. The basic allocation of land was to be 100 *mou*, or approximately 13½ acres, for each adult between the ages of eighteen and sixty; and other categories of persons, such as the old and the disabled, were to get smaller allocations in view of the fact that they were not liable to tax. One-fifth of the 100 *mou* was to be held in perpetuity and so became hereditary, but four-fifths were to revert to the state when the occupier reached the age of sixty. The reason for allocating some land in perpetuity was so that the peasants could plant trees, and especially mulberry-trees, which were important because they provided food for silkworms. Nobody might own more than the amount of land to which he was legally entitled. Merchants and artisans, monks and nuns, and other categories of persons were to be given smaller allotments of land. Officials, on the other hand, received large grants of land in accordance with their rank, together with other lands the produce from which formed part of their salary and provided for such expenses as the upkeep of public buildings.

The purpose of this apparently unrealistic scheme was to prevent the growth of large estates as well as to give the peasant a minimum level of subsistence so that he could pay the taxes the state required. But equality of land-ownership could only be an ideal rather than a reality. Such a scheme could be introduced in newly developed areas in which the conditions of physical geography were such that equal division of land was possible, and at Turfan and Tunhwang, which were military outposts set in Central Asian oases, there is evidence that the letter of the law was honoured to a remarkable degree. But the impossibility of putting the scheme into practice equally throughout the country was recognized in the rule that inhabitants of districts in which there was not enough land to enable the people to receive their full legal entitlement only received half of the recognized allotment of 'personal share' land. In practice even less was available in a densely populated area, especially in a region like Kuan-chung, where there were many officials who were entitled to large holdings in respect of their rank. Nor was any allowance made for differences in the quality of the land, although this was to be a characteristic of programmes of agrarian reform undertaken later in Chinese history. But the major flaw in the scheme was the fact that large parcels of land, amounting to a hundred times the size of peasant holdings, were being allocated to officials in perpetuity, while monastic communities were also being enriched by receiving grants of land in respect of their monks although there was no corresponding call on them to pay taxes. By introducing schemes of this kind Chinese lawgivers have been concerned to put forward ideals, preferably based on the revered precedents of an imaginary antiquity, as much as to cope with realities; and it is not surprising that a system which would have taxed the resources of a huge and efficient bureaucracy should soon have yielded to the private desires and needs of individuals. Frequent decrees issued soon after this legislation was passed in 624 forbade peasants to sell their lands, a sure sign that hardship was already forcing many of them to take this very step. Another reason why big changes were bound to occur despite legislation of an essentially conservative type is that the whole system of taxation was suited to an agrarian type of society in which most people were primary producers. Taxes were reckoned in terms of grain, cloth and labour; and the peasant population bore the major burden, although there was a great development of commerce and handicraft industry during the T'ang period. Another weakness was that the taxation system was geared to a conception of a rather primitive economy in which commodities rather than money could be treated as the basic currency.

To provide a body of officials to administer the country the T'ang rulers were to place growing emphasis on the Confucian civil service examination system recreated by the Sui. Li Yüan himself inclined to favour Taoism and, possessing the same surname as the reputed founder of that religion, claimed descent from that ancient sage, for it was wise not to neglect any device which could give an aura of legitimacy to the dynasty. Nevertheless he saw the virtue of encouraging Confucian ideas, and in the year after his accession he symbolized his support for the doctrine by having a temple built at the capital and jointly dedicated to Confucius and another ancient sage, the Duke of Chou. On the other hand no attempt was made to stamp out Buddhism, although this was proposed by the Grand Astrologer, Fu I, who thought that a brand of Confucianism reinforced with Taoist ideas would form a powerful system of thought and religion which would make it possible to dispense with the foreign faith. Now that China had at last triumphed again after centuries of division and alien rule, it was time to banish this outlandish creed, which he felt was a heavy burden on the state's economy. It was also a political menace, since it had been responsible for the disintegration of China after the Han and continued to be a subversive element in society. But Fu I's proposals obtained little support. The religion was too powerful, and the last disastrous attempt to suppress it under the fanatically Confucianist Northern Chou emperor was too recent a memory.

The T'ang founder's brief rule came to an end in 626. The problem of the succession had soon posed itself, since the able and ambitious Li Shih-min was only the second son. For some years before 626 the Emperor had entertained the idea of recognizing Shih-min's abilities by appointing him crown prince in place of his elder brother. The inevitable consequence was that the elder brother plotted to eliminate his more talented rival. The plot was foiled, and in the ensuing struggle the elder brother is said to have been shot by Li Shih-min himself who, having survived another attempt on his life a few months previously, was very much on his guard. Another brother was killed by one of Shih-min's main supporters, who after his death became, together with another loyal T'ang general, a tutelary deity of doorways. This came about because these two had been so effective in guarding their master's door against evil spirits, that he had likenesses of them painted and suspended on either side of the entrance to the palace. The emperor, who was now sixty, had been powerless to stop the feud between his two sons, and when fighting broke out between the two factions, he was out sailing on a pond in the palace grounds blissfully unaware of what was going on. Within three days he had appointed Shih-min crown prince and within two months he had abdicated in the latter's favour. Shih-min's rise was undoubtedly due to the fact that his military successes had given him great prestige with the officers and important officials at the capital. The crucial factor was that he had control of the Imperial Guard, which, like the praetorian guard in imperial Rome, was an essential ally in palace struggles.

When Li Shih-min ascended the throne, years of warfare had left the country in an impoverished condition, but a few excellent harvests in the opening years of his reign did much to restore the situation. A further blessing was the support of some excellent and loyal ministers, notably Chang-sun Wu-chi, the brother of his empress, who was the Emperor's chief adviser for more than thirty years. Major matters of government policy were generally decided by the sovereign in consultation with an informal group of such senior advisers. This group would include the heads of the three main branches of the central government, the imperial chancellery, the imperial secretariat and the department of state. The function of the imperial chancellery was to receive reports from members of the central and provincial governments and supply the emperor with whatever information and advice he needed for the conduct of affairs. The imperial secretariat was mainly concerned with the drafting and promulgation of imperial decrees and with the custody of official documents. The compilers of official history were also subordinated to this department. The department of state controlled the six boards, which were the executive organs of the government. The senior of these six boards was the Board of Civil Office, which was charged with all matters concerning the staffing of the civil service, including promotions, postings and the conduct of examinations, although the latter function was taken over by the Board of Rites in 736. The Board of Finance was concerned with the collection of taxes and the administration of state resources. The Board of Rites was concerned with religious matters and with the reception of foreign envoys (for the Chinese had no separate ministry of foreign affairs until nineteenth-century Europeans insisted on proper channels for the reception of their diplomats). The control of foreign subject peoples, however, came under the Board of War, in addition to its responsibility in military matters. The Board of Punishments was responsible for the administration of justice, fulfilling the functions of a judiciary as well as of a government department. Finally, the Board of Works had control of public buildings and state projects, such as irrigation and river-control schemes.

Another major organ of government was the Censorate. Hallowed Confucian tradition gave an honoured place to the minister who remonstrated with an erring sovereign, who was expected to heed his advice. This basic Confucian concept was formalized in the institution of the Censorate, which was charged with the responsibility of criticizing the policies and actions of high officials and even of the emperor himself. This body also had the job of inspecting the whole bureaucratic machine, and investigating cases of injustice and corruption; and these duties made it one of the most powerful offices in the empire. Such an organ was essential if the Confucian administrator, who enjoyed much freedom of action and was trained to think of himself as the 'father and mother' official, responsible for the welfare of the people in his own area, was to be relied on to put into effect policies which he did not personally consider wise. Under honourable rulers the power and vigilance of the Censorate did much to ensure the integrity of the bureaucracy, and in dark times its members provided examples of conspicuous courage in the face of tyranny.

Beneath these three major institutions – the three departments, the six boards and the censorate – were numerous minor departments of the civil service, and above them stood the emperor, who could exercise very considerable power, especially as it was he who chose his senior ministers. On the other hand the emperor daily consulted his group of favoured elder statesmen, and many major policy decisions were not initiated by the government at all, but were made in answer to suggestions submitted in the form of memorials by individual officials acting on their own responsibility.

This pattern of central government survived in broad outline throughout the T'ang Dynasty, although later in the dynasty, as we shall see, much power was exercised by groups, such as the palace eunuchs, which were outside the formal bureaucratic organization. Gradual changes would also take place in the provincial administration. In Han times China had been divided into just over a hundred provinces, but in early T'ang there were more than three times this number, largely because the Chinese now occupied the country more intensively, especially in the south, where Chinese communities had previously been dotted like small islands in a barbarian sea. This number of local units was obviously too unwieldy for efficient administration, so from time to time senior officials were commissioned to inspect the provinces in a certain area of the empire. During the early part of the seventh century this arrangement was gradually formalized until the provinces began to be grouped into ten separate circuits, subject to inspection by ten itinerant representatives of the central government. But it was several centuries before the empire came to be formally divided into the big provincial units which have existed in modern times.

The method of recruitment by competitive examinations was still in its infancy and in the early T'ang there were fewer than ten graduate entrants a year, so that the old aristocratic families were still successful in holding on to their privileged position. The situation of Confucianism was considerably strengthened under the Grand Ancestor, who fostered the growth of colleges in which studies were concentrated on the Confucian Classics. In 630 he decreed the establishment of a Confucian temple in every one of the provinces and counties of China. (The county was the lowest level of provincial authority and there were over fifteen hundred of these in T'ang times.) In these temples sacrifices were offered by the local officials, and Confucius thus became virtually the patron deity of the civil government. In 647 the emperor developed his Confucianizing policy further by making these temples into national shrines commemorating not only Confucius but also those who had best served the Confucian cause by their scholarship. Tablets commemorating twenty-two men of great literary attainments were placed in the Confucian temples. This precedent was followed by all later dynasties. Tablets were added and removed by imperial decree, and the temples became shrines to Confucian orthodoxy. The stone stelae which are still kept at the Pei Lin ('Forest of Tablets') at Changan (present-day Sian), with some of the Confucian Classics engraved from the Grand Ancestor's own handwriting, are a monument to that emperor's interest in Confucian studies.

But although T'ai-tsung's civil accomplishments were of lasting importance, they were outshone by his military glory. As a very young man he had played a major part in the wars which had established the dynasty. After he had ascended the throne the strongest military threat was the frequent incursions of the Turks across the northern frontiers. The only long-term solution of this problem was the conquest of all the country south of the Gobi Desert: this might guarantee lasting peace at tolerable cost, but no Chinese ruler since the Han had been in a position to contemplate such action. Indeed the traffic had all been in the other direction. The Turkish chieftains had been especially hostile towards China since the Emblazoned Emperor of the Sui had tried to sow dissension among them, and it was only natural that, when T'ang strength grew apace and their support was no longer needed, they should become bitter enemies of the new Chinese régime. Their hostility was fomented by the Sui princess, I Ch'eng, who, during her remarkable career as wife to four successive khans of the eastern Turks, had used her good offices to keep them on friendly terms with China while the Sui lasted (and is even said to have helped the Emblazoned Emperor escape from the siege of Yenmen), but took the reverse attitude after the T'ang successes. From the moment of his accession in 620 the last of these four husbands of I Ch'eng, Qadir Khan, had launched a series of invasions which so embarrassed the Chinese that in 624 there was even a proposal that Changan should be abandoned and the capital sited where it would not be an attraction to Turkish raiding parties. But the following year saw Li Shih-min succeed against the Turks, partly by sowing dissension between Qadir and his nephew, who should rightfully have succeeded to the throne instead of Qadir. The tragic events at the T'ang court in the summer of 626, which led to Shih-min's succession to the throne, were a signal for Qadir to make a fresh invasion on a grand scale. This time he was able to reach a point ten miles from the capital, but in the face of a bold show from the new emperor which fooled the khan into thinking his opponent much stronger than he really was, the Turks were unwilling to do battle so far away from their home territory, and a peace treaty was arranged. The Turkish menace was not serious if boldly faced by a reunited China.

A year later the severe winter brought famine to the Turks, and this sowed the seeds of discontent among Qadir Khan's people. The losses caused by the bad weather were increased when he failed to crush a revolt of disaffected tribesmen, but the Grand Ancestor would not take advantage of the situation to break the treaty. But he did consider himself free to attack Liang Shih-tu, the last surviving pretender to the imperial throne, who controlled the territory in the loop of the Yellow River where it runs north of the Great Wall, since Liang had not been included in the peace treaty. Liang was, however, an ally and vassal of the Turkish khan, who consequently went to his assistance, thereby incurring the just hostility of the T'ang without being able to save his ally from annihilation. The rebel hordes now elected a new Great Khan as rival to Qadir; and he, in return for T'ang recognition, acknowledged Chinese suzerainty. In 629 the Grand Ancestor, feeling that the treaty was no longer binding, decided that it was time to mount an offensive operation against Qadir, who suffered a series of disastrous defeats, leaving the whole of Inner Mongolia up to the edge of the Gobi Desert subject to the emperor, who became the 'Heavenly Khan' to his Turkish vassals. Two large garrisons were established to keep watch on the hordes, which were administered by their own khans acting as Chinese officials. This success came to T'ai-tsung and his generals only four years after the enemy had been encamped within ten miles of Changan. In this campaign Qadir's famous Chinese wife I Ch'eng was slain. Qadir himself was taken alive and, after publicly confessing his faults at the imperial court, he was given the indignity of a minor post in the imperial stables, where many of the defeated Turkish nobles were employed. Some years later one of these organized a conspiracy against the emperor's life, but a night attempt on the palace failed, and henceforward all these Turks were compelled to leave China and settle in Inner Mongolia.

Although the northern frontier problem was solved, away in the west the restless nomadic people called the T'u-yü-hun were causing trouble with their border raids on Chinese territory. These people, who dwelt in the mountainous country of what is now northern Chinghai, to the south of the Kansu trade-route, had been briefly under Sui domination; but now they were again harassing Chinese lines of communication with the far west, and their seizure of a Chinese ambassador who was on his way to Central Asia prompted the emperor to take firm action. But, undismayed by the fresh forces pitted against them, the T'u-yü-hun severely ravaged the district of Liangchow in the present province of Kansu. A full-scale expeditionary force was accordingly dispatched to attempt the permanent conquest of these troublesome neighbours. Heavily defeated near Sining, the barbarians retreated, adopting a scorched earth policy, so that it was difficult for the Chinese armies to follow them because there was no pasturage for their animals. However, half the army took up the pursuit and, inflicting a series of defeats on the enemy as they headed westward, captured huge herds of animals. In the meantime the rest of the army, under the leadership of a distinguished general called Hou Chün-chi, had been making its way on a great southern detour through an uninhabited land of such altitude that the snow lay thick on the ground in the middle of summer. After toiling through seven hundred miles of such terrain, they surprised a T'u-yü-hun force on the shores of a lake (either Tsaring Nor or Oring Nor) and totally defeated it, driving the remnants north-west till they met up with the other imperial army, with whose assistance they mopped up the remaining barbarian forces. Envoys begged for peace, which was granted on condition that the T'u-yü-hun accepted Chinese suzerainty, and afterwards there was no more trouble from that quarter.

In spite of this resounding victory, whose fame spread far and wide in Central Asia, the Chinese still had to put up with some trouble from Tibet, which had only recently, in 607, become a unified state. Irritated by a refusal to supply their king with a Chinese consort, the Tibetans invaded territory which is now in the province of Szechwan, only to be repulsed by Hou Chün-chi, the same brilliant general who had been in charge of the long southern march which had led to the utter defeat of the T'u-yü-hun. Having put the Tibetans firmly in their place, the emperor acceded to a later but much more polite request for a Chinese princess, and the latter, it is recorded, had a somewhat civilizing influence on the Tibetans by inducing them to give up the primitive practice of painting their faces in various colours.

In the distant north-west, more than twice as far from Changan as the T'u-yü-hun and the Tibetans, lay the oasis kingdoms which lined the important trade routes to the far west, which in antiquity had carried precious cargoes of silk to Rome. This region had come under imperial rule during the Han period, when Chinese military might had held sway over two thousand miles from the capital, and thus had reached further than the distance from contemporary Rome to the remotest outposts of the Roman empire, in spite of the harsh conditions of mountain and desert which had to be overcome. During the period of disunion after the fall of the Han the Chinese had naturally lost their political influence in this region, but the Sui had made some attempt to restore the position and the T'ang had been able to improve on their efforts so that by 630 the frontier post on the northern of the two main trade-routes was Hami, which surrendered to the Chinese in that year. The next main station upon this route was Turfan, the capital of a large and powerful kingdom under a dynasty which had been founded by a Chinese from western Kansu at the beginning of the sixth century. The state was governed on Chinese lines and there was even a college at which the Confucian Classics were taught, although the local language was Indo-European. Buddhism was also firmly entrenched, as in all these Central Asian kingdoms (which were, it will be remembered, the channel through which Buddhism originally flowed into China), and when the famous pilgrim Hsüan-tsang passed through on his way to India in 630 the king of Turfan tried to persuade him to settle there as head of the Buddhist church in his country.

The kingdom had long enjoyed friendly relations with China. The king's father had accompanied the Emblazoned Emperor of the Sui Dynasty on one of his Korean expeditions and had been honoured in return by the bestowal of a wife from the imperial clan, and on the accession of the Grand Ancestor there had been an exchange of gifts between the two royal houses. When the boundaries of the Chinese empire drew nearer with the acquisition of Hami, the king of Turfan wisely offered tribute; but cordial relations came to an end in 639 when the king not only stopped paying tribute but also gave shelter to Chinese political refugees. He had banked on distance and the desert saving him from T'ang vengeance, but in Hou Chün-chi, the conqueror of the T'u-yü-hun and the Tibetans, T'ai-tsung had a general who was used to overcoming such difficulties of terrain. The news that a Chinese army was actually approaching across the desert so dismayed the king that he fell ill and died, and his son soon surrendered. The surprising outcome of this campaign was that the emperor decided to annex this remote and large country, similar in size to Norway, instead of making it a subject state under a vassal ruler. It was garrisoned by Chinese troops. This may seem surprising in contrast with the treatment of the much more troublesome Turks, whose raids had been a constant menace. Turfan offered no military threat to China. On the other hand Hou Chün-chi's successes in the west had shown that anything was possible, while the Han Dynasty pattern of imperial power must have beckoned to the Grand Ancestor's ambition. Moreover these oasis settlements, in country which was much more fertile than it is today and which could be made still more fertile by irrigation, offered an environment more congenial to the Chinese than the frozen north, in which their agricultural way of life would not flourish at all. During the next decade other states further to the west, even in the Oxus valley beyond the Pamirs, fell to Chinese forces or offered their allegiance, notably Khotan, whose king came to the capital to make his submission. Chinese prestige was now enormous, and ambassadors came from Persia, from the states of India, and from other countries far and wide. It was in these times too that wandering Syrian missionaries found their way to China and were permitted to establish a Church of Nestorian Christianity under imperial patronage. The strength and stability of the T'ang régime now meant an increasing flow of trade and of people throughout the China-centred world. From now on it would also be easier for the techniques pioneered by the Chinese to find their way across to the West, and the Middle Kingdom's political system would also be imitated by neighbouring peoples.

A Turkish invasion in 641 was repulsed with very heavy losses to the enemy, a victory which ensured that there would be no serious danger from that quarter for some time to come, but it was not long before the Grand Ancestor became involved in Korea. Disastrous Korean campaigns had been the ruin of the Sui Dynasty, and in this same theatre T'ai-tsung was to experience his one major military failure. In 642 a revolution had taken place in Koguryo; the king had been murdered by a powerful nobleman, who had thereupon put a puppet on the throne but exercised the supreme authority himself. In the following year Silla and Paikche, the other kingdoms on the Korean peninsula, were threatened by this new régime, so they appealed to T'ai-tsung for help. The emperor promised his assistance and decided to take personal command of the campaign. Very careful preparations were made. Mindful of the fate of the Emblazoned Emperor's troops, starving to death in the desolate Manchurian wastes, the Grand Ancestor had a fleet of four hundred large ships built so that he could send part of his force straight across the Yellow Sea to offer a direct threat to the Koguryo capital. This would divert the enemy's attention from the main force which would meanwhile be making the long overland march. The plan met with some success when it was put into operation in 644, but although T'ai-tsung scored one brilliant victory which made him send back a triumphant message concluding, 'When I am at the head of the army, what else should we expect?', his progress was delayed by strongly defended cities, and with the approach of winter he had to retreat back to China. Although he had annexed a number of cities and brought 70,000 captives back to settle in the area of modern Peking, he had failed in his purpose of toppling the regicide. His later attempts to subdue Koguryo were equally unsuccessful.

An unfortunate legacy of the Korean campaign was a deterioration in the emperor's health, and although he was still only in his middle forties he had not long to live. His declining years were darkened by the fact that the crown prince, his eldest son by the Empress Chang-sun, was not the worthiest candidate for the succession, so that the situation was tragically reminiscent of the circumstances immediately before his own succession to the throne. Unfortunately the crown prince, whose name was Ch'eng-ch'ien, was an unbalanced young man with an exotic taste for the practices of his remote barbarian ancestors, which found little favour with the tutors who were trying to imbue him with the polite civilization of China. He had an elder half-brother, named Li T'ai, Prince Wei, who was a talented young man, strongly approved by the emperor, but ruled out for the succession because he was the son of a concubine and not of the emperor's beloved consort. T'ai, however, had one fault: he was ambitious, and he saw in the Grand Ancestor himself an example of a worthy prince who had succeeded to a throne to which he was not entitled. When his ambitions were brought to the sovereign's notice, the latter tried to put an end to intrigue by announcing that if Ch'eng-ch'ien died, his son would succeed him as crown prince. In an attempt to improve Ch'eng-ch'ien's character a most respected minister called Wei Cheng was appointed as his tutor, but unfortunately he died early the following year. The conduct of the heir to the throne now became even more outrageous. There was a notorious affair with a dancing-boy, which made the emperor so angry that he had the boy put to death. Ch'eng-ch'ien was desolated by his loss. He had already entertained murderous designs against his ambitious brother, and now his thoughts could easily be turned in the direction of taking vengeance on his father for the bereavement he had suffered. The man who prompted him was none other than the great general Hou Chün-chi, who had now fallen into disgrace. But before the plot could be put into effect, the man whom Ch'eng-ch'ien had hired to murder his half-brother turned king's evidence and the whole affair came out into the open. Hou Chün-chi was executed. Ch'eng-ch'ien was degraded to the status of a commoner and sent into exile, where he died a year later. Li T'ai, Prince Wei, also died in exile shortly afterwards.

In the final years of the Grand Ancestor's life several of his most trusted advisers also died, but Chang-sun Wu-chi was still there to attend him at the last when he passed away in 649. Li Shih-min had been a man of great all-round ability, uniting in himself the finest qualities of his barbarian and Chinese forbears. From the former came his great love of horses and skill with the bow. He celebrated his six famous war-horses in prose and verse and commissioned the stone reliefs of them which later adorned his tomb. His accomplishments did not stop short at military glory, but also embraced the arts of peace. For although much of his youth was spent in the saddle, he had been given a traditional education in Chinese literature, and as emperor he not only became a renowned patron of Confucian education, but also achieved distinction as a calligrapher, whose work engraved on stone tablets has survived to this day and been admired as a model of style. His patronage of Confucianism did not mean that Buddhism was neglected. Indeed during the last years of his life he sought especial consolation in this faith, having fallen under the spell of Hsüan-tsang after that worthy monk had returned from India amid great acclaim. When he first gave him audience, the meeting lasted until evening, in spite of the fact that the Grand Ancestor was busy making final preparations for his Korean campaign. Later, in 648, when the sick emperor withdrew to his rustic retreat, the Jade Flower Palace, he had Hsüan-tsang join him, and expressed deep regret that his busy life had left him little time for the study of Buddhism and that he had not met Hsüan-tsang sooner. Although, in the earlier years of his reign, he had favoured Buddhism out of political interest, patronizing temples so that monks would pray for the empire's welfare, it was only in his last years that he regarded Confucianism and Taoism as 'mere puddles beside the mighty ocean' of Buddhism.

It is difficult to rely on official histories for the accurate character portrayal of great founders, who are as likely to be described with adulation as bad rulers are to suffer vituperation, but there seems to be no doubt that Li Shih-min was a great emperor who inspired much loyalty in his subordinates whom he treated with something of the respect expected from a Confucian monarch. Thus it is recorded that on the death of Wei Cheng he declared: 'In my life I have used three mirrors. One of bronze to adjust my dress; the records of history to correct the mistaken policies of the present; and Wei Cheng who served to reveal the faults of my character.'

3

One of the unfortunate hazards of the system of hereditary monarchy is that the heir to a great sovereign is more than likely to be a weakling. The prince who eventually followed the Grand Ancestor was the youngest of the Empress Chang-sun's sons. He succeeded, in his early twenties, as the emperor who was to be canonized after his death as Kao-tsung ('High Ancestor'). When he attended his father during his last illness he made the acquaintance of the concubine Wu, who had been a member of the Grand Ancestor's harem for the past ten years. He fell in love with her, and it was even rumoured that he was intimate with her before his father's death. When the emperor did die, the concubine Wu, together with all the other members of the harem, had to have her head shaved and enter a Buddhist convent where, according to the usual fate of such persons upon the death of their imperial master, she was destined to pass the rest of her days. The lady Wu, however, was back in the palace again in little more than a year. Kao-tsung's empress was childless and, worried at the increasing favour shown by the new emperor to one of his concubines who already had a son, she persuaded him to have the concubine Wu restored to the palace, thinking that she would provide a safe diversion for him, since the gratitude she would feel at her release from the convent would ensure that she did nothing detrimental to the empress's own position. Thus in 650, at the age of twenty-five, there returned to the palace one who, despite her sex, was to play a leading role in the state's affairs for the next half century.

Notwithstanding the extreme irregularity of her position, she rose steadily in the emperor's favour. The High Ancestor was of a lustful disposition and he further strengthened his ties with the Wu family by having relations with her widowed sister. Meanwhile the lady herself showed none of the gratitude which the empress had expected of her. Indeed in 654 she went so far as to accuse the unfortunate woman of murdering her baby daughter, and in 655 she denounced her for engaging in sorcery against her. In the same year, after some ministerial opposition to the proposal, the elevation of the lady Wu to the position of empress at last became acceptable. As a preliminary step, the original empress was found guilty of plotting to poison the emperor, and was imprisoned within the palace. Then a decree was issued white-washing the lady Wu's earlier connections with the palace and she was duly installed as empress. Before long her hapless rival had suffered a terrible death on her instructions.

By the end of the decade all the elder statesmen who had opposed her elevation had been removed. Even the great Chang-sun Wu-chi, the brother-in-law of the Grand Ancestor who had held high office for thirty years, was exiled on a charge of plotting to poison the emperor and finally harried to suicide. All influence was now in the hands of the Empress Wu and her supporters. In 660 the High Ancestor suffered a stroke and it was necessary for him to have her help in dealing with state papers, and in this way much official business came into her hands. Before long she was attending imperial audiences, seated on a throne as elevated as that of the emperor, but hidden behind a screen. By this time she already had three sons, and the emperor having no other sons of any seniority, her future and that of her offspring now seemed secure. Until the High Ancestor's death twenty years later, she maintained control of affairs, and in the words of the historian,

The whole sovereign power passed into her hands. Life and death, reward and punishment, were determined by her word. The Son of Heaven merely sat upon his throne with hands folded, and Court and country alike named them the Two Holy Ones.

The ultimate symbol of legitimacy was given to the régime of the Empress Wu and her ailing husband in 666 with the celebration of those most holy rites at the sacred mountain of T'ai-shan, which, as we have seen before, were meant to mark the complete pacification of the empire and its contented submission to the sovereign. The occasion was marked by the presence of foreign envoys, including even a representative of the rising Japanese empire and the son of that dictator of Koguryo whom T'ai-tsung had vainly attempted to overthrow. The auspicious event was celebrated by the grant of a general amnesty and followed up by a court visit to the birthplaces of Confucius and Lao Tzu, the reputed founder of Taoism.

At the time when a representative of Koguryo was present at the T'ai-shan sacrifices, no solution had yet been found to the Korean problem, which had defeated even the great T'ai-tsung. It was an affront to China that this large and prosperous state, occupying territory which had formed part of the Han empire and enjoying a high level of civilization which owed much to Chinese influence, should remain independent. In his will, however, the Grand Ancestor had ordered his successor to abandon the Korean war, and it was not until 655 that hostilities were resumed, when Silla, having been invaded by Koguryo and Paikche, successfully appealed for Kao-tsung to intervene. After several years of indecisive border campaigns on the Liao, the Chinese decided to strike at the weaker partner by sea, and Paikche was conquered in one brief campaign in 660. Encouraged by this success, the imperial forces planned to complete the downfall of Koguryo by means of a two-pronged attack, striking north from Paikche while simultaneously advancing along the usual overland route; but their plans were thrown out of gear by a revolt in Paikche, which necessitated a further conquest of that country in 662. It was during this campaign that China and Japan came into direct hostilities for the first time, for Paikche had appealed to the Japanese for assistance. The Paikche and Japanese forces were totally defeated and four hundred Japanese ships were burnt. The Korean campaigns had, however, been too costly for the Chinese to contemplate a further attack on Koguryo, so the next few years were given to the pacification and

rehabilitation of Paikche. In 665 a treaty of friendship was concluded between Silla and Paikche, and the following year envoys
from Silla and the still independent Koguryo were present at the
great ceremony at T'ai-shan, which has just been described. But
in the same year the dictator of Koguryo died, his death being
followed by dissension among his sons, which had possibly been
fomented by Chinese agents. The T'ang government rapidly took
advantage of the situation, winning a complete and final victory
in 668, when the king of Koguryo and other captives were presented at the Grand Ancestor's tomb. The state of Koguryo had
been in existence for more than 700 years. After this the Korean
peninsula was unified under the rule of Silla, which soon settled
down to be a loyal vassal of the Chinese.

For the High Ancestor and his empress another fruit of victory
was the glory of succeeding where the great T'ai-tsung had
failed. But the cost was great, and Kao-tsung's last years were a
period of economic crisis, with serious inflation leading to widespread distress and tax evasion. These difficult campaigns, which
had involved long and costly siege operations, also hastened
changes in the organization of the armed forces. During the
reign of T'ai-tsung and in the early years of Kao-tsung, the
frontiers had been guarded for the most part by a large number of
small garrisons, manned generally by militiamen, although in the
more remote outposts condemned criminals were sometimes used.
When the need for a large army arose, an expeditionary force
would be especially created to deal with the emergency. Such
forces would consist of militiamen together with conscripts from
parts of the empire which did not come within the militia system,
and contingents supplied by barbarian allies. But now, starting
in 678, large armies were kept together as units to become a
regular feature of frontier organization.

It was not only in the Korean theatre that Chinese armies were
brought into action. Although the Tibetan court was becoming
increasingly sophisticated and sinicized, the people had not lost
their habit of plundering Chinese frontier districts, and in 663 an
infringement of Tu-yü-hun territory led to an open clash with a
T'ang army which resulted in a surprising and thorough Chinese

defeat. To deal with continued Tibetan raids punitive expeditions were sent with varying degrees of success, and it was not until the end of the reign that a former Korean general serving in that theatre was able to perfect a system of defence which could contain the situation. But by this time the Tibetans had expanded their sphere of influence enormously. In the north they had wrested control of the Tarim basin from the Chinese, and in the south and east they were asserting overlordship over the tribes in what are now northern Yünnan and western Szechwan. At the same time the Turks, who had remained quiet for twenty years, began to cause trouble again towards the end of Kao-tsung's reign.

A further drain on the empire's resources was the increasing amount of wealth being spent on Buddhism. In the closing years of his life, T'ai-tsung had been deeply impressed with the wisdom of Hsüan-tsang, who had been greeted with tremendous popular enthusiasm when he returned from his pilgrimage to India, his route into Changan being lined by dense throngs of citizens. Among the new religious buildings put up in the capital during Kao-tsung's reign was the great Hsi-ming ('Western Brightness') monastery, which had more than four thousand cells. One of these was occupied by Hsüan-tsang, and while he stayed there he was constantly visited by high officials and palace eunuchs bearing gifts. One official complained to the throne that 'Present day temples surpass even the imperial palaces in design, embodying the last word in extravagance, splendour, artistry, and fineness.' The famous Wild Goose Pagoda was also built, to house the texts and images Hsüan-tsang had brought back from India. The chief purpose of imperial patronage of Buddhism was to secure prayers for the prosperity of the state, and nationwide supplications were ensured when it was decreed, in 666, that each prefecture in the empire should have a Buddhist and a Taoist temple. Thus all of the 'three doctrines' were now represented in every corner of the country, under official patronage. But it was not only for reasons of policy that Buddhism was patronized by the court. The lady Wu herself was a fervent Buddhist, and already during the High Ancestor's reign she had begun the

85

famous carvings of Buddhist figures in the grottoes at Lungmen near Loyang, which she was to continue when she came to wield the supreme power in her own name.

In the last few years of Kao-tsung's reign matters fell out in such a way that the lady Wu was able to continue to dominate the court after his death. In 675 the emperor tried to have her appointed regent in view of his failing health. This proposal was dropped when it met with ministerial opposition. But in the same year, the crown prince, the lady Wu's eldest son, Li Hung, who gave promise of being an excellent ruler when his turn came, died in circumstances which threw suspicion upon his mother, who was known to differ from him on matters of policy and would have lost all influence if he had succeeded to the throne. The next holder of this dangerous position was disgraced in 679 when a large store of weapons was found at his residence; after being accused of plotting rebellion, he was degraded and exiled. The next available son of the Empress Wu was the future emperor Chung-tsung, who accordingly succeeded as crown prince. But when the High Ancestor finally died at the end of 683, his will stated that his successor should refer all disputed matters of great importance to the empress dowager for her decision. Only three days after his death the head of the imperial chancellery proposed that, since the crown prince had not formally ascended the throne, all urgent matters should be dealt with by the empress dowager. Thus she continued to handle all business. The weakling Chung-tsung was deposed after less than two months and replaced by the Empress Wu's youngest son, whose imperial name was Jui-tsung ('Sagacious Ancestor'). But his position was purely nominal. He neither occupied the imperial apartments, nor exercised the functions of an emperor. Instead he was virtually a prisoner in the palace.

One of the Empress Wu's first actions was to transfer the capital from Changan to Loyang, which was re-named the Divine Capital. This was a sensible move, since in time of crop failure it had been proving impossible to provision Changan and the Kuanchung area because of the obstacle to communication up the Yellow River presented by the Sanmen rapids, especially now that standing armies were replacing the old militia, so that there were more mouths to feed in the metropolitan area. In years of scarcity the court and the whole administration with its bulky files and records had had to be transferred to Loyang, and this had happened in eleven out of the last twenty-six years of Kao-tsung's reign. The main obstacle to a permanent move had been the fact that most of the important families came from the Kuanchung area, but the Empress Wu was not so interested as her predecessors in relying on the support of the old aristocratic families.

It was now the empress's task to consolidate her position, and being a woman in a totally unprecedented situation, she had to be even more ruthless than a man. Ex-Crown Prince Li Hsien, a possible focus of revolt, was harried to suicide; and her nephew Wu Ch'eng-ssu soon became leader of a party working for the establishment of a new dynasty under her. As a necessary preliminary to this she promoted her ancestors to royal rank and established an imperial ancestral temple for them at Loyang. This move touched off a revolt aimed at restoring Jui-tsung to full imperial power, but within three months all opposition was crushed. She was now able to go right ahead with her preparations for the day when she would ascend the throne in her own right.

Although the rebellion had soon been crushed, it had made the empress very suspicious, so she instituted a system of secret police and informers in order to detect and suppress conspiracies against her. A school was established to offer instruction in these squalid arts, and many undesirable characters obtained prominent positions in the state, like the cake-seller whose prowess as an informer won him the rank of general. At the same time, to counterbalance the power of the old aristocracy, the empress favoured the promotion of talented men from the less privileged classes, and this policy eventually gave her a solid base of support among the intellectuals. Already in the High Ancestor's time she had been an active patron of learning and literature, collecting together a group of literati known as Scholars of the North Gate. At first they had been given literary commissions, but later they had been entrusted with the secret inspection of all memorials and documents before they were submitted to her imperial husband, so that the empress could feel sure that no intrigues were being carried on against her.

In the meantime predictions and prophecies were preparing the way for the usurpation. In 688 a stone was found in the River Lo bearing the inscription: 'The Holy Mother has come among men to rule with perpetual prosperity', whereupon the Empress Wu took the grand title of 'Holy Mother Divine Imperial One'. A feeble and badly co-ordinated revolt of the T'ang princes in the same year was soon crushed, giving the empress and her secret police an excuse for securing the conviction and execution or exile of almost the entire imperial family. In January 689 two great ceremonies were staged, the first at an altar especially erected for the veneration of the sacred stone from the River Lo, and the second in the new Hall of Light, which had been completed only the previous month. This great and costly building, the most imposing edifice of its day, based on hallowed and shadowy precedents from the Chou Dynasty, was regarded as the most sacred building in the empire. Here she presided in imperial robes and, after sacrificing to the Supreme Deity, she next paid honour to the High Progenitor and the Grand Ancestor, founders of the T'ang, and then to her own father, a plain indication that he was to be regarded as the founding ancestor of a new dynasty.

Confucian writings provided no sanction for a female ruler, but in the great store of Buddhist literature men found justification for her succession. The Great Cloud sutra, which was available in Chinese translations, referred to a female divinity destined to be reborn as a monarch ruling over a wide area, so the empress's Buddhist supporters interpreted the sutra to mean that she was the incarnation of Maitreya, whose coming would inaugurate a better age. The work was circulated throughout the empire, and the message must have deeply impressed the populace. Soon a censor submitted a petition openly suggesting the change of dynasty. This the empress refused in accordance with propriety. But the portents continued to be favourable: it was related that a phoenix, emblem of the empress, had alighted on the roof of the imperial palace. Another petition, this time headed by Jui-tsung and backed by the whole court, was graciously accepted, and on 24 September 690 she was proclaimed emperor. Members of the Wu clan were given princely rank and her other supporters were duly rewarded with promotions. The censor who first proposed the change of dynasty had been promoted so rapidly that he had worn robes of four different colours in the course of one year, and so was nicknamed 'Official of the Four Seasons'. For the first and last time a woman had ascended the throne of the Chinese emperors to reign in her own right.

In this unique situation it is not surprising that this was a period of rapid social and political change. The Empress Wu needed new kinds of support for her régime, so, although the outline of government organization remained largely the same, the court and administration had been taking on a new look throughout the period of her ascendancy. With recruitment by examination now running at a much higher level than it had been early in the T'ang period, high office had been getting an infusion of new blood, particularly from the rapidly developing south-eastern part of the country. There was also a considerable growth in the size of the bureaucracy. Indeed the country was undergoing an important social revolution in which the intellectuals were ousting the aristocracy as the governing class. At the same time other organizations outside the normal bureaucratic machinery were having an important influence on political affairs. During Kao-tsung's reign the Scholars of the North Gate had been employed to inspect memorials before they reached him, and later a system of secret police had been introduced to protect the empress from conspiracies. Fortunately the end of the system of delation came with the downfall of its protagonist Lai Chün-ch'en in 697, but during the period of its activity it had not only brought many people to ruin, but had also undoubtedly served as a corrupting influence in society.

Another evil influence at court and an offence to the dignity of political life was the series of favourites who achieved great influence over the ageing empress and were rewarded with quite unprecedented honours. The first of these was Hsüeh Huai-i, a pedlar of cosmetics renowned for his strength and virility. One of the women with whom he had dealings happened to be the maidservant of the eighteenth daughter of the Emperor Kao-tsu, who eventually introduced him to the empress. She is said by the malicious historians to have bestowed her favours, at the age of sixty, on this lowly representative of a rather unrespectable profession. However this may have been, she certainly had him made a monk so that it was easy for him to visit her in the imperial palace. She also compelled her son-in-law to adopt this upstart hawker as his own father. Not content with this, she made him abbot of the White Horse Monastery, the oldest Buddhist foundation in China; and although one would not have thought him any better qualified for this than for the Buddhist priesthood, he was also appointed palace architect. The empress ignored a suggestion that, before taking up such a post, it would be more seemly if he were made a eunuch. She did not do things by halves and, just as she had made him abbot of the most venerable Chinese monastery, so she also commissioned him to create the most grandiose Chinese building, the Hall of Light, which, as we have seen, had a part to play in the preparations for the usurpation.

Hsüeh Huai-i continued in favour after the empress's elevation to the imperial throne. Pedlar of cosmetics, monk, architect, he now added yet another profession to his list, that of soldier, again entering at the top without serving any apprenticeship. In 694 he was appointed commander-in-chief of the northern frontier armies, to repel the Turks who had been raiding across the border. This time he was more patently a figurehead, for what he lacked in experience was made up for by the quality and seniority of the staff attached to him. It was not long before an attempt was made to bring about his downfall: he had gathered young rogues about him at the White Horse Monastery, and this was made the basis of a charge of treason. But though his followers were exiled, Huai-i himself remained unscathed. One night shortly afterwards there was a conflagration at the Hall of Light, the blaze illuminating the capital like daylight, and it is said that Huai-i had set fire to it out of pique because others seemed to be succeeding him in the empress's favour. Nevertheless it was he who was instructed to rebuild it. This was the last commission. Overbearing because he had been loaded with favours but at the same time discontented because he was no longer at the summit of the empress's esteem, he now treated her so un-civilly that the imperious old lady decided to get rid of him. Having owed his rise to the maidservant of a princess, he now met his downfall and death at the hands of the palace women, the sturdiest of whom were chosen to overpower him and put him to death.

Hsüeh Huai-i's encounter with the Turks had only been of slight importance, but there was a more serious conflict in 696 when a new and more vigorous khan attempted to extract some concessions from the T'ang court, including the hand of a royal prince for his daughter and the return of some of the Turkish tribes which had previously submitted to the Chinese. He was encouraged to press for these concessions by the fact that the Khitan, a tribe on the north-eastern frontier which was to play an important role in later Chinese history, had been provoked into a powerful revolt by the unreasonable conduct of the Chinese frontier commander in their area. The force sent against them had been hastily got together from slaves and criminals and had been heavily defeated. A further invasion by the Khitan in 697 was also to inflict a defeat on a T'ang force under the command of the empress's nephew Wu San-ssu. In view of the Khitan threat the empress acceded to the Turks' demands, but the khan grumbled at the fact that his daughter was offered the hand, not of a Li, but of the empress's great-nephew, a Wu. This crisis in foreign affairs resolved the conflict for the succession which had been raging between the supporters of the Wus and the Lis. The Wus had proved so deficient in military prowess that the great minister Ti Jen-chieh was emboldened to propose that Chung-tsung should be brought back to Loyang and restored to the position of crown prince. The imminent danger of another Turkish invasion helped to persuade the empress to take this step, and his restoration and appointment as nominal commander-in-chief was apparently enough to improve recruiting drastically and rally the morale of the Chinese troops who, with Ti Jen-chieh as field commander, forced the Turks to retire. The year 696 had also seen a serious defeat for the Chinese at the hands of the Tibetans. Four years previously a Chinese force had recovered the important Central Asian oasis towns of Kucha, Khotan, Kashgar and Karashahr, but now they reverted to Tibetan control.

The succession to the throne was a perennial source of trouble in the Chinese state even in normal circumstances, and the uniqueness of Empress Wu's position meant that the matter was more complicated than usual. During the years prior to the restoration of Chung-tsung it had been one of the main political problems. The Wu family tablets had replaced those of the Li family in the Temple of the Imperial Ancestors; but on the other hand an earlier T'ang emperor, Jui-tsung, had been titled Imperial Heir, and so was the presumed successor of the empress. Jui-tsung's own position was highly ambiguous because, although he was a son of the High Ancestor and his succession would therefore imply the restoration of the T'ang dynasty, he had taken the surname of Wu and so been adopted into that family. Many other Lis had adopted the Wu surname, and to complicate matters still further there had been some intermarriages between the two families.

As Imperial Heir, Jui-tsung had been the chief target of Wu machinations, and in 693 both his former empress and a favourite concubine had been put to death on a charge of using sorcery against the Empress Wu. Soon Jui-tsung himself had been accused of conspiracy and the leading informer Lai Chün-ch'en had been put in charge of the investigations. But the Empress Wu had eventually had the case against Jui-tsung dropped, and it was not long before Lai Chün-ch'en met his downfall and death. Meanwhile the Wu clan had continued to press that the empress's nephew Wu Ch'eng-ssu should be made her heir, but, as we have just seen, opinion against the Wu clan hardened because of the débâcle on the northern frontier, and Wu Ch'eng-ssu himself died in 698, disappointed at the final failure of his ambitions. Soon after Chung-tsung had been made crown prince, the empress, fearing that the Wu clan would be exterminated at once after she passed away, made her children and the Wu princes swear a solemn oath to live in harmony after her death. This ceremony took place in 699 in the Hall of Light, but oaths are often broken, however solemn the setting, when thrones are at stake.

Meanwhile in 697, two years after the architect of that grandiose edifice, the ex-pedlar of cosmetics, Hsüeh Huai-i, had died, the ageing empress entered into another grotesque relationship, this time with a certain Chang Ch'ang-tsung, a young man of extreme beauty and musical talent. He and his half-brother both soon became firm favourites of the empress, and would frequent the palace, powdered and rouged and dressed in gaily coloured silks. The historians say that the old empress, now seventy-two, graciously permitted both her young favourites to become her lovers. However this may be (and it has been argued that the story is probably true, since a female sovereign was just as much entitled to such diversion as a male emperor was to his harem), she clearly ceased to concern herself very seriously with the future, conscious that there was not much of it left for her to enjoy, and was content to pass her time in the company of these men in the seclusion of her summer palaces. Poets were invited to sing Ch'ang-tsung's beauty, and handsome youths were engaged to attend him. A nephew of the empress having flatteringly opined that he was a reincarnation of an ancient sage who ascended to heaven on a crane, a pageant was staged in which he was appropriately dressed for the part and raised to the roof by mechanical means, playing the flute as he went. Before long the power, arrogance and greed of these two brothers, which might have been tolerated had they been accompanied by talents which were of service to the state, began seriously to weaken the empress's authority. Ministers vied with one another to flatter her favourites, and the depths of indignity were reached in 702 when her sons, the two ex-emperors, so far lowered themselves as to take part in the general adulation, when together with their sister, the Princess T'ai-p'ing, they petitioned their mother to make Chang Ch'ang-tsung a prince, and she actually made him a duke.

A serious crisis developed when the empress decided to instal a younger brother of her two favourites in the important post of governor of Changan. This appointment was resisted by her chief minister, Wei Yüan-chung, and the Chang brothers realized that they would not survive long if the empress died while Wei remained in high office. They made the usual attempt to concoct a charge of treason, but their success was limited to securing his exile. The case only served to weaken the prestige of the empress further in the eyes of the increasing number of people who were looking to a restoration of the T'ang as the main hope for the future. In late 704 the empress became so ill that she could not see her ministers for two months at a stretch, but she was still attended by the Chang brothers, who were the only channel of communication between the court and the empress. If events were left to take their course and the old woman died, there were obvious dangers that her young favourites might fake decrees in a desperate attempt to secure their future, so early the following year some of the leading ministers conspired to put Chung-tsung back on the throne. The conspiracy was successful, for the two Chang brothers were caught in the palace and summarily decapitated, and the Empress Wu was forced to abdicate.

After she had been deposed, she was taken to a palace just outside Loyang, where she spent the remaining months of her life, still treated with respect and paid formal visits by Chung-tsung at the head of the entire court. But the removal of the aged empress did not mean the end of feminine domination of the throne, for Chung-tsung's empress manipulated her weak husband just as determinedly as her predecessor had managed the High Ancestor. At the same time Wu San-ssu had not relinquished hope of power, and he managed to engineer an alliance between his son and Princess An-lo, daughter of Chung-tsung and his empress, an especially important match since the imperial couple had no surviving sons, all Chung-tsung's remaining male offspring having been born of low-ranking concubines. This ambitious girl, inspired by her imperial grandmother's example, was aiming at her own appointment to the unprecedented position of Crown Princess. Before long, to clear the way for this novel development, the five leading ministers who had conspired to restore Chung-tsung had been eliminated on various charges, and by the time that Empress Wu died at the end of the year, Wu San-ssu was skilfully manipulating the imperial family.

The Empress Wu had seen many changes during her lifetime, and one which owed much to her own presence on the throne was the continuing growth of Buddhism, which had an immeasurable effect on social and cultural life in China. It is true that Buddhism flourished primarily because it responded to the religious needs of the people and because tax-exemption and other economic factors favoured the prosperity of monastic institutions, but with a woman on the throne the growth of the religion was bound to be further stimulated. Herself an ardent Buddhist, she had used Buddhist sacred literature to justify her usurpation, and in her extravagant patronage of the religion she showed lack of the restraint and economy which were deeply implanted in all who had had a Confucian education.

Her own patronage of Buddhism was not only shown by the increased activity of the sculptors at Lungmen. On her accession she sought to establish herself more securely throughout the empire by decreeing that each prefecture should have a temple named after the Great Cloud sutra which had been used to justify her rule. In the following year she decreed that Buddhism should take precedence over Taoism, which had formerly had priority because the Li family claimed descent from Lao Tzu. Chapels were established within the imperial precincts at Changan and Loyang, a reversion to a practice which had existed under some of the Northern Dynasties. In 694 Buddhism was brought within the jurisdiction of the Bureau of National Sacrifice under the Board of Rites, having previously been officially treated as a foreign religion. Shortly afterwards the famous pilgrim, I-tsing, returned to China from India, whither, like Hsüan-tsang, he had gone in search of sacred texts. Unlike the latter he had been unable to go by the overland route because of the growth of Tibetan power in Central Asia, and was the first important pilgrim to go by the sea-route, leaving Canton in 671. When he returned in 695 he was greatly honoured by Empress Wu and provided with a group of scholars to assist him in his work of translation. Apart from their contribution to the understanding of Buddhism in China, both great monks wrote works describing the countries through which they had passed, which enormously increased the geographical knowledge of the Chinese.

4

The death of the great empress, whose achievements in consolidating the T'ang Dynasty were on as heroic a scale as her vices, and whose ruthlessness was mitigated by a genuine understanding of the demands and possibilities of political life, left a gap which could be filled only by a series of bloody palace revolutions. These brought about in turn the deaths of Wu San-ssu, Chung-tsung (poisoned by his empress) and the three ambitious women, Chung-tsung's empress and the T'ai-p'ing and An-lo princesses. Jui-tsung was briefly restored to power, but he soon abdicated in favour of his ablest son Li Lung-chi, who is known to history as the Emperor Hsüan-tsung ('Mysterious Ancestor').

In these troubled years the financial situation of the empire had rapidly deteriorated. Under the Empress Wu the extravagant building schemes, the drain on resources for frontier warfare, and the growth of the bureaucracy, which next to the upkeep of military forces was the most expensive item in the budget, were eroding the country's wealth and causing the spiral of inflation and tax evasion to operate. Chung-tsung made things worse by rewarding his supporters with the revenue from a certain number of households, which meant that there were that many fewer households from which the state revenues could come; and this meant increased taxes, followed by further evasion and decline in the number of registered households. The notorious imperial princesses vied with one another in extravagance and sold offices and Buddhist ordination certificates to pay for their luxuries. Venality brought the whole bureaucratic apparatus into disrepute, and the civil service entrance examination was reduced to a farce.

On his accession to the throne the Mysterious Ancestor was therefore confronted with an urgent and serious economic problem. He took immediate action to curb some of the worst abuses, restoring to lay life large numbers of monks and nuns who had purchased ordination certificates, getting rid of supernumerary officials, who enjoyed sinecures through the favour of the corrupt court, and reducing the revenues of princes. But the really serious

problem which had to be solved was the faulty method of taxation. The land equalization system imposed at the beginning of
the dynasty had proved a failure for several reasons: it unreal-
istically ignored the economic facts of life, and it depended for its
operation at the higher levels on administrators who were law-
breakers themselves, and at the lower levels on local village elders
who were not themselves part of the official bureaucratic machine
and were thus in too weak a position to thwart the widespread
illegal acquisition of property. Furthermore, the penalties for
breaking the law were too light. Nevertheless no attempt had
been made to reform the system. As time went on more and more
land was being absorbed into large estates, either through the
illegal purchase of peasants' lands or through the occupation of
properties deserted by their owners in time of war or famine, or
by various illegal means. At the same time there was a great
increase in the number of vagrant families, which had left the
districts in which they were registered; and these included not
only those who fled to avoid paying taxes, but also those who
wished to escape military service or were driven from their homes
by flood, drought, invasion or other disasters, together with the
growing numbers of those who were simply attracted by the
greater prosperity of the south. Indeed such was the strength of
this movement that by 742 a third of the empire's population
lived in the southern provinces although the comparable figure in
the Sui period had been only twelve per cent. In 723 an attempt
was made to tackle the problem of the migrant population. A
certain Yü-wen Jung, who was descended from the imperial
family of the Northern Chou Dynasty, was given a special
appointment as Commissioner for the Encouragement of Agriculture to supervise an arrangement whereby unregistered squatters
who contacted the authorities would be given six years' exemption from normal taxation and only be subject to a special light
tax. This measure seems to have been successful, for so many
families were anxious to regularize their position that the newly
registered households formed about twelve per cent of the whole.

Nevertheless this plan did not suit everybody. It was resented
by the established bureaucracy because Yü-wen Jung had been
given special powers which overrode the normal administrative

machinery. Moreover, the new men who had entered the bureaucracy through examination and who relied on their newly acquired lands for economic security resented the fact that conditions which had worked in their favour were now being terminated by a man who was a member of the old aristocracy. Indeed his appointment had been partly motivated by the desire to curb this new political force, for Hsüan-tsung was anxious to demonstrate his departure from the policies of the Empress Wu, who had been responsible for nurturing this new element in politics. The opposition which Yü-wen's role aroused should have made it obvious that no permanent solution could be found by merely bolstering up the 'land equalization' system instead of introducing some more sophisticated taxation policy; but in 735 an edict formally re-imposed the system, merely providing harsher penalties for offences against it. The great estates continued to grow, for land was now often being presented as a reward for services to the state, and such land could be freely disposed of.

Another growing problem which had not been seriously tackled throughout the seventh century was that of the transport of grain to the Kuanchung area. This area was over-populated and crop failures were frequent because of the variable climate. Much of the land was increasingly taken up by the large estates acquired by the official families of the locality, and was therefore used partly for recreational rather than productive purposes. The area available for intensive cultivation was thus sharply reduced. In the early days of the T'ang Dynasty, the water transport system instituted by the Sui for importing grain from the southeast had been adequate, largely because at that time the large number of troops in the Kuanchung area were organized according to the militia system and were virtually self-supporting. Parts of the Sui system, including the canal linking Changan with the Yellow River, had even been abandoned at that time. But the replacement of the militia system by regular standing armies which had to be clothed and provisioned by the state, together with the growth in the number of the civil service personnel at the capital, had placed such a severe strain on Kuanchung's resources that, as we have seen, the court had frequently had to move to Loyang, which the Empress Wu had eventually adopted as her permanent seat. Hsüan-tsung restored the capital to Chang-an, but found he had to undertake the appallingly cumbersome and expensive operation of transferring the court to Loyang in nine out of his first twenty years. If Changan was to remain the capital it was high time someone was given the task of improving the transport system, so in 734 the emperor asked a certain P'ei Yao-ch'ing to turn his mind to the problem. P'ei's reforms included the introduction of transit granaries at various points, particularly at the junction of the Yellow River with the great canal route to Yangchow, so that crews could return south from that point and leave their goods to be transported further by crews more used to coping with the difficult waters of the Yellow River. They also included cutting out the expensive eighty-mile overland haul between Loyang and Shanchou, upstream of the Sanmen rapids, and reverting to the route which entailed only a five-mile overland journey to avoid this difficult stretch of river. It seems that these modest improvements were extremely successful and Loyang was no longer needed as an alternative capital. In 742–3 a further improvement was made by the opening up of a canal between the Yellow River and Changan, following the lines of the old Sui Dynasty canal. Soon it became possible to use this transport system not only for the movement of tribute grain, but also for the shipment of luxury goods from the south. In 734 a great pageant of boats carrying fine local produce from all parts of the empire was staged before the emperor at Changan.

The appointment of such specialist commissioners as Yü-wen and P'ei marked a new departure, since an important feature of the Chinese bureaucratic system had been lack of specialization. This meant that local officials were normally overburdened with a great variety of tasks, and had inadequate staff to deal with matters of detail, so that they had to depend on the assistance of the local elders, who were not members of the bureaucracy at all and naturally put local interests above everything else. Now under Hsüan-tsung a great step forward was taken with the appointment of commissioners to plan and co-ordinate certain specialized governmental operations. In the past such problems of co-ordination had been dealt with by the dispatch of censors, and it was an obvious improvement that they should be handled instead by special officials appointed at a high level and given adequate staff. The earliest commissionerships were held concurrently with other posts, the prefects of Shanchou, for example, being appointed transport commissioners for their area. Yü-wen Jung was the first commissioner to be given empire-wide authority. It was not originally intended that these commissioners should set up large permanent organizations, but the manifold responsibilities of P'ei Yao-ch'ing's transport commission, which had granaries as well as land and water transport under its care, made it desirable that it should become a permanent body with its own staff. At about the same time the minting of coinage, which also required more expert treatment than it had been receiving, was put under the control of a permanent agency.

The conflict between the old aristocrats such as Yü-wen Jung and the new class of scholar-bureaucrats entering through the examinations was an important feature of political life during the early part of Hsüan-tsung's reign. During the first decade affairs were largely under the control of the latter group, who with their Confucian morality were inclined to make politics into a more gentlemanly and less ruthless business and treat defeated opponents with more generosity than had previously been the case. But the aristocrats gradually won the upper hand, and their successful economic policies appealed to the emperor's desire for a strong, centralized and financially sound government, so he increasingly gave his support to them. From 736 onwards the aristocratic party was firmly in control and with one of their number, Li Lin-fu, virtually acting as dictator from that time until his death in 752 the literati could only hope to get on by attaching themselves to him or to some other aristocrat.

Another basic conflict in Chinese political life was that between the court and the bureaucracy, reflecting the contrast between the arbitrary, autocratic tendencies of the sovereign and the impetus towards systematic, universalized administration represented by the civil service. Hsüan-tsung's policy at the beginning of his reign was to keep court and bureaucracy from mutual involvement. He did not allow his empress or her family to obtain any influence in affairs of state. Naturally afraid that the series of conspiracies which had preceded his succession to the throne might continue, he would not allow members of the imperial family to associate freely with outsiders. If there was an infringement of the rule, the outsiders were punished, but the members of the imperial family were left unmolested.

On the other hand the Mysterious Ancestor's reign saw an increase in the political power of the eunuchs, who were no longer restricted to their original role as servants in the imperial harem. For many centuries castration had been an official punishment in China, but after the abolition of this penalty in the sixth century, the needs of the court had to be supplied by means of raiding parties to capture boys from aboriginal tribes in the south and south-west. This informal arrangement was eventually regularized so that officials in the southern provinces submitted a quota of castrated boys as part of their annual tribute. Later a richer source of supply was found in the flourishing slave-markets of the southern region, where eunuchs were purveyed to private households as well as to the court.

At first they were used for purely menial tasks in the palace. They were all brought up in the Buddhist faith, and the great majority were illiterate, but a few acquired some literary education and were even employed in teaching ladies of the imperial harem. Gradually their status improved. Under Empress Wu they were allowed to take wives and under Hsüan-tsung they were able to set up their own establishments outside the palace, and some acquired large mansions and estates in the metropolitan area. Their influence grew considerably during the time when Chung-tsung and Jui-tsung were deprived of the throne. Having little contact with the outside world they and their families, including the young Hsüan-tsung, spent much time in their company. As purveyors to the palace, they made much money, and more found its way into their pockets from the sale of commissions to repair temple buildings, and similar perquisites. By the end of the Empress Wu's reign many eunuchs were holding extraordinary appointments of a bureaucratic nature, and this development continued under Hsüan-tsung, although he had made attempts to curb it at the beginning of his tenure of the throne. Moreover the ranks of the lower eunuchs were swollen because of an increase in the number of imperial palaces, the harems of which contained 40,000 ladies during the Mysterious Ancestor's reign. At the same time their political influence was growing quite naturally out of their increasing usefulness. They had first been employed outside the palace as official messengers under T'ai-tsung, an example being the eunuchs who bore gifts from the emperor to Hsüan-tsang. Gradually their missions became more important and confidential until eunuchs were being used as unofficial political envoys.

Among the eunuch protégés of Hsüan-tsung was Kao Li-shih, who had particularly endeared himself to his master by his services at the time of the struggles preceding his succession. He was obviously a very able man, and he remained a friend and confidant of the emperor throughout his reign. From the beginning he attended the highest councils of state and had the privilege of reporting imperial decisions to ministers after the meetings had ended. Largely through his agency the political influence of the eunuch body increased considerably. The policy of using eunuchs as intermediaries between emperors and their ministers was obviously convenient because they were always at hand, and it chimed in with Hsüan-tsung's centralizing, autocratic preferences, but it was to cause much trouble in Chinese political life. One important innovation which strengthened the eunuchs' power was an arrangement whereby a considerable proportion of the revenues of the empire came to be paid direct into the emperor's personal treasury, which was under eunuch control.

The eunuchs are also said to have been responsible for the downfall, in 731, of the commanders of the Northern Palace Army, which was a rival for power and influence within the palace. This force had won the favour of the emperor because it had helped set him on the road to the throne. Its officers had received rich rewards, which further stimulated their ambitions, and led to their downfall. The Northern Palace Army was part of the Northern Army, which originated as the force used by the High Progenitor and the Grand Ancestor when they had advanced on Changan in the campaign which led to the founding of the dynasty. The army was kept in being in the expectation that it would show especial loyalty to the throne, and to maintain its proud traditions vacancies were filled by sons and nephews of the original members. Its responsibilities included the control of the strategic northern gate of the capital, and its officers held in their hands the key to the success or failure of palace revolutions. Consequently their permanent duties at Changan proved in the long run to be a guarantee not of their lasting loyalty but rather of their involvement in the political intrigues of the moment and of their succumbing to the arrogance given them by their privileged position.

Powerful though Kao Li-shih had become, he remained a faithful and devoted servant and never dominated his emperor, as eunuchs later in the dynasty succeeded in doing. On the other hand the emperor's plan to keep his consorts in their place was not entirely successful, and women played an unfortunate role in his life, and he was too much swayed by their influence. His first empress, née Wang, was unfortunately childless and, fearing the rivalry of the concubine, Wu Huei-fei, sought occult cures for her barrenness. To consult sorcerers was very dangerous and this rash move led to her degradation and death. Wu Huei-fei then became his favourite. Being a great-niece of Empress Wu, she was not given the title of empress because the sovereign's advisers objected to such an honour being conferred on a member of the family which had usurped the T'ang throne. Hsüan-tsung had seven children by Wu Huei-fei, and one of these, called Mao, was an especial favourite of the emperor, so Wu Huei-fei conceived an ambition of having the crown prince deposed and replaced by him. One obstacle to this plan was the fact that Mao was only the emperor's eighteenth son, but on the other hand Crown Prince Ying, his second son, was only the offspring of a provincial singing-girl who had long been dead. In 736 Wu Huei-fei succeeded in persuading the emperor that the crown prince and two other sons were plotting to kill Mao, so they were degraded and ordered to commit suicide. She is said by the historians to have obtained the complicity of Li Lin-fu in return for assisting him to attain power. However this may be, this was a black stain on Hsüan-tsung's record, and it was uncharacteristic of him to deal so harshly with his own family. The unscrupulous concubine did not live to complete her machinations, for she died in the same year and eventually the emperor's third son, the future Emperor Su-tsung, was made crown prince.

This same eighteenth son of the Emperor Hsüan-tsung had a wife of the Yang family which could trace its lineage back to the emperors of the Sui Dynasty. The emperor must have met her when she paid her formal respects to him after her marriage in 736. Before long Wu Huei-fei had died and the Mysterious Ancestor had taken over from his son this girl of the Yang family. In 741 he had her registered as a Taoist official and moved to a residence within the palace grounds, and in 745 she became an official member of his harem. She was one of the most famous women in Chinese history, and is known as Yang Kuei-fei (Kuei-fei, 'Precious Consort', being the name of her rank in the imperial seraglio).

Before this the emperor had liberally bestowed his favours on his concubines and is known to have had fifty-nine children. It is said that the girls competed to see who could pick the most beautiful flower, and then the emperor would release a butterfly and watch to see on whose flower the insect would settle. The owner of that particular flower was the winner of this charming game, and the reward of victory was to be the next one to enjoy the imperial favours. But when Yang Kuei-fei entered his life, all this changed and the two became inseparable companions. They shared a taste in music and in the court orchestra they played together, he on the drums and she on the guitar-like p'i-pa. They had their lovers' tiffs and at least twice Kuei-fei was expelled from the harem, but she remained remarkably close to the emperor throughout the last ten years of his reign. Their liaison has been romanticized by the Chinese and it is easy to forget that, even when they first met, Hsüan-tsung was already in his fifties and so debilitated by his earlier debaucheries that none of his fifty-nine children seems to have been born in the last twenty years of his reign. Yang Kuei-fei is also said to have been plump and not to have conformed with the conventional standards of fragile Chinese beauty, but it was perhaps more important that she came from a distinguished Chinese family. She had three sisters who were married to members of prominent clans, and they had free access to the harem; and Hsüan-tsung lavished gifts on all the sisters, giving them a huge annual allowance for cosmetics alone. Another member of the Yang family was destined, as we shall see, to attain important political office. But his story must be left because it is involved with the tragedy which brought Hsüan-tsung's reign to an end.

Under Hsüan-tsung Buddhism continued to flourish and present a serious economic problem. In the critical situation which he faced when he came to the throne, he had immediately put a stop to the sale of ordination certificates and returned a large number of unworthy monks and nuns to lay life. He also prohibited private individuals from constructing new temples and from handing over property to monasteries, and limited the size of monastic estates on the basis of the number of monks. But the abuse of private ordination remained: this not only meant that monasteries could conduct ordination ceremonies, but even that certain individuals, including imperial princes and princesses, retained the right to conduct ordination ceremonies which they had earlier been granted. It was not until 747 that these abuses were stopped and a system of official ordination was introduced. But unfortunately, before this new system was working properly, the government was forced to resort to the sale of ordination certificates to raise funds to cope with the rebellion which was to end Hsüan-tsung's reign.

Nevertheless, like his predecessors, the Mysterious Ancestor was aware of the political value of Buddhism under imperial patronage and, in addition to continuing the practice of sponsoring official temples in each prefecture, he inaugurated in 730 the Festival of the Thousand Autumns to celebrate the imperial birthday, and the vegetarian feasts to mark this occasion were held throughout the empire in these state-sponsored temples. Nor was it possible to succeed in cutting down the flow of immense wealth into monasteries. Even the emperor's friend, Kao Li-shih, spent much of his enormous fortune on the construction of religious buildings, and also arranged a conspicuously extravagant funeral for his wife, although the practice had been expressly attacked by his royal master. The religion was also taking ever deeper root in the lives of the people and it was already the almost invariable practice in high society to have Buddhist services for the dead. At the same time Buddhist influence was affecting other cults. It was in Hsüan-tsung's reign that, for the first time, images replaced tablets in the Confucian temples, and this alien practice survived right through until the sixteenth century. Confucius was now definitely being worshipped as a god, and at the same time official recognition was being given to the popular worship of honoured soldiers and administrators. More importantly from the point of view of imperial policy this practice led to the casting of images of the sovereign for worship in every county of the realm.

Under the Mysterious Ancestor Taoism also enjoyed imperial favour, and in 741 new civil service examinations were introduced for candidates who chose to be tested on Taoist rather than on Confucian texts, and in the following year it was decreed that the main Taoist works should be given the same status as the Confucian classics. Early in his reign the emperor himself had obtained a diploma of proficiency in the Taoist doctrine, and the contemporary poet Li Po also possessed such a diploma.

Literary men such as Li Po have also added lustre to the Mysterious Ancestor's reign, for he was a great patron of scholars and poets, one of his most important acts being the creation of the Hanlin (literally 'Forest of Writing-brushes') Academy, a kind of national academy which had a continuous history until modern times. This was certainly an age of supreme aesthetic genius, born perhaps because the new confidence and broadened horizons of the times had quickened men's imaginations; although Hsüan-tsung has even sometimes been given some credit, as if patronage and relatively settled political conditions were preconditions of the flowering of literary talent. In any case the great Li Po was an outsider. Although he was for a short time a member of a pool of court poets, he was the only well-known literary man of the age who neither went in for the civil service examinations nor succeeded in securing a regular official post. As a young man he had been a knight-errant, running his sword through quite a number of people to redress the grievances of the wronged, and in later life he was a drunkard, too unreliable to be given office. He was a strong believer in Taoism, and lived much among the mountains; and his poems reflected that love of the wildness of nature, which owes nothing to mortal ruler, but is more likely to flower in turbulent or disappointing times.

A tipsy regret at the swiftness of the passage of time is a common mood of his poetry, reflected in the following lines:

> See the waters of the Yellow River leap down from Heaven,
> Roll away to the deep sea and never turn again!
> See at the mirror in the High Hall
> Aged men bewailing white locks –
>
> In the morning, threads of silk,
> In the evening, flakes of snow.
> Snatch the joys of life as they come and use them to the full;
> Do not leave the silver cup idly glinting at the moon.

This was the golden age of lyric verse, and the trio of Li Po, Po Chü-i and Tu Fu are unrivalled in the affections of their country-men. But the products of their genius were merely the peaks on a high plateau of literary endeavour. Since literary skill was the chief road to a distinguished career, writing was a highly prized activity, and to be able to compose poetry was an essential in-gredient of the civilized man. The related art of calligraphy was already regarded as an important vehicle for the expression of aesthetic genius. This art in turn already exerted a powerful influence on painting technique, as may be seen in the bold and economical brush-strokes of the monochrome landscapes which played an increasingly important role in the history of Chinese art.

The strong tradition of landscape painting, which was to sur-vive throughout imperial Chinese history, owes nothing to foreign influence but is rooted in Chinese soil, for it reflects the Taoist attitude of wonder at nature, with human beings shown as tiny as insects crawling on the surface of its vast expanses. So, in spite of the fact that Buddhism provided additional subject-matter for painting and sculpture, the native traditions in art were little distorted by the foreign influences which had poured into China, and the flowering of culture at this time was largely the result of careful husbandry by the Chinese of their own heritage throughout the centuries, even in the face of the political and economic disruption which their country had suffered in the period of disunity. This was true not only in literature and painting, but also in the applied arts. The potters, for example, were using their long heritage of skill to perfect the manufacture of porcelain, a process which would culminate in the matchless wares of the Sung period. At the same time the long-established practice of placing pottery figurines in tombs since it was imagined that they could be of service to the dead in after-life still flourished. Works of very high quality were produced, and the servants, dancing-girls, horses, camels and other subjects manufactured for burial purposes during the T'ang period are highly prized by collectors.

Jade-carving also provides a good illustration of the gradual development of a very ancient tradition. The great hardness of the material makes it unworkable without the use of an abrasive, and even the simplest operations require great time and patience; but in antiquity there had been one major innovation, when the use of iron tools first made it possible to carve three-dimensional figures and to hollow out bowls and other vessels. Jade-carvers had also begun to exploit flawed and multi-coloured pieces of stone, so that a blotch of red on a dull-coloured pebble might be turned by the imaginative eye and skilled hand of the craftsman into a dagger dipped in blood, or a brown patch on a white stone might be transformed into a dragon soaring among the clouds. In antiquity jade had been regarded with great reverence, its qualities being summed up in an ancient dictionary in the words:

Jade is the fairest of stones. It is endowed with five virtues. Charity is typified by its lustre, bright yet warm; rectitude by its translucency, revealing the colour and markings within; wisdom by the purity and penetrating quality of its note, when the stone is struck; courage, in that it may be broken but cannot be bent; equity, in that it has sharp angles which yet injure none.

Held in such regard, jade was often used for ritual objects; but in medieval China, although it became a popular material for Buddhist figurines, the reverence for the stone because of its ritual purposes began to fade, and its appeal for the Confucian gentleman lay in its antiquarian associations and in its beauty and attractiveness to the sense of touch. One manifestation of the growing antiquarian interests of the Sung and later periods was the making of jade copies of ancient bronze sacrificial vessels. Also throughout the centuries there was increasing use of the material for everyday purposes. It was used for jewellery, such as hair-ornaments and pendants; dress accessories, such as belt-hooks; and items of personal adornment, like the sheaths the scholar used to protect his long finger-nails. For the banquet jade vessels and chopsticks might be used, and in the study the accoutrements of scholarship, like inkstones, brush-pots and brush-rests, were often made of the stone. These uses of jade reached a climax in the eighteenth century, but already in T'ang China jade played its part in the increasing elegance of the lives of the well-to-do.

Whereas Europe had fallen apart after the collapse of the Roman empire, China had surmounted similar difficulties and had built a civilization unrivalled in the world at that time. But a people's forward march may be halted by the frailties of its rulers. Hsüan-tsung's own golden days came to an end long before the conclusion of his reign. From 736 onwards he had been content to leave matters largely in the hands of the trusted Li Lin-fu, who at first kept control by relatively mild methods, but eventually in the face of growing opposition to his power launched a series of purges in 746 and hounded many of his opponents to their deaths. One threat to Li Lin-fu's power was the danger that he might be outshone by rivals acquiring too much prestige through victories on the frontiers, especially since the ageing emperor was setting his heart on military glory. He himself had played an important part in army reform. Large armies, it will be remembered, had become a regular feature of the frontier organization as a result of the long and difficult Korean campaigns. By 742 there were forty-seven of these units, kept in permanent readiness to perform the tasks which had formerly been given to specially raised expeditionary forces. By the end of the seventh century armies in a particular area were being grouped under overall commanders, and this practice was regularized under Hsüan-tsung with the institution of the office of military governor. It was Li Lin-fu who, in 737, gave final shape to this new organization and at the same time introduced other military reforms. Before this time conscription for an average period of three years had been the basic method of recruitment. This was obviously wasteful, since men were lost as soon as they had become thoroughly competent. Efforts had been made to induce conscripts to remain in the army as veterans, and convicts also provided some long-service troops; but now arrangements were made for the permanent enlistment of frontier soldiers, and in future conscription was only used in case of emergency. The creation of permanent professional armies meant that it was possible to pursue a more aggressive foreign policy, but the control of large military forces on the frontiers could be a grave danger in the hands of ambitious men who might plan revolt, and it is a tribute to the internal stability of the state under Hsüan-tsung that such a development could even have been contemplated.

Early in his struggle for power Li Lin-fu had obtained the key post of President of the Board of War, and it was in this capacity that he introduced the above-mentioned reforms. Between 738 and 740 he obtained close personal control over a large number of armies by becoming Military Governor of Lungyu and Hohsi, which covered the western and north-western frontier regions. After the purges of 746–7 he obtained the emperor's approval of a new policy, which was to appoint barbarians as military governors. Reared on the hard frontier life and inured to battle, unfitted to hold high civil office and unaccustomed to political intrigue, they would make much safer and more effective military governors than the Chinese.

Conspicuous among the barbarian generals in the service of China was An Lu-shan, a pure soldier, so it seemed, and, being illiterate, unqualified to play an important role in civil affairs. An Lu-shan was the son of a Sogdian who was an officer in the army of the northern Turks, and his mother was a member of a noble Turkish clan. His family had had to flee to China because of a purge when An Lu-shan was a boy. As soon as he was old enough, he joined the army. In 733 he was already one of the chief subordinates of the Military Governor of Yuchou on the north-eastern frontier. He held the rank of general and had won commendation for his courage and efficiency in the face of the Khitan and Hsi tribesmen who threatened that sector of the frontier. He continued to serve in this area and in 744 was made military governor of Yuchou, which had been renamed Fanyang. Li Lin-fu seems to have considered him an unsophisticated soldier who was loyal and reliable. During the next few years he was heaped with honours, and in 750 was even made a prince, a title which had been previously restricted to members of the royal family and foreign potentates. In the same year a victory over the Hsi tribesmen enabled him to present 8000 prisoners at court, and the emperor had a new house built and furnished for him at his own expense.

The Mysterious Ancestor and Yang Kuei-fei seem to have made rather a pet of An Lu-shan, who amused them because he had become enormously fat and was extremely gauche in matters of court etiquette. They showered him with gifts, and on his birthday in 751 he was adopted as a son by Yang Kuei-fei, who had the grotesque general dressed as a new-born infant, to the intense amusement of the emperor, who now seems to have been more interested in frivolities than serious affairs of state.

In the following month he was given the additional post of military governor of Hotung, which meant that he had control of the whole of the eastern half of the northern frontier and commanded 200,000 troops, about forty per cent of the country's forces. Nevertheless in a full-scale expedition against the Khitan under his personal command, his army was completely routed.

This same year saw other serious military setbacks for the Chinese. An encounter of the utmost importance was the Battle of Talas, in which Kao Hsien-chih, a general of Korean birth, was disastrously defeated by the Arabs, whose power had been spreading widely throughout the previous century, encompassing North Africa and part of the Iberian peninsula to the west and gradually reaching eastward to absorb the states of Balk, Bokhara, Samarkand and Ferghana. In 738 the Chinese had recovered from the Tibetans the supremacy over the Tarim Basin, and states beyond the Pamirs had even acknowledged their suzerainty because of threats of Arab invasion. In 747 Kao Hsien-chih also inflicted a defeat on the Tibetans in the same area. But this defeat at Talas meant that the Tarim Basin again passed under Tibetan control, and before long the whole of this region was to fall permanently under the influence of Islam.

At the same time Chinese armies were suffering another setback in the south-west. Here the general T'ang policy had been to enfeoff conquered chieftains with their own former territories and leave them to administer their own internal affairs. In course of time, as a result of conquests which had Chinese approval, an able chieftain had been able to create a large kingdom called Nan-chao in the area now occupied by the province of Yünnan. Hsüan-tsung honoured the Nan-chao ruler, whose friendship offered a useful counterbalance to Tibetan hostility. But in 750 a dispute with the Chinese flared up into war, and two very heavy defeats for the T'ang forces in 751 and 754 paved the way for the existence of an independent Nan-chao kingdom that was to last for five centuries.

This unfortunate conflict in the south-west may have been sparked off by the activities of Yang Kuei-fei's second cousin, Yang Kuo-chung, who was beginning to emerge as Li Lin-fu's chief contender for power. He had originally come from the south-western frontier area, and may have been trying to build a power base there to rival the strongholds of the northern military governors. He did eventually succeed in getting himself appointed military governor of the area, and when Li Lin-fu died at the end of 752, Yang Kuo-chung succeeded him as chief minister. The next three years were given over to a struggle between the new chief minister and An Lu-shan, which culminated in the open rebellion of the latter at the end of 755.

Most serious rebellions started when the peasants found their lot intolerable, and certainly there was widespread famine in the years immediately preceding the An Lu-shan rebellion, which the government took inadequate steps to relieve, prompting the poet Tu Fu to contrast the luxury of the court with the hunger outside: 'From the vermilion gates comes the smell of wine and flesh; in the roads are the bones of men who froze to death.' But there was no sign of the serious peasant unrest which normally sparked off such an uprising, and the armies which An Lu-shan headed

were not untrained mobs but seasoned frontier soldiers. He may
have been tempted to move because he felt seriously threatened
by the enmity of Yang Kuo-chung, but clearly the most com-
pelling reasons can be found in the history of the Hopei region.
This was a proud and independent district which had in the past
gloried in being the centre of Chinese culture in the north. It had
been the most prosperous part of the Northern Wei state and
continued to be the strongest area of the north in the sixth
century when it flourished as an independent state (under the
Northern Ch'i Dynasty) until 577 when the Northern Chou,
rapidly followed by the Sui, switched the centre of power to
Kuanchung. Again, at the end of the Sui it had been the north-
eastern warlords who had held out longest against the T'ang.
Mutual suspicion between Changan and Hopei continued, and
this important frontier defence area was kept surprisingly short
of troops and seems to have suffered several serious invasions in
consequence. When larger military forces were made available to
An Lu-shan, the area began to enjoy more security and economic
prosperity. This would give the people of the Hopei region more
power to redress their long-cherished grievances. Perhaps An
Lu-shan was not the prime mover, but merely the tool of the
north-easterners' separatist ambitions.

An Lu-shan's movements do not seem to have been very well
planned. Within a month he had captured Loyang, and at the
beginning of 756 he proclaimed the inauguration of a new
dynasty, but he seems to have made no attempt to gain control
of the vital waterway from the south-east, nor did he secure his
lines of communication with his base in the north-east. In the
latter half of 756 he took Changan. The writings of Tu Fu,
living there at the time, capture the atmosphere of the occupied
capital. As Waley wrote,

One evening in spring he steals to the Serpentine, the fashionable
pleasure-resort of Changan. The great houses on its shores, all shut-
tered and barred, stand empty. He recalls the gorgeous fêtes and
carnivals held here in honour of Yang Kuei-fei. Once more the gardens are in all their glory, but foreign cavalcades fill the evening air
with blinding dust. The poet, as though he were in a strange city,
loses his way in the dust and dark.

Thus ended a glorious era in the history of this fine city, which was a thriving commercial centre at the end of the Central Asian trade-routes as well as the capital of the greatest state and civilization of the contemporary world. Its precise rectangular plan, intersected by great north-south and east-west thoroughfares, was a perfect symbol of the control the government tried to maintain over society. The blocks divided off by these imposing boulevards were separate walled villages closed off at night. In the north was the Imperial City, the sight of whose splendid palaces would provide Chinese bureaucrats and tributary envoys alike with an awe-inspiring culmination to the long approach up the broad avenue from the monumental gate in the centre of the southern wall of the city. But although the design of the capital seems to suggest that medieval China was a totally planned and closed society, dominated by a supreme monarch, the early T'ang had been exposed to all kinds of new influences from outside. Among the million people who filled the city were many who flocked from all over Asia, bringing with them their own religions and customs and the exotic products of their own countries, all freely accepted by this open-minded and confident people as an enrichment to their lives, and merging into a truly cosmopolitan culture which was reflected in the great literature and art of the period.

Shortly before this great city had been entered by An Lu-shan's troops, the Mysterious Ancestor together with members of the imperial family, Yang Kuei-fei, Yang Kuo-chung and other members of the Yang clan, some eunuchs and an escort of soldiers had left en route for Szechwan. They arrived at a place called Ma-wei in a hungry and exhausted condition. There the troops slew Yang Kuo-chung and demanded the death of the Precious Consort herself. The old emperor told her, and then granted her last request, which was that she meet her death by strangling in front of a Buddhist shrine. After viewing her corpse the troops swore eternal allegiance to the T'ang. The emperor was heartbroken, and abdicated in favour of the crown prince, the Emperor Su-tsung ('Reverent Ancestor'). The story of the imperial romance and its dramatic ending is one of the most famous in Chinese history, capturing the popular imagination and inspiring poets. In Po Chü-i's version, called *Everlasting Remorse*, the old emperor is so stricken with sorrow that he employs a magician to search the universe for his favourite. Her spirit form is at last found, and she sends poignant messages to her beloved, but their great days in Changan together can never return again.

5

The An Lu-shan rebellion destroyed the greatness of the T'ang but failed to put anything in its place. An Lu-shan himself was murdered by his son in 757, and before long the son too was assassinated and another barbarian general took command. Local revolts broke out and it soon seemed as if the country might disintegrate into a number of warlord régimes. Even Li Po found himself caught up in the war when he acted as a kind of unofficial poet-laureate to one of the rebel régimes, with the result that he was arrested as a traitor and had to spend some time in prison. Peace was finally restored in 763, when the rebels were defeated with the aid of barbarian allies, notably the Uighurs, who had rebelled from the western Turks in the mid-seventh century and had now built up a large and powerful empire.

The dynasty was now gravely weakened, and never recovered its former glories. The country was impoverished, and the central government was never able to control the strong centrifugal forces which had been released when great power was given to military governors, and which had been further strengthened by civil war. For the rest of the T'ang period some parts of the country were to contribute taxes only irregularly, and the Hopei and Shantung areas were to become virtually independent, contributing no revenue to the central government. This was a serious setback since these were rich agricultural regions and also the most important silk-producing areas of the country.

The more immediate effect of the rebellion was that the machinery of land registration and taxation broke down so seriously that by 760 the number of registered households was only a fifth of what it had been five years earlier. Not only did much of the country slip from government control, but also large areas were virtually depopulated as a result of the fighting, and migration to the south again increased. The inevitable consequence was a great increase in land-grabbing and the building up of large estates, which now became a permanent and widespread feature of the Chinese scene, although the T'ang government did nothing to acknowledge their existence and land equalization officially remained in force. The estates were farmed by dispossessed peasants and migratory workers, and it is estimated that by the end of the eighth century free and independent peasants constituted not more than five per cent of the population.

During the fighting various desperate attempts had been made to raise additional revenue, including the sale of ordination certificates for the Buddhist and Taoist priesthood, a very shortsighted measure, completely undoing Hsüan-tsung's recent attempt to restrict the number of clerics. Ranks and titles were also sold, forced loans were extracted from merchants, and the coinage was debased, but the only emergency measure which was to have any long-term success was the introduction of a monopoly tax on salt.

Even after peace had been restored the country was militarily so weak that the Tibetans, who had occupied large areas of western China which had been denuded of troops because of the demands of the internal conflict, were able to advance on the capital and occupy it for a short time in 763, and large armies were needed to keep them in check in the future. In the north-east rebel generals retained control of their territories as officially recognized military governors, but paid no taxes to the central authorities. Beyond the frontier to the north-west the Uighur empire hovered like a great cloud, and T'ang forces no longer exercised any authority outside China proper. Even in the capital itself the government was in poor shape, for Su-tsung had to rely largely on the handful of officials who had accompanied him when he fled to escape the rebel advance. Just as Hsüan-tsung had given much influence to eunuchs who had been close to him during the troubled times which had preceded his reign, so Su-tsung became increasingly dependent on the members of his immediate entourage, especially Li Fu-kuo, a former stable-boy who became the most powerful figure in the government. A eunuch secretariat was now formally established, and this gradually assumed greater powers as the dynasty continued.

One instance of the increasing power of eunuchs was their employment to keep watch on army commanders. From the beginning of the dynasty it had been the practice of the government to appoint a censor to accompany expeditionary forces to keep an eye on the general's conduct of affairs and ensure that the reports he sent back were truthful. Eunuchs had sometimes been employed in this capacity even under Hsüan-tsung, and now eunuch supervisors were appointed to all armies, not only in the provinces, but also at the capital. Eventually the regular commanders of the palace armies were to be entirely replaced by these eunuch supervisors, and this accretion of power enabled the eunuchs to dominate the court for the remainder of the dynasty.

Su-tsung's brief reign did not last into peace-time. He was succeeded by his eldest son Tai-tsung, during whose reign the government made attempts to adjust to the new situation of restricted central control. One of the hardest problems was to secure the necessary revenues. In the provinces, local authorities raised money by taxes of their own invention, and at the capital the main new source of taxation was the salt monopoly, which within twenty years of its inauguration was producing over half the annual revenue of the state.

The reason for the success of this tax when central authority was weak was that it was only necessary to control the areas where salt was produced. These areas were fairly limited and therefore easily inspected. Moreover, salt production could not be carried on in secret very easily because of the amount of capital equipment needed and the obviousness of the salt pans. The way the system worked was that merchants had to pay the monopoly tax when buying their stocks from the government and then pass the burden on to the consumer in the form of higher prices. Since salt was a necessity of life, not only because of its value in preserving food but also because it is a physical requirement for a people with a predominantly cereal diet, the government was able to impose a very high tax without fear of boycott or reduction in consumption. The Salt Commission, based on Yangchow, grew into a very powerful institution, eventually becoming the dominant financial authority in the south, so that the authority of the government departments ordinarily concerned with finance was restricted to the north.

At the same time as the state was having difficulty in putting its financial affairs in order, the Buddhist community was becoming an increasingly heavy burden. It not only meant a loss of revenue because of tax-exemption, but also was a positive expense, since it has been calculated that the upkeep of official monasteries absorbed up to one-fifth of the revenues of the state at the end of Tai-tsung's reign. At this time the chanting of sutras could be heard regularly within the palace, for hundreds of monks were attached to the royal chapel. Commissioners of Religion were now established to take over supervision of the monastic community from the Bureau of National Sacrifice under the Board of Rites. These posts were generally occupied, not by monks, but by eunuchs, who seized the opportunity to amass great fortunes for themselves.

The reign of Tai-tsung's eldest son, Te-tsung (779–805), saw some hope of a genuine revival of the dynasty, with a renewal of intellectual life at the capital. Further fiscal and administrative reforms were evidence that the state was gradually adapting itself to its new situation, and the shock which the dynasty had suffered served to stimulate thinkers of the time to a more fundamental consideration of contemporary problems. The most important and enduring of the financial measures introduced during his reign was an entirely new method of direct taxation, known as the two-tax system.

The old system of taxing people equally (since in theory they were equally capable of paying because they had equal amounts of land) was finally scrapped. It was replaced by a household levy geared to the size and property of every household, and a land levy based on all lands under cultivation in 779. This was a much fairer system since it took into account people's different capacities to pay. At the same time matters were simplified by the abolition of numerous miscellaneous taxes which had recently been imposed. The new system was made easier and fairer to administer when it was decided that the central government should merely fix the overall quotas for each province and each prefecture in consultation with the local authorities, who should determine the actual tax rate, varying it, if desired, from prefecture to prefecture, taking into account their different productive capacities. The provincial and prefectural authorities were, of course, entitled to retain a fixed proportion of the revenue for their own purposes. Now that the tasks of tax assessment and collection were delegated to the local authorities, the central government's inability to enforce its mandate throughout the provinces was recognized in a manner which at the same time brought great benefit to it by simplifying its role in financial matters.

The success of the new system was unfortunately marred by an outbreak of rebellion in Hopei and Shantung, which seriously threatened the dynasty and finally put paid to the central government's hopes of exercising control over those areas. The emperor had attempted to reassert the authority of the central bureaucracy, stop the hereditary succession of provincial governors, and reduce the strength of the armies. The rebels were joined by a powerful governor in Honan, and in 783 Te-tsung was forced to flee the capital. The leaders of the rebellion had adopted princely titles and a new dynasty was inaugurated. But their incompetence and jealousies proved to be the emperor's salvation, and he was able to return to his capital in the following year.

The passage of time also accentuated defects in the new taxation system, such as the lack of effective machinery for keeping assessments up to date and for keeping a check on changes of ownership, which were stimulated by the fact that newly cultivated lands were exempt from taxes. A further source of trouble was the fact that the household levy was assessed in money terms; so that the system was thrown out of gear by the sharp changes in the value of money which took place at this period. In trying to cope with these problems, the government was hampered by lack of understanding of the full implications of assessing taxes in money terms. Nevertheless the reform did provide the government with a system of direct taxation which was to survive until the Ming Dynasty.

One of the problems which had to be solved if taxes were to be assessed in money terms was the chronic shortage of coinage from which the country suffered during the T'ang Dynasty. The copper coinage was of one denomination only, and for large transactions, for which the quantity of copper would have been too bulky, silk or silver ingots were used as currency, the latter predominating after the An Lu-shan rebellion. Counterfeiting was always a serious problem, in spite of the fact that the death penalty was imposed during the seventh century, and this was one reason why attempts to introduce larger denominations of copper coinage failed, since counterfeiters could simply melt down the old coins in order to produce pieces of higher denomination. In the latter part of the eighth century, as a result of the gradual economic development of society and the obvious convenience of money as compared with commodity currencies, the demand for money greatly increased, but there was great difficulty in maintaining production of coin at the right level because of the acute shortage of copper. This metal was much used in the production of utensils, mirrors, Buddhist images and many other objects; but during the latter part of the T'ang Dynasty there were a number of edicts proscribing the use of copper for these purposes in order to save it for minting coins.

The general effect of the financial reforms was to increase and ratify provincial autonomy. In the capital too the reign of Te-tsung saw a weakening of the authority of the central bureaucracy. Eunuch power had already achieved formal recognition in the constitution of a eunuch secretariat. Now the Hanlin Academy, which had previously merely been a body of experts on whom the emperor might call for literary composition or other expert assistance, developed into a group of close confidential advisers, who stood between the emperor and his chief ministers.

But at the same time Changan began to recover as a centre of intellectual life. The An Lu-shan rebellion had prompted large numbers of intellectuals to take refuge in the south, where their enforced leisure and remoteness from the capital stimulated fundamental thoughts on the state of society and how it might be improved. The most prominent outcome of these reflections was a movement to advocate the reform of prose style in an effort to achieve the simpler qualities of the Chou and Han Dynasty writers, as an essential prerequisite of moral regeneration and a revival of the Confucian tradition. Originally this was a reactionary movement prompted by the proud Confucian-minded northerners' resistance to southern influence, but eventually their rather purist attitude was modified by the influences of southern Buddhism until a new synthesis of Confucianism strengthened by an admixture of Buddhist metaphysics began to emerge. At the same time the Confucian Classics were subjected to a new criticism in an attempt to get at the true meaning of the sage: this was a reaction against the orthodox interpretation which had been established in the reign of the Grand Ancestor and it foreshadowed the critical scholarship which was to flourish under the Sung.

The examination system was now firmly entrenched as the orthodox means of entering the bureaucracy. Inevitably there was a reaction against it and men began to feel nostalgia for the time when true merit had been discovered by the simpler procedure of personal recommendation. It therefore became the practice for examiners to rely not only on the evidence of the candidates' scripts, but also on estimates of their ability proffered by distinguished patrons. Candidates now made energetic efforts to curry favour with the great in the hope of obtaining their support, and these new practices opened the way to favouritism and corruption; but they do represent the beginnings of a formalized system of sponsorship which was to prove an extremely valuable feature of the civil service system when it reached the height of sophistication under the Sung.

During this period much thought was also devoted to political and economic theory. Two of the most famous books of the time were encyclopaedic works which provided a classified digest of important official documents, constituting a great reservoir of source material on the political and social history of China. The more important of these two works was the *T'ung Tien*, on which Tu Yu, himself a distinguished official, worked for thirty-six years of his life. He was an independent and original thinker, who was even prepared to take the view that the ancient Chinese had been very much like the barbarians, and that their progress had not been due to the supernatural achievements of the sages but to geographical advantages. He also saw that progress was a continuous and cumulative matter and that even men like the ancient unifier of China, the founder of the Ch'in Dynasty, whose cruelties had been universally reviled by the Confucians, had made their own contribution to the development of society.

Towards the end of his reign Te-tsung became increasingly autocratic and avaricious. He treated the bureaucracy in an off-hand manner and relied on favourites to fill the treasury by irregular and unscrupulous methods. A reform group including among its adherents many of the most brilliant young men at the capital began to be active in political affairs in support of the crown prince, and when the latter succeeded his father in 805, this group was for a short time in control of the government. But unfortunately the history of China depended greatly on the fate of emperors. The new monarch, known to history as Shun-tsung, suffered a stroke which deprived him of speech. The reformist cause was irreparably weakened, and the resistance to change of eunuchs, military governors and reactionary bureaucrats brought about the downfall of the party, the death of its leader, Wang Shu-wen, and the exile of his chief supporters, while Shun-tsung was forced to abdicate in favour of his son, who was posthumously known as Hsien-tsung. The most serious charge against the reformers was that they had attempted to deprive the eunuchs of control of the palace armies. If they had succeeded in this, later tragedies would have been prevented, but the eunuchs were clearly now in too strongly fortified a position to be easily overthrown.

After the downfall of the reformers, the impetus to a true renaissance of the T'ang Dynasty seems to have fizzled out, and intellectuals tended to retreat into the consolations of literature and Taoism. Under Hsien-tsung there was some strengthening of the position of the central government vis-à-vis the provinces and some attention to administrative efficiency, notably in the reform of the salt commission under the aforementioned Tu Yu : but the north-eastern areas still remained practically independent and, in defiance of the central government, most of the frontier commands became hereditary. In 809, for example, the government was compelled to launch a campaign against Wang Ch'eng-tsung, a Khitan tribesman by origin, who had just inherited the control of Western Hopei. But they achieved nothing.

In the west it had proved impossible to restore the frontiers to where they had been before the An Lu-shan rebellion had enabled the Tibetans to make widespread gains of territory in the area of present-day Kansu. They had pushed forward their frontier till it was not much more than a hundred miles west of Changan, and great Chinese cities, such as Liangchow, with 120,000 inhabitants, had remained under Tibetan control. In 783 Te-tsung had had to rely heavily on the Tibetans' support to secure his restoration, and in return was compelled to accept their views on the demarcation of the frontier. However, the Tibetans continued to put pressure on the Chinese, and it was not until Hsien-tsung's reign that relations genuinely improved. The reason why the Tibetans were now more ready to come to some agreement with the Chinese was that in 808 the Uighurs drove them out of part of Kansu, including Liangchow, and they had also previously been involved in serious hostilities with the Arabs and with Nan-chao.

Throughout this period the T'ang authorities had done their best to keep on good terms with the Uighurs. The relationship was cemented in the conventional way with a marriage between a Chinese princess and the Uighur khan in 788, but more practically by an agreement for the exchange of Chinese silk for Uighur horses. This trade became an embarrassment for the Chinese because it imposed a great strain on their industry to supply the appropriate amount of silk in repayment for the increasing number of horses sent, but at this time of weakness it was important to keep peace on the northern frontier, which had often proved vulnerable; and China did in fact succeed in avoiding disasters there for as long as the Uighurs were the dominant power in the north.

But in the latter part of Hsien-tsung's reign there was serious internal trouble. A rebellion in central China dragged on for three years and was a serious threat to the vital waterways linking the Yangtze with the Yellow River. There was also further trouble in Shantung, and as soon as these uprisings had been put down Hsien-tsung died suddenly at the age of forty-two. Some blamed the eunuchs, but others claimed that he had succumbed to an elixir of immortality prepared by Taoists.

His two successors had brief and inglorious reigns. Mu-tsung, who was mainly interested in hunting and theatricals, died in 824 at the age of twenty-nine after a four-year reign and was succeeded by Ching-tsung, an unruly lad of sixteen, who would turn up late to court and rush off as soon as he could to play ball. He was killed two years later in a drunken brawl, and was succeeded by his seventeen-year-old brother, who is known to history as Wen-tsung. He at once gave promise of better things by pruning his own establishment: he got rid of Buddhist parasites and drastically reduced the imperial harem. He proved to be a patron of Confucian studies and a lover of poetry.

But the new emperor's good intentions were of no avail, since the eunuchs had been able to take advantage of the weakness of his two predecessors to entrench themselves more securely than ever. In 830 he planned an armed coup d'état against them, but they got wind of the plot and frustrated it by concocting evidence that the emperor's chief confidant had really been intending to depose the emperor himself. A later conspiracy to get rid of the eunuchs also failed with disastrous consequences. The original idea had been to round them up when they attended the funeral of a prominent eunuch leader, but this plan was shelved in favour of a hastily conceived scheme to decoy the leading eunuchs, including the two generals of the palace armies, into a barracks where an ambush had been prepared. It was announced at court that sweet dew, the Buddhist nectar of immortality, had fallen near the barracks, and the chief eunuchs were sent to investigate. But as they entered the barracks gate a squall of wind blew aside the curtain behind which the assassins were hiding, and the eunuchs retreated. Soon the palace army arrived with its eunuch generals in command, and began slaughtering all those supposedly connected with the plot. The three chief ministers were executed, and many officials were massacred. The eunuchs were now in full control, and executions without trial went on for several weeks, while the capital was given over to rioting and looting. When Emperor Wen-tsung died in 840 at the age of only thirty, they were strong enough to set aside the duly appointed crown prince and install their own nominee, a younger brother of Wen-tsung, whose temple name was Wu-tsung.

During these troubled decades lived one of the most famous figures in Chinese literature, Po Chü-i, whose typical career may reflect the character of the age more vividly than many pages of generalization. Civil servant as well as poet, he became a member of the Hanlin Academy quite early in his career, and was much employed in composing important official correspondence with neighbouring states, dispatched in the emperor's name. In 809 we find him courageously protesting to the emperor at the unprecedented proposal to put a eunuch in supreme command of the force attacking Wang Ch'eng-tsung. A few years later he was banished to a minor post at the city which is now called Kiukiang, where the strange sound of the local speech, the shamanism practised by the people, and the unfamiliar flora and fauna combined to create an exotic atmosphere, although this was only the Yangtze valley, which in modern times has been the heart of China. But he soon tired of the primitive life, the constant diet of salted fish, the simian quality of the local aborigines, and the outlandish nature of the local music, although he found some compensation in the taste of the lychee and the sight of the magnolia. The latter was still so unfamiliar in the north that he commissioned a painting of one to send to a friend in Changan. Later he led a very different life as governor of Hangchow, by now a very prosperous city with a big trade in luxury goods, happily spared the devastation which rebellions had brought to so many parts of the country. Many retired officials made their homes there and were among Po's friends. Finally he settled down to spend the last seventeen years of his life in Loyang.

Po was a devout Buddhist, particularly in the later part of his life, and his poetry is full of compassion. In a famous ballad he described how an old charcoal-seller was set upon by the agents of the eunuch Commissioner for Palace Marketing and given a ludicrously inadequate return for his whole load of charcoal. He often expressed shame at his comfort when others were so poor. His poems were very popular, being relatively free from archaisms and allusions, and his ballads were on the lips of singing-girls and monks, old women and officials. We are told of a street labourer whose whole body was tattooed with lines from Po's poems illustrated by pictures, and of a singing-girl who put up her price because she could sing the *Everlasting Remorse*. Po tried to make use of his popularity. He wrote:

The duty of literature is to be of service to the writer's generation; that of poetry to influence public affairs... Where I believed I could bring alleviation to the sufferings of the people or remedy some defect of policy it was impossible to broach the matter directly, and instead I wrote a ballad, hoping that it would be passed on from person to person till it finally reached the emperor's ear.

Into old age he retained his compassion, and his love of nature, and the never-failing excitement he felt when spring came. Like most of his kind, he felt that a quiet and private life was more agreeable than being an official:

> Happier far the owner of a small garden;
> Propped on his stick he idles here all day,
> Now and again collecting a few friends,
> And every night enjoying lute and wine.
> Why should he pine for great terraces and lakes
> When a little garden gives him all that he needs?

For a short time in the early 820's Po Chü-i had been on friendly terms with the other great literary figure of the day, Han Yü, who is famous alike for trying to introduce a simple 'ancient style' of prose writing to counter current artificialities and for his thorough-going Confucian orthodoxy. He saw himself as a Confucian teacher in the direct line of descent from Mencius, and would have none of the compromise with Buddhism which other thinkers were favouring. He made a very famous attack on the religion in a memorial to the throne which particularly criticized it for its foreign origin. This was presented in 819 on the occasion of the emperor's annual reception of a relic bone of the Buddha, which was usually kept at a temple outside the capital: 'Why,' he inquired, 'should his decayed and rotten bones, his ill-omened and filthy remains, be allowed to enter the forbidden precincts of the Palace?' For this indiscretion Han Yü was banished, but he was soon recalled.

In Wu-tsung the state at last had an emperor who was himself interested in suppressing Buddhism which, in its serious economic effects, could be as harmful to the state as the eunuchs whose power his predecessor had failed to curb. The sale of ordination certificates resorted to in the financial crisis imposed by the An Lu-shan rebellion had been continued for their own profit by the warlords who had governed the frontier areas after this time. In 845 a whole village of tonsured Buddhists was found in Szechwan, all living with wives and children. Such abuses could not be allowed to continue. A first sign of the emperor's disfavour was that Taoist priests were given privileges denied to the Buddhists at the celebration of his birthday in 841. For the next few years the anti-Buddhist movement gained momentum, encouraged by the machinations of prominent Taoists. At first only certain categories of monks were laicized, then monks were cleared out of the imperial palace, and finally in 845 the emperor ordered a census of the monastic community as a prelude to the wholesale repression of the religion. The census showed that there were 260,000 monks, 4600 temples, and 40,000 shrines. In the same year Wu-tsung ordered the destruction of all Buddhist establishments, except that one temple was to be preserved in each of the major prefectures, and four at each of the two capitals. The vast majority of monks were to return to ordinary life, and for administrative purposes Buddhism was to be treated as a foreign religion again. Much valuable monastic land was now restored to the state and, in addition to the laicized monks, many laymen in temple employment were released to become full tax-paying members of the community. The enormous quantities of images, bells and other copper artefacts in the monasteries were to be melted down and cast into money, which would not only have general economic benefit, but also relieve the perennial shortage of coin.

There were also moral and xenophobic reasons for the suppression of Buddhism. As the edict summing up the results of the persecution said, 'Its strange ways have become so customary and all-pervasive as to have slowly and unconsciously corrupted the morals of our land.' In the late T'ang the Chinese were not so willing to accept free intercourse with foreigners as they had been in the happier, more confident days of the dynasty. Thus Nestorians, Zoroastrians, and Manichaeans also suffered persecution during the time of Wu-tsung, and afterwards their religions never thrived as they had done before.

The main supporters of the Manichaean church in China were the Uighurs, whose power was now in decline. In 840 their capital had been sacked by their northern neighbours, the Kirghiz of Western Siberia, with whom they had long been at war. In 842 they were forced by a food shortage to make repeated raids into Chinese territory, so that several hundred of the Uighurs who had long been resident in Changan were arrested and executed, and the Chinese also undertook a successful expedition against them. At the same time the Tibetans were much weakened by internal dissensions, so at least China's external problems were not serious at this period.

It is remarkable that the emperor could carry through his anti-Buddhist measures in spite of the religion's many highly placed supporters. The eunuchs were capable of no more than a delaying action, perhaps because the security of the frontier meant that the power of the palace armies which they controlled weighed much less against the regular armies since these could now be spared from frontier duties.

The year after the full-scale persecution was initiated, the emperor died and was succeeded by his uncle, Hsüan-tsung (his name being written with a different character from that of the famous 'Mysterious Ancestor' who reigned in the first half of the eighth century). He immediately cleared out his nephew's supporters, including the Taoists who had been influential at his court, and reversed his anti-Buddhist policy. Instructions were even given that the new coins which had been made out of Buddhist images should be taken out of circulation and cast into images again. But it is clear that this regulation was not strictly enforced and, although the new emperor issued an edict of tolerance the following year, permitting the repair of temples damaged in the persecution, the suppression of 845 had dealt a crippling blow to Buddhism in China and definitely marked the beginning of its decline. At the same time changes in the nature of Chinese society also meant that the religion was suffering some loss of vitality: otherwise it would not have been possible for the state to inflict such a decisive setback.

6

In its heyday Buddhism had had a profound impact on Chinese civilization, not only in the obvious spheres of religion and art, but just as importantly in social and economic matters. Although the enrichment of monasteries was remote from the primitive Buddhist ideal, the religious community's dependence on gifts from the pious for its basic necessities sowed the seed of an eventual accumulation of wealth which would give scope for commercial and capitalistic activities. By presenting gifts to the Buddhist community, the layman stored up merit which, according to the unsophisticated popular version of the religion, would ensure future blessings both in this life and in the one hereafter, so at times of great religious fervour much wealth would pour into the monasteries. The relationship between the religious community and the layman had originally involved a simple exchange in which the former received the necessities of life in return for the religious gifts it bestowed on the latter. When it became the practice to give land, silk, metal and other nonessentials, these were regarded as impure and so were not immediately usable by the monks. Commercial transactions were therefore necessary in order to convert these gifts for the benefit of the community. This was the essential factor in the commercialization of Buddhism, although throughout the history of Buddhism in China there had been close contacts between it and the commercial world. The new religion had come in along the Central Asian trade routes, and had developed in the commercial settlements of foreigners in China, while merchants who had embraced the Buddhist faith doubtless placed their commercial expertise at the disposal of the religious community. Alongside the ordinary traffic of the trade routes came the pious commerce in religious texts and relics. The Buddhist community was also at the very centre of economic growth because it stimulated the manufacture and sale of objects of piety, and many skilled artisan occupations found expression in the construction and furnishing of monasteries. Religious festivals also provided an opportunity for holding fairs, so they too made their contribution to the commercial life of the times. Perhaps the most surprising role of the Buddhist community was that of money-lender. The earliest pawnshops in China existed in monasteries, and their origins can even be traced back to the pre-T'ang period. It was not only money that the poor peasant needed to borrow. His existence was so precarious that, when sowing time came round, he often needed to borrow seed, and monasteries with large granaries were able to lend this out at usurious rates of interest, thus keeping the peasants in a state of dependence upon them.

Monasteries also had the capital to engage in industrial activities and equip themselves with such machinery as rolling-mills and oil-presses. The latter were very necessary since many monasteries were in remote places and the consumption of oil in a religious community was large as it was needed for ceremonial as well as for cooking purposes. Surplus produce was sold to lay customers. Monasteries also profited by serving as hotels for lay travellers as well as for monks and pilgrims. This had been a very necessary service at the isolated staging posts in Central Asia, and the practice soon spread to China proper, where travelling merchants, officials and examination candidates were glad to avail themselves of the monks' hospitality.

In addition to being centres of commercial and industrial activity, Buddhist communities stimulated important social changes. We have already seen how the growth of large monastic estates was part of a general revolution in land-ownership which had meant that the class of free peasants had been much reduced by the end of the eighth century. The work on these estates was not done by the monks themselves, but mainly by slaves, who were recruited from among criminals, orphans brought up by the monastic community, people who had been tenants on the land when it came into the possession of the monastery, and unemployed migrants. 150,000 of these slaves were freed at the time of the suppression in 845.

Since slavery has not been discussed before in this narrative, it is necessary to say something about the place of this institution in Chinese society. Slaves never formed more than a very small proportion of the population. The chief source of supply was the enslavement of members of the families of criminals who had been condemned to death, and the only slaves strictly recognized as such by the law were such people and their descendants. The state could emancipate slaves, so the number of people in this category did not grow enormously. Those who were surplus to its needs could be given away or sold to private individuals, but the chief source of private slaves was destitution, which forced individuals to sell themselves or their wives and children. The selling of children into domestic servitude because of famine persisted until modern times. Because of the penal origin of the institution and because punishment in ancient China primarily involved degradation in the form of mutilation or disfigurement, such as castration or the cutting off of limbs, rather than the deprivation of freedom, slaves were thought of as a degraded class of human being at the bottom of the social scale, rather than as people who had lost their liberty. The owner had no right to misuse his slaves, but crimes committed against them were comparatively lightly punished, and, conversely, especially severe penalties were meted out to slaves who had committed crimes against ordinary members of the community. Under barbarian influence there had been large-scale enslavement of prisoners-of-war during the Northern Dynasties, and later foreign dynasties would also bring about a temporary growth of the institution in conformity with their own customs, but throughout imperial Chinese history slaves were generally employed in domestic service. However, in monastic communities they were employed on the land, as we have just seen.

Just as important was the influence of Buddhism on the social life of the lay community. It acted as a social cement which bound all classes together in an entirely new way. This happened because it was a religion of compassion and salvation and because the great festival occasions brought the whole community together in a convivial atmosphere. At the same time smaller groups of people got together for religious purposes. Such religious societies, formed with the aim of acquiring merit by contribution to some collective act of piety, such as the financing of rock-carvings at Lungmen, had been known before the T'ang Dynasty. The institution developed during the T'ang, with increasing emphasis on financing more modest activities, such as the copying or recitation of sutras or the holding of vegetarian feasts. It was a natural development that these groups should become mutual aid societies providing for secular as well as religious needs. The monastic communities also developed various welfare activities, and right down to modern times such institutions as hospitals, dispensaries, old people's homes and bathhouses often owed their origins to Buddhists. Community projects such as road and bridge building, well-digging and tree-planting were also sponsored by the monasteries.

Religious festivals offered the ordinary people the excitement of the crowd, the attraction of extravagance and spectacle, and an opportunity for relaxation from the normal restraints of life. The extravagance and spectacle also appealed to those members of the upper classes who were not influenced by the doctrines of restraint and economy which formed part of the Confucian ethic. Hence it had much influence at court, especially among the palace women and eunuchs. Many religious establishments were patronized by the court, and emperors knew how to use the paraphernalia of Buddhist ceremony to stimulate loyalty to their régime; and they also sought to ensure that they and their régimes would receive the benefit of the prayers of the religious, so that even when economic necessities forced an enormous reduction in the scale of Buddhist operations temples were allowed to survive all over the empire in order to carry out the official cult. From the orthodox Confucian viewpoint the religion could be tolerated if practised on a small scale: morally it was not totally repugnant for, although it was irreconcilable with the important Confucian virtue of filial piety, at least compassion and charity were not alien to the Confucian tradition. It was the economic threat of the religion which was the major reason for its suppression. It could also be dangerously subversive: it sometimes inspired messianic uprisings, with remote monasteries serving as convenient places in which rebel supplies could be stored; and the close-knit religious societies which had developed were units of social organization which were entirely outside government control and might be manipulated for subversive purposes.

After the suppression of Buddhism in 845 the steady decline in T'ang fortunes continued until the dynasty was irreparably damaged by the Huang Ch'ao rebellion, which broke out in 875. Two years earlier the eunuchs had placed on the throne a boy of eleven, the Emperor Hsi-tsung, who was only the fifth son of the previous emperor, I-tsung. To add to the growing difficulties of the administration, the Honan area suffered a severe drought, and the people, driven to despair by a combination of human folly and natural disaster, rose in revolt. When their leader was defeated and killed in 878, the command of the insurgents was taken over by Huang Ch'ao, who was probably a frustrated intellectual who had graduated to salt-smuggling after repeated failures to pass the civil examinations. In the following year his force moved south and captured Canton and the surrounding area.

Canton was in the deep south, that strange area of China which had nominally been part of the country for a thousand years, but which had had sparse Chinese settlement in pre-T'ang times. Even military colonization was not carried out on a large scale until the eighth century, and a civil posting was tantamount to exile with a fair prospect of an early death from malaria or some other tropical disease. If Po-Chü-i found the inhabitants of the Yangtze valley outlandish, it is not surprising that the northern Chinese regarded the denizens of the far south as savage and even sub-human, and wrote their tribal names with characters which indicated that they were related to animals rather than to mankind. To the metropolitan Chinese this region presented problems which were in complete contrast with the challenge of the northern frontier. Instead of a country of vast open spaces lined by the Great Wall to mark the boundary of the northern nomads' legitimate sphere of influence, there was an immense area of haunted forest and spectacular mountain scenery, whose lush greenness made a very different impression from the familiar yellow earth; and Chinese settlements were sprinkled frugally over this alien terrain. Because the aborigines were thought not to be properly human, the T'ang Chinese could with a clear conscience carry them off into slavery, so that they could be sold for service in aristocratic households, or used to replenish the supply of eunuchs for the court. Later a more humane attitude began to prevail, and in the ninth century schools were built and the people were introduced to some of the benefits of Chinese technology, for it was felt that even these benighted barbarians, like others elsewhere, might in course of time embrace the eternal truths of classical doctrine and begin to think and behave like Chinese. To administer these savages sometimes even men of ability found themselves sent to the deep south, for this was a common posting for disgraced officials exiled from metropolitan comforts. Eventually some of those Chinese who survived and lived out their lives there had their imaginations stimulated by the rich hues of tropical vegetation and the wealth of unfamiliar flora and fauna and the spectacular scenery, so that the world of the T'ang imagination was enriched by the addition of these new experiences. At the same time many exotic southern products made their way as annual tribute to the distant north via Canton, which was itself an old town and trading centre although most settlements in the extreme south were recent.

Much of the commerce here was in the hands of the large foreign community, which mainly consisted of Muslims. Arab writers had remarked on the peace and security of their lives: the trade was carefully regulated by the government's inspectorate of maritime trade, but the Muslims were given the privilege of dealing with their own legal disputes. Now the dark shadow of dynastic decline fell over Canton, for when Huang Ch'ao's men arrived they put many of the inhabitants to the sword. Arab writers claimed that over 100,000 members of the foreign community perished and, although this figure must be regarded as a great exaggeration, the rebel occupation of the city certainly had a disastrous effect on Sino-Islamic trade relations.

Canton was a valuable prize, and it was a long tradition that the Chinese governors in this still insalubrious area expected to do very well for themselves out of their appointments. Unfortunately malaria, which was the dread of men exiled to these southern regions, struck a deadly blow, and cost the rebel leader about a third of his force. Returning north from the city, Huang

Ch'ao was heavily defeated by an imperial general, but there was too much discontent in the provincial armies for him to be able to pursue the defeated rebels and put a stop to the uprising. This dissatisfaction had been boiling up for some time, particularly since barbarian cavalry had been used to put down a mutiny in 868–9. Since 875 there had been a series of mutinies, and some provincial governors had even been removed by disaffected troops. To deal with these troubles the government had to commit its reserves, leaving Huang Ch'ao an easy march on the two capitals, which he occupied in the winter of 880–81, having recruited fresh men on his march north. The boy emperor and his court had fled to Chengtu and Huang Ch'ao was proclaimed emperor. But although several provinces had now been taken over by army officers who declared their allegiance to Huang Ch'ao, the court retained sufficient influence to mount a counter-attack on the rebel. Huang Ch'ao managed to hold on to Changan for a couple of years, an occupation memorable only for the bloodbath to which he treated its inhabitants and the desperate food-shortage which marked the end of his régime. Finally in the spring of 883 he was expelled by the imperial forces with the aid of cavalry supplied by Li K'o-yung, leader of the Sha-t'o Turks, who dwelt to the north-west of China where the Yellow River curves north of the Great Wall. Huang Ch'ao fled eastward but met his death the following year when his supporters had been reduced to a handful, and the emperor duly directed that his severed head should be presented at the imperial ancestral temples.

But the defeat of Huang Ch'ao did not mean the end of trouble for the T'ang. By now the government's loss of control was almost complete. Army officers had seized power in many places, and those generals who were ostensibly loyal were almost as unreliable as the régime's most desperate opponents. Indeed the court was so anxious to be conciliatory that it would reward surrendered rebels with provincial governorships, a policy which did not make loyalty seem a very attractive proposition. Thus Chu Wen, one of Huang Ch'ao's generals, surrendered in 882 and within six months found himself appointed military governor of Pien prefecture, an area of great strategic importance in Honan. In the south the repercussions of Huang Ch'ao's campaigns were still felt, and a former commander-in-chief of the imperial forces arrayed against the rebel was defying the court and supporting uprisings in various places south of the Yangtze. Nearer the capital, the three prefectures closest to Changan were a constant menace since their governors were not men who had been chosen by the court. In the east Chu Wen had to cope with a dangerous rebellion which went on for three years after the death of Huang Ch'ao, so that for all that period Honan was virtually cut off from the capital. The court's influence over the prefectures which it nominally controlled gradually got weaker. Many governors dispensed with court-appointed officials altogether and gave office to their own supporters, and in many cases loyal army commanders were rewarded with important civil appointments. The military forces were just as much out of control of the central government as the civil administration, since the eunuch supervisors found it simpler and more rewarding to become the tools of provincial governors and intrigue for them at the capital instead of presenting the emperor with reports of irregularities which he had not the power to punish. Indeed diplomacy and intrigue were the only weapons left to the court as a means of dealing with the powerful provincial warlords, but as always such weapons proved dangerous to those who wielded them.

The two most important figures in the dying decades of the T'ang Dynasty were Chu Wen and Li K'o-yung. They had been mainly responsible for the defeat of Huang Ch'ao, but afterwards they had quarrelled and Chu had attempted to assassinate Li, so henceforward they were bitter enemies. They each built strong centres of power in their respective regions, Li K'o-yung away to the north in Hotung, and Chu Wen in Honan. Pien prefecture was of great economic importance because of its situation on the Grand Canal and its control of granaries which had been established as part of the chain of stations in the grain transportation scheme. It was also a key strategic point because it could guard against rebellion in Honan and also act as a bastion against Hopei, that long-dissident area of the empire which had been out of the control of the central government since the rebellion of An Lu-shan. Chu Wen's appointment here therefore gave him control of a large army, which he was forced to increase to withstand the rebels who continued to be a menace after Huang Ch'ao's death. At one time they became so strong that they were able to take Loyang and besiege him in Pien, leaving him entirely dependent on his own resources to build a force sufficiently strong to crush them. To this end he formed alliances with other governors and recruited reinforcements as and where he could. Over the years the Pien prefectural army was gradually moulded into a rigorously disciplined force which owed strong personal loyalty to Chu. Many of his relatives and adopted sons held important positions in it.

In 888 Hsi-tsung died and the eunuchs put his brother Chaotsung on the throne. His whole reign was as ignominious as its inception. Li Mao-chen, governor of the prefecture of Ch'i, not far west of the capital, taking advantage of the fact that Chu Wen and Li K'o-yung were preoccupied with a bitter struggle for control of the Hopei area, marched on the capital and forced the court to flee. There had been other imperial retreats in this unhappy period, but this was the most humiliating. The Son of Heaven took refuge with Han Chien, governor of the small and weak neighbouring prefecture of Hua. But although Han Chien was weak, his imperial master was weaker. Han reduced him to a mere puppet by disbanding his personal bodyguard, executing his ablest commanders, absorbing into his own forces the armies of the imperial princes, and finally having the princes murdered. This was all pointless folly, for Li Mao-chen and Li K'o-yung soon insisted that the emperor be restored to the capital. Two years later it was the eunuchs' turn to depose their wretched sovereign, but within a couple of months he had been restored again with the backing of Chu Wen, who now dominated the scene for the remainder of the dynasty. The area under his control gradually expanded and he put soldiers in charge of all the subprefectures, so that each one became a strong garrison town under a soldier-administrator. By 903 the processes of war and intrigue had reduced the number of independent governors to twelve, and the only three of these who had direct access to the capital were Chu Wen, Li K'o-yung and Li Mao-chen, and of these three, Chu Wen was much the most powerful. He was now strong enough to make his distinctive contribution to Chinese history. Succeeding where many others had failed, he had all the court eunuchs killed and forced the emperor to order the killing of all the eunuch army supervisors in the provinces. Their removal cleared the way for an entirely fresh start, but this could not be made under the totally discredited T'ang. In the following year the emperor was removed to Loyang, and on the journey every one of his men down to the humblest palace servant was killed and replaced by one of Chu Wen's own supporters; and later that year the emperor himself was killed and replaced by a boy of twelve. The next few years saw many executions, and Chu Wen, having dallied as long as he could, finally took the throne in 907 after half a lifetime of campaigning, at an inauspicious moment when his armies were being driven back and it was far from clear that his butcheries had entitled him to claim the Mandate of Heaven.

The departure of Chao-tsung from Changan marked the end of that city's career as capital of China. It had already been very seriously damaged during Huang Ch'ao's occupation, and soon peasants would move back in to reclaim the land on which had stood the city which for three centuries had been the greatest in the world. By contrast with the Romans, who built for eternity, the Chinese emperors constructed their cities of more fragile material, seeking immortality instead in the pages of the dynastic histories which would ultimately be compiled from the day-to-day records which were kept by court and government. So the old Changan was swept away, and even the modern city of Sian which stands on its site is but an eighth the size of the old capital.

The T'ang Dynasty had reached the height of its glory in the expansive and cosmopolitan days before An Lu-shan when China was dominant in East Asia. Then it had enriched itself materially through trade and conquest in remote lands, and intellectually and spiritually with its new knowledge of strange countries, exotic customs and religions, and fresh aesthetic experiences, just as Europe did later during the great age of overseas exploration. The decline in the dynasty after the rebellion had meant not only a shrinking of China's physical frontiers and a loss of strong central control over what remained, but also a less tolerant attitude to foreigners and foreign religions, and a sentimental nostalgia for the great days of the past, while a desire to escape from the world motivated many of the finest intellects at a time when there was little glory in serving a government which was in the humiliating control of eunuchs. Even so, to the outsider, like the Japanese monk Ennin who visited the country in the middle of the ninth century, China still gave the impression of being a great and well-ordered society. Although on the surface the political history of the period was squalid and frustrating to men of good will, institutions had a remarkable capacity for survival at a local level. Sweeping social changes were taking place, which would be very important for the country's future. Indeed, the very independence from central control of provincial areas had contributed to the building of a state in which there would be many important centres of population instead of the one great capital city which had dominated earlier régimes. The improvement of communications, including not only the canals, but also the network of posting stations which had flourished in the early part of the dynasty, had contributed to this development. So also had the growth of international trade, which still prospered during the ninth century in places like Canton, where there was a large colony of foreign merchants. The expansion of commerce not only fostered urbanization but also brought greater freedom to merchants and traders, who had previously had to conduct their business in strictly controlled markets in the cities. But the dynasty's most striking export was its culture and style of government. The country was surrounded by peoples which had adopted the T'ang model, from Tibet and Nan-chao in the west to the Tungusic kingdom of P'o-hai in Manchuria on the north and Korea and Japan to the east. Never has Chinese prestige stood higher among its neighbours than in the heyday of the dynasty whose ignominious conclusion has just been described.

3

The Five Dynasties period and the Sung Dynasty

1

As the destroyer of a great dynasty Chu Wen has been condemned as one of the villains of Chinese history, and the period of disunity which he ushered in has been regarded as the inevitable consequence of the abandonment of Confucian principles and a dire warning to future generations of political leaders. During this period five short-lived dynasties in turn held sway in the north, while the south was fragmented into several separate states, so that this epoch of Chinese history is traditionally known as the age of the Five Dynasties and Ten Kingdoms. But it is wrong to treat this age as an unrelieved orgy of iniquity terminated by the heroic and miraculous achievements of the great founder of the Sung Dynasty, because some of the developments of this troubled era can be seen to have smoothed the path towards the re-establishment of unity. Indeed the period of the Five Dynasties should be seen as a preparation for reunification rather than as the final degradation after the destruction of T'ang. It was an era in which the seeds of future greatness were sown. Even in the south, where relative peace and security compensated for fragmentation of the country, some of the states could boast significant contributions to China's cultural history.

Even the much maligned Chu Wen, after the three decades of brutal struggle which had brought him to the throne, had something more positive to give to Chinese history than the butchery of his opponents and the annihilation of the palace eunuchs. A considerable contribution towards the future physical reunification of the country was the integration of the prefectures in the Honan area, which remained free of significant rebellion throughout the Five Dynasties period. Chu Wen's old base of Pien in

Honan now became his capital under the name of Kaifeng. He also embarked on a policy of trying to secure greater control of the prefectures by splitting up the large and powerful ones, and in his first three years on the throne he created seven new prefectures in this way. In the capital the removal of the eunuchs had meant that the posts which they had traditionally held were made available to minor local officials who had served under Chu Wen and to officers who had begun their careers in his private army. The control of affairs was generally in the hands of palace commissions. The status of the commissioners was secured by the use of sinecure army titles, a practice which had apparently not been totally discredited by its application to eunuchs during the T'ang. Palace commissions were not merely concerned with appropriate palace matters: they were even put in charge of such important concerns of state as military affairs and finance. The ranks of the official bureaucracy had been seriously depleted because many members of literati families had been executed at the end of the previous dynasty and others had fled the metropolitan area because of the troubled times. The few who remained had small influence. Nevertheless the civil examinations were held in thirteen out of the sixteen years of Chu Wen's dynasty, which was known as the Liang, and this helped to keep alive the bureaucratic tradition and give some respectability to the administration. But the tragic struggle in the imperial family weakened the dynasty at a time when unity within the palace was essential if any kind of unity outside was to be imposed. In 912 Chu Wen was murdered by an illegitimate son, who seized the throne only to be murdered eight months later by the supporters of another son. During this period of struggle several prefectures fell out of the court's control, and other losses of territory soon followed. The principal gainer was Li Ts'un-hsü, the son of Chu Wen's old rival Li K'o-yung, from whom he had inherited in 908 the tribal army of the Sha-t'o Turks and three prefectures. Within nine years he had gained territories in the north-east which were almost as extensive as the Liang had ever controlled. In his drive to replace that dynasty he rallied support by appealing to a programme of restoring the T'ang. This could not fail to attract the old T'ang official families which were uneasy with Chu

Wen because he had the blood of many bureaucrats on his hands.

When he did conquer the Liang in 923, Li made some attempt to put the clock back by reverting to the old capitals of Changan and Loyang and by restoring some power to aristocrats and re-placing some palace commissioners by eunuchs, but since he himself was imbued with the style of the provincial governor he continued to place much reliance on his powerful retainers and departed very little from the Liang pattern of administration. Although he continued to be militarily successful for a time and even conquered the southern kingdom of Shu (present Szech-wan) in 925, his policies had aroused too much discontent and in 926 his armies mutinied and killed him. One of the chief griev-ances against him was that he had even resurrected the system of eunuch army supervisors. With his downfall came the end of power for the eunuchs again, for they could not survive long without the military influence which they had exercised during the T'ang. One of the next emperor's first acts was to order the execution of the eunuch army supervisors and discontinue their use. The Later T'ang Dynasty had soon reverted to a style of government not dissimilar to that of the Liang, which might be described as the transference to the larger theatre of state affairs of the apparatus of prefectural government as it had developed towards the end of the T'ang, with heavy dependence on staff owing personal allegiance to the governor. The failure of both these dynasties to develop strong central control was due to the fact that the governors of the prefectures were able to build up their own apparatus of personal retainers on the same pattern.

The next emperor, Li Ssu-yüan, was an adopted member of the Sha-t'o Turk imperial family and a general of great seniority who had first seen service with his predecessor's grandfather and now rather unexpectedly found himself on the throne at the age of fifty-nine. Following the usual pattern of the times, he appointed a group of local officials to the highest palace commissions, in spite of their ignorance of imperial government. But he had to compensate for their defects by giving more responsibilities to the old scholar-bureaucrat element in his administration in order to provide experience and continuity, and this proved to be a turning point in the recovery of bureaucratic influence. Another important step taken by Li Ssu-yüan was the creation of a new military unit known as the Emperor's Personal Army. Serving the emperor in the same way as the military governors had been served by their own private armies, it was soon to play a vital role in the power struggle. Outside the capital the new emperor had great successes in regaining control of North India, which had been thrown into turmoil by the mutinies against his predecessor. By now many fewer governors had the resources to defy the central government, and at the time of his death in 933, only four still held out against him. But the dynasty did not long survive the death of this effective administrator, and after two short reigns the Later Chin Dynasty was established in 936 by a son-in-law of Li Ssu-yüan, named Shih Ching-t'ang.

The last Later T'ang emperor had been a usurper, placed on the throne by the army, and since the army did not get the promised rewards and owed him no personal loyalty, Shih Ching-t'ang, then governor of the important northern frontier prefecture of Ping, which had been Li K'o-yung's power base, was able to rebel and establish a new dynasty, with its capital at Kaifeng. Shih Ching-t'ang, who under his father-in-law had once held the important post of Commander of the Emperor's Personal Army, managed to gain firm control of the imperial armies by 938, and was consequently able to institute a stronger policy towards the prefectures, his aim being to keep the resources of the governors to a minimum and to try as far as possible to reassert the principle that local government should be under the supervision of the central bureaucracy. At the same time he continued to build up the Emperor's Personal Army so that it became strong enough to cope with any rival force from outside the metropolitan area. This policy increased the effectiveness with which the court could begin to impose its will on the provinces, but meant that the strength of frontier defences was dangerously reduced. The Khitan were now becoming increasingly powerful in the north, and the emperor had already rewarded them for the support they had given him in his bid for the throne with the present of sixteen prefectures on the northern and north-eastern borders. Nevertheless he had done much to achieve the necessary job of strengthening the central power. Another sign of growing health and strength at the centre was the continued revival of bureaucratic influence and confidence. Although the retainer palace commissioners remained powerful, it was becoming increasingly clear that no stable government could be built simply on personal loyalties and that the expertise and continuity provided by the traditional bureaucracy was essential to the well-being of the state. At the same time its great traditions ensured that the more ambitious of the palace officials wished their sons to acquire the prestige of belonging to it.

Unfortuntely, however, the presence of a powerful army at the capital is no guarantee of stability. One danger is that the commander will become too powerful and seek to impose his will. This is what happened after Shih Ching-t'ang's death in 942. His nephew and successor, Shih Ch'ung-kuei, was dominated by the commander of the Emperor's Personal Army, who insisted that Shih should assert his independence of the Khitan and stop the regular payment of tribute to them. A disastrous and costly war raged from 943 until 946, when the Chinese forces surrendered, leaving the empire at their opponents' mercy. For five months the Khitan actually ruled northern China but they had not the resources to impose their will for a longer period.

During the first half of the tenth century the Khitan had developed from a confederation of tribes into an imperial state, and more than any of the other border peoples had shown themselves capable of profiting from the Middle Kingdom's weakness. In the very year when Chu Wen established the Liang Dynasty a powerful and vigorous chieftain called Yeh-lü A-pao-chi had declared himself emperor of the Khitan, and nine years later he founded a dynasty, scrapping the nomad custom of choosing the ablest man to rule for a limited period. To establish a centralized state instead of the loose confederation which was so often the weakness of these nomadic peoples, he clearly had to look to China which, despite its present troubles, provided the obvious pattern of a workable centralized political organization. Accordingly he not only instituted the system of hereditary monarchy, but also took over the Chinese scheme of reign titles and adopted Confucius as the supreme sage. Although the Chinese subjects of the Khitan had been given inferior status by an edict of 921, their value to the state gradually asserted itself so that, soon after the alliance between A-pao-chi's successor and the emperor of the Later Chin had led to the cession of the sixteen prefectures, a civil service examination system was introduced. At the same time there was a wave of cultural influence from China, encouraged particularly by this alliance with the Later Chin and by the occupation of 947 : the emperor began to wear Chinese clothes and adopt the paraphernalia of the Chinese court, surrounding himself with eunuchs and court ladies. The first two emperors were post-humously known as the Grand Progenitor and Grand Ancestor after the fashion of founders of Chinese dynasties. At the same time Buddhist beliefs and practices began to sweep their domains.

In the meantime Khitan power had also been growing in other directions. In 926 the important sinicized Tungusic state of P'o-hai had been conquered, and in the previous year the emperor had received tribute missions from Silla and Koguryo, and even a delegation from Japan. The Khitan indeed kept in close touch with two of the Ten Kingdoms, Southern T'ang and Wu-yüeh, receiving tribute and military intelligence from them, and Wu-yüeh even adopted the Khitan calendar.

In 947, the year of the occupation of the Later Chin capital, the Khitan adopted the dynastic name of Liao, under which they have been recognized as one of the official Chinese dynasties, although they only occupied a small proportion of the country. The interest of this frontier society arises from its dual nature : for climatic reasons it was impossible for the tribal and pastoral north to fuse with the agricultural and settled south mainly populated by Chinese, so that the old tribal ways survived in spite of the attractions of Chinese culture. The dual nature of the country was recognized in the division between the northern and southern regions into which the territories were organized after 947. As capital of the southern region, the city which is now Peking made its bow as a capital city.

The long war against the Khitan had severely weakened the state's resources. The only commander with the military strength to make an effective bid to establish a new dynasty was Liu Chih-yüan, the governor of Ping, the old Sha-t'o Turkish stronghold which had been the power base in turn of the founders of the Later T'ang and of the Later Chin Dynasty, and which was kept strong by these Turkish imperial houses as a bastion and a refuge in time of trouble. The Chin generals had all been discredited by their failure in the Khitan war, but Liu had been sufficiently strong to hold out and resist the Khitan demand for his presence at court. As the Khitan forces, stretched beyond their capacity, began to fall back, Liu was in a good strategic position to threaten them and to fill the military vacuum created by their withdrawal, which was speeded by the sudden death of the Khitan emperor and the necessity to decide the choice of his successor back at the capital. Having declared himself emperor earlier in the year, Liu Chih-yüan marched south and entered Kaifeng in the summer of 947.

The new dynasty was called the Han, but it was not destined to rival in duration the glorious ancient dynasty of that name. But during its life of less than four years it became clear that the prefectures had been so weakened by the recent conflict that the court now occupied the position of relative strength which it had been the aim of previous governments to secure. It was now strong enough not only to appoint bureaucrats to serve in the prefectural governments but even to attach army officers to supervise the governors' personal staff, and it was able to secure acceptance of this new arrangement by sending powerful units of the Emperor's Personal Army to patrol the prefectures to keep a check on the governors' military authority at the same time as they were dealing with the problems of bandit suppression and border defence.

The Emperor's Personal Army, which had been rebuilt by Liu out of Later Chin army units recalled from the prefectures, was now clearly the dominant force in the empire, and in 950 it had its will by enthroning its commander Kuo Wei in place of Liu's successor (the founder having died soon after establishing the dynasty). The Han court had to take refuge at Ping, and with the support of the Khitan it was able to survive in this stronghold for another twenty-eight years as a separate régime known as the Northern Han. The new dynasty, founded by a military usurper, adopted the most hallowed of all Chinese dynastic names, the

Chou, which was the period of Confucius and the ancient sages. One of the main preoccupations of the two men who reigned during the mere decade of its existence was to try to ensure that they did not suffer the same fate as the Han. To this end they introduced some army reforms, including the establishment of a palace corps under the close personal control of the emperor, but ironically it was the commander of this force, Chao K'uang-yin, who stepped in on the death of the second Chou emperor, removed the child who had briefly succeeded him, and at last managed to establish a viable régime.

As the founder of the glorious Sung Dynasty, Chao K'uang-yin has traditionally been given the credit for a miraculous feat of reunification but, just as the skilful policies of their predecessors in alliance with the chance course of events had been preparing the way for this recovery of Chinese power and prestige, so the work of the two Chou emperors must be given due credit. Indeed Ch'ai Jung, the adopted son of the founder Kuo Wei, seems to have been a remarkably energetic and effective ruler. During his reign eleven of the eighteen new governors appointed were officers in the Emperor's Personal Army. These retained their army commands after their appointment, so that for much of the time they were away on service and the prefectures were mainly being run by court-approved bureaucrats in their absence; while when they were actually in their prefectures, their membership of the emperor's army was some guarantee of their administering them in the sovereign's interest. This system had been in existence since 947, but it was made much more widespread by Ch'ai Jung, who thus ensured a further strengthening of central control.

Ch'ai Jung was also responsible for energetic measures to improve the country's financial situation. He dealt with the Buddhist burden on the economy by closing over thirty thousand monasteries in the first year of his reign. In the following year he tackled another method of tax evasion by issuing a warning against the production of poor quality linen and silk. It is also clear that he was responsible for the resumption of large-scale water-control activity. The capital city of Kaifeng was now growing into a great commercial centre, and this development was fostered by the government, which constructed in the vicinity twelve huge warehouses in which merchants could store their goods. Industrial development was also stimulated, particularly by a big shipbuilding programme in which several hundred vessels were ordered for a projected campaign against the large and prosperous state of Southern T'ang, although it was the Sung founder who was to reap the benefit of these preparations. A further reflection of growing strength and confidence is the fact that there is little record of any tribute being paid to Liao, and all in all the Chou Dynasty is a striking example of the not un-familiar phenomenon of a state devastated in war almost immedi-ately making great progress in the constructive arts.

Before we contemplate the great edifice which Chao K'uang-yin, who was to be posthumously known as T'ai-tsu, the Grand Progenitor of the Sung Dynasty, built on the foundations laid by the Chou, some brief notice should be taken of the development of Chinese civilization in the southern Chinese states during the period which we have just been discussing. Although these short-lived states played no essential part in the story of the growth of the Sung political system out of the ruins of the T'ang which we have just been tracing, some very important cultural developments demand our attention.

The areas of especial importance in the south were the kingdom of Shu, based on what is now Szechwan, and Southern T'ang, with its capital at Nanking, but stretching away far to the south-west. Shu was a populous and self-contained area which had been independent as one of the Three Kingdoms, and since then its capital, Chengtu, had been a favourite retreat for emperors in difficult times. Hsüan-tsung had fled there at the time of the An Lu-shan rebellion, suffering the heartbreaking loss of Yang Kuei-fei en route, and the hapless Hsi-tsung had also taken refuge there when his capital was seized by Huang Ch'ao; so it was only natural that, when the T'ang Dynasty collapsed, it should become a separate state. Enjoying a relatively high level of material prosperity, and strengthened by the presence of many of the literati who had fled the harsh treatment suffered by their kind during the closing years of the T'ang, the state prospered. Poets and painters flourished at its court, and the tomb of its first emperor, which was excavated during the Second World War, bears witness to the high quality of the jades, silverwork, sculpture and wall-painting being produced in this peaceful haven while the north was still torn by conflict.

Shu also played a very important role in the history of printing in China. As has already been mentioned in the first chapter of this book, the Chinese were responsible for the inventions of those two basic essentials of world civilization, paper and printing, the former providing a cheap and plentiful writing material, and the latter a means of the wide and rapid dissemination of ideas. Before they knew how to make paper the Chinese had used rolls of silk or strips of wood tied together, the former too expensive a material, and the latter too bulky for convenience. Although the traditional date of its invention is early in the second century A.D., archaeological evidence shows that it was in existence long before that; but it was not until the capture of Chinese papermakers at the Battle of Talas in 751 that this skill made its way from East to West, and there was clearly a gap of ten centuries between its first uses in China and in Europe. The early development of printing in China was stimulated by the country's two main intellectual traditions, Confucianism and Buddhism. Ever since the Later Han Dynasty it had been thought the solemn duty of government to have an accurate edition of the Confucian Classics given permanence by being engraved in stone, from which copies could be taken by a process comparable with brass rubbing. The transition from this procedure to block-printing required that characters be carved in relief rather than incised and cut back to front so that they came out the right way round on the printed copy. It is clear that the technique of block-cutting developed considerably in Shu during the first decades of the tenth century, printing having been a speciality of the region in the closing decades of the T'ang. This process came as something of a novelty to the government of the Later T'ang during the brief period between 929 and 934 when it extended its domains to incorporate Shu. It was proposed that the technique should be used as a makeshift way of recording a new orthodox text of the Classics, since the state was at present unable to undertake the engraving in stone which imperial dignity properly demanded. In this rather casual way the printing of the Classics was started, and the official who had proposed this makeshift method was even honoured later as the inventor of printing, although he should only be credited with the responsibility of bring this hitherto obscure art into the service of the state.

Strangely enough, little regard seems to have been paid in official circles to the development of Buddhist printing which had been taking place over the previous two centuries. One of the more debased aspects of Buddhism is the belief of the Pure Land School that the repeated calling upon the name of Amitabha or the mechanical repetition of formulae had great religious efficacy. Similarly a device for reproducing large numbers of small images and charms would be a means of accumulating a great store of merit. Moreover seals with characters on them had been used since antiquity for such purposes as the authentification of documents, the Chinese having for centuries been especially skilful in the techniques of hard-stone carving which had to be employed. From this it was a short step to the reproduction of brief passages of text from wood-cut plates and from there to the printing of whole books. Although it was not until the fifteenth century that printing eventually reached Europe, in China a high standard of craftsmanship had been achieved long before the end of the T'ang period, for the world's oldest extant datable printed book, the *Diamond Sutra* of 868 now in the British Museum, is a beautiful piece of work. It was found in the important ancient library discovered at Tunhwang at the beginning of this century, having been walled up for nearly nine hundred years. At a slightly later date than this comes the first evidence of the secular printing already being carried on in the Szechwan area, which was to develop into such an important activity during the time of the Shu state.

Another haven of culture in these troubled times was the Southern T'ang based on Nanking, an area which had also been a refuge for intellectuals after the An Lu-shan rebellion. The last emperor of this dynasty, Lo Hou-chu, was himself a poet and a great patron of artists, and during his reign flourished both landscape painting and also figure-painting, a famous example of which is the *Night Entertainment of Han Hsi-tsai*, commissioned because the emperor wished to know whether this accomplished man was sufficiently decorous to employ in affairs of state despite the rumours of his dissipation. The special interest of this picture is that it is an early illustration of the fact that the change to the use of chairs instead of mats for sitting on indoors was now complete. This point is worth dwelling on since the Chinese were the only Far Eastern people to use chairs before modern times. Moreover the adoption of the chair means all kinds of domestic changes. The design of other furniture, not only tables but also such things as cupboards and mirrors, must reflect the fact that people no longer sit on the floor. Costume is also affected, because it is no longer necessary to wear garments which are seemly and comfortable for sitting on the floor (like the Japanese kimono, which bears a close resemblance to T'ang Chinese dress). Nor is it necessary to wear shoes which can easily be discarded on entering the house so that the mats are not soiled.

The chair was in use in ancient Egypt five thousand years ago, but its evolution in China was slow and complicated. In antiquity the northern Chinese already used the *k'ang*, the big brick bed heated by flues, which occupied the whole end of a room and could accommodate several people sleeping side by side. It was possible to sit cross-legged on this, resting one's back against the wall. In the Han period a kind of large folding camp stool came into use. This article of furniture evidently reached China from the Roman Empire where it was in common use, but the Chinese continued to sit cross-legged upon them, their main usefulness being that they prevented contact with cold and damp ground. Thus they were normally used out of doors, as items of military equipment or garden furniture. It was a long time before the Chinese hit upon the idea of an article of furniture which not only had a back to lean on, like the room-wall at the back of the *k'ang*, but also a seat short enough to enable the sitter's legs to dangle over the edge and rest on the ground. The first illustration of people sitting on such structures in the European manner dates from the late eighth century, but in this case they are still being used in the garden and have not yet been let into the house. It is not clear what caused the breakthrough to the European style of chair, but the possibility of foreign influence cannot be ruled out, especially since there were resident in China people like the

Nestorians for whom chairs, or thrones, had religious importance. However this may be, the use of the chair had been spreading throughout the late T'ang period and early tenth century and it would soon be in common use among all classes in society, and the use of mats for sitting on would be obsolete. The Chinese language, however, would continue to reflect the fact that for most of their history the Chinese people had sat on mats. 'Chairman Mao' is literally 'Mat-master Mao'.

2

History records that Chao K'uang-yin became emperor reluctantly, since when he was on a campaign against the Khitan, he was forced to don the imperial robes by his officers, who had no confidence in the future under a child emperor, with the real power in the hands of the empress regent. However this may be, he soon proved to be an even more energetic ruler than the second Chou emperor, and set out to make quite sure that the Sung which he established would not turn out to be one more ephemeral dynasty like the last. To this end he must first continue his predecessors' policy of strengthening the centre and devising some machinery of government for controlling the outlying regions, and then bring once again within the frontiers of the empire all those territories which traditionally belonged to it.

At the start of a new dynasty it was still wise to give priority to religious matters, and the Grand Progenitor's attempts to get both Confucian and Buddhist sentiment on his side are reminiscent of the religious policies of the Cultured Emperor of the Sui who similarly had the task of making a usurping dynasty respectable after a long period of disunity. From the first year of his reign the emperor paid regular visits to the temple of Confucius and personally sacrificed to the sage. In the same year he showed his regard for Buddhism by ordering that his birthday be celebrated by the ordination of eight thousand monks. The Later Chou had persecuted the Buddhists just like their namesakes who had preceded the Sui and, like the Sui, Chao K'uang-yin was able to benefit from a timely tolerance which contrasted strongly with his predecessor's harshness. He often entertained monks in the palace, and he also established a translation bureau under his patronage, and dispatched a large mission to the west in search of Buddhist scriptures for it to translate.

To secure the future of his dynasty and free it from the perennial threat of usurpation, he succeeded in inducing the prominent generals who had supported his own usurpation but who might become rivals in the future to accept handsome pensions in return for their disappearance from the active political scene. The next requirement was the construction of machinery whereby the bureaucrats, who had gradually regained much of their prestige and some of their power towards the end of the Five Dynasties, might play their full part in a stable and viable system of government. At first much depended on the emperor retaining firm personal control, and fortunately his experience as a general had made him fit and willing to take a heavy responsibility on his own shoulders. A man of great vigour, he seems to have taken most of the important decisions himself and used his ministers rather as if they were his subordinate officers. At the same time he ensured that his officials were well treated, well paid and respected. With remarkable speed he and his advisers introduced some of the highly sophisticated procedures for the organization of the civil service, which proved to be among the most impressive achievements of the dynasty.

Procedures for appointment and promotion were worked out in detail in the first few years of the reign, so that officials no longer felt that their careers depended on chance. Registers were kept at the capital containing relevant information on all civil servants, and by 962 a sequence of offices which the bureaucrat could normally expect to hold in the course of his career was established, the cursus depending partly on whether he had entered by examination or other means and partly on the merit ratings he had been awarded during his previous appointments. The system of merit ratings was also worked out very early in the Grand Progenitor's reign. These ratings were generally made the responsibility of the official's administrative superiors, but every effort was made to relate them to objective and verifiable criteria. For example, if the official's concern for popular welfare had resulted in a certain percentage increase in population, this would earn him high marks. High ratings generally led to rapid promotion.

The emperor was able to ensure increasing control of the provinces by continuing the policy of keeping the best military units at the capital and by replacing the old military governors, as they died or retired, by civil officials from the state bureaucracy. A further improvement in the standards of local government was secured by an important reform of 964, which provided that graduates, however distinguished, should all commence their careers in one of the lower posts in local administration, which had previously been filled by men whose quality was not high because they were irregularly recruited and had little prospect of advancement. This measure also had the merit of ensuring that eventually the men at the top of the civil service would all have had some experience of administration at the level where it closely touched the interests of the people as individuals.

Another feature which was developed very rapidly during the first decade of the Sung Dynasty was the system of sponsorship. This proved to be an effective method of making appointments with some guarantee of their being successful, since, if the appointee committed a crime, his sponsor stood to suffer a punishment only slightly less severe than the guilty person himself. Again, under the Grand Progenitor, the main use of sponsorship was to fill appointments at the lowest level of local administration because of the vital importance of improving the standard of official at this level, but later the system came to be much more widely used. Underlying the device of sponsorship was the ancient Confucian ideal of government through the promotion of men of worth recommended to the ruler by his advisers, so there were plenty of precedents for this kind of procedure; but it is another sign of the government's energy and skill that all the detailed regulations should have been worked out in the first busy decade of the dynasty, so that later practice was a modification of that introduced by the Grand Progenitor. A man of great administrative ability and extraordinary powers of leadership and reconciliation, deeply concerned to see that the machinery by which men were appointed and promoted worked properly, the Sung founder was less interested in the content of the examinations, which now at last provided the major source of recruitment. But even in this field he showed that he liked to exercise personal control of affairs by introducing the palace examination as the final rung of the civil examination ladder: to combat the danger of personal favour being shown to candidates by examiners at the highest level, the emperor henceforward examined them himself.

The main effort to reunify the empire waited until the emperor had put his administrative house in order. The very small state of Southern P'ing in the area of the Yangtze gorges had capitulated to a show of force in 963, but it was not until 965 that he completed his first major military campaign, the conquest of Shu. Here a vital role was played by the navy which he had inherited from the Chou Dynasty and had continued to build and train. One important effect of this conquest was that the book-printing activities based on Chengtu were now brought within the orbit of the empire. The Grand Progenitor soon showed his continued patronage of Buddhism by ordering the printing of the Buddhist canon, a massive undertaking since the whole collection was 130,000 pages long.

The coastal state of Southern Han fell in 971, and its former capital, Canton, was made the headquarters of a Maritime Trade Commission, designed to revive the profitable overseas commerce which had flourished in this area during the T'ang period and to ensure that a proportion of the proceeds entered the imperial coffers. The large state of Southern T'ang was not subjugated until 975, and here again the Grand Progenitor's navy was put to good use. The only remaining independent régimes at the end of his reign were Wu yüeh, a small state with its capital at Hangchow, and Northern Han, the succession state of the short-lived Han dynasty on the northern frontier, and both of these succumbed early in the following reign.

The Grand Progenitor himself had wisely made no move in a northerly direction, for the Liao state was too hard a nut to crack until the resources of the whole empire could be gathered together and mobilized. The Sung might successfully defend itself against further Liao incursions, for the nomad horsemen were more suited to mobile warfare than to the protracted siege of walled cities. Equally no Chinese force could happily contemplate an encounter with the Khitan tribesmen on their own ground. The most that they could do was to maintain relations with Korea, which by this time had accepted the status of vassal to the North Chinese reigning house, in the hope that they might strengthen their position against the Khitan by diplomatic means. In 918 a certain Wang Kon had established a new dynasty called the Koryo, which is a shortened form of the ancient Koguryo and the word from which Korea is derived. He had supplanted Silla and he and his successors had been recognized by the Northern Dynasties. Koryo, although cut off by the Liao state from the close cultural contact which had formerly existed with China, adopted a system of government closely based on the Chinese; and a salaried bureaucracy for which recruitment was carried out by means of an examination system on the Chinese model had been introduced shortly before the Grand Progenitor came to the throne in China. A mission from Koryo was received by the new emperor in 962 and close relations between the two countries were maintained for the next seventy years.

Thus when the emperor died in 976 he bequeathed his successor an empire which was united and peaceful and firmly controlled from the centre for the first time since the middle of the eighth century. But this is no mere revival of T'ang greatness, for we are in a new world. The cumbersome methods of government which had involved those repeated treks backwards and forwards between Changan and Loyang have now given way to a most sophisticated bureaucratic apparatus; and where court intrigues, the machinations of eunuchs, the interference of palace favourites and the internecine struggles of the ruling family occupied the centre of the stage, we now feel that government is being conducted by remarkably rational and civilized means. As a corollary of this, the military glories of the T'ang were never recaptured, and not only Central Asia but even the northernmost areas of China proper were to remain beyond the Sung armies' capacity to recover.

The Grand Progenitor did not make the mistake which had brought about the end of the previous dynasty. Instead of leaving a child on the throne, he appointed his brother to fill his shoes.

The Grand Ancestor, as the latter was posthumously called, was an experienced administrator who resembled his brother in taking much personal responsibility for the conduct of affairs. But no one could have matched the vigour shown by the late sovereign, and the reign is marked by a definite decline in effectiveness after the successful campaigns in the north against the Northern Han and in the south against Wu-yüeh. Hostilities take place along the northern frontier, but neither Liao nor Sung can gain the advantage. The navy, having fulfilled its urgent tasks, is allowed to decline rapidly after only one more major campaign, an unsuccessful expedition against Annam, and before long is only capable of performing a ceremonial role.

Nevertheless the relative peacefulness of the times and the effect of unification, which brought wide opportunities for trade, ensured a marked increase in the country's prosperity. The money economy continued to develop rapidly, and the rich resources of copper, tin and lead made available to the state by the conquest of Southern T'ang ensured a more plentiful supply of copper cash to meet the increasing demands for currency, so that by the end of the Grand Ancestor's reign the number of copper cash minted annually reached two-and-a-half times the maximum amount minted in a year during the T'ang period. At the beginning of the reign the government introduced a very profitable arrangement for dealing with imported goods by purchasing them directly from the importing merchants and monopolizing the resale. At the same time trade missions were sent to countries in South-east Asia to try to secure a further expansion of commerce with this area, and the resulting increase in business led to the establishment of further offices of the Commission of Maritime Trade at Hangchow and Ningpo.

The capital, Kaifeng, and other commercial centres were already expanding rapidly. The T'ang capital of Changan had been a four-square walled city dominated by imperial and princely palaces and great Buddhist monasteries, a great monument to imperial dignity in which traders were kept out of the way in large walled markets under close official supervision. Commercial prosperity had come after the city's establishment as a capital. But by contrast Kaifeng was an important strategic, commercial and communications centre which had grown into a capital city. In such a community the prestige of the merchant class was bound to rise, and in the face of their great wealth and ostentation and their desire to combat social discrimination, it was impossible to retain the sumptuary laws determining the dress to be worn by different classes and they had to be repealed. Rigid class distinctions continued to break down as the great landowners became more deeply involved with the industrial and commercial world when some of their number were able to develop large-scale mining or metallurgical operations on their estates, like the great landowners in the mining areas of England. As the city of Kaifeng grew at an enormous rate, problems of supplying its huge population accumulated: for example, an acute shortage of charcoal for heating and cooking was felt as early as the Grand Ancestor's reign and the government had to make regulations controlling its distribution.

The Grand Ancestor made few innovations in administrative practice, and had enough to contend with in trying to enforce the arrangements that his brother had made for improving the standards of the local administration. He did his best to follow the path laid down by his brother. Like him he paid honour to Confucius, and showed a frugality of conduct appropriate to a Confucian monarch, wearing his clothes until they were threadbare and refusing to enlarge his palace. He showed more interest in learning than his brother had done and patronized scholarly projects. Like the Grand Progenitor, he took too much on his own shoulders and showed a fussy attention to detail which should have been left to subordinates, but at least he appreciated that after his departure there would have to be a change in the style of government. 'My children,' he said, 'are brought up in the seclusion of the palace. Not being familiar with the affairs of the world they will need the advice and guidance of good scholars.' More responsibility was henceforward to pass to the scholar-officials, and the emperor made sure that his heir was brought up to acknowledge the authority of Confucian ideology, to delegate power to his counsellors, and to heed the observations of the organs of policy criticism, which had hitherto not played a very important role in affairs. By the end of the Grand Ancestor's reign it was fortunately possible for the administrative machinery which his brother had created to work smoothly with less personal attention from the sovereign; so before turning to the reign of his successor, it would be appropriate to give an outline of the structure of the government, which had changed much since the great days of the T'ang.

The administration of the empire was now split between three main bodies, the Secretariat Chancellery, the Finance Commission and the Bureau of Military Affairs. The responsibilities of the Finance Commission very roughly corresponded with those of the T'ang Boards of Revenue and Works. The Bureau of Military Affairs had general responsibility for defence matters, while the Secretariat Chancellery had under its control all the agencies concerned with the whole range of other governmental activities.

Set above these three bodies was a Council of State consisting of between five and nine of the most senior members of the staffs of the Secretariat Chancellery and the Bureau of Military Affairs. This Council was concerned with formulating measures in all fields of governmental activity which were of sufficient importance to require the emperor's approval. It was given technical assistance in the drafting of measures by a Bureau of Academicians, while criticism of its actions might come from the Censorate and various other organs which were created for the purpose of policy criticism. This most important and distinctive feature of the system, providing a channel for complaints, suggestions and criticisms from all sources, was weak under the rather autocratic brothers who had the task of establishing the dynasty, but under the third emperor it began to play the full part for which it was designed. The emperor at the top was final arbiter, but was conditioned by Confucian teaching to accept the advice of his counsellors and welcome criticism and suggestions coming from the appropriate bodies or even from private individuals.

In local government the large provincial areas which had begun to take shape during the T'ang had not yet developed into the formal provinces of the later empire, and the main unit of administration was still the prefecture (*chou*), of which there were over three hundred at the end of the tenth century. Grouped under the prefectures were the subprefectures or counties, which numbered over twelve hundred at this time. The subprefect, operating at the grass roots level, was concerned with public safety, justice, taxation and education, as well as – in keeping with Confucian ideals – the general moral and economic well-being of the people; and he also commanded the local military garrison. Although the prefects were in direct administrative contact with the capital, the arrangement whereby circuit intendants performed the function of oversight and inspection on behalf of the central government was taken over from the T'ang. In the early Sung there were from fifteen to twenty circuits. Intendants were of four kinds, fiscal, judicial, military and exchange. Fiscal intendants were originally charged with supervision of financial matters, but later came to have more general authority in affairs of civil government. The duties of judicial and military intendants are self-explanatory. The primary responsibility of the intendants of exchange was the handling, storage and transportation of goods and commodities, the most important of these being the grain supplies. They also operated state monopolies, and supervised mints. Intendants were sometimes appointed *ad hoc* to deal with special emergencies.

The most important development in personnel administration during this period was the growth in the use of sponsorship, which now became a much more normal method of filling appointments. Originally much emphasis had been placed on the personal qualities of the sponsor, for it was thought that only men of true worth were capable of recommending people of similar calibre. But afterwards sponsors were selected by more objective criteria, and a regulation of 1010 obliged all court officials to recommend one man a year, while senior provincial officials might recommend as many as they saw fit. Although his two predecessors had been very concerned to limit military power, under Chen-tsung, who had succeeded in 998, it became possible for military officials to sponsor men for civil office. Although sponsorship often served the state well in providing the right man for the job and acted as a general stimulus to good work in the civil service, it probably also contributed to the growth of factionalism, which was already beginning to be a problem during Chen-tsung's reign.

However, at the same time as the growth of sponsorship was increasing the dangers of favouritism, every effort was being made to wipe out the risk of such abuses in the civil examinations. The principle of the anonymity of candidates was adopted and put into operation for the major examination, and in 1033 was even extended to the prefectural examinations. In 1015 a Bureau of Examination Copyists was established, to copy out the candidate's scripts so that there was no fear of the handwriting being recognized. To guarantee a fair assessment each script was marked independently by two examiners and the marks were reconciled by a third. Careful precautions were also taken to certify the identity of candidates and prevent them from illicitly substituting persons whom they thought more capable of passing the test than themselves. The meticulous attempts by the government to devise fair means of recruiting and promoting its civil servants are a most remarkable feature of the age: though they antedate the Norman Conquest, they would be a credit to any contemporary society. It is not surprising that by the reign of Chen-tsung some very talented men were forcing their way to the top, so that the role of the emperor became less dominant and more genuine responsibility fell upon the shoulders of the Council of State.

The first few decades of the eleventh century seem to have been very prosperous. At the beginning of the dynasty inducements had been offered to the unemployed to rehabilitate lands laid waste or deserted during the recent upheavals; and an effective agrarian policy had ensured that the countryside was in a better state than it had been for many generations. It would not be long, of course, before this very prosperity would bring its own problems. The great urban development at Kaifeng and gradually at other centres imposed a strain on resources, and in very severe winters there was a serious shortage of charcoal. A rapid increase in population put pressure on the country's agricultural productivity, while the tradition of equal inheritance would soon put the small farmer into difficulties again. But for the moment the country enjoyed one of its rare periods of calm development, especially after the long hostilities against the Liao were terminated by the Treaty of Shan-yüan in 1004. The Sung had suffered a serious defeat at their hands in 986 and had been getting the worst of exchanges since then. In 991 they had been unable to do anything when asked for help by the Jürched, a Tungusic people from Manchuria, who consequently had to submit to the Liao régime, although they were destined to play an important part later. The war had dragged on and a further serious defeat had forced the Sung to come to terms. The Treaty of Shan-yüan guaranteed the Liao an annual payment of a hundred thousand taels of silver and two hundred thousand bolts of silk. This was not a very heavy burden upon the state, representing probably less than one per cent of the national income; nor was it a serious humiliation, for even the great Han Dynasty had resorted to the practice of buying off barbarians, which was condoned by the Confucian scriptures. The more serious consequence of the Sung military weakness was the failure to recover the sixteen lost prefectures and the inability to help Liao's other opponents, not only the Jürched, but also Koryo. The Khitan people also benefited immediately from the termination of hostilities on their southern front by forcing the Hsi tribes to give up their semi-autonomous status and integrating them into their own state. Their old royal capital was walled and filled with Chinese settlers and made into the new central capital of the Liao state.

In the years since the Khitan had temporarily occupied the Chinese capital in 947 it is clear that they had had to modify their attitude towards the Chinese, cease discriminating against them, and make increasing use of their talents. They were driven to this mainly by the need to keep their population fairly contented during the long years of intermittent warfare against the Sung. Now that peace prevailed there could be a growth of trade between the two countries, so that, abandoning restrictions on the export of cattle, felt, silver and gold, the Liao were now prepared to let them cross the frontier freely in order to satisfy the increasing demand for the import of Chinese luxuries, especially silk, for the annual silk tribute was evidently insufficient to fulfil all need for the commodity. The Chinese population of the Liao state gradually became more prosperous and influential, but intermarriage between the peoples was limited. Chinese became the *lingua franca* of the tribes which had been subjugated by the Liao and was even used by the educated Khitan themselves. On the other hand the great majority of Khitan tribesmen remained little affected by Chinese culture, and the basic division between the nomadic tribesmen and the sedentary Chinese remained. Although used for ceremonial purposes, Chinese clothing was not generally adopted. Confucianism did not catch on, but Buddhism did flourish and gain a firm hold on the ruling family. As a result the country was covered with a sprinkling of buildings more permanent than the tents of the nomads, and the large number of monks became an embarrassment to the state. Nevertheless the Khitan still clung firmly to their own traditions, and never abandoned themselves to total sinicization.

In 1008, not long after peace had been arranged with the Liao, Chen-tsung followed the hallowed tradition of a pilgrimage to make the great sacrifice at Mount T'ai, and to visit the temple of Confucius at the sage's birthplace, which was not far away. History records that, unlike previous emperors who had merely bowed, Chen-tsung showed his extreme veneration for Confucius and Classical learning by performing the kowtow. But unfortunately in his later years he came under the influence of an unscrupulous Taoist and was involved in the kind of absurd trick which had been used to herald the usurpation of the Empress Wu: it was alleged that a letter had been received from Heaven expressing approval of Chen-tsung's government. Towards the end the emperor's mind was unbalanced. At one time such a tragic situation would have resulted in a disastrous struggle for the succession, but now there were wise ministers who could steer the state safely through these troubled waters and see the son and heir safely on the throne.

Still only a boy less than twelve years old when the time came for him to succeed, Jen-tsung ('Humane Ancestor') was as carefully indoctrinated with Confucian ideals as his father had been. On the instructions of the empress dowager, scholar-officials compiled for his special edification a story-book containing accounts of exemplary instances in history of the proper relationship between an emperor and his ministers. Soon after he had attained manhood it became the practice for him, amid all the burdens and cares of state, to receive regular lectures on the Confucian Classics. At this time Mencius was achieving a position of high honour, and the *Book of Mencius* insists almost to a tiresome degree on such salutary principles as the right of ministers to criticize their rulers, maintain their independence and only serve a good sovereign, or at least one prepared to take their advice. The new breed of scholar-officials was now firmly in power: they exerted constant pressure towards a system of government in the Mencian manner, with the emperor accepting almost as a formality the proposals of the Council of State; and during the Humane Ancestor's minority there was ample opportunity for them to strengthen their position in relation to the throne.

Was China then on the point of reaching that happy state of affairs which some of the later Jesuit visitors thought they saw, when the government would be entirely in the hands of the philosophers? No, for since they did not have to contend with difficulties arising out of eunuch machinations or palace intrigue, they naturally found refuge in conflict among themselves, and there was a dangerous spread of factionalism within the bureaucracy. There were various controversial issues. Now that a civil service examination system based on the Confucian Classics was firmly established, what more natural than that some men should perversely question whether this was, after all, the best way of recruiting civil servants? Now Confucianism was firmly in the saddle, should one not question it and see whether the Confucian education was really giving the country what was needed? And now that the Sung state had been consolidated, was it not time to look round and see what could be reformed? Now that intellect has prestige and power again, a lively period of intellectual activity follows and is the chief interest of the ensuing decades.

The renaissance of Confucianism during the Sung period has generally been identified with its ultimate flowering in the philosophy of Chu Hsi, the great Southern Sung philosopher, whose most significant achievement was to provide a kind of metaphysical basis for the eminently practical and this-worldly teachings of Confucianism. But in fact much Sung Neo-Confucian thinking was vitally concerned with the immediate problems of Chinese society. The T'ang scholar, Han Yü, whose main purpose had been the revival and reassertion of Confucian teachings to secure the moral reform of a decadent age and who had condemned sterile concentration on the Classics for the mere purpose of passing examinations, was the fore-runner of those Sung scholars who devoted themselves to the ideal of Confucianism as a living faith and a guide to practical conduct in all spheres of human activity.

The first figure to emerge as leader of the Confucian renaissance was Hu Yüan (993–1059), who made a great reputation for the excellence of his exposition of the Confucian Classics as guides to the moral life and whose contemporaries bore witness to the remarkable moral influence he had over his students. Like Han Yü he criticized the literary examinations as a perversion of scholarship, and tried to instil into his pupils the idea that the Confucian Classics were not mere repositories of ancient lore but had vital messages which must be brought to bear on the solution of contemporary problems. In the tradition of Mencius he stressed the importance of economic measures to improve the livelihood of the people, and he also concerned himself with the promotion of practical studies such as mathematics, astronomy, and military defence against the barbarians.

Hu Yüan was the head of a private academy, and a contemporary of his called Sun Fu opened a similar institution at Mount T'ai, the sacred mountain near Confucius's birthplace, where he also upheld the need for a revived appreciation of the Classics. A pupil of his called Shih Chieh wrote a book called *Strange Teachings*, which even lumped the mastery of conventional literary forms for the civil examinations together with Taoism and Buddhism as the three heresies. A reform in the examination system was therefore held to be necessary before men of true learning and wisdom could get into the government. But such a reform could not easily be introduced unless it was pressed by a substantial group of people, who would probably be labelled a subversive faction by the conservative majority.

The first person to try to introduce a broad programme of reform was Fan Chung-yen, who originated from a gentry clan of modest importance and rose to become a distinguished general. Fan's famous maxim that the scholar 'should be the first to worry about the world's troubles and the last to enjoy its pleasures' testifies to his crusading spirit. His fearless outspokenness often got him into trouble: early in his career he was so rash as to protest that the young Emperor Jen-tsung should not have to knee before the empress dowager on her birthday, and later he criti cized the emperor himself for divorcing his empress. Both these protests earned him demotion, and he suffered a similar fate again in 1036 when he submitted to the emperor four famous essays advocating the need to employ the virtuous and at the same time produced evidence that the emperor's chief councillor Lü I-chien had been exercising favouritism in the appointment of officials. This last demotion led to a hardening of the division between the conservative northern bureaucrats under Lü and aspiring scholar-officials friendly to Fan, many from the south. The old north–south conflict which had existed under the T'ang was still important, since the northerners had monopolized high office in the early part of the dynasty, and the southerners from the independent states, coming later into the empire, had not had the chance to catch up and obtain a full share of power. Thus the chief means open to Fan and his friends to have a say in affairs was through the prerogative of criticism, but the consequences of Fan's latest indiscretion was that officials were forbidden to speak on matters outside their jurisdiction.

This ban was, however, rescinded four years later when increasing military dangers forced a reconciliation between the two sides. The northern frontier had been relatively quiet since the Treaty of Shan-yüan, but now serious trouble threatened from Tangut tribesmen, who had been expanding their territories in the north-west until in 1038 they adopted the Chinese dynastic name of Hsia and became known to the Chinese as the Hsi Hsia (Western Hsia). In 1040 they declared their independence of vassal status and began invading the north-west border areas. Fan Chung-yen was put in charge of the defence of the frontier. Years of peace had softened the martial spirit of the troops, and generals had been hampered by the central government's fear of a recrudescence of warlordism. The Chinese suffered several defeats in the early campaigns, but eventually weight of numbers told, for numerous militiamen were recruited, and soon the state had more than a million men under arms. The Chinese also now had the advantage of the use of gunpowder for military purposes, and a kind of hand-grenade was in use during these campaigns. The Tangut were eventually defeated but, fearing that the Liao would take the opportunity to make fresh attacks, the Chinese strengthened their defences along the northern frontier. The Liao regarded this as a provocation and extracted an agreement from the Sung that they should pay an additional hundred thousand taels of silver and a hundred thousand bolts of silk annually. The Tangut too had to be bought off with a promise of tribute, which amounted to about half what the Chinese were now paying to the Liao.

Trouble also soon broke out internally. Bandits became a menace, and for the first time the dynasty had to cope with a serious rebellion. In view of the marked decline in the state's fortunes brought about by the war and its aftermath, Fan, whose military successes had brought him back into increased favour with the emperor, was invited in the summer of 1043 to submit proposals for reform. He put forward a ten-point programme, primarily aimed at improving the quality of the administration by eliminating incompetent officials, by reducing high officials' privilege of recommending relatives for appointments, by reforming the examination system so that emphasis should be placed on the discussion of practical problems of statecraft rather than on literary qualities, and by attaching more land to local appointments to provide a sufficient income for officials and stamp out peculation. The remaining measures were concerned with land reclamation and dyke repair for the benefit of agricultural production and grain transport, the creation of peasant militias and the reduction of corvée labour. By winter the programme was being implemented, but after he had made a final peace agreement with the Hsi Hsia state in the following year the emperor seemed to lose interest in the reform policies, and Fan and some of his supporters were dismissed from their positions. Early in the following year most of the measures were rescinded, and the only one of Fan's schemes to have a marked long-term effect was the establishment of a national school system, with a school in each prefecture and subprefecture being maintained and staffed by the local officials.

This attempt at reform having largely failed, the government was once more in the hands of safe conservatives. But the need for change was made evident by the country's serious economic circumstances, which had been aggravated by the war. Writers of the time tell of the old injustice of unfair distribution of land, with the large estates growing while peasants' holdings dwindled in size as they were split up among sons, and the familiar spectacle of destitute peasants having to work as agricultural labourers or fleeing the land to adopt less essential pursuits. The national income had increased remarkably in the first sixty years of the dynasty, but was now falling off, although fortunately for the peasants there was a continued increase in revenue from the taxes on commerce and from the salt, wine and tea monopolies, which were a more severe burden on the town dwellers, if only because evasions could be more easily detected. At the same time expenditure rose considerably, partly because many men were kept under arms in the interest of national security and also because of the inflated number of civil servants. Despite the increased military expenditure, the annual payments to the Tangut and Khitan continued to be made.

One institution which was to cushion members of the upper classes against economic difficulties and especially against the absence of the principle of primogeniture was the clan charitable estate, which had its origin during this period. The charitable estate was held corporately by the family, and therefore was not subject to fragmentation on death as the ordinary great estate was. It was an investment, the income from which formed a fund which could be used for such purposes as wedding and funeral expenses, the relief of needy clan members and the provision of educational facilities. The obvious model for the charitable estate was the permanent endowments in land held by Buddhist monastic communities. The system was invented by Fan Chung-yen, who had been educated in a Buddhist monastery and came from the Soochow area, which was a stronghold of Buddhism at this time. It proved not only to be very beneficial financially, but also a very potent means of bringing solidarity to the clan group.

There was certainly a need at this time for institutions which could provide some cohesion for the ruling class. During the early T'ang the ruling aristocracy had formed a close-knit group, and the privilege of hereditary employment had helped to preserve this cohesion; while during the period of the late T'ang and the Five Dynasties powerful families had usurped hereditary authority for themselves in the provinces as the result of the weakness of the central government. Now there was a need for some fresh means of welding together the new ruling class, which came from a more varied social background. Furthermore the disorders of the last two centuries had made people acutely aware of the need for institutions which would secure harmony in society, and so a conscious attempt was made by the Sung Confucianists to use the clan as a basis for social order. This was in line with ancient Confucian doctrine, which stressed the importance of the family unit and regarded the state as the family writ large. Some of the most important writers and thinkers of the period made a contribution to the movement by stressing the ethical importance of the family, while others laid down standards by which genealogies should be compiled.

The scholar who contributed most to the study of genealogy was Ou-yang Hsiu, who made outstanding contributions in several different fields and was a peerless example of Sung renaissance man. As a historian he was solely responsible for one of the great corpus of dynastic histories, and was joint compiler of another, apart from making distinguished contributions to bibliography and doing pioneer work in the study of archaeology. He also played a full part in the reappraisal of the Confucian Classics, which had been pioneered by Hu and Sun, and joined in the attempt to get away from unthinking memorization and a narrow concern for textual problems and seek out the essential truths and use them for the moral reform of society. In the field of literature he won distinction as a poet, and also played the key role in ensuring the dominance of 'ancient style', which Han Yü had not succeeded in permanently reviving, but which was seen as essential to the programme of moral regeneration. He was active too as a political theorist and played a full part in the events leading up to the Fan Chung-yen reforms of 1043–4, and even before this had written an important essay entitled 'On the difficulties of being Emperor', which urged the moral and ideological independence of officials, stressed their privilege of loyal criticism, and pleaded that they be delegated sufficient authority and responsibility to do their jobs properly. As a pen-name he adopted 'Liu-i', meaning 'six ones', referring to one library, one archaeological collection, one musical instrument, one chess set, one pot of wine and himself, one old fellow who enjoyed their company.

By the time that Ou-yang reached prominence in the state the Humane Ancestor's health had begun to decline. Like his father he suffered from mental instability. It has even been suggested that the illnesses of these two emperors were partly brought on by their heavy responsibilities for endless decision-making. What cannot have brought any pleasure to the emperor and may have caused him extreme melancholy in a society which set great store by the bearing of sons to maintain the ancestral sacrifice was the fact that he had thirteen daughters, but no son. The ailing emperor was slow to appoint an heir apparent, but in 1062 he heeded the pleas of Ou-yang Hsiu, and installed in this position a cousin, who was known to history as Ying-tsung ('Heroic Ancestor'). But only a few days after his succession in the following year, the Heroic Ancestor became mentally ill, crying out hysterically that someone wanted to murder him. The empress dowager acted as regent and a difficult situation arose because she and the emperor were not on good terms with each other. Fortunately the emperor recovered, but immediately the ranks of the bureaucracy were torn by a violent dispute about what posthumous honour should be given to his father. Many officials objected to the new sovereign's wish to confer the title of emperor upon him, since this would imply a lessening of the gratitude which he ought to show to his predecessor who had so graciously adopted him. Their counter-proposal was that he be given the title of Imperial Uncle, although there was no historical precedent for such a solution. For supporting the emperor in this controversy Ou-yang was accused of shamelessly ingratiating himself with the new sovereign at the expense of his loyalty to the old, and since this kind of issue, which seems of no practical importance, aroused violent passions in a society much concerned with ritual, the stability which Ou-yang and his colleagues had been building up was destroyed.

3

In 1067 the Heroic Ancestor died and was succeeded by his eldest son, Shen-tsung ('Inspired Ancestor'). The new emperor was only eighteen at the time of his accession. Early in 1069, on the advice of a former tutor, he summoned to court Wang An-shih (1021–86), who was then Governor of Nanking. Deeply impressed with his ability, he soon entrusted him with a sweeping programme of reform which was to occupy the next five years. Wang's so-called New Policies represent a culmination of Sung Confucian revivalism, and were inspired by the desire to go back beyond the errors of the Han and T'ang and recover the essential truths of the Confucian Classics, and accordingly all his policies are given Classical authority. But in fact they grappled with some of the urgent and fundamental problems of contemporary statecraft.

The fiscal problem was, as often, the most pressing, and in recent decades there had even been a decline in revenue from taxation. To try to introduce some positive planning into these matters, one of Wang's first actions was to create a Finance Planning Commission. Practical measures soon followed. A new scheme was introduced to dispense with the cumbersome and antiquated procedure whereby tribute in grain or other goods was transported to the capital. Instead local officials were empowered to resell the tribute commodities and procure in their place the goods actually needed by the government. Thus heavy transportation costs were avoided, and it was also possible to develop a state marketing system such that the prices of all basic commodities were stabilized by means of a storage system like that of the traditional 'ever-normal granary', which was designed to prevent severe price fluctuations as a result of glut or scarcity. At the same time he also instituted a system of state farming loans to enable peasants to buy seed and other necessities in the spring, which they would repay at harvest time. The peasants were required to pay a much lower rate of interest than that which would normally have been extracted by private usurers, so the arrangement benefited both the peasants by keeping them out of the hands of the usurers and the state by producing revenue in the form of interest on the loans.

In order to make the tax burden fairer he had a new system of land registration and assessment introduced, so that the tax payable depended not simply on the area of land owned but also on the productive capacity of the soil, which was graded. The plan was originally introduced in the northern areas, where many large land-owners had been indulging in tax evasion on a big scale.

Another economy measure which would in the long run have military advantages was to replace the standing professional armies, which had not in any case proved very effective because they had been recruited from the poor and destitute, by a militia force. To this end Wang introduced the *pao chia* system, whereby families were organized in units of ten which would be responsible for providing certain quotas for the local militia. The primary purpose of this device was the maintenance of local law and order by a system of self-policing, for the members of each group of families were made responsible for the misconduct of any individual. This was a system which also had precedents in antiquity, but the authority for it was Legalist rather than Confucian. Further measures to improve national security included an attempt to repair the long-standing weakness in cavalry by assigning a horse with fodder to each family in the frontier regions of the north and north-west, so that one member of each family could serve in the cavalry militia in time of emergency. A Directorate of Weapons was also established, with the responsibility for improving quality.

Wang An-shih was also deeply concerned with improving the quality of the civil service. At the lowest level of local government people from the neighbourhood were drafted to carry out the work, but not recompensed for their labours. Because this arrangement bore heavily on the individuals and families concerned and hardly made for efficiency Wang replaced it with a graduated money tax, bearing more heavily on the rich, to pay for the hiring of the necessary personnel.

Wang also saw the vital need to improve the quality of the clerks employed both at central and at local level. These men were of greatly inferior status compared with the members of the bureaucracy proper, they had no prospect of advancement, and their pay was quite inadequate. On the other hand, as administration became more complex, they were performing skilled and important tasks and, since they remained in the same place throughout their careers, they could often use their local knowledge to influence the decisions of their superiors, who were posted from place to place. Not unnaturally they were a hotbed of corruption. Wang tried to improve the situation by cutting down the number of clerks and increasing the pay of those who remained. He also made it possible for clerks of high ability to take a test for entry into the ranks of the bureaucracy proper. In return for these improvements in conditions he insisted on more effective supervision and heavier penalties for corruption.

He was also concerned to improve the quality at the top of the civil service, so he greatly expanded the number of government schools, particularly in the north, which had been lagging behind in this respect. He insisted that the civil service examinations should be less devoted to literary tests and more concerned with practical problems of administration, and that the Classics should be offered from the point of view of a general understanding of Confucian principles rather than as a sheer memory test. It was only now that the movement to stress fresh thought on practical subjects in the examinations came out on top.

Apart from the reforms which came specifically under the heading of Wang An-shih's New Policies the early years of the Inspired Ancestor's reign were noteworthy for a renewal of energy in other activities. The navy, which had long been in decline, was reorganized in 1068, and for the first time for many years saw action in 1077 in an inconclusive war against Annam, which it failed to win because it was still short of sea-going vessels. To make good this need the government then embarked on a large programme of shipbuilding, opening new yards for the purpose.

For the Annam War they had had to call on the assistance of the merchant marine, reimbursing the merchants for the damages suffered by presenting them with monk-certificates, which were by now virtually a form of paper-currency, increasing numbers being distributed by government policy from the beginning of Shen-tsung's reign onwards. But the government did not merely call on the merchants in time of emergency. It actively promoted foreign trade as a further means of increasing revenue. In 1074 the merchants were urged to organize trading missions and successful importers whose business was worth more than a certain amount in import duty to the government were rewarded. More maritime trade commissions were set up to deal with the increased business and the volume of seaborne commerce had more than doubled by the end of the century.

During these years the state also pursued a more active foreign policy. For forty years there had been no relations with Korea, but contacts were resumed on the Sung initiative in 1071. Negotiations were conducted by a merchant, and trade was one of the reasons for the resumption of relations, but Wang An-shih also considered it important that China should be able to claim some show of allegiance from such a traditional vassal in order to have the prestige to compel the submission of lesser border peoples. Nevertheless his Korean policy came in for considerable criticism. It was seen to be an extravagance, for special ships were constructed to carry the first Sung embassy, and special hostels were built along the overland section of the route in order to entertain visiting envoys, the lavish scale on which they were treated causing considerable hardship to the localities through which they passed. And since the Koreans now acknowledged Liao suzerainty it was suspected that they might pass on vital information. Indeed there were strong objections to the Korean envoys going off sightseeing because of the useful intelligence they might get hold of.

Wang was not in favour of large-scale military adventures, since it was more important to make the country strong economically; so, while there were various successful campaigns against small border peoples during his period in power, he would not contemplate action against the Liao empire or the Hsi Hsia kingdom, although the Inspired Ancestor found China's military weakness to be a source of embarrassment. Nevertheless defences against the Liao were improved: fortifications were built, garrisons were increased and trees were planted to serve as obstacles to the nomad cavalry, unfriendly activities which drew an official protest from the Liao in 1074.

During Wang's period in power extensive irrigation works were undertaken in the region of the capital. By this time Kaifeng had grown so large that it imposed an enormous problem of feeding and supply, and the more that could be done to improve the yield of agricultural land close to the city the better. Its population was now about a million, which is not far short of the total population of England under William the Conqueror, who was the exact contemporary of the Inspired Ancestor. Apart from the large numbers of people who were employed in government or who got their livelihood from supplying and servicing the palaces, there were 150,000 troops stationed in the suburbs, also providing employment for a large civilian population. Kaifeng was not only the administrative centre and chief garrison city of the country, but also a most important commercial centre, because of its position on the waterway network. It was also an important manufacturing centre, its products including textiles, metalwork and porcelain, and it was a centre of the printing industry. Like other overcrowded ancient cities it was subject to disastrous fires, so that the manufacture and maintenance of fire-fighting equipment became a major enterprise. Enormous supplies of material were needed to house the people and keep them warm, and by this time coal was beginning to replace charcoal as the means of domestic heating and cooking. Urban life meant a great growth in the entertainment industry, and amusement centres, theatres and taverns sprang up to cater for the city rabble and the soldiers in their off-duty hours. Changan had been a solid, dignified place, designed to conform with cosmic principles and symbolize imperial power, with commerce kept well out of sight in walled markets, the principal pleasure-grounds being the gardens of Buddhist monasteries. Now the jostling and bustling urban mob had taken over, and the whole appearance of the capital was quite different from that of its T'ang predecessor.

Imperial China

The switch from charcoal to coal is an important example of the industrialization which was a prominent feature of the Northern Sung period. Charcoal production is a very ancient occupation which can be carried on by individuals, but for the coal industry considerable capital investment and concentration of labour is necessary. During the period between the reign of the Inspired Ancestor and the end of the Northern Sung China reached a peak in the consumption of coal, for both domestic and industrial purposes, which was not surpassed until modern times. The iron industry had also developed rapidly, and by 1078 125,000 tons of pig iron a year were being produced in north-east China, where it had first been a source of commercial prosperity in antiquity. The deforestation of certain areas and the pull of growing urban centres had led to the concentration of the industry into a small number of enterprises with vastly expanded output, mainly in the Honan–Hopei border country. The techniques employed were very advanced, still being unsurpassed by the Chinese iron and steel industry in the nineteenth century. The scale of production at individual establishments was also probably unequalled anywhere in the world until the nineteenth century.

This production of iron was stimulated by a variety of demands. The iron currency which was circulated in some border regions in order to prevent copper cash flowing out of the country demanded over 4000 tons a year. There also seems to have been a remarkably high demand for iron for agricultural implements, and it is thought that the Chinese farmer of this period made more use of iron implements than his counterpart at the beginning of the twentieth century. Armouries were also established in the mining areas and much iron was used for weapons of all kinds and for other military purposes, while the expanding shipbuilding industry needed iron for anchors, nails, armour, etc. Iron was also used for bridges, gates, pagodas, Buddhist images, and the heavy pans needed by the salt industry. By this period some other industries, notably shipbuilding, printing, paper-making and salt processing, were conducted on a scale greater than in any other country before the late eighteenth century. This was plainly the most highly developed country in the whole medieval world, and it is surprising that the growth now achieved was not sustained in later centuries.

As was only to be expected, Wang An-shih's reforms provoked widespread opposition. Among the critics were some of the most famous names in Chinese history, including the veteran statesman Ou-yang Hsiu, who had himself been a reformer in his young days and had included Wang among the many promising young men whom he had sponsored; and Ssu-ma Kuang and Su Tung-p'o, both distinguished statesmen, but even better known for their contributions to literature, the former as a historian and the latter as a poet. Wang might easily have been swept aside but for the continued support of the emperor, who demoted his most relentless opponents one after another. Many entrenched interests were affected by Wang's measures and the sufferers could not be expected to stand idly by and put up with efforts to stamp out the tax evasion in which they had been indulging. The state farming loans and the state trading system took money out of the pockets of money-lenders and merchants and put it into the coffers of the government, and merchants were now not without allies in officialdom, especially at Kaifeng. Moreover, there were ideological objections to Wang's programme, for in the old-fashioned Confucian view the government's economic role was merely to spend less so that there was more available for the people, and this was at odds with Wang's positive economic planning. But the biggest obstacle of all to success was the poor quality of the clerical staffs which underpinned the bureaucracy, whose efficiency was essential for carrying out detailed procedures at the lowest level. Unfortunately by this time corruption was also quite widespread among the officials themselves, who would employ various methods of supplementing their inadequate salaries, such as the misuse of office expense accounts, or engaging in trade although they were not officially allowed to do so. Wang did secure a salary increase for the civil service and, although he also reduced office expense funds, thus impairing the goodwill he might have expected from this measure, there was a temporary improvement in the civil servants' position.

Mounting dissatisfaction at the operation of some of the reforms was heightened by famine in the northern areas, which suffered badly from locusts in the years 1073–6. Discontent at the capital led the empress dowager Hsüan-jen and the eunuchs to join in the attack on Wang, and he resigned in 1074. The emperor restored him after less than a year, but he no longer had his sovereign's full confidence, so he finally retired at the end of 1076.

This sinister revival of eunuch influence in politics is attributable to the guild exemption tax which, together with the state trading system, was the main cause of resentment in the capital. The guild exemption tax was paid by guilds or associations of merchants to secure exemption from the iniquities of the previous system whereby goods were requisitioned by the government from merchants as they were needed, with the government paying less than the market price and the merchants also being responsible for the cost of transport. Now that this tax had been instituted, the government was expected to pay the market price for goods supplied. The merchants and traders apparently felt that they were nevertheless much worse off under the new scheme; but the people who definitely suffered were the palace eunuchs who lost their lucrative role as intermediaries between the palace and the market. Their resentment led them to intrigue against Wang, and they found a ready ally in the empress dowager, who was a northerner and had been opposed to the reform right from the beginning.

Matters deteriorated further in 1085, when the Inspired Ancestor died at the age of only thirty-six. As his heir was only ten, his grandmother, the empress dowager who had been bitterly opposed to Wang's reforms, acted as regent until her own death in 1093. She soon began to undo Wang's work, and many supporters of the reform were denounced as members of an undesirable faction. The reformer himself only survived his imperial master long enough to contemplate in a last sad year the turn events had taken since the Inspired Ancestor's death. Under feminine rule eunuch influence inevitably grew, and the old woman's favourites were entrusted with her imperial seal and the handling of state papers when she herself fell ill.

The new emperor, Che-tsung ('Wise Ancestor'), greatly admired his father and bitterly resented his domineering old grandmother, not least because he did not like the woman, named Chao-tz'u, whom she had forced him to take as his empress. He recalled the reformers to power and most of Wang's policies were revived, but the atmosphere was embittered by increasing hostility between the conservatives and reformers, and many of the former were exiled to remote and humble government posts. The new leader of the reformers, Chang Ch'un, also played a squalid part in palace politics by informing the young emperor that his grandmother had intended to dethrone him. This charge eventually resulted in the execution of Hsüan-jen's chief eunuch supporter and the exile of some of her other favourites. Soon Che-tsung's consort was being accused of using black magic against the lady who was the young emperor's favourite and, after eunuchs and palace maids had been tortured to extort confessions, the empress was banished to a nunnery. With the bureaucracy increasingly rent by factions, the worst evils of palace politics are rife again, and the general atmosphere recalls the worst abuses of T'ang political life.

The Wise Ancestor died at the age of twenty-three and was succeeded by his seventeen-year-old brother, who was to be posthumously known as Hui-tsung ('Excellent Ancestor'). He came to the throne in 1100. The reign-title adopted was Chien-chung, meaning 'Establishment of the mean', and some attempt was made at a policy of reconciliation by the emperor's chief adviser Tseng Pu, a former associate of Wang An-shih, but this succeeded neither in pleasing his fellow reformers nor in conciliating the anti-reformers. In keeping with the policy of letting bygones be bygones, the Empress Chao-tz'u was restored to the palace, but even this move ended in tragedy, for her rival, Empress Liu, committed suicide. It is not surprising that the Excellent Ancestor, a man of cultured tastes, soon grew weary of politics and preferred to make a reputation as a patron of arts rather than follow his brother and father in a vain attempt at reform. His hapless brother and predecessor, having had the misfortune to inherit the throne as a child, had had to endure being lectured to on the Confucian Classics by the formidable Ch'eng I who, fully conscious of his standing as an eminent philosopher, had insisted that he be seated in the emperor's presence and that the lectures must continue daily without vacation. Not unnaturally Hui-tsung turned to painting and calligraphy rather than the Classics, and preferred the company of Taoists to that of Confucians.

Political power soon fell into the hands of Ts'ai Ching, who was a brother of a son-in-law of Wang An-shih and who succeeded in remaining in control from 1101 to 1125, practically the whole of Hui-tsung's reign. The emperor had a weakness for luxuries and it was easy to keep him happy by pandering to this. Ts'ai consolidated his power by a disreputable alliance with the leading eunuch T'ung Kuan, who was even allowed to take command of the army.

Under Ts'ai Ching books written by the anti-reformers were banned and people who expressed themselves openly in favour of the anti-reform were required to correct their thoughts in rooms at the prefectural school which were called 'studios for self-indictment'. According to an authority on the period, 'the imposed conformity reached a point where thousands of examination papers all read alike'. The Palace Guard Commission, which was in charge of intelligence work in the capital, used *agents provocateurs* to trap people into voicing criticism. The creative Confucianism of the early Sung had given place to increasingly bitter wrangling over policy, which had in turn led by an almost inevitable process to a stifling uniformity.

But if words could not safely be used, perhaps artists were more free to practise their skills. The powerful and passionate landscape painting of the early eleventh century had given way to a more detached attitude, less involved with nature, which was cultivated by the scholar painters. They considered that painting, like literature, music and calligraphy, was one of the polite accomplishments contributing to the art of moral self-cultivation. They felt that, since a painting is a revelation of the nature of the man who paints it, the best paintings would be produced by men of refinement and nobility of character. This attitude made for an avoidance of obvious visual appeal and a certain individuality of approach and technique, which the Excellent Ancestor would not tolerate among his court painters. On the contrary, he handed out subjects for them to paint as if he were setting papers for examination candidates, and the rigid orthodoxy he imposed established a palace style which was characterized by thoroughly painstaking, detailed and realistic pictures of birds, flowers, and animals, but which was totally devoid of inspiration. Hui-tsung was not only a painter and patron of painters. He was also a keen collector, and it is not easy to refuse the powerful anything they want. Consequently the palace became filled with ancient masterpieces, which did not survive the disasters which were to bring the Excellent Ancestor's reign to a close.

The most remarkable artistic achievement of the Chinese during the Northern Sung period, a marvel both of artistic sensibility and of technological advance and a testimony to the high degree of industrial development which we have already ascribed to this period, is the exquisite porcelain which it produced. At this time wares of unsurpassed beauty were being created in a material the secret of whose manufacture was not even known to Europe for another seven hundred years. The most perfect of these wares takes its name from a prefecture called Ting in Hopei. The shapes are elegant, the glaze is a lovely creamy white tinged with brown, the decoration, incised with remarkable skill and artistry, often features plants, flowers and birds, the very subjects taken by Hui-tsung's painters but depicted with a marvellous vigour and rhythm which is quite absent from the paintings. The emperor, however, was blind to their merits and did not think that they were good enough for palace use, so he set up new kilns to make a fresh official ware.

Although the great days of the Northern Sung were now past, the reign of the Excellent Ancestor was not entirely devoid of benefit for the people. Progress was made in the provision of relief for the poor and needy. Public assistance had not been organized on a regular nation-wide scale until the Excellent Ancestor's predecessor, within two years of his death, had decreed that relief homes should be established all over the empire. These were to give shelter during the cold months to the aged, infirm and destitute, and supply them with rations and a small dole. For a short time after the Excellent Ancestor's accession relief was distributed rather extravagantly at such institutions, and in 1102 relief clinics were also established. These were administered by monks, and staffed with state doctors who were recompensed in accordance with the percentage of their patients who survived. Two years later the emperor gave his approval to a proposal for the establishment of public cemeteries in all parts of the empire to house the remains of paupers and people who had died a long way from home. Unfortunately, however, as the reign progressed, corruption in the relief administration steadily increased and much of the benefit probably failed to reach those who most needed it.

Hui-tsung's father and brother, both reforming emperors, had died young; but he himself, who had let the affairs of state get into the hands of a Ts'ai Ching, lived on longer and reigned for a quarter of a century before great changes in the north brought an end to his tenure of the imperial throne. The power of the Khitan was now waning fast, and in 1122 the eunuch T'ung Kuan even attempted to recapture Peking from them. The attempt was a dismal failure, but the city did not stay in Khitan hands for much longer. Beyond their eastern border lived the Tungusic people known as the Jürched, who paid tribute to the Liao empire. Every year the Liao emperor would come to fish in the frontier rivers and feast the border chieftains and ask them to dance for him, to symbolize his power over them. In 1112 the Jürched chieftain A-ku-ta had refused to dance. It rapidly became clear that the world would no longer dance at the Liao request. A-ku-ta gained control over near-by tribes and by 1114 was able to inflict a serious defeat on a huge Liao army. In 1115 he established an empire named Chin ('Golden') and, after haggling with Liao over terms for recognition of his new status, began an advance in 1120 which rapidly brought control of half the Liao empire and finally snuffed out the Liao Dynasty in 1125. The Chinese offered little resistance in the north of the country, and the Excellent Ancestor abdicated the same winter, only to be captured together with his successor the following year when the Jürched took Kaifeng. Not for the first time the Chinese state would have to start up a new life in the south.

But before we turn to the Southern Sung let us put into perspective the achievements of the early Sung, one of the most remarkable epochs in Chinese history. Throughout this period the centre of gravity continued to move southward, so that by the end of the Northern Sung seventy per cent of the nation's tribute money and goods was coming from the Lower Yangtze valley, a region of the country which was now very densely peopled compared with the rest of China. The shift of population during the centuries covered by this book had had several causes. Most obviously the Chinese had been under pressure from the northern barbarians, and the devastation wrought by warfare in the north had proved more horrifying than the greater disease prevalent in the south, which had earlier been a deterrent to migration. The rice-growing areas of the south had indeed proved their superiority in fertility and attractiveness over the cold dusty plains of the north, where climatic changes had brought more severe winters and diminished rainfall, so that rivers became shallower, irrigation became more difficult, and the land became less fertile. Much of the country on the south-east coast was, however, too hilly for the people to gain a prosperous living, so large numbers had flocked to the towns, where they were employed in the rapidly developing industries, swelling the cities so that by the end of the Northern Sung several of them rivalled the capital in size.

This was, as we have seen, a period of great commercial development. The coinage of copper reached levels never again approached during the history of the Chinese empire, and paper money also came into common use. The merchant class became more socially acceptable, and scholar-officials would themselves indulge in commercial activities. The value of overseas commerce to the state and the increased income from government monopolies compared with the decline in income from land taxes was a significant change, while the growth of the armed forces and the devotion of considerable resources to the building of a navy was a great stimulus to industry. The basic coal and iron industries consequently expanded enormously, and unprecedented technological development took place, not only in the coal and iron industries, but also in such fields as shipbuilding, bridge-building, hydraulic engineering, architecture and armament manufacture (including the use of gunpowder).

The great development of the economy and the consequent

draining of surplus labour off the land into the towns, and the comparative peacefulness of much of the Northern Sung period, meant that peasant discontent never rose to the level of large-scale revolt. The tenant farmer was very dependent on his land-lord, being tied to the land so that he passed to the new owner when the land was sold. He also bore a heavy burden, for he not only had to pay the landlord a fixed share of his crop, but also had to contribute his labour in the lord's service. Nevertheless the landlord did have some interest in not treating him too harshly, since he helped to provide protection against bandits; the close interdependence of lord and retainers remaining as a legacy from the troubled decades of the Five Dynasties period. Among the middle range of landowners absence of primogeniture caused much instability and sudden changes of wealth and status, so that this was a period of marked social change. Old families faded into obscurity, to be replaced by new families whose rise had been dependent on land-grabbing or on commercial and in-dustrial wealth.

Men from new families were also attaining high positions in the state as a result of the great spread of education. Many schools had been opened by the state to provide a stream of candi-dates for the rapidly expanding civil service, and other such establishments were sponsored by private individuals, since men would now put their money into this sort of venture instead of contributing to Buddhist monasteries as they had done in earlier times. The development of printing had also made material for study much more widely available, and greatly increased the pool of literati from which the country's administrators could be drawn. At the same time this invention stimulated a great era of literature and scholarship, and polymaths like Ou-yang Hsiu were typical of the age.

The most remarkable development of all was the growth, right at the beginning of the dynasty, of the most mature and subtle methods of recruitment and promotion of civil service personnel which ever existed in the world before modern times. The task of governing this enormous empire had proved ultimately too diffi-cult even for the great Han and T'ang, and the Sung founders were determined to do everything possible to find the right men for the job. Indeed the country became so thoroughly accustomed to the system of bureaucratic government on earth, that men even began to organize the gods into a kind of extension of this system of civil government, such that the emperor had authority not only over the earthly bureaucracy, but also over the official pantheon: deities could be promoted or demoted at his command, and after their deaths worthy human beings could be selected to fill vacancies in the bureaucracy of the gods. With this new kind of religion gaining increasing hold on the popular imagination, Buddhism grew weaker and, for the mass of the people, eventually merged into an amorphous popular religion consisting of a hotch-potch of elements from Buddhism, Taoism and other cults. The situation was welcome to the government since the powerful Buddhism of an earlier age had been a challenge to the state itself.

So a much more modern edifice has been built by the Sung out of the ruins of the medieval T'ang state. A system of government dependent largely on aristocratic privilege and at times clumsy and antiquated in operation, especially when the whole court trundled backwards and forwards between the two capitals, has given way to a most sophisticated and modern-seeming political machine (although human weaknesses still ensured that it often worked far from perfectly); the reign of eunuchs, of palace favourites, or of provincial warlords has given way to that of an emperor advised by his scholars; successions to the throne are no longer determined by a series of bloody palace coups, but by the natural order; the great cities are hives of industry rather than monuments to imperial power; the heartlands of the society are in the warm, humid rice-fields of the south rather than in the cold windswept plains of the north; eyes are no longer turned towards the trade routes of Central Asia, but gaze out to sea and seek profit from commerce with South-east Asia, and the southern ports no longer house large communities of foreign traders, but are the headquarters of state maritime trading commissions; a spirit of military venturousness has given way to a loathing of the martial virtues, and a desire to explore new territories has yielded to a concern with new realms of science and technology; and a willingness to absorb a foreign tradition has given way to an urge to breathe new life into the native one. But for all the greatness of the Sung achievement, men still had not – nor have they yet – founds means to guarantee permanence for their advances. The old economic problems had set in by the middle of the eleventh century, and under Hui-tsung the government was resorting to desperate measures such as the over-issue of paper money, and inflation was rampant. The political problem had proved in the long run to be insoluble, perhaps because of the lack of any machinery for grouping like-minded people into recognized parties. If everyone spoke with his individual voice, and there were only occasional and undisciplined attempts to talk in unison, the result would be cacophony, and decisions taken and measures introduced by previous administrations would be regularly scrapped as power shifted and the bitterness of controversy increased, and finally the harsh rule of a Ts'ai Ching would restore order and absolutism again. But what dealt the final blow to the Grand Progenitor's great achievement was the failure to solve the state's security problem: although vast sums had been spent on the armed forces, and at one time during the dynasty eighty per cent of total government expenditure was being allocated to military purposes, the founder himself had sown the seeds of eventual defeat by ensuring strength at the centre at the cost of inability to defend the border against an enemy that was not content just to receive tribute, as the Hsi Hsia and Liao had been, but was in the full flush of victory and was spurred on by the impetus of its own advance.

4

Just as the T'ang Dynasty had been divided into two by the An Lu-shan rebellion, which gravely weakened the state, so the Sung was cut into two equal parts by its removal to the south. In the remaining century-and-a-half of its existence we cannot expect to discover the dynamic contributions to the history of human society in China which characterized the early part of the dynasty. Although shame and anger at the country's disgrace prompted some minds to concern themselves with drastic reform, the keynote of the age is the continued growth of the commercial

prosperity of southern China. Many were content to resign themselves to their country's fate and enjoy the fruits of this new
prosperity, while the growing cities were flocked with a new
urban pleasure-seeking society, which stimulated the growth of
new entertainments.

When the Jürched horsemen captured Kaifeng, they took the
emperor and his court into captivity, but a twenty-year-old son
of the Excellent Ancestor escaped and proclaimed himself
emperor in 1127, and he was to be known to history as Kao-tsung
('High Ancestor'). But his court led a fugitive life before the
nomad invaders, and it was not until a decade after the fall of
Kaifeng that the High Ancestor finally settled on Hangchow as
his capital. Hangchow was a suitable site since it was in an area
of lakes and rice-paddies, in which enemy cavalry could not easily
be deployed. It was also – and still is – one of the most beautiful
places in China, with its gently curving tree-clad hills and its
famous West Lake whose shores were dotted with temples and
pleasure-pavilions. But at this time it was a provincial town of
modest size and, although it had served as the chief city of the
Wu-yüeh state in the early part of the tenth century, it was
many miles away from the areas where the Chinese had
previously set up their capital cities, so it was very long before
the court could accept this as anything other than a purely
temporary retreat and make proper and dignified provision for
housing itself there. The name 'temporary residence' even stuck
to Hangchow after the Mongols had seized it and put an end to
the Sung Dynasty, and it was under this name, transliterated as
Quinsai, that the city was to be known to Marco Polo. The loss
of the north was a constant reproach to those in power and they
could not officially admit that Hangchow was to be recognized as
the permanent capital of the Middle Kingdom.

In the early days of Kao-tsung's reign the dynasty had hardly
survived and in 1130 the emperor was even forced to take to his
ships off the South China coast to flee from the enemy, but after
this the Sung forces began to rally and win back possession of
the south. Energetic steps were taken to build up the naval forces
both by the conversion of merchant vessels for military purposes
and by the building of new warships, and fresh impetus was

given to this programme when Chin forces, returning laden with booty from their successful advance south which had driven the emperor to put out to sea, were held up for three months by a Sung naval force on the Yangtze. On the high tide of enthusiasm a bold scheme was concocted for a seaborne invasion of Korea, which could then be used as a base from which to carry out naval attacks on the Chin empire. One leading minister called the sea and the Yangtze the new Great Wall of China and the warships its watch-towers. Previously the government had been mainly concerned with river defences, but the emphasis shifted to sea-borne forces and coastal defence as fears grew of an enemy attack across the sea. In 1132 a permanent agency was created for the direction of naval forces at sea, which were now administratively separated from the river squadrons, and this marked an important step forward in the establishment of Sung naval power. Equipped with iron rams, rockets, and catapults for hurling incendiary missiles, the naval vessels of the day were formidable engines of war.

The military situation on land during these early years of the Southern Sung was very confused. In the powerful enemy thrust south which led to the flight of the Chinese emperor in 1130, the commander-in-chief of the army had surrendered, leaving Sung military units cut off in the north. Several of the leaders of these units turned bandit and tried to carve out independent territories for themselves in the areas south of the Yangtze. One of the northern commanders was an exceptionally skilful and dedicated general called Yüeh Fei, who had first seen action in the vain attempt of the Chinese to recapture Peking in 1122. His patriotism won him a special place in the affections of the Chinese people, for he was one of only two warriors who won a place in the official list of gods.

Having earlier been mainly concerned with wiping out military bandit leaders and suppressing other local uprisings fomented by peasant distress and secret society activities, Yüeh Fei later took part in co-ordinated imperial campaigns against the Chin and a puppet state of Ch'i which the Chin had established as a buffer between themselves and the Chinese. These campaigns took place in the area between the Yangtze and the Yellow River, and the most penetrating advance, in 1140, was against Loyang and Chengchow, when Yüeh claimed that the Chin were so hard-pressed that they considered withdrawing beyond the Yellow River.

But the more successful the Sung forces were in driving back the enemy, the more bitterly raged the controversy whether the Chinese should now seek peace or should endeavour to drive north and regain their lost territories. The peace party was led by Ch'in Kuei, and the leader of the hawks was Yüeh Fei. Now, at the moment of greatest success, the Sung government, weary of the war, decided to reach an agreement with the Chin, leaving the territory north of the Hwai River in the hands of the barbarians. An undoubted reason for reaching peace at this stage was that the Sung state was still afraid of generals becoming too successful. After one victory against the puppet state of Ch'i, the High Ancestor is said to have remarked that 'what makes me happy is not that Ch'i has been defeated, but that the generals have obeyed orders'. Centralized power was still more important to the Sung ruler than the recovery of lost territories. Thus, at the time of greatest victories it was the peace party of Chin K'uei which was uppermost. Shortly after the conclusion of peace the three principal Sung generals were done to death, Yüeh Fei being murdered in prison and the other two publicly executed. The Sung were quite prepared to accept tributary status, and hence-forward a quarter of a million ounces of silver and a quarter of a million rolls of silk crossed the northern frontier each year as token of homage to the Chin court.

An uneasy peace now reigned for two decades. Another strong reason for avoiding further military ventures was the heavy cost of the war. By the time that the peace was signed the Sung had an army of a million-and-a-quarter men. The land forces were protected by armour made of leather and metal and were trained in archery, the crossbow, swordsmanship, wrestling and boxing, and also equipped with a variety of huge catapults for hurling stones and bombs. Although interest in the navy had declined because the threatened seaborne invasion had not materialized, the ship-building programme must also have been very costly. Because of the great decline in revenue from other sources to meet this heavy expenditure, the government took energetic measures to increase foreign trade. By 1131 annual government income from this source already amounted to two million strings of cash, as much as twenty per cent of its now much reduced income. Honorary ranks were awarded to merchants who were especially successful in promoting foreign trade and inducing foreign merchants to bring their wares to China. The government benefited not only by imposing import tariffs, but also through profits on the resale of goods brought into the country, for merchants were compelled to sell about half their imports to the government at fixed prices. New maritime trade commissions were opened to cope with the increased volume of traffic, and it was possible for the government to maintain an income of two million strings of cash a year from this source, although this gradually dropped to a much smaller percentage of the total state revenue.

Following efforts which had been made during the Northern Sung, the government continued to improve facilities for merchants by providing better and safer harbour facilities, repair-docks, storage-yards and warehouses, as well as a system of coastal beacons to fulfil the function of lighthouses. Methods of protecting merchant shipping from pirates were also improved. Under the Northern Sung Canton had been the main centre of maritime commerce, so protection against pirates had been afforded by a network of naval stations and observation posts centred on this city, together with a naval unit known as the 'convoy escort squadron'. But the opening of new sea-ports, the growing coastal traffic, and the wealth of the coastal cities aggravated the problem, and the Southern Sung were soon forced to take more positive measures for the suppression of pirates. Naval squadrons were dispatched on regular anti-pirate missions, and groups of merchant vessels were made mutually responsible for each others' activities to try to curb the conduct of unscrupulous merchants who had dealings with the outlaws. The government also did its best to induce the pirates to join the regular naval forces by offering amnesties but, although this policy had some successes, it also meant that the more hardened criminals could feel able to continue their nefarious activities with impunity. Many pirate chiefs did rally round to offer resistance to the Chin when war broke out again in 1161, but after the emergency they drifted back to their old pursuits.

The threat of further invasion had been in the air for ten years before it finally struck. In 1150 the Chin emperor had been murdered by a cousin who, on seizing the throne, declared his ambition to conquer South China, and began to build and train a navy with the aid of Sung deserters. When these activities came to the ears of the Sung government, it stopped merchantmen from sailing to the north lest they be seized by the Chin authorities, and embarked on a new programme of building ships and also of requisitioning them from the merchants.

When the Chin invasion finally came in 1161, there were three separate attacks, an advance into Szechwan with a small cavalry force, an attempt to drive across the Yangtze near Nanking, and a seaborne assault by an armada of six hundred ships, which had Hangchow as its target. Fortunately a Sung fleet of 120 ships was at sea and, receiving reports that the Chin force was rounding the Shantung promontory, it was able to sail north and intercept the enemy not far south of where the modern city of Tsingtao lies. By effective use of their incendiary weapons they were able to destroy the Chin fleet, which at the time was strung out in a long line.

The Chin land forces met with no better success because, though the Sung troops were thinly spread out along the south bank of the Yangtze, the naval forces, which included a large contingent of huge sea-going merchant vessels adapted for military purposes known as whales, were able to frustrate two attempts to cross the river, using rockets, bombs and fire-rafts to good effect. When the Chin emperor, who was personally in charge of operations, marched eastward to make a further attempt at a crossing, he found himself faced with a Sung war-fleet which included a hundred whales. Rather than contend with these, the Chin soldiers mutinied and killed their emperor, and thus their short-lived attempt at conquest came to an inglorious end and their forces were withdrawn. For river operations the Sung navy not only had the advantage of superior weaponry, but also had a better method of propulsion because they had now perfected treadmill-operated paddle-wheel boats, which were extremely effective in these campaigns. Boats of this type had already been mentioned in fifth-century literature and had been used on a large scale as early as the eighth century, although it was not until the sixteenth century that the paddle-wheel boat was to be first tried out in Europe. Chinese war-junks with the same method of propulsion even went into action against the British in the nineteenth century, and were supposed by the Europeans to be mere copies of a Western invention.

By now the High Ancestor had been on the throne for thirty-four years. His reign had seen some successful attempts to strengthen the country militarily and economically, but the emperor himself seems to have been more concerned with cultural than with political matters. He had inherited his father's interest in painting, and established a National Academy at which the surviving artists from his father's court eventually gathered. The National University and Imperial Academy were also re-established at Hangchow and a School of Medicine was opened. The mood of the time was affected by a nostalgia for the glories of early Sung, and even the old Empress Dowager Chao-tz'u, consort of Che-tsung, the Wise Ancestor, was on the scene as a symbol and reminder of past greatness. Now, shortly after the defeat of the Chin, the High Ancestor abdicated in favour of Hsiao-tsung ('Filial Ancestor'). He survived another twenty-five years and died at the age of eighty.

The new emperor was anxious to restore peaceful relations with the Chin, but there was again a conflict between peace and war parties at the court, and it was not until 1165 that a peace treaty was signed. It was clear that, both for the sake of security against the Chin and to keep down piratical depredations, the state needed to maintain strong water-borne forces, so during the next forty years the Sung navy was at the peak of its efficiency. The recent victories over the Chin had brought the Sung a rare taste of military glory, and the emperor himself keenly supported the improvements to the navy, which he referred to as the country's 'strong arm'. All the coastal fleets were put under the direct command of the court and given the title 'imperial', and new naval bases were established, the two largest

1. This portrait of the Ch'ien-lung emperor, shown wielding the writing-brush and surrounded by objets d'art and elegant furniture, reflects the fact that civil rather than military virtues were the chief criterion of imperial excellence. To prove their right to the throne the Manchu monarchs had to show themselves to be learned in traditional Chinese culture. The five-clawed dragon is the emblem of imperial power, and is shown on the dragon robe lording it over earth, sky and sea.

2 and 3. Kaifeng and Peking are among the cities emperors have chosen as their capitals. 2 shows a busy street scene in the former city in the Northern Sung period. 3 shows the Forbidden City at Peking. The photograph is taken looking due south from Coal Hill, where the last Ming emperor committed suicide. Like Changan, the T'ang capital, Peking is built on a due north-south axis.

4. Although the audience halls in the Forbidden City are imposing buildings standing on marble terraces (4a top), the private quarters are on a more intimate scale, not unlike the typical Peking house built round a courtyard (4b top right). Early evidence of the appearance of domestic architecture is provided by pottery tomb models (4c bottom right).

5. Hangchow, the capital of the Southern Sung Dynasty, was renowned for the beauty of the West Lake just outside the city.

6. Surrounded by luxury during their lives, the emperors after their death reposed in huge mausolea. The tombs of thirteen of the Ming emperors are spread over a wide area north of Peking. Beyond the 'soul tower', which encloses the tombstone (6a above) there is a huge mound covering vaults containing priceless treasures buried with the dead. Guarding the approach to the tombs are rows of stone figures of civil and military officers (6b left) and animals.

7. Also in Peking is the Altar of Heaven, where the emperor
sacrificed to Heaven at the winter solstice, the most solemn annual
event in the state ritual. The circular, three-tiered altar is in the
foreground of the picture.

8. The cult of Confucius played an important part in the state religion and the study of Classics associated with him also constituted the backbone of the educational system. Classical scholarship was the mainstay of the intellectual tradition (8a above shows scholars collating Classical texts). Civil servants were mostly recruited from scholars who passed examinations in these works, which they sat in row upon row of individual cells (8b below).

9. *Success brought much prestige, and friends flocked with their congratulations. On this plaque conveying wishes for examination success (9a above) the two crabs and the reeds represent by a rebus a title conferred on top seconds at the Palace Examination, and the swallows similarly stand for the feast given to successful candidates. The wings of the dragonflies are reminiscent of the silk gauze hats worn by successful scholars. P'ai-lou, memorial arches (9b below), were a common means of commemorating examination success, and they were also erected in honour of philanthropists, centenarians, virtuous widows and other local worthies.*

10. Many successful candidates were employed as district magistrates. As 'father and mother of the people', the district magistrate had wide responsibilities, including the administration of justice (10a above). He also had some responsibility for inculcating Confucian values, such as filial piety and brotherly affection. Three stories illustrating the latter virtue are to be seen on this ivory arm-rest (10b left).

11. A common form of punishment for petty crime was having to wear the heavy square wooden collar known as the cangue.

12. Apart from Confucianism, the other important native system of thought was Taoism, which according to tradition had been founded by Lao Tzu, here depicted riding on a buffalo (12b below). Taoist monasteries were often sited in remote mountainous places, like this one on a peak of the sacred mountain Hua-shan, near Sian (12a left).

13. Taoist beliefs and practices smoothed the path for the acceptance of Buddhism, which made a powerful impact on Chinese society in medieval times, but the economic strength and independence of the monasteries provoked persecutions of the religion, and from the ninth century onwards it declined and tended to merge into an amorphous popular religion incorporating cults from various sources. This illustration shows carvings on the cliff-face at Lungmen near Loyang, where Empress Wu of the T'ang Dynasty was an enthusiastic patron of the work.

14. Ever since the Shang people had produced magnificent bronze sacrificial vessels, religion had stimulated the skill of Chinese craftsmen. 14a (left) shows a gilt-bronze figure of Kwanyin, dating from the twelfth century. 14b (below) is a Ming Dynasty blanc-de-Chine porcelain figure of the God of War, who was a deification of a famous hero of the Three Kingdoms period.

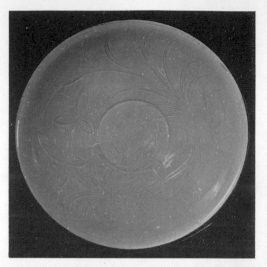

15. Porcelain had reached a high point of excellence in the Sung period, notably in the wares which came from Ting prefecture in Hopei (15a top). The less refined art of the period is well represented by the Tz'u-chou stoneware pillow decorated with a painting of a carp (15b below).

16. The jade-carver worked with a variety of treadle-operated tools (16a top). The altar-set of green jade (16b below) illustrates the archaistic character of many jade objects. The cauldron and the two vases are modelled on ancient Shang Dynasty bronze shapes.

17. Many objects of daily use, such as tableware and jewellery, were made of jade. This illustration shows a green jade pot used for holding writing-brushes.

18 and 19. *The brush was the tool alike of the scholar and of the painter. The method of gripping the brush is shown clearly in this picture of a portrait-painter in action (18 above). Painting was also closely related to calligraphy, as is apparent in the very secondary use of colour and the bold economical brush-strokes used, for example, in this painting, Bamboo in Wind (19 overleaf). This was a common theme of Yüan Dynasty painters, and was intended to symbolize Chinese courage in the face of Mongol oppression.*

20 and 21. Landscapes were the main interest of
the Chinese artist, who was not concerned with
a restless search for new subjects but aimed at a
perfect understanding and representation of the
forces of nature, while man was generally
depicted as a tiny figure at the foot of a vast
mountain (20). The mountain in the photograph
(21 overleaf) is the sacred mountain, Hua-sham.

22 and 23. Paintings and music contributed to the pleasure of the scholar in this Yüan Dynasty painting. (Notice that the scholar in the picture within the picture is not sitting on a chair, but is squatting on a large couch, with his books on a smaller stool set upon it.) 23 shows the grosser pleasures of a mandarin's banquet, with a theatrical entertainment being provided in the background.

24 and 25. Out of doors the garden provided much pleasure. 24 (left) is in Soochow, which is famous for its gardens. 25 shows the top of a stand in famille verte enamels, depicting the Seven Sages of the Bamboo Grove, a famous group of eccentrics who lived in the third century A.D. The two in the centre are playing wei-ch'i, the most highly regarded game among the Chinese.

26. From antiquity music and dancing had been common entertainments at the courts of princes. 26a (above) shows palace musicians of the Sung Dynasty, and 26b (below) shows two pottery dancing-girls dating from the seventh century.

27a (above). Hunting was traditionally the main outdoor entertainment, but polo, introduced from Iran, was one of the many foreign innovations popular in the T'ang. 27b (below). For many centuries after the invention of the stirrup the cavalryman was the dominant force in warfare in North China. This seventeenth-century blue-and-white jar shows a cavalry officer in full charge.

高轉筒車

28. A high level of technology in agriculture and industry was also reached at an early period. Here is shown a device for raising water to irrigate a paddy-field at a higher level.

汲鹵

運載滇川

29. *The salt industry was an important source of revenue because of the salt monopoly tax. 29a (above) shows brine being raised from the bottom of a salt well, and 29b (below) shows salt being transported and loaded on boats.*

30 and 31. For transporting tax grain and other goods, China relied heavily on its rivers and canals. 30 shows a waterside scene at Kaifeng in the Northern Sung. 31a rather exaggeratedly illustrates the difficulties of navigating the Yangtze River, and 31b shows Chinese barges of the Macartney Embassy going through a sluice on the Grand Canal, the 1100-mile-long waterway which had been created during the Yüan Dynasty.

32. Commerce brought many foreigners to China, especially in the T'ang Dynasty when there were Arab trading communities at Canton and many merchants from the west in Changan, like this wine-merchant (32a right). But throughout imperial Chinese history the great majority of people were peasants, like this girl with a winnowing basket (32b below).

being situated so as to protect the mouth of the Yangtze and the capital.

The reign of the Filial Ancestor coincided with the period when Chu Hsi, the most distinguished and influential of all Chinese philosophers since antiquity, was at the height of his power and fame. Born in 1130 when the dynasty was struggling for survival, he began to play a part on the national stage as soon as the Filial Ancestor had come to the throne. One of the emperor's first acts had been to invite memorials from scholars and officials. Chu Hsi had obliged by submitting one, and so had been granted an imperial audience, at which he gave his sovereign lofty advice about the moral duties and political principles which should inform his conduct of affairs. From then on his career was a supreme example of the code of behaviour adopted by the moral, but often exasperatingly self-satisfied, Confucian gentleman.

The classical precept was that a scholar should not take office except under a virtuous régime, so Chu Hsi repeatedly refused to accept employment at the capital, making no bones of the fact that he did so because he did not wish to get his hands dirty. A series of sinecures did permit him to get on with his own private writing, with incalculable consequences on the future history of Chinese thought since his interpretation of the Confucian Classics was to become orthodox early in the fourteenth century and remain so until the dying years of the Ch'ing Dynasty. When he did bring himself to accept office as prefect of Nanking, he performed very creditably, gaining a reputation as a relief administrator, but before long he was at his old business of telling the Son of Heaven that he was surrounded by an unscrupulous clique of favourites and sycophants. He kept up this attitude right to the bitter end of the Filial Ancestor's rule, for in 1188 he lectured the emperor in a long memorial which condemned his whole government and entire reign, explaining that the general atmosphere of moral turpitude pervading both the palace and the civil service was due entirely to the sovereign's failure to rectify himself. Chu Hsi's theory was that the whole process of the moral regeneration of society must start with the rectification of the emperor, but since it was Confucian doctrine that sovereigns needed the guidance of wise ministers and it was only an already rectified sovereign who could be expected to appoint wise ministers, it was not easy to see how the process of regeneration could really be started. Moral purity was needed to reform politics, but it could not survive if it were tainted by politics. Lesser men, doing their best in an imperfect world, naturally became rather irritable with Chu Hsi, so he was attacked by his political adversaries, and it was a remarkable testimony both to his own prestige and to the Filial Ancestor's tolerance that he was able to say such disagreeable things so repeatedly to the occupant of the throne and get away with it. Indeed his staying power was greater than that of the emperor, who, perhaps thinking that the effort of self-rectification was totally beyond him, wearily abdicated in favour of his son in 1189 at the age of sixty-one.

The new emperor, Kuang-tsung ('Luminous Ancestor'), showed himself to be even less capable of cultivating his virtue than his father had been. A sick man when he inherited the throne, he came increasingly under the domination of his empress, who had a violent antipathy towards her father-in-law, and even forced the Luminous Ancestor to break completely with him. When the old ex-emperor died in 1194 matters came to a head, for the Luminous Ancestor would not perform the mourning rites, and this flagrant breach of filial duty was widely condemned and resulted in a political crisis in which the Luminous Ancestor was manoeuvred into abdication in favour of his son Ning-tsung ('Tranquil Ancestor'), who was to occupy the throne for the next thirty years. Kuang-tsung had been the third successive emperor to vacate the throne by abdication.

The Southern Sung is not a period of startling and dramatic changes produced by sweeping reforms, sudden political events, or foreign wars. From the time when peace was reached with the Chin in 1141 the frontiers remained more or less the same, and no dynamic event occurred to cause a great upheaval in the state. Instead it was a period of steady, but eventually very thorough, change in the nature of Chinese society.

The last time when a Chinese dynasty had been driven south, at the beginning of the Eastern Chin in A.D. 317, this was still a frontier region with a sparse Chinese population confined to certain very limited areas, but now it was the most populous part of the country. Between the eighth and the eleventh centuries the population of South China had tripled, and the victory of the Chin barbarians ensured the continuation of this southward movement: among the northerners who settled in the south were the forebears of the so-called Hakka people (the name means 'guest families'), who came and made their homes in Kwangtung and Kwangsi and have until modern times remained separated from their neighbours because of their dialect. The Southern Sung domains fortunately covered a very large and rich area, including not only the fertile lands of the south-east, but also the prosperous Szechwan region, which had always been capable of strong economic independence and self-sufficiency. After they had recovered from the initial shock of defeat and the costly military campaigns against the Chin, it was possible to build a prosperous state with a very different ethos from the old northern Chinese pattern, and to fashion a new style of life suited to the warmer climate and to a more urbanized type of society, which depended for its wealth on trade and industry as much as on land, and faced out to sea rather than towards Inner Asia.

One of the most serious problems was the shortage of land and houses. New land was brought under cultivation, particularly in the south-west, but one method of increasing the amount available was the reclamation of marsh-land. For example, refugees from the north were given the task of reclaiming the marshy terrain in the Soochow area soon after the Chin troops had withdrawn and it was possible to resume normal life. The people were given free seed and charged no rent for three years until they had got the land on its feet. Work of this kind involved much digging and repair of dikes and cutting of irrigation channels, so the Southern Sung sources record a very high level of water-control activities. Unfortunately, however, the lake-bottom land reclaimed in various parts of the country proved to be so fertile that rapacious landlords were tempted to drain and reclaim land for cultivation without caring that this might cause flooding on the properties of their less fortunate neighbours. The government does not seem to have been strong enough to prevent this, especially in the time of the powerful minister Chin K'uei, who is alleged to have been one of those who profited most from possession of lake-bottom lands.

Further increases in productivity were secured by technical improvements in farming. New tools and implements were invented, including complicated water-driven machinery for pumping irrigation water, draining fields, threshing and milling. Illustrations of this machinery – such as the big bamboo water-wheels which can still be seen in the Chinese fields – appeared in printed manuals of the late Sung period which are still extant. New kinds of seed also came into widespread use, especially an improved variety of quickly maturing drought-resistant rice which had been imported during the Northern Sung from Champa, a state in Central Indochina. Officials played their traditional role of instructing the farmers in the new techniques.

The introduction of some of the new methods and machinery was of course dependent on the possession of capital, but owners of large estates could afford to put the requisite resources into these improvements and the result was a boom in agricultural production. Even the lot of the tenant farmer was probably better than usual, at least in areas near to the rapidly growing cities where there were opportunities of selling vegetables for cash, which was all profit since rents were paid simply as a proportion of the rice crop.

The great rice-producing areas were the Yangtze delta, the Kan and Hsiang River valleys, which led south from the Yangtze in Kiangsi and Hunan, the Szechwan Basin and the Pearl River area. In other parts of the country rice production was neglected, notably in Hupei and the Hwai River region, which had suffered greatly from the desertion of its people and the destruction and neglect of irrigation facilities during the war with the Chin, and which presented a picture of gloom and devastation throughout the remainder of the twelfth century. In Chekiang and Fukien rice production was also low because of the hilly terrain. These areas of deficient rice production now began to develop industry and to produce goods which they could exchange for the heavy surpluses of the cereal which would pour in from the rice-producing areas, while the government encouraged these commercial exchanges as a means of revenue. Although previously the seaborne trade had only involved luxury goods, great quantities of rice now started to be transported along the coast from the rice-growing areas of the Yangtze and Pearl River deltas, and rice was even imported by the Chin empire from the Yangtze region.

In this way an exchange economy gradually developed, with the rice-importing areas being able to pay for their imports through the proceeds of such industries as mining, fishing and salt-production, or such handicrafts as silk-weaving and pottery, while the coastal ports were developing as overseas trading marts. In earlier times the transport of commodities from one area of the country to another had generally taken the form of the movement of tribute-goods under government supervision. The consequences of this new private-enterprise exchange system were undoubtedly beneficial for the general health of the country's economy, and it would no longer be necessary for peasants in poor agricultural areas to try to scratch a living from the soil when they could import rice from elsewhere through the products of their labour. This diversification of the economy continued to produce all kinds of social changes. In the countryside there was a spontaneous growth of markets, which developed into small market towns. Cities expanded rapidly, and changed in character as they sprawled beyond their ancient walls. Commercial life became more complex, giving scope to brokers, wholesalers and all kinds of middlemen. Without this growth of the national economy the heavy defence expenditure undertaken by the Southern Sung would not have been possible, nor would such splendid cities have been built. After southern China had developed into a prosperous conglomeration of interdependent communities a division of the area into separate states like the Ten Kingdoms seems a less viable possibility; and in fact, after the end of the Southern Sung, China was never again under divided rule until the twentieth century.

Overseas trade also flourished, as we have seen, but unfortunately much of the wealth that entered the country came in the form of luxury goods. Incoming cargoes included rhinoceros horn, ivory, pearls, coral, agate, rare woods, incense, spices and other goods which would appeal to the taste of the rich merchants, who had grown wealthy on the trading and shipbuilding boom or had done well out of government contracts to supply the armed forces. Such men, who had no regard for Confucian frugality, rivalled each other in vulgar display, and in the big cities and especially at the capital it was possible to buy all kinds of exotic products, not only from all over China, but also from the South Seas, India and the Middle East. China's main exports were manufactured goods, notably silks and porcelains. There were important porcelain factories in the capital itself, as well as in various other places in the south-east, and Sung wares have been excavated in places as far afield as Egypt, as well as in the Philippines and South-east Asia and on the coasts of India and East Africa. There was also much export of copper coins to several countries of the Far East, although this was illegal, and raw materials such as gold, silver, lead and tin were also sent abroad. The great development of overseas trade owed something to the big improvements in shipbuilding and navigation which were being made at this time : for example, the principle of water-tight compartments was already used in the construction of Chinese vessels although it was not adopted in Europe until the early nineteenth century, and the magnetic compass was already in use for navigation by this time. The peoples of West Asia had also played their part in the great growth of international commerce and in T'ang times much of the trade had been in the hands of Arabs and Persians, but by the late Sung the Chinese were dominating the East Asian trade-routes. Commercialism was the keynote of the age, and the government itself made much of its revenue out of commerce. The increased availability of credit and banking facilities and the widespread use of paper money facilitated these new developments.

As might be expected, the more spiritual side of Chinese experience was in decline. Although the splendid monuments of Buddhism throughout the country bore witness to the great days of that religion, it now lacked the capacity for further development. It had deeply affected beliefs and customs and made an indelible impression on the Chinese outlook on the world, but extreme devoutness was no longer a characteristic of the religious life. It was the common thing for Buddhist services to be held for the dead and the Buddhist practice of cremation was widespread, particularly in crowded cities like Hangchow, where there was little room to bury people; but the level of mass religion is shown by the popularity of manuals which enabled people to work out how much merit they had accumulated, while the widespread belief in a kind of infernal bureaucracy dealing out rewards and punishments is not indicative of a very high-minded religious fervour.

Among the intellectuals the heated controversies which had marred the closing decades of the Northern Sung had not died down, and indeed defeat and disgrace accentuated the need for some kind of reform of the body politic. There were many political battles on the proper course to be pursued : in the early stages these generally hinged on the issue of peace and war, but later the issues broadened to include a wide range of practical problems of statecraft. The biggest difference of outlook emerged between those who still believed that immediate practical reforms were possible and those who now saw these as a much more distant prospect which could only be achieved after a long period of moral and educational rehabilitation had prepared both the governors to institute proper reforms and the governed to accept them. The failures of the Wang An-shih reforms were regarded as due to defects of character, and men like Chu Hsi were driven to the more basic problems of human nature and the cultivation of the human personality so as to produce a better world; and these topics caused them to explore still more deeply and consider metaphysical problems, which had not previously played a very great part in Confucian thinking, but whose examination enabled the revived Confucianism to stand on firmer foundations for the future. The term Neo-Confucianism has often been used narrowly to apply to the metaphysical philosophy, particularly associated with the name of Chu Hsi, which under the influence of Buddhist metaphysics brought an entirely new element into the Confucian tradition; but this was only part of the thorough reappraisal of the Confucian tradition which had developed during the Sung period. This Confucian revival, which was in part a result of the decline of Buddhism, was always moved by a practical and reforming rather than a contemplative spirit. But the feeling that a more fundamental rehabilitation of the human spirit was a necessary antecedent to reform meant that, although during the Northern Sung the best minds had been concerned with politics, under the Southern Sung some of the greatest intellects were reluctant to play an active part in the immediate political controversies. Moreover, the spirit of free interchange of ideas had not revived from the repression of the later Northern Sung, and non-conformist opinions were coldly looked upon.

In these circumstances no progress could be expected towards eradicating the weaknesses of the bureaucratic system. Wang An-shih's energetic efforts to improve the clerical staff had not met with success, for the problem was too big to deal with, and now, with the use of hired personnel to perform tasks which in the days before the Wang reforms had been required as service by the local community, the ranks of the clerical service were larger than ever. There are signs, too, of a steady deterioration in the standards of the bureaucracy proper. The old method of entry by hereditary privilege had never been entirely done away with, and patronage and nepotism seem to have become a serious problem. At the same time wealthy merchants were permitted to buy rank to assist the depleted treasury and, by usurping the right to wear official dress, they ate into the unique position of the mandarinate. The rising tide of luxuries available in the capital and other great towns made the mandarins ambitious to increase their standard of living at a rate faster than their salaries would allow, so many of them placed capital in commercial enterprises although this was illegal. Corruption spread even into the ranks of senior civil servants. This resulted in the maladministration of such institutions for social relief as the people's dispensaries which had been organized under the Northern Sung, so that medical supplies did not get through to the common people as they should have done.

On the other hand there was so much money in private hands that some of it was dispensed in the form of charity. The *nouveaux riches* did not spend all their wealth in vulgar display and in attempting to imitate the cultured tastes of the scholars.

To keep themselves on the right side of the gods, they would also give lavishly to the poor. Moreover there was enough money to spare to ensure that education flourished at this time. Apart from the state schools which had been established in all prefectures and countries in the eleventh century, there were numerous private establishments ranging from the small seminaries run by retired officials or unsuccessful examination candidates to the big academies, which were often sited in the kind of idyllic mountain retreats also favoured by monastic establishments.

Although the Southern Sung court had been half-hearted about making Hangchow its capital, it flourished so vigorously that within a century or so it had become the richest and most populous city in the world. Compared with the spacious older capitals of China, which had large unbuilt-up areas within the walls, it was a very crowded city, and houses several storeys high – a new phenomenon in Chinese domestic architecture – had to be constructed to accommodate the teeming population, although wide main thoroughfares and splendid official buildings set off the overcrowded conditions in which many of the people lived. Since the houses were built of wood and bamboo, serious fires were frequent, and over three thousand troops had to be employed in an elaborate fire-fighting service modelled on that of Kaifeng. To protect goods from the danger of fire, warehouses surrounded by water and also carefully secured against thieves were constructed by wealthy persons, including empresses and palace eunuchs, and rented out to prosperous merchants. In this marshy area of China water transport was preferred to land transport, so numerous canals ran through the city and formed the main thoroughfares both for goods and passengers. Carts were to be seen only on the main Imperial Way, and goods which did not go by boat were generally conveyed by porter or pack-animal. Among the well-to-do, the men rode on horseback and the women were transported in sedan chairs. In the city centre there were shops specializing in luxury goods from all over China and the rest of the known world, and to cater for the multifarious needs of the populace there were many different kinds of specialist trade which did not exist elsewhere. For entertainment there were taverns and tea-houses, singing-girl establishments, and many different kinds of restaurant, specializing in their own variety of food. Outside the city the people could stroll in the gardens beside the West Lake, or hire boats for an excursion on the water to admire the scenery. The beauty of the lake, whose shores were studded with temples and pavilions, was lovingly preserved, and care was taken to ensure that any new building blended in with the scenery, while military patrols looked after its maintenance and ensured that people did not dump rubbish into it or otherwise interfere with the amenities. The lake was thronged with gaily painted and skilfully carved boats of all kinds, some carrying singing-girls, and others providing meals on board. Within the city, for the amusement of the civilian population and of the numerous soldiers garrisoned there, pleasure-grounds provided all kinds of entertainments, theatrical and musical, together with acrobats, story-tellers, jugglers, wrestlers and all the fun of the fair.

One of the least attractive features of the new city life was the decline in the status of women. It became more common for members of the upper classes to take concubines, and the practice of foot-binding was also introduced. In early childhood girls had their feet tightly bound in cloth so that they assumed a severely deformed, hoof-like shape. This custom had snob appeal, since it showed that the male could afford to have women who were handicapped and incapable of the kind of physical labour which the peasant woman shared with her menfolk in the fields. Although women who had been subjected to this absurd practice walked in a stiff and awkward manner, small feet came to have erotic attractions, so the fashion caught on among the lower classes too. It has only been eradicated in the present century, and there are still many elderly women hobbling about in China today, victims of this strange affliction.

The bustling, pleasure-seeking world of the city-dwellers, contrasting sharply with the dull routine of peasant existence to which many of their fellow-countrymen were committed throughout their days, fostered new trends in the arts. Literature was enriched by the development of short story, novel and drama, which appealed to the taste of those among the urban populace who were literate but not geared to the more austere classical tradition, the mastery of which led to an official career. At the same time a growing interest in the collecting of paintings, calligraphy and antiques, which had previously only appealed to the scholars, but now attracted wealthy people who wished to better themselves by affecting cultural interests, resulted in a new commercialization of art and expanding trade in art objects which had its only precedent in the flourishing trade in religious art in the heyday of Buddhism. The élite and the common people were being brought together by sharing the many pleasures of city life and the old rigid class barriers were breaking down, while the new more diversified culture was spreading from Hangchow to other cities and enriching the life of the whole country.

But at the same time as the old aristocratic and exclusive Chinese taste and culture was being broadened and was acquiring a fresh accretion of vitality through the creation of material which had more of a mass appeal, the development of printing was also making more widely available the products of élite culture and there was a great proliferation of scholarly work, particularly in the field of history and archaeology. The Sung was an age which was not only characterized by the growth of commercialism: it was also the time when the stage of history was graced by the Confucian ideal of the all-round man, who appeared in the roles of statesman, scholar, poet and perhaps painter or philosopher as well, men like Ou-yang Hsiu and Chu Hsi, who can stand comparison with the greatest human spirits of all times and all places. It was the period when, with the decline of Taoism and Buddhism, Confucian learning really came to the fore again. But unfortunately an alien force was soon to destroy its supremacy.

4

The Mongols

1

During the reign of the Tranquil Ancestor the initiative of history in East Asia was grasped by a new and terrible force, for out of the constant rivalries and conflicts among the northern nomads there now emerged the greatest conqueror the world has ever known. When Genghis Khan came on the scene, it had been three centuries since anyone had been able to impose unity on all the peoples beyond the Gobi Desert. Back in 840 the relatively civilized Uighur had lost the hegemony of Outer Mongolia to their less civilized Kirghiz vassals from the Yenisei River region, but the latter's empire had scarcely survived until the end of the ninth century, and since then the constant struggle for supremacy had thrown up no dominant figure among the rival chieftains, while Chin authority in the north had never extended beyond the eastern half of Outer Mongolia. When Genghis Khan first came to the notice of history, he was a vassal of the Kerait prince who was the Chin Dynasty's chief vassal among the nomads, and so through him a vassal of the Chin also.

At this time it so happened that the Mongol tribes were weakened by constant fighting among themselves, and needed a leader who could bring them together by an appeal which transcended the claims of tribal allegiance. Genghis Khan was such a man and, after a series of bloody battles, he eventually conquered the Kerait and became the most powerful figure in the steppe. The simple purpose of his campaigns was enshrined in the words: 'A man's greatest pleasure is to defeat his enemies, to drive them before him, to take from them that which they possessed, to see those whom they cherished in tears, to ride their horses, to hold their wives and daughters in his arms.'

The same simple philosophy characterized the words of his followers when he was proclaimed khan:

When you are khan we shall be in the front in every battle against your foes, and if we capture beautiful girls and women, we shall give them to you. If in battle we disobey your commands, or if in time of peace we do any injury to your interests, then you will take from us our wives and chattels and leave us to our fate in the empty wilderness.

It was in 1206 that he was proclaimed Genghis Khan, or universal ruler, of the Mongols, and at the same time a general assembly of chieftains, known as a *kuriltai*, was held, at which a new Mongol state organization was introduced. It was to be run on military lines, with the men being divided into units of ten, one hundred, one thousand and ten thousand men, and they and their families were under the command of their officers in peace time as well as in war.

Now that Genghis Khan had succeeded in unifying his people, the next inevitable step was to move south in search of booty from the rich lands of China, for the prospect of unlimited plunder was a certain way of maintaining popularity. People who like grand impersonal explanations for the great movements of history have tried to explain the Mongol tide which washed across most of Asia and Europe in terms of the decline of their traditional grazing lands, but it is clear that there was no climatic change sufficient to spoil their capacity to support the sparse population of Outer Mongolia. In the Mongol triumphs personal genius weighed more heavily than impersonal forces. A leader who combined personal magnetism and military prowess with skill at negotiating profitable alliances and at benefiting from strokes of good fortune, could succeed in forming a confederacy of nomad peoples which would not easily be checked by any civilized, sedentary state. In their daily round the Mongols were always in touch with war conditions, for they were constantly in the saddle wielding the bow, which served them for the hunt as well as in the field. Their women and children, who were always migrating with their great wagon-carried tents, even in time of peace, could just as easily move backwards and forwards in answer to the demands of war. Settled peoples, on the other hand, depend for their livelihood on the protection of their crops and, on an exposed frontier, may prefer to depend on the assistance of a nomad chieftain in return for the payment of tribute rather than rely on the declining power of the remote authorities of their own state. And, by a coincidence, the states of Chin, Sung and Hsi Hsia were all in decline at this time.

In its early days Chin had been a fairly strong and prosperous state. There had been no problem of peasant unrest to pose a threat to security, if only because many people had fled south to Southern Sung; and the economy was helped by the tribute which was received from Sung and by the fact that the hostility between Sung and Chin did not prevent a flourishing trade being carried on between the two countries. But things had changed for the worse by the end of the twelfth century. In 1194 the Yellow River had burst its banks and changed course, causing much havoc, while further economic disorders were brought about by the government's failure to cope with the system of paper currency inherited from the Northern Sung. Serious inflation was made worse by heavy military expenditure on renewed warfare with Southern Sung, which distracted Chin from the mounting Mongol menace until peace was signed in 1208.

After coming to terms with Sung the Chin emperor Madaku (Chang-tsung, 1190–1208) sent his uncle on an embassy to the Mongol court to investigate the situation; but he got such an unfriendly reception that he recommended an early attack on the Mongol ruler, who was at the same time being advised by renegade Chinese officers to make a swift move against Chin. Instead, Genghis Khan decided that he would first deal with the Tangut kingdom of Hsi Hsia, against which he had already mounted two exploratory expeditions in 1205 and 1207. With his trade-routes cut by the invading armies and his capital surrounded, the Tangut ruler felt bound to accept the suzerainty of the Mongol chief, although the Mongols were not yet adept at siege warfare since this was their first venture against settled populations. Now it was Chin's turn. Pleading ancient wrongs which the Mongols had suffered at the hands of the Jürched, Genghis Khan launched a series of campaigns against them. His aim was to capture booty and break Chin prestige, for occupation of territory was not yet a concept which fitted in with the nomad Mongols' pattern of thought. The campaigns of 1211 and 1212 were enough to bring about a palace revolution in which the Chin sovereign was murdered by a general and replaced by another member of the royal family, and the ensuing confusion made it possible to overrun large areas of the country rapidly during the winter of 1213–14. Bought off by Chin presents when at the gates of Peking, Genghis Khan withdrew again, but the shock of this campaign was enough to make the new emperor shift his capital and take up residence at Kaifeng, which was not only less exposed than Peking but also had the advantage of being in richer territory at a time when famine and economic distress were beginning to threaten the régime. This change of capital also marks the culmination of Jürched sinicization: earlier rulers had deprecated the abandonment of Jürched customs, dress and speech for Chinese, but now their Chinese possessions were clearly more attractive to the Chin court than their ancestral lands.

It was not long before Peking, demoralized by the court's departure, fell to the besieging Mongol army. The great city was sacked and many thousands of its inhabitants slaughtered. Insurrection and famine were now rife in the Chin state and it seemed that its fall was imminent, but at this stage Genghis Khan himself became preoccupied with other wars. Although he resolved to open the final offensive in 1217, the Chin state was to prove a tough and obstinate opponent and survive for another decade-and-a-half, in spite of the fact that it also got itself involved in a further war with Southern Sung because the latter had thought Chin involvement with the Mongols made it safe for them to discontinue their tribute payments.

Genghis Khan's other preoccupations at this time were in campaigns far away to the west. He defeated the Kara-Khitai kingdom, which had been established by survivors of the defeated Liao ruling family a century before. It covered a vast area stretching from the borders of the Hsi Hsia kingdom in what is now Kansu westward beyond the Pamirs to the River Oxus. He then overran the great Khwarazmian empire east of the Black Sea, and even further afield he campaigned in Georgia, the Crimea and the Ukraine. Thus at this time famous centres of Islamic culture like Bokhara and Samarkand came into his power. To the north also the Chin dominion in Manchuria had been destroyed and Korea made tributary. Genghis Khan's final operation was the punishment of the Tanguts who had refused to fulfil their obligation to assist an earlier campaign. When he died in 1227 during what was one of the most destructive campaigns ever fought by the Mongols, the final onslaught against the Chin had to be postponed yet again.

The success of Mongol arms over such an enormous area of Europe and Asia in such a short time is one of the wonders of history and we are bound to ask why they achieved so much. The explanation certainly does not lie in strength of numbers. The word 'horde', which is used to describe the Mongol armies, has developed in English the connotation of 'multitude', but the word 'ordu' from which it is derived, means a camp. Certainly the Mongols, for the sake of psychological warfare, spread rumours that their forces were much greater than they really were, but in fact they were almost always heavily outnumbered by the enemy. In their onslaught on Chin in 1211 they deployed a force of only 110,000 men, which was less than a quarter of the size of their opponent's army, and at the time of Genghis Khan's death the total strength of the Mongol army proper was only 129,000. Indeed the total Mongol population was only about a million, approximately equivalent to that of a single Chinese city like Hangchow.

The explanation for the Mongol victories must lie in the superior military skill of their cavalry. In this field they were building on a long tradition: as long ago as the third century A.D. the invention of the stirrup had greatly increased the effectiveness of cavalry by giving the horseman a firm foothold while shooting in the saddle, and in recent centuries the Khitan had improved cavalry technique by adding discipline and co-ordination to its great mobility and striking power. The Mongols developed these skills even further, and were also better equipped than any previous invaders of China because of the supplies of iron and weapons which reached them. Before the Chin there had been an embargo on the sale of iron and weapons to the north, but later they had been exported in large quantities. The Mongol tactic was to advance in columns which were widely separated from each other but which could unite speedily when the need arose. They sought to encircle the enemy like trapped game but avoided closing with him until he was weakened and demoralized by fire. They made use of simulated flight and ambush, and they followed up their victories by a relentless and annihilating pursuit. These nomad warriors showed that far-ranging cavalry did not need to depend on a stable infantry base. Nevertheless it took the Mongols sixty-nine years to complete the conquest. The terrain of mountain and lake in southern China was not congenial to their horsemen, and the numerous walled cities posed problems of siege warfare which were quite novel to a people completely unfamiliar with urban life. To help to solve the former problem they even developed an instinct for naval warfare, which was very remote from their own military traditions. For this they depended mainly on Chinese experts, and when attacking cities they relied heavily on the help of foreign experts in siege warfare. To help them with their manpower problem they were able to reinforce themselves with allies who were glad to share in the rich booty of the Chinese campaigns, and they also forced their captives to take part in storming cities.

Before he undertook a campaign Genghis Khan took great care to build up a picture of the military, political and economic situation in the state he was about to attack. His sources of information were not only scouts and spies and deserters, but also the Muslim merchants who traversed the transcontinental trade-routes in safety because of Mongol power.

But the lifeblood of Mongol successes was the discipline and cohesion of the army organization. At its apex was the Imperial Guard, which consisted of ten thousand men, recruited by a process of sifting from the entire army. Even a private in it ranked higher than a commander of a force of one thousand men. The units of the army were headed by men whom Genghis Khan knew personally and trusted and those under their command were generally kinsmen, so Genghis Khan was adapting the clan organization to provide a strong and cohesive military force.

The Imperial Guard served as a training ground for future military leaders and a means of strengthening Genghis Khan's hold on the aristocracy. Military discipline was very severe.

The conquest of the Chin state not only posed serious military problems which took more than twenty years of bloody conflict to solve, but also confronted the conquerors with novel administrative tasks, especially after 1219 when for the first time the Mongols received voluntary submission of an extended area of North China and had to deal with the unfamiliar problems of settled occupation of a large and populous conquered territory. In the steppe, relationships between conqueror and conquered had nothing to do with the possession of land, but rather with personal servitude. It would have been impossible to transfer such a system to Chinese terrain, so the compromise which emerged was a system in which the country was split up into appanages held by members of the Mongol imperial family and other nobles. These appanages consisted partly of certain social groups, especially various kinds of artisan, who were much in demand by the Mongols, and partly of the inhabitants of whole areas, who remained attached to their own neighbourhoods since it was impracticable to make the sedentary Chinese attach themselves to the mobile Mongols. Thus North China was in process of being broken up into a number of independent local administrations under foreign overlords.

One of the main tasks of government was the collection of taxes, but as the traditional Chinese bureaucratic apparatus for exploiting the populace no longer functioned, the Mongols had to resort to the expedient of tax-farming. The privilege of collecting the revenues was sold to the highest bidder. These tax-farming concessions generally fell into the hands of groups of Central Asian Muslim merchants, and the system operated not only in China but throughout the Mongol empire. The Central Asian peoples had, as we have seen before, a long tradition of commercial expertise because of their position on the transcontinental trade-routes; and the nomads always produced a surplus of animals which they needed to have pushed on to the markets of the settled societies in exchange for weapons and other products which they required. Once conditions became relatively settled again, there was a great expansion of commerce in North China, for the large amount of wealth extracted from the settled population gave the conquerors a big surplus to exchange for the commodities they needed; and the increased demands for goods stimulated the arts and crafts, and gave further scope to the commercial groups which had moved in from Central Asia and were becoming an increasingly powerful force in society. At times when China was controlled by a powerful bureaucratic machine merchants were generally kept under control by such devices as taxation, but under the Mongol régime the growth of commercial interests could flourish unchecked.

As the founder of a great empire, Genghis Khan also promulgated his famous *yasa* or system of laws, a codification of existing practice together with some additions of his own invention: written down by scribes in the form of the Uighur alphabet which had been adopted by the Mongols, it was to be revered by generations of the conqueror's people. Apart from legal and administrative matters it contained moral precepts and also prescribed religious tolerance and respect for the learned and wise of all peoples.

The Mongols' own religion was a form of shamanism, together with a kind of simple monotheism of a type which is found among many primitive peoples, but which must have increasingly owed something to the knowledge of Christianity, which in its Nestorian form was a powerful influence among the Keraits, who were to provide many wives and ministers to future Great Khans. Of the Chinese religions Genghis Khan seems to have been most attracted to Taoism. Indeed in 1219 when he was engaged on his great campaign in Western Asia, he summoned to his presence from remote Shantung an illustrious adept of that religion named Ch'ang-ch'un ('Eternal Spring'). But his summons was not prompted by the loftiest religious feeling. He made it clear that he desired two things of this Taoist master who performed this great journey at the age of seventy-one, firstly the long life which he believed that he could procure through his Taoist arts and secondly the counsel in political matters which he thought the sage would be able to offer. As a reward for his advice and his prayers Taoists were exempted from taxation by a decree of 1223, and in a message to him after he had returned to China Genghis Khan besought him to recite the scriptures each day on his behalf and to pray that he might live long. But clearly the great conqueror's deepest religious conviction was in the divine nature of his own mission. 'Heaven has ordered me to govern all peoples,' he declared, and the ideology behind his conquests was that he had been commissioned by God to conquer and rule the world, so that those who resisted Mongol demands for submission were rebelling against God.

2

It was the Mongol custom for the eldest son to be given the remotest grazing lands, while the youngest son inherited the home territory on his father's death. This arrangement arises naturally out of conditions in the steppe, for as each son married, he would be allotted a proportion of the family herds to support his separate establishment. On Genghis Khan's death this custom, which was the seed of future political weakness, had the effect of splitting the empire into four segments, each under a son (except that in the case of the senior branch of the family the inheritance went direct to a grandson, Batu, since the eldest son was already dead). The youngest son, Tolui, who had inherited the Mongolian homeland, held the regency until 1229, when a *kuriltai* was held, which ratified the wishes of Genghis Khan that the supreme rule should go to his third and most intelligent son, Ögödei.

It was agreed that one of the most urgent tasks awaiting the new ruler was the completion of the war against the Chin state, which had now dragged on for nearly twenty years. Indeed in recent years the Chin had not only been able to maintain themselves in the area of their new capital at Kaifeng, but had even regained some territory in the important strategic area of the Wei River valley. Now a series of brilliant campaigns culminated in the capture of Kaifeng in 1233 and the destruction of the Chin empire. The Mongols now shared a frontier with the Sung state, which they rewarded with some small concessions of territory in exchange for assistance rendered during the war. Dissatisfied with this recompense the Sung government committed the supreme folly of attacking the Mongols. They even succeeded in occupying Kaifeng and Loyang, but they were soon chased out of these cities by their adversaries, who then decided at a *kuriltai* in 1235 that the Sung empire should also be conquered. But although initial successes were scored by the three armies which then invaded the Sung territory, the pressure was not maintained because of the demands of other campaigns, for at the very same *kuriltai* it had been decided to make war in Korea, in Iran and in Russia. The completion of the conquest of Iran and Southern Russia was enough to set beside the victory over the Chin for one short reign, and the final defeat of the Sung would have to wait for another forty years.

The reign of Ögödei also saw many administrative developments, much of the credit for which was due to the efforts of the famous Yeh-lü Ch'u-ts'ai, a sinicized member of the old Liao Dynasty royal family. Taken prisoner by the Mongols at the capture of Peking, Yeh-lü had been employed by Genghis Khan, first as his astrologer and later as his chief minister. He sought to establish a bureaucratic system on traditional Chinese lines, and to reconstitute as much as possible of the old apparatus of government. One of the essential steps was to hold a census. This not only established the population of North China but also set up certain fundamental categories for taxation purposes. The main distinction was between households which were directly subordinate to the emperor and whose taxes went to the imperial government and those which were assigned to the Mongolian nobles. The system of taxation was extremely complicated; firstly because Yeh-lü was opposed to and tried to modify the nomad conqueror's policy of dividing North China into appanages; secondly because tax farming was still practised to some extent and no serious attempt was made to do away with it until the following reign; and thirdly because there were different systems for the conquering race and for their Chinese subjects. The Mongols had to pay a tribute to their personal lord, whether the Great Khan himself or an imperial relative, in accordance with the size of their herds; and they also had to render other goods and services, including the maintenance of the postal relay system in the domain to which they were attached. In the case of the Chinese, the artisans had to pay taxes in the form of their own products, and the rest had to pay poll-tax and household tax plus innumerable additional levies collected for special occasions. In traditional Mongol society the subject had to furnish the lord with the goods and services necessary to enable him to function as a lord, but in a settled society of the Chinese type the fiscal obligations of the inhabitants were geared to the functioning of the state, so it took some time for the Mongols to adapt to this very different situation. Indeed under Genghis Khan the view of the Mongol generals had been that most of the northern Chinese should be exterminated and their land turned over to grazing, and Yeh-lü had had to persuade them that it would be more profitable to the Mongol state for them to be taxed rather than slaughtered.

The old commercial taxes, which were not only very profitable, but also easier to administer than taxes dependent on a census and on dealing with every household in the state, had already been in operation for some time before the great census of 1235–6. The salt monopoly was already in full working order by 1230 and, despite the difficulty of operation, a liquor monopoly was introduced as early as 1231. Yeh-lü Ch'u-ts'ai also made some attempt at currency reform. Under the Chin rapid depreciation of successive issues of paper money had brought silver ingots into popularity as a basic medium of exchange, but in the early years of the Mongol occupation attempts were made to stimulate a re-growth of trade by the issue of paper currencies, which merely circulated in the locality in which they were issued. In 1236 Yeh-lü made an attempt to re-introduce a national paper currency, while issuing warnings against a repetition of the mistakes in monetary policy committed by the Chin.

At this stage the Mongols were only just beginning to show an interest in Chinese culture, and their understanding of it was very superficial. Marco Polo, who visited the Great Khan at a later stage, was struck by their great mistrust of the Chinese. They were extremely suspicious of Confucianism, especially because they wished to escape the fate of earlier foreign rulers of China who had had to submit to Confucian administrators in the end. They tended to treat Confucian literati as if they were the clergy of a religion on a par with Buddhism and Taoism; and the business of government, which was their métier, was kept firmly in the hands of the conquerors and their foreign advisers and ministers such as Yeh-lü Ch'u-ts'ai. To the disgust of Confucian scholars there was no attempt to restore the civil service examinations. But the practical benefits which could be conferred by experienced Confucian administrators encouraged some movement towards more enlightened policies. Thus in 1237 a Confucian scholar of Tangut origins triumphantly succeeded in persuading a son of Ögödei who was garrison commander in western Kansu to hold an examination so that the talents of the scholars who were doing manual labour could be put to better use. This resulted in over four thousand scholars being employed in a manner more suited to their capacities. Ögödei saw the virtue of recognizing the state cult of Confucius and of re-establishing the national academy. But, as we shall see later, Taoism and Buddhism were now the main rivals for supremacy in religious matters.

Ögödei undermined his health by indulgence in wine and women and died prematurely in 1241, at a time when the Mongol empire had spread as far as Hungary. This was the furthest west the Mongols ever reached, for Batu had to give up his campaign in Eastern Europe and return for the customary *kuriltai* to elect the new Great Khan. This assembly took place at Karakorum, the capital which Ögödei had built in Mongolia. Before this Ögödei's widow had held the regency for several years; and eventually she contrived the succession of her own son Guyug, which was neither in accordance with the wishes of her late husband nor to the satisfaction of other powerful Mongols, including Batu. During her regency several of her husband's distinguished foreign advisers, notably Yeh-lü Ch'u-ts'ai, were removed from government. Yeh-lü died shortly afterwards at the age of fifty-five. His achievement was remarkable, for he had guided the Mongol rulers along the path to government of a settled community and had shown them that their empire 'gained on horseback could not be governed on horseback'. Had he not curbed some of the conqueror's baser instincts the results could have been appalling for the civilization of East Asia and of the world.

The *kuriltai* at which Guyug was eventually elected did not take place until 1246, when it coincided with the arrival in the Far East of the first of several notable visitors from Europe who left accounts of their journeys. This was an elderly Franciscan named John of Plano Carpini, sent by Pope Innocent IV with only one companion to brave the hazards of an immense journey to a people whose widespread conquests had given them a dreadful reputation and who had seemed to offer a dire threat to Western Europe after even Hungary had been occupied for more than a year. The purpose of this and later missions was to enlist Mongol support against the Saracen. The travellers' attempts to get on terms with the Great Khan proved fruitless. Arguing that the success of the Mongols' arms proved that they had divine support, he bluntly demanded the Pope's submission, viewing him as a kind of Great Khan of the West with all other European kings as his vassals. 'Thanks to the power of the Everlasting Heaven,' said Guyug,

all lands have been given to us from sunrise to sunset. How could anyone act otherwise than according to the Command of Heaven? Now you must say with upright hearts: We will be your subjects and will place our powers at your disposal. You in person at the head of the monarchs, all of you without exception, must come to tender us service and pay us homage; then only will we recognize your submission.

Guyug had only accepted the succession on condition that the throne became hereditary. He showed signs of being a stern, uncompromising, authoritarian ruler, but within two years he was dead at the age of forty-three, allegedly because the severity of his nature had not prevented him meeting an early end through the same indulgences as had proved too much for his predecessor. At the time of his death an armed clash with his great enemy Batu, the head of the senior branch of Genghis Khan's family, seemed imminent, and a new crisis of succession followed under the regency of Guyug's widow. Eventually, as a result of the powerful influence of Batu, the succession went to Möngke, son of Tolui, the empire thus finally passing out of the hands of the Ögödei branch, which at the time had no members of sufficient age and experience to stake a claim to the throne, but which nevertheless resented its displacement.

Möngke proved to be a most able ruler, concerned to govern in the spirit of Genghis Khan and maintain a firm grip on the whole empire. Although Batu in the far west had been practically independent, after his death in 1255 Möngke was firmly in control, and succeeded in combating the powerful centrifugal forces which would inevitably result in the break-up of the empire. During his reign the ambitious plans of conquest were still to be pursued, especially in China, where little progress had been made since the destruction of the Chin a decade-and-a-half before. The Mongol army had by now reached its peak of about a million men, including the auxiliary forces recruited from subject peoples. After the victorious conclusion of the campaign against the Chin, Chinese had been recruited in large numbers. Möngke held a census in 1252, which included the classification of households by occupations, which were henceforward to be regarded as hereditary. The purpose of this was partly to ensure that the Mongol élite did not become submerged in the mass of the Chinese population, and partly to ensure that specialist skills were always available to the state. Households classified as military had to furnish a certain number of men for military service according to their means. The soldiers were garrisoned in military communities supported by agricultural colonies. These were now no longer merely an institution for manning the frontier, for the whole country had to be garrisoned. Since the Mongols were unused to agriculture, the labour was provided by Chinese soldiers and their families. The Mongols' continued enjoyment of their privileged position depended heavily on these military communities.

At a *kuriltai* in 1253 it was decided that Möngke himself and his brother Khubilai should be in charge of the renewed attacks on China. Khubilai had already been appointed governor of the occupied parts of China and had been given Honan as his appanage, where he had done much to restore agriculture by distributing seeds and tools to the peasants and employing soldiers to work in the fields. The main strategy adopted was for the western flank of the Sung line to be turned by Khubilai in a great march through Szechwan, which had been the centre of much bitter and inconclusive fighting since the fall of the Chin. His armies penetrated as far as the non-Chinese state of Nan-chao in the area of what is now the province of Yünnan. This area, which had never yet been part of the Chinese empire, was taken over by the Mongols, although the king was allowed to remain as vassal ruler. By now Khubilai himself had returned north, but one of his lieutenants attacked the kingdom of Annam, which had formerly been part of China, and its ruler concluded in 1258 that it would be prudent to acknowledge Mongol suzerainty.

Later that same year Möngke decided to take personal charge of the operations against Sung, and led an assault with the principal Mongol army from the direction of Szechwan, but at the time of his death in the summer of 1259 he was still held up at a place not far to the north of Chungking. At this time Sung was being threatened from three directions, for Khubilai had been advancing from the north and was besieging the city now known as Wuchang in the central Yangtze region, while the southern army had passed from Yünnan into Kwangsi, where it had attacked Kweilin and afterwards advanced on Hunan to besiege Changsha. With the death of Möngke all this had to be dropped so that Khubilai could secure his own succession. He made a truce with the Sung and marched north again for the customary *kuriltai*. Although he had failed to achieve the final victory over the Sung, Möngke's campaigns in Western Asia had been more decisive.

Möngke had close contacts with Christianity since he was the son and husband of Nestorian princesses, his chief minister was a Nestorian, and he himself attended Nestorian services. At the same time it is reported by the dynastic history and borne out by William of Rubruck, another missionary who set out to convert the Great Khan, that he had great faith in the traditional shamanism of the Mongols. The religious situation was very complicated. Within Möngke's empire, even within the borders of China itself, all the great religions of the medieval world were to be found: there was Christianity in its Nestorian, Roman and

Byzantine forms, Islam, Judaism and Manichaeism, not to mention the three major faiths of the Chinese themselves, Confucianism, Taoism and Buddhism. Möngke's attitude to these Chinese doctrines was formed largely by political considerations. Under Guyug a monk called Hai-yün had been put in charge of the administration of Buddhist affairs in North China and he was confirmed in his position by Möngke, who also made a similar arrangement for the administration of the Taoist religion, so that now both religions were officially recognized and controlled by the state. At the same time Tibetan Buddhists had been gaining influence at court. Their religion, which included a certain amount of miracle working of a kind that had commended Buddhism to earlier barbarian rulers of China, was more suited to the Mongol mentality than some of the more sophisticated Chinese branches of the faith; and a lama called Namo was appointed to administer Buddhist affairs throughout the whole Mongol empire, thus apparently being made superior to Hai-yün.

In view of the great prestige and influence at court wielded by these advisers, there was naturally a powerful struggle between the old rivals, Buddhism and Taoism, for imperial favour. Representatives of the two religions were summoned to debate before the emperor in 1255, an event which had flattering precedents in the great religious discussions held before kings and emperors throughout Buddhist history. The Taoists were adjudged defeated, but they refused to yield, and further conferences were held in 1256 and 1258, the latter being attended also by Confucians, who sided with the Buddhists. The Taoists again lost, and some of their books were proscribed and burnt in the presence of the authorities at Peking. Möngke thought little of the Confucians, reduced in this episode to mere allies of the Buddhists. He took a severely practical attitude, and once, impatiently interrupting a Confucian in the flow of his discourse on the great ethical principles of his philosophy, demanded what use the Confucians were in magic and the art of war. He was interested in religious adepts because he knew they had influence with the people, and as it became clear that Buddhism was the most powerful force among the Chinese, so he favoured it increasingly. He told William of Rubruck that, just as God had given the hand several fingers, so he had given Man several religious paths, but later he referred to Buddhism as the palm and the other religions as the fingers. But all the time the supreme religious power, as far as these Mongol emperors were concerned, was the God of their own destiny. 'There is only one eternal God in heaven and one sovereign on earth,' Möngke wrote to Louis IX via William of Rubruck.

Before Khubilai Khan could continue his Sung campaign he had first to establish himself firmly at the head of the Mongol empire, for apart from himself, Möngke had left two other brothers. The previous changes of ruler had been marked by long regencies, prior to the grand *kuriltai* at which the emperor was finally proclaimed, but now in the summer of 1260 Khubilai hastily had himself declared Great Khan at Shang-tu (Coleridge's 'Xanadu'), where he had established his summer residence. His youngest brother, who had control of the Mongolian homelands, likewise had himself proclaimed ruler at Karakorum. The ensuing struggle was not resolved until his rival was defeated and captured in 1264. Khubilai established his winter capital at Peking and in 1271 adopted the Chinese dynastic title of Yüan, to symbolize his intention of finally superseding the Sung. Yüan means 'origin', a departure from the usual practice of using a local name.

Meanwhile in southern China the defences were not in a very healthy state. In particular the great days of the Sung navy were over and the advances of the Mongol forces in Möngke's reign had found it in a shocking state of unreadiness. The government put heavy pressure on private shipowners to supply ships to make up the deficiency, and this succeeded in alienating the merchant class at a time when the Mongols were making valuable propaganda out of their favourable treatment of such people, especially by releasing captured Chinese traders and sending them south with stories of the commercial opportunities under Khubilai's rule and his patronage of the merchants.

In 1265 the long but undistinguished reign of Li-tsung came to an end, and he was succeeded by his younger brother's son Tu-tsung, who was even more ruthlessly dominated by an unprincipled minister called Chia Ssu-tao than his predecessor had been. The Mongol forces, when Khubilai was free to deal with the Sung, chose to exert their main pressure by an advance along the Han River, but they were held up for five whole years by the twin fortress cities of Siangyang and Fancheng. But by autumn of 1275 they had fought their way down the Han and eastward along the Yangtze, and in the process had inflicted some heavy defeats on the Sung navy. By the end of the same year these people, who had only recently been introduced to naval warfare, had at their disposal a large sea-going fleet; for they had seized over a thousand ships, mainly at Shanghai, and had received from Chu Ch'ing and Chang Hsüan, a pair of pirates and salt smugglers turned respectable merchants, a fleet of five hundred vessels together with several thousand men to handle them. It was thus possible for the Mongol forces to make a combined land and sea attack against Hangchow, which capitulated in February, 1276.

Two years earlier Tu-tsung had died and been replaced on the throne by his four-year-old son. This infant and his mother were taken as prisoners to Khubilai's court, but his two younger brothers had been smuggled out of the doomed capital, and one of them was proclaimed emperor at Foochow. But the Mongol advance continued, and the Sung cause received a crushing blow with the defection of the Persian P'u Shou-keng at Chuanchow. He was the most powerful man in the region, being not only commander of the naval forces, but also Commissioner of Maritime Trade and a dominant figure in the civil administration, as well as the possessor of a large fleet of sea-going ships in his private capacity as a wealthy merchant. He ensured victory for the Yüan forces in the final battle against the Sung remnant at the island of Yai-shen near Canton early in 1279.

3

The social and economic structure of the south was little affected by the Sung defeat, for the Mongols had now become fully aware that the best way to exploit a country was to leave its traditional institutions undisturbed. In great contrast with their earlier habit of plundering defeated enemies, they won the willing submission of the local gentry by taking steps to safeguard their property rights. Even before his accession Khubilai had been accused of being soft on the Chinese, and his removal of the capital from Karakorum to Peking symbolized his intention of taking his duties as Son of Heaven just as seriously as his responsibilities as Great Khan. The clash between him and his younger brother had been not simply a conflict between two ambitious rivals, but a confrontation between two different attitudes to the Mongol future. A further embarrassment to Khubilai was the revolt in 1268 of Khaidu, a grandson of Ögödei, who seized the Khanate of Chaghadai: this new war cut him off from his western dominions and became so serious that, as soon as Hangchow had been captured his greatest general, Bayan, had to be rushed back to deal with the situation although there was still much to do to complete the conquest of China. Khaidu was to be a continual menace until his death in 1301.

Khubilai certainly did not abdicate his responsibilities as Great Khan. Indeed throughout the rest of his life he was to be waging war in defence of the principle that he was the heir to Genghis Khan and presided over a united Mongol empire. But this very civil war compelled him to depend more and more on the resources of China itself, and at the same time he was forced to appreciate that this great settled civilization could best be governed by its own highly developed bureaucratic methods, and that all the Mongols needed to do was to exercise firm control at the top level. So under Khubilai the separate powers of the ruling Mongol nobility were abolished and a strongly centralized Chinese state was reconstituted. The Mongol nobles still took care to keep themselves apart from the Chinese and did not merge with the Chinese gentry, and they and their foreign employees retained firm control of the upper echelons of the political structure, although the local basis was Chinese. They helped to preserve their separateness by grading the people into four classes, the Mongols themselves, their non-Chinese allies, the northern Chinese and finally the southern Chinese, who had been the last to capitulate; and different systems of law applied to the different classes.

The organization of civil government superficially followed T'ang and Sung precedents, but there was a major innovation in the division of the country into a dozen large provinces in the modern manner, and the whole complex structure became much more authoritarian and centralized than it had hitherto been. One of the basic features of the Chinese bureaucratic system which Khubilai did not re-introduce was the examination system. Instead the mandarinate was hereditary. It was composed of Mongols, foreigners and former officials of the Chin and later of the Sung dynasties; and mandarins of the first seven of the nine classes were entitled to transmit on retirement or bequeath at death the right to hold official employment. At the very beginning of his reign Khubilai had introduced a system of official salaries, which were drawn in the form of rent on specially allocated 'office lands'. But in view of inflation and rising prices he had great difficulty in keeping remuneration at a level which would prevent officials from indulging in venality and corruption. Mandarins were subjected to traditional Chinese regulations: they were not allowed to hold office in their native provinces, nor could they marry anyone from the district they were administering, and they were required to adhere strictly to the rules governing retirement during the three-year mourning period. In most respects the new political system which evolved under Khubilai was Chinese in principle, and it was recognized that the attempt to impose Mongol patterns on this alien society had proved to be a failure.

An important step towards the assertion of stronger central control was taken in the very first year of Khubilai's reign when 'pacification offices' were established for each of the provinces into which North China had been divided since the time of Ögödei. In tightening the state's control over outlying districts they became especially active in enforcing the new taxation system which was in operation now that the right of collecting taxes in their appanages had passed out of the hands of the nobles. It now also became possible for the state to cut down on the privileges of the powerful merchant groups, which had not only benefited from the lucrative tax-farming concessions they had enjoyed, but had also been exempt from taxation themselves; and in the fourth year of Khubilai's reign they were deprived of this latter privilege. But even after Khubilai had carried out some rationalization of the tax system the population still suffered from having to pay out not only the traditional Chinese taxes, designed to finance the functioning of the state (consisting of land taxes, payments in lieu of corvée labour, together with commercial taxes and taxes imposed on commodities like salt which were monopolized by the state), but also the Mongol-style levies devoted to the support of the ruler or lord. The salt tax was at this period still the most profitable source of government income.

Khubilai's government also made big efforts to get agriculture back on its feet. In the first year of his reign the pacification offices were ordered to select agriculture-encouragement officials, whose activities were later co-ordinated under a board of agriculture. The state adopted a programme of organizing the countryside into *she* or communities, which were to supplement the existing village organizations in the promotion of agriculture. The *she* were not only charged with providing instruction in agricultural methods, but were also given the task of arranging such matters as pest control, irrigation, pond maintenance and tree-planting schemes. Moreover they were required to establish 'charity granaries' and schools at which a traditional classical education could be given in slack seasons. After the conquest of South China, the government tried to introduce the same system in this area but the extent to which these *she* functioned successfully is not entirely clear.

The government also faced the problem of ensuring that the products of their agricultural policy reached their destination. Once Peking had become the centre of government it grew enormously, and in 1267 Khubilai began the building of a new city there. By 1270 there was already a population of four hundred thousand registered citizens and by 1272, when the city was completed and named Ta-tu, the Great Capital, it had already outstripped its food supply. Despite all efforts to increase agricultural production and make the distribution fairer by a system of ever-normal granaries, famines occurred almost every year. Production in war-ravaged North China was still below normal. Khubilai had forbidden the confiscation of agricultural lands for conversion into pasture, but much land had been turned over to grazing purposes before this, particularly in the area of Peking, and this was one important reason for the grain shortage. Much of this land was to be restored to private ownership and put under cultivation again before the end of the dynasty.

No complete solution to the problem was available, until Bayan conquered the fertile Lower Yangtze valley, and then the task of transferring the surplus grain from this region to Peking could at last be tackled. The old canal system was completely out of action, for not only had serious damage been done during the fighting between Sung and Chin, but in certain areas the channels had silted up early in the twelfth century, and houses had been built and crops grown on the old canal beds. In any case what was now needed was a direct link between Peking and the Lower Yangtze. In the T'ang period the northern canal route had gone towards Peking in a north-easterly direction from the area of Loyang, and under the Northern Sung a water route had been established as far north as Tsining, but further north the land was not flat enough, so that it was necessary to construct many locks (a skill at which the Chinese engineers were proficient many centuries before their European counterparts), and even then the waterways still remained too shallow to transplant large quantities of grain and they were always likely to silt up.

Supporters of the canal route were bitterly opposed by those who advocated maritime transportation. Prominent among the latter were the ex-pirates Chu and Chang, who had not only won the gratitude of the Mongols by going over to them at a very useful moment during the war, but had also demonstrated the feasibility of the sea route by transporting Bayan's spoils of war from Hangchow to the capital in 1276. So the difficulties of canal construction led to the inland routes being abandoned. A system involving the use of private shipping rather than the impersonal navy to transport the grain was worked out, and Chu and Chang were now to be seen in the dual role of officials operating the scheme and of private individuals furnishing the ships and seamen at a very profitable rate. But unfortunately in 1286, when there was a very bad harvest in North China, a quarter of the grain transported by sea was lost in a typhoon. In the following year Chu and Chang were deprived of their authority and inland transport again came into favour, and although the two ex-pirates were again restored to authority and a new improved sea-route made it possible for the grain fleet to complete two voyages a year, work went ahead on completing the famous Grand Canal, which made it possible to go by water direct from Hangchow to Peking, a distance of 1100 miles. A paved highway was also built along the whole distance, and despite the difficulty of maintaining this waterway, it remained a key feature of China's system of communications until modern times.

Now that the civil war had cut off land contacts with the west and the Sung had been conquered, maritime commerce became the most important branch of the Yüan Dynasty's foreign trade. The government's first maritime trade commission was established in Chuanchow soon after the port's occupation. It remained the greatest emporium of southern China, but other trade commissions were soon established, notably at Shanghai, which now began to develop into a leading port. As in Sung times, a flourishing trade developed with India and South-east Asia, and luxury goods were even exchanged with the remote khanate in Persia.

Commercial stability during the early part of Khubilai's reign had been much assisted by the monetary reforms which were among the new measures introduced in his very first year. Previously many different paper currencies had circulated in North China, and now that a unified currency had been issued, it proved to be extremely successful for a couple of decades owing to the cautious policy of the government, and it was not until the late seventies that inflation set in.

A sure sign of the change in Mongol methods achieved under Khubilai was the readiness with which his rule was accepted in the south and the ease with which the final take-over took place. He had learnt to disturb the status quo in the conquered domain as little as possible, and he had succeeded in enticing the Sung navy and the private ship-owners to defect to his side. His propaganda was also effective in religious circles, and he was quick to make use of this device, just as the Sui founder had been when he conquered the south to reunify China after a long period of dis-unity. Although Taoism had suffered a setback in the north, Khubilai lost no time in cultivating good relations with the head of the Taoist religion in the south. Even before the conquest of Sung was complete, he confirmed him in his position, and thus the Taoists recovered a certain influence at court although there were further burnings of Taoist books in Khubilai's time.

The other religions were similarly exploited to help secure political stability. Like his brother Möngke Khubilai showed most favour to Buddhism, and soon after his accession he made gifts of land to Buddhist temples. Nevertheless an edict of 1271 forbidding people to present slaves or land to monasteries was a sign that Buddhist establishments were already growing too wealthy at the expense of the state. Meanwhile in political affairs Buddhists had obtained influential positions. The Uighur Sengge, who seems to have been the most powerful man in Khubilai's government from 1264 until his disgrace and death in 1291, was a lamaist; and a young monk called 'Phags-pa', who had impressed Khubilai when he came to court at the age of eighteen and was still only in his twenties, became head of the Buddhist church throughout the empire soon after his succession. In 1264 he was concurrently entrusted with the political administration of Tibet, which had acknowledged Mongol suzerainty. When Hangchow fell in 1276, Khubilai immediately stepped in to take control of the Buddhist church in the south, which he soon put in charge of a Tibetan lama. The power of the lamaists in the south was not devoid of scandal, and the fiscal privileges enjoyed by the monks led to the same disastrous economic consequences as during the T'ang Dynasty. Heavily taxed to pay for increasing state expenditure, more and more of the population sought refuge in monasteries or merely claimed to be monks while carrying on their normal family life. At the end of Khubilai's reign the Buddhist clergy numbered 200,000 and many peasants attached to ecclesiastical lands also evaded tax. Another unfortunate consequence of Khubilai's patronage of Buddhism was that much of the wealth accumulated by the monasteries flowed into Tibet, the home country of the powerful lamas. Towards the end of the reign steps had to be taken to tighten up and prevent all but the genuinely religious from becoming monks, and one indication of the debasement of this vegetarian religion is an edict of 1291 pro-

scribing the slaughter of sheep and cattle for Buddhist feasts!
As before in Chinese history, the attempt to use Buddhism as an
ally and support of the throne had got out of hand.

Confucianism, on the other hand, continued to make little progress, although Khubilai recognized the cult of the sage and
ordered that a Confucian temple be built in his new capital, so
that sacrifices would be offered in spring and autumn. Among
strict Confucian scholars, especially in the south, there was much
hostility to the idea of serving the alien dynasty. Some carried
their Sung loyalist sentiment to absurd lengths, showing their
attitude by refusing to use the Yüan calendar and referring to
the former emperor as if he were still reigning; and one famous
scholar, who had been a bitter critic of the Sung in its last days,
nevertheless remained so loyal to it after its demise that he refused to serve the Yüan and even starved himself to death on
being taken to the capital in the hope that he would accept office.

Christianity was also well represented in the Far East at this
time, although in China it seems to have been the religion only
of foreigners and not to have penetrated to the Chinese themselves. The Nestorians were easily the most numerous representatives of the religion and they were extremely influential since the
Kerait and Ongut tribes, which were Nestorian, provided empresses and chief ministers for the Great Khans. A Nestorian
archbishopric had been established at Peking in 1275, and the
adherents of the religion were so numerous that in 1289 Khubilai
Khan created a special government office to deal with their
affairs, ranking it on the same level as the Taoist office. There
were also some Byzantine Christians who were mainly soldiers
from the Caucasus who had been recruited by the generals of
Genghis Khan and had served in the imperial guard of his
successors. The few Catholic Christians who had found their
way to the Far East had mainly been taken prisoner during the
Mongols' European campaigns, and it was not until after
Khubilai Khan's death in 1294 that John of Montecorvino, the
founder of the first Catholic mission in China, arrived in Peking.
He baptized several thousand converts, trained a choir which
sang Gregorian chants for the imperial pleasure, and in 1307 was

appointed Archbishop of Cambaluc, the name by which Peking was known to Europeans.

As if he were not fully enough occupied with such great undertakings as the conquest of Sung and the civil war against Khaidu, Khubilai indulged in reckless overseas adventures. By the time he came to the throne Korea had been completely subjugated by the Mongols, who were to dominate the country for the next century, during which time the Korean ruling house intermarried so much with the Mongol that it became virtually part of it. The next step in this direction was to force the Japanese to accept the Mongols' suzerainty; and when they repeatedly refused to yield, the wretched Koreans were pressed into supplying large quantities of provisions and ships and some men for a Mongol invasion of Japan in 1274. This onslaught was repulsed with heavy losses, but since the leaders of the expedition were able to blame this on the weather as much as on Japanese swords, Khubilai repeated his demands for submission, and in 1281 utilized the resources of the recently acquired Sung navy to mount a much more formidable attack. Containing 140,000 men, this was the largest overseas expeditionary force which had ever been dispatched in the history of the world, but it could not conquer the hostile elements encountered in these treacherous waters. A typhoon struck and the invaders suffered appalling loss of life : some were drowned and others made their way ashore but fell easy prey to the Japanese soldiers. Khubilai even wished to make a third attempt, but his advisers were not happy about this and the scheme was dropped. Other foreign adventures in South-east Asia also failed to win permanent success, and, although some petty princedoms in this part of the world acknowledged Khubilai as suzerain, Mongol forces suffered heavy defeats in trying to impose their will in such places as Burma, Champa, Annam and even Java.

So in one remarkable personality Khubilai combined the Mongol urge for world domination with a wise understanding of how domestic policies would have to accommodate themselves to Chinese circumstances and traditions. But, at the very time when he was trying to play the role of Great Khan, he was even accelerating the inevitable process of fragmentation of the Mongol empire, which was shown up not only by hardening political divisions between the khanates, but also by the conquerors' increasing acceptance of the cultures of the conquered peoples. In the west of the Mongol empire the Islamic culture was dominant, while in China the successors of Genghis Khan had increasingly absorbed the Buddhistic culture of the country and had even begun to take an interest in Confucianism.

Khubilai's own knowledge of Chinese was rather poor and he had to make use of interpreters. This was not surprising, for even the famous Venetian traveller, Marco Polo, who was in the Far East for seventeen years and was one of the many foreign administrators employed by the Yüan government, apparently needed to know little Chinese since the upper echelons of the civil service consisted mainly of foreigners. But such was his appreciation of Chinese culture that Khubilai made sure that his heir apparent and the other imperial princes had a literary education. The heir had to practise Chinese writing every day, and he studied the Chinese *Classic of Filial Piety* and received lectures on Chinese history from former Sung officials.

Khubilai was, however, eventually succeeded by his grandson, Temür, who was not a good Chinese scholar. He governed firmly and more cautiously than Khubilai, eschewing reckless overseas adventures. He was the last strong Yüan ruler, for after his death in 1307 six brief reigns followed in rapid succession before the last Mongol emperor ascended the throne in 1333, to preside over the final thirty-five years when the dynasty's power had disintegrated beyond hope of recovery.

Of these short-lived emperors, Buyantu, who reigned from 1311 to 1320 and had the Chinese posthumous tide of Jen-tsung ('Humane Ancestor'), had a keen interest in Chinese learning and a considerable knowledge of Chinese poetry. It was in his reign that the civil service examinations were at last re-introduced, and this was obviously the real break-through in the sinicization of the Mongol régime. His nephew Togh Temür (alias Wen-tsung, 'Cultured Ancestor') had a singularly appropriate posthumous name, for he cultivated literature and the arts like a typical Chinese gentleman. He not only painted and wrote poetry, but also became a distinguished calligrapher with an insatiable desire to cover objects, however precious, with samples of his work, and even an expert in such a recondite branch of aestheticism as ink connoisseurship. The martial vigour of the Mongol rulers had now completely withered away, and no greater contrast can be imagined than between this young aesthete and the terrible conqueror who had laid the foundations of Mongol power. He died at the age of twenty-eight, but in his short three-year reign he founded an academy to which famous literary men, painters and calligraphers were attached, and established himself as a patron of the arts. These activities were continued by the final Yüan emperor, Toghan Temür, and, after an attempt on the part of his chief minister to eliminate Chinese influence had failed, the court was the centre of intense traditional Chinese literary and artistic activity.

When the civil service examinations were re-introduced by Buyantu in 1313, the system of hereditary entitlement to office continued side by side with it and the number of candidates who entered by examination was small. Those who submitted themselves to examination were entitled to enter the service at a grade higher than they would otherwise have done, so there was a certain incentive even for members of established bureaucrat families to compete. There was also racial discrimination in the treatment of the successful examination candidates. Mongols entered the service at a level two grades higher than the Chinese, while the various foreign collaborators of the Mongols entered one grade higher than the Chinese. The interruption of the civil service examination system, which had now been restored, but only in a partial and invidious manner, has been seen by the Confucian tradition as the hardest blow which the Mongols dealt to Chinese civilization. Just as harmful was the fact that, when they re-introduced the examinations, they prescribed Chu Hsi's commentary on the Classics, so that a stifling orthodoxy marred the educational system throughout the rest of imperial Chinese history. As a symbol of their new eminence, the tablets of Chu Hsi and other Neo-Confucian masters of the Sung period were placed in the temple of Confucius.

It should be emphasized that, although some educated Mongols were influenced deeply by Chinese culture, the ordinary people preserved their own distinctive culture rather tenaciously, and continued to use their own language, consume their traditional food and drink, such as the cheese and fermented liquor made out of mare's milk, and wear the leather and furs their forebears had worn on the steppe. Since non-Chinese were greatly favoured over the Chinese during the Yüan Dynasty, there was every incentive for members of the conquering race not to merge into the far more numerous conquered population and become Chinese. Indeed among the ordinary people the influence generally worked in the opposite direction, and there was much imitation of Mongol ways, especially among the northerners, and this even affected such serious matters as marriage customs. The fashion for imitating Mongol manners was to continue after the fall of the Yüan and give concern to the Ming.

These developments were all part of the enormous spread of cultural influences released by the success of the Mongol conquerors in uniting such a large area of Asia under one rule. Thus some Central Asians who came to serve in China developed into distinguished Confucian scholars or made worthy contributions to Chinese literature and the arts. At the same time their own home regions were receiving a strong cultural influence from the many Chinese who travelled to these areas, and many of the technological advances of the Chinese found their way to Western Asia and thence, often by a slow process, to Europe as a result of the freedom of travel at this time, while the export of Chinese porcelain had a profound influence on Japan, South-east Asia and even the Arab world. In return Islamic culture came to China to stay, and in Kansu and Yünnan the Muslim faith has remained powerful ever since, while in the sea-ports on the southeastern coast Arab traders continued to live in their own separate communities according to their own customs.

Some Europeans also found their way to China and sent back accounts of their experiences, although Sino-European contacts at this period of history were of very slight importance compared with the interchange between the various parts of the Mongol empire. Carpini had little to report about the Chinese when he returned to Europe, but William of Rubruck began to unveil the mystery of Cathay by being the first to identify it with the country occupied by the Seres, or 'silk people', as they were known in antiquity. He also told of the quantities of silk used there and the great skill of Chinese craftsmen and physicians. He mentioned paper-money and brush-writing, and tried to explain the Chinese script.

The fullest account of China in Mongol times came from Marco Polo, a member of a Venetian merchant family, who departed for China in 1271 together with his father and uncle, who had made a previous trip and had been requested by Khubilai to return with a hundred Christian friars. They set off with only two, and both of these fell by the wayside. The story of his seventeen years in the Far East only reached the world because some time after his return he had a chance meeting with a professional romance writer called Rustichello. The encounter took place in a gaol where they both happened to be incarcerated as prisoners of war, so Polo had plenty of time in which to tell his tale. Some parts of the narrative owe more to the romance-writer than to the traveller, notably one of the most memorable passages in the book, the account of Polo's welcome at the Great Khan's court, which is modelled on an Arthurian romance by Rustichello. On the other hand there are many fascinating glimpses of the true China of the time, particularly in the description of Hangchow; and although Polo was sometimes guilty of exaggeration, even the plain truth would have been sufficient to cast doubts on his veracity, so great was the contrast between the tiny city state of Venice and the vast, prosperous, highly cultured and populous country of China. Fortunately there were some who were inclined to believe Polo's account, and soon ideas of world geography began to reflect his discoveries. One who took him seriously was Christopher Columbus, who possessed a copy of the book, which he annotated in such a way as to indicate his interest in Cathay, which he wanted to reach by sailing westwards.

Another traveller who wrote a vivid account of his experiences was Friar Odoric of Pordenone, who was in China in the 1320s and lived for three years at Peking. He delighted in curiosities and was the first of many travellers to mention foot-binding, long fingernails (a sign of gentility) and cormorant-fishing, which involved the use of tethered cormorants with rings round their necks to prevent them swallowing their catch. His account was extensively borrowed and heavily embroidered by Sir John Mandeville, whose fantastic description of his imaginary travels throughout Asia was extremely influential and was taken at its face value by some people as late as the eighteenth century. Although they made their mark on European intellectual history, these medieval travellers had no impact on China, except for the small mission established by John of Montecorvino, which faded out long before the Catholic fathers arrived in China at the end of the sixteenth century. And it was not until the Jesuit accounts reached Europe that the Europeans would begin to have a deeper understanding of Chinese civilization. The medieval travellers had had much to say about the look of China, the crowded and prosperous cities, the rivers teeming with vessels of all kinds, the skilled craftsmanship, the variety of natural products and the strange customs; but, not being familiar with the literature of the country, they were in no position to enter into the spirit of Chinese civilization.

Despite the increasing Mongol attempt to come to terms with Chinese civilization, exemplified by the re-introduction of the examinations in 1313, the dynasty began to go into a rapid decline at about this time. The lack of a strong ruler of the calibre of Khubilai and a weakening of military vigour meant that it was no longer possible to hold down this enormous population. The army had long been in decline because in the totally alien agricultural milieu officers had become land-owners and had exploited their men and used them as farm-labourers, so that the prestige of being a soldier and the ties of loyalty which had formerly bound a Mongol to his unit were lost. The Mongols had also been too oppressive and unsympathetic towards the traditions and institutions of the Chinese to win their willing collaboration, and when it became necessary to increase taxation to support a growing bureaucracy and an increasingly avaricious imperial household, the landholders of Central and South China, who provided most of the revenue, began to grow restive, and the support which they had originally accorded to the dynasty began to evaporate. Matters were made worse because the continued growth of Buddhist power and effrontery was, as usual, a drain on the economy. The first serious revolt broke out in 1315 and was directed against the implementation of a new land survey, and thereafter the rebellions grew in intensity. After 1330 grave economic difficulties were caused when shipment of rice to the metropolitan area from the south was seriously disrupted by a series of uprisings: the consequent sharp increase in prices led to growing economic distress, which was made worse by flood and famine in the Yellow River region. Towards the end of the dynasty even some of the intellectuals who had on the whole remained aloof but passive began to take an active part in hastening the Mongols' downfall. There had long been dissension among the Mongol princes, and since they insisted on trying to destroy each other instead of preserving a united front against the successful rebels in the south, the final victory of the Ming was easy and rapid.

The main heritage left by the Mongol rulers was that in future the state would be run in a more centralized and autocratic way than previously. A similar influence was felt by all the other sedentary societies which had suffered Mongol rule. In the countryside the lot of the peasant had not been improved by their régime, and the number of independent landowners continued to decline by comparison with the huge armies of tenants who now became liable to be sold and mortgaged as if they were slaves. The lower classes in the cities were subjected to the restrictions imposed by hereditary registration of their occupation, and this practice was to continue in the succeeding dynasty. It had taken the Mongols nearly seventy years to conquer China, but for all the suffering they had caused they were unable to compensate with a period of lasting prosperity: in another seventy years the dynasty was on its last legs and within less than ninety it had faded away. But although the Mongol conquest had brought little benefit and much harm to Chinese society, traditional Chinese culture was not irreparably weakened by it, nor was it greatly modified by the impact of foreign cultures: it merely continued to develop in a more private fashion. The great tradition of landscape painting survived, but the Yüan masters painted for their own personal pleasure rather than to meet the criteria of an academy or the approval of a court; and in the realms of literature and scholarship, although lack of opportunity and patronage meant that the public tradition was carried on in more muted fashion, some of the intellectuals turned to the novel and drama as a means of self-expression. The age is noted for the great progress made in these two varieties of vernacular literature, which appealed to the less highly educated audiences of the big cities. The theatre had already become popular in Peking and Hangchow, the capitals of the Chin empire and Southern Sung respectively, but now the art reached its peak. The Chinese drama has many facets. It is really a form of opera, and its appeal depends not only on the skill of the dialogue but also on the complicated conventions of stylized movements in the acting, the highly trained technique employed in the singing and dancing, and the brilliance and special significance of the various costumes. The novel had antecedents in the Buddhist stories told by evangelical monks in T'ang times, samples of which turned up in the Tunhwang finds. There was also a long tradition of secular story-telling, and the material used reached its first written form in the guise of prompt-books for professional story-tellers which eventually developed into the fully-fledged novel. The earliest surviving novel dates from the fourteenth century and is a romanticized account of the Three Kingdoms period, but many other novels which did not reach their final form until much later were current in an earlier version during the Yüan Dynasty. So, in spite of Mongol oppression, the Yüan is an important period in the history of Chinese art and literature. Indeed there is even one conspicuous example of Mongol patronage in the splendid capital which Khubilai had built at Peking, on which Chinese architects, painters and craftsmen had lavished all their traditional skills.

5

The Ming Dynasty

1

The last great native Chinese dynasty was founded in 1368 by a man of humble origin named Chu Yüan-chang. A long career as a rebel lay behind him when he finally attained the throne at the age of forty. As usual, the rebellions of the late Yüan period were sparked off by the poverty and discontent caused by the inefficiency of a dynasty in decline. Chu was not motivated by any strong anti-foreign sentiment, or any powerful urge to liberate the country from foreign oppressors. Indeed the arch-enemies of the revolutionaries were just as much the rich Chinese, particularly in the southern part of the country, where they had been allowed by the Mongols to retain their power to exploit the masses. But once on the threshold of power Chu adopted, at the instance of his scholarly advisers, the old Confucian myth of the highly civilized Chinese surrounded by admiring barbarians, a doctrine which had to be asserted with fresh emphasis now that there had been this rude interruption to the natural order. The Chinese sense of their own superiority, which they felt was due to the possession of superior virtue, had been developed in the Han and T'ang Dynasties, and had been preserved during periods when it squared much less neatly with the facts of history. Foreign domination over the whole of China was a traumatic experience, because it proved that the sheer fighting ability of the Mongols could overcome the Will of Heaven. The only consolation was that the relative shortness of the Yüan Dynasty was proof that power without virtue could not survive for long, just as virtue without power had been the downfall of the Sung.

In his youth the founder had been forced by poverty to embrace religion and, as a mendicant Buddhist monk, he eventually became the co-ordinator of the activities of secret societies of a

religious character which often played an important part in rebellions. But the real seeds of his later power were sown in 1352
when he entered the service of an important military official
in the Hwai River valley, and soon afterwards became his son-in-
law. Within four years Chu's father-in-law was dead, and Chu
had usurped his brother-in-law's military patrimony. Assuming
the title of Duke of Wu (the ancient name for this area of China
which had also been used in Three Kingdoms and Five Dynasties
times), he established his seat at Nanking, although formally he
subordinated himself to the revel Sung régime which claimed to
be the legitimate successor of the last Chinese dynasty. During
the next decade the regions of Chekiang, Kiangsi, Hunan and
Hupei were added to his domains, and his régime began to take
on the attributes of imperial sovereignty, until finally the new
dynasty was formally proclaimed at the beginning of 1368 under
the name Ming ('bright'), a title which, in the manner inaugurated by the Yüan, was of religious rather than regional significance. In the same year military campaigns brought much of the
rest of the country under control, the only areas remaining to be
absorbed being Shensi, Szechwan and Yünnan, which were added
in 1369, 1371 and 1382 respectively. As had now become the regular practice, the founder was destined after his death to be given
the temple name of Grand Progenitor (T'a-tsu), but it has become
customary to refer to the Ming and Ch'ang sovereigns by the
names of their reign-periods. From now on each reign is known
by the reign-title expressing some pious hope for the style of the
period, such as Eternal Contentment (Yung-lo) or Prosperous
Tranquillity (Chia-ching). In earlier times a similar device had
also been used, but era-names had often been changed during the
course of a reign, sometimes as many as a dozen or more times,
so it was only with the inauguration of the Ming that it became
convenient to refer to emperors in this way. These reign-titles
are commonly referred to in the dating of Ming and Ch'ing porcelain, since the names appear on the underside of vessels; and
consequently they are not totally unfamiliar in the West. At
a time when much fighting remained to be done Hung-wu
('Boundless Valour') was chosen as the name of the Ming founder's reign.

Like the Sung founder, who gave the country a new start after a long period of division and warfare, the Hung-wu emperor had a splendid opportunity before him. If he could fill the vacuum left by the incompetence of the declining Yüan with a period of firm and positive government, the country would respond out of weariness with recent anarchy and enthusiasm for the richer opportunities which might come under a native dynasty. Unfortunately however the Sung founder had been accustomed to holding high office on merit, whereas the Hung-wu emperor was a man who, although he possessed great qualities, could not surmount his humble origin and the early hardships which had embittered him towards members of the more prosperous classes in Chinese society, and emerge as the wise and level-headed leader the country needed.

An early mistake, which ignored the lessons of history, was to give too much power to his own sons. Chu became a conspicuous member of that ironic fraternity who in their youth fight against entrenched power and wealth, but in their maturity are concerned to establish or perpetuate a system for preserving the power and wealth, newly acquired, of their own families. For a man of humble origin who had also been a Buddhist monk, the Hung-wu emperor had acquired a large family even before he attained the throne, and he proceeded to increase it until it totalled twenty-six sons and sixteen daughters. To secure their future, he introduced in the second year of his reign a system of enfeoffing his sons with principalities scattered throughout the empire, at which they would reside after reaching maturity. Each of these principalities was given an appropriate ancient territorial name, and the princes were each to have a retinue of as many as nineteen thousand men, including very substantial military forces. Although the area was to be administered by an office staffed by the central government, which was to have the responsibility for general supervision of the principality as well as for advising the prince and dealing with his communications with the central government, these principalities provided great scope for aggrandizement, especially when the emperor decreed that princes based near the frontier should have absolute power to deal with the Mongols, who were still a menace to the northern areas of the country. So, although the original intention was that the princes should have no administrative or judicial function, their control of troops and other retainers gave them a great deal of power and they were in a strong position to usurp more.

Apart from the immediate danger to internal security, this arrangement also entailed a long-term drain on the country's economic resources since these princedoms were handed down in perpetuity through the eldest sons, and each new emperor also created fresh first-degree princedoms for his sons. Moreover, sons of all these imperial princes received lesser princedoms, and in fact every direct descendant of a Ming emperor received some title and salary. Thus, though no later sovereign was quite as prolific as the founder, it has been estimated that the number of imperial clansmen reached six figures by the end of the dynasty, which meant that the Chinese had to pay a considerable price to maintain the imperial family in a manner appropriate to its prestige.

Although the Hung-wu emperor was bound to avail himself of the services of the literati in running the state, he had none of the genuine respect for them evinced by the Sung founder. Consequently many members of this class, who might have been expected to take very happily this new opportunity of serving under a native dynasty, kept well out of the way and did their best to avoid serving in the government. Indeed Mongol despotism still cast a dark shadow over the new emperor, who would even go so far as to have his officials flogged at court, in sad contrast with the punctilious treatment meted out by the early Sung rulers. As he grew older and more suspicious, he would sometimes have men put to death for quite imaginary insults, so that no poet could make an allusion to natural harshness or calamity without fearing that the occupant of the throne might see it as a veiled reference to his own tyranny, while according to one contemporary writer, officials took the precaution of bidding a final farewell to their wives and children every morning before setting out for the court audience.

But it was not only the scholar-bureaucrats who suffered. The power of the rich landowners of the Lower Yangtze was broken by the removal of 45,000 members of these well-to-do families to

Nanking, where they were kept under close government surveillance. These had been old enemies of the Hung-wu emperor, but his erstwhile friends were also to suffer. Not only did he suppress the secret societies, which had helped to put him where he was and might do the same for some future pretender to the throne; he also began to eliminate individuals who might seem a threat in view of their eminence and who because of the great loyalty they had shown him during his rise to power might, once spurned, prove to be most dangerous and implacable enemies. One of these, Hu Wei-yung, an invaluable adviser before the establishment of the Ming and now chief minister, seeing that his own days were numbered, made a bid for the throne in 1380: his failure merely meant that he met his death at the hands of the executioner rather more quickly than he might have done if he had allowed things to take their course. Others, innocent and guilty alike, were to share his fate, as the Hung-wu emperor seized the opportunity for a wholesale purge. A similar attempt was crushed in 1393, and tens of thousands of people are said to have been put to death as a result of these two attempted coups.

But the consequences of the Hu Wei-yung affair cannot only be measured in the deaths of the victims. The Hung-wu emperor changed his style of government in a manner which was to have far-reaching effects on the administrative history of the period and on the fate of the dynasty. He decided not only to get rid of the unfortunate Hu Wei-yung, but also the office which he held, and indeed the whole of the Secretariat, which was proving to be a tiresome check on his absolutism. The Secretariat had had considerable influence on imperial decisions and had served to integrate the nation-wide civil service apparatus. Now there was nobody to stand at the apex of the government structure and co-ordinate the activities of the six ministries and the other organs of state, except the emperor, who held the executive authority entirely in his own hands. Furthermore he was not content to regard this as an administrative experiment. On the contrary he prescribed the death penalty for anyone who might have the effrontery to advocate the re-establishment of the Secretariat. In later times the Hung-wu emperor was bitterly criticized for this reform, which undoubtedly helped to weaken the dynasty. Certainly no emperor who was not both vigorous and conscientious would be able to cope with the amount of paper-work now involved, and in making this alteration the Hung-wu emperor was inflicting upon himself, through inability to trust others, the kind of crushing work-load which the early Sung emperors had had to endure.

The administration of this great empire was now beginning to settle into its final shape. At the core of the civil administration were the six ministries, which were the same as they had been in the T'ang period. The Board of Civil Office was responsible for all civil service personnel matters, such as appointments, honours, promotions and demotions, and for keeping records of the civil servants' careers and evaluating their performances. The Board of Revenue was responsible for the census, for the assessment and collection of taxes, and the handling of government revenues, and it included a separate office for each province. The Board of Rites was principally concerned with state ritual and ceremony, with the reception of envoys from tributary states, and with the control of the Buddhist and Taoist priesthood through central registries which were required to examine and certify priests. Numbers of these were now severely limited, and since the two religions were declining forces, there was not much need for imperial patronage of them. The Board of War's main sub-divisions were the bureaux of personnel (responsible for appointments and promotions), of operations, of equipment, and of provisions. The Board of Punishments was, like the Board of Revenue, organized on a territorial basis. It was concerned with the judicial review of important cases, for although judicial matters were generally handled by officials as part of their ordinary duties, in some cases ratification had to be sought from the judicial authorities, and in some cases even from the emperor. The Board of Works was in charge of such matters as government construction projects, the manufacture of equipment for the government, the maintenance of roads and waterways, and the standardization of weights and measures. Most of these ministries had numerous specialist offices attached to them. There were also a number of independent agencies at the service of the central administration, such as the Office of Transmission, which acted as a message centre for the government, the Directorate of Astronomy, the Directorate of Imperial Parks, the National University and the Hanlin Academy, whose job was to provide scholarly assistance for the emperor and court.

As the Hung-wu emperor brought different areas of the country under his control, he put them in charge of Branch Secretariats modelled on the metropolitan Secretariat, but in 1376, even before the abolition of the metropolitan Secretariat, he abolished the twelve Branch Secretariats which had been set up to control the provinces liberated by that time. In future the affairs of the provinces were to be in the hands of a trio of agencies, which were to act independently of each other: the Provincial Administration Office, the Regional Military Commission and the Provincial Surveillance Office. Henceforward nobody was to have complete authority over a province and fulfil the role of provincial governor, just as there was to be no chief minister in the central government.

The three-fold pattern of the provincial administration was paralleled in the central government, for alongside the civil administration, which has just been briefly described, was the military organization and the various surveillance agencies. The most senior of the surveillance agencies was the Censorate, which in the reform of 1380 was reorganized and given the new name of Chief Surveillance Office. A popular name for the censors was 'ears and eyes of the emperor', and they were responsible for keeping under surveillance the operation of the entire governmental machine and with initiating preventive, corrective or punitive measures where necessary. For example, regional inspectors from the Censorate toured their areas inspecting all agencies of local government, observing the conditions of the people, and interrogating officials and commoners alike. They had access to all government records, and were able to advise, admonish, command or impeach as they saw fit, and even inflict punishment on low-ranking officials without trial or ratification. Other censors had more specific tasks, such as the inspection of the military service, or the supervision of famine relief; while those who remained at the capital were occupied with routine checks on the activities of the many government agencies there, as well as with attending imperial audiences and top-level discussions of policy at the court. Surveillance was not the only responsibility of the censors, for there still survived the time-honoured and hazardous function of remonstrating with the emperor and criticizing his policies, a tradition which had the blessing of Confucius and Mencius.

In addition to the Chief Surveillance Office or Censorate there were six Offices of Scrutiny, one for each of the ministries : their principal job was to keep a check on the flow of documents to and from the appropriate ministry and re-phrase or return for further consideration any material which seemed unsuitable or inconsistent with government principles. Outside the metropolis, apart from the periodical inspections conducted by regional inspectors from the Chief Surveillance Office, there were also the provincial surveillance offices to keep a check on all local government personnel. For much of the Ming period there were thirteen provinces, fewer than the eighteen provinces of the Ch'ing because there were two large metropolitan areas, one based on Nanking and comprising Anhwei and Kiangsu, and one in the north round Peking, which became an auxiliary capital in 1403 and directly administered a large Northern Metropolitan area. At this auxiliary capital there was much duplication of central government agencies.

To fill all these posts officials had to be rapidly recruited, and in the early days some were appointed merely on the recommendation of people who were already in the civil service. Another method of recruitment was to have pupils sent up from the state-supported Confucian schools which the Hung-wu emperor had ordered to be established in each prefecture, subprefecture and county, and have them examined by members of the Hanlin Academy. If they passed, these so-called 'tribute students' were enrolled in the National University and appointed to government posts after a period of study there. But both these methods of recruitment were soon to be overshadowed by the state examination system which was re-introduced at the beginning of the dynasty and, after a brief suspension, began to flourish again in the 1380s, when it took the form which was to survive until

the final abolition of the examination system in 1905. This consisted of three separate degrees: the first, popularly known as
the *hsiu-ts'ai* ('Flowering Talent'), was taken at the prefectural
city. This entitled the holder to compete in the triennial examinations at the provincial capital, leading to the degree of *chü-jen*
('Recommended Man'), taken at the great examination arenas
with their rows of cells, one for each candidate. The final hurdle,
reached by fewer than one per cent of those who contested at the
provincial capital, was the metropolitan examination leading to
the degree of *chin-shih* ('Presented Scholar'). Those who were
successful at this level were summoned to the palace and finally
tested by the emperor himself. Even those who only passed the
hsiu-ts'ai test acquired considerable prestige. They were expected
to maintain their status by sitting additional periodic examinations, so they were enrolled in prefectural or county schools for
further instruction. In addition to exemption from corporal
punishment, to which their new status entitled them, they were
given free board and a modest stipend, together with exemption
from corvée duties for themselves and as many as two other
adult males in their families. In a period of general upheaval this
simple arrangement for subsidizing scholars meant unusual
opportunities for people to rise in the social scale. On the other
hand another method of recruitment much used at the beginning
of the Ming did favour established families: this was the hereditary privilege which entitled officials of the top seven ranks to
obtain civil service status for their sons. But this method of entry
soon declined in importance, for the privilege not only came to
be restricted to the top three ranks but also lost prestige, so that
civil servants who had entered by this means could not attain
high office.

When the examination system got into its stride, it was found
that there was a heavy predominance of southerners among the
successful candidates, which was not surprising since the
economic and cultural centres of gravity had for some centuries
been in that area of the country. Matters came to a head when
there were bitter complaints from northerners after the metropolitan examinations of 1397, so it was decided to introduce
broad regional quotas in the ratio of forty per cent for the north

and sixty per cent for the south. It was particularly necessary to appease the northerners in this way since a long period under alien rule meant that they did not feel any strong sense of loyalty towards a Chinese régime based on Nanking.

It was generally necessary to pass the metropolitan examination before embarking on an official career, but many Recommended Men who failed at the third hurdle obtained appointments at the state schools which had been established as a result of imperial exhortation. There were as many as twelve hundred of these by the time of the Ming founder's death. But although the emperor was approaching closer to the Confucian ideal of equality of educational opportunity than any of his predecessors had done, the education provided was rigidly orthodox. In his decree announcing the inauguration of the examination system the emperor had left no doubt about his view of the purpose of education: he prescribed the commentaries of the Sung Neo-Confucianists and stressed the need for orthodoxy in the writing of essays. Quality was being sacrificed to quantity, and instead of fostering a genuine commitment to Confucian ideals, the examinations now produced graduates with limited intellectual attainments who had succeeded in memorizing the Classics and the commentaries upon them.

If the Hung-wu emperor was not an outstanding success in his management of the civil government, perhaps we can expect greater achievements in military matters, which had occupied much of his time before his accession. The main defence problem was how to cope with the Mongols, not only beyond the frontier, but also in China itself, where many members of the conquering race had been left stranded when their dynasty collapsed. Under the Yüan there had been many Mongols and other foreigners in the civil service, and at the beginning of the new dynasty these were retained, in view of the strong need for trained personnel; and a few new Mongol recruits even entered the service after 1368, as interpreters and in other special capacities. If the Ming claimed to be heir to the world empire of the Mongols, it was right that they should absorb the Mongol civil servants into their own administration. Some Mongols even attained positions of distinction, as heads of civil service ministries or as generals in the Chinese army, and one was even appointed tutor to an imperial prince.

The great majority of Mongols who stayed behind in China were enrolled in the army. This was no great hardship to them since they belonged to a society in which every able-bodied man was automatically a soldier. Prisoners taken in the fighting at the end of the dynasty seem to have been incorporated immediately into the victorious armies, in which they served in their own units under their own officers, as part of larger Chinese groupings. The fact that the Mongol soldiers were generally accompanied by their wives and children, who lived in special quarters in or near the towns where Mongol troops were garrisoned, was a guarantee of their loyalty. They were stationed in all parts of the empire, and even as early as 1370 the emperor was prepared to permit the settlement of Mongol prisoners-of-war in the northern borderlands which were their natural habitat, and there seems to have been surprisingly little fear of subversion. Indeed, loyal Mongol troops were often used in campaigns against other Mongols and proved to be very useful defenders of the northern frontier. But the Chinese were generally very careful to limit the Mongol command to the lower levels, and not to give any authority to people who had wielded power in Mongolia before the surrender and who might therefore still command personal allegiances and be a potential danger. Similarly members of the royal family and other Mongol dignitaries were kept in honourable custody at the capital, where they could be watched over and perhaps, after suitable indoctrination, used at some future date to head a vassal Mongol régime. In 1374 a possible heir to the throne was sent back to Mongolia in the hope that he would eventually succeed and bring the whole of Mongolia under Chinese suzerainty, but when his father, the Great Khan, died in 1378, the succession went to a younger brother.

Apart from the Mongols who were already living in China and those who came over from Mongolia in small groups and surrendered and those who were taken as prisoners of war, there were also large groups of Mongols living in their own territories on the border whose rulers switched their allegiance to the Ming. Mongolia was in a state of disorder for many years after 1368, so it was natural that some petty chieftains should look to the south in search of a better deal. The Chinese did their best to encourage this, their avowed purpose being to try to sinicize the Mongols and any other foreigners they could attach to the Ming. These Mongol groups were allowed to continue living in their own territories and were incorporated into the military organization of the Ming empire, but the civil administration was left entirely in the hands of the chieftains, in conformity with the policy adopted towards tribal chieftains on the other frontiers of the empire.

With North China under the control of foreign dynasties there had been no frontier separating the Chinese from the northern nomadic peoples for several centuries, so at the beginning of the dynasty the situation remained fluid. The collapse of Mongol power meant that the Chinese were able to surge far to the north. On the other hand pockets of Mongol resistance did survive for some time in the north-west of China itself, and in the mountains of Shansi guerrilla warfare was waged by Mongol princes, with some assistance even from the local Chinese population, for twenty years before it was finally stamped out. But gradually, as resistance inside China was quelled and Chinese north of the Great Wall tended to move south for greater security or else disappear among the Mongol population and become Mongolized, the line of the Wall re-asserted itself as the natural frontier; and although some Chinese communities continued to live north of the Wall the Hung-wu emperor paid great attention to re-building the fortifications along this line, which was well sited on the natural bastion of the mountainous terrain overlooking the Mongolian plateau. Although he did conduct some aggressive campaigns against the Mongols, his attitude towards barbarians was summarized in the dictum 'Resist them when they invade us, but do not pursue them relentlessly when they withdraw', which had a powerful influence on Ming foreign policy. In the first year of his reign he had urged the people of non-Chinese ancestry who had supported the Yüan to become his subjects and had promised them fair treatment and equality with the Chinese. Later he declared:

Human nature can always practise good, and to reform the barbarians through China's customs is the teaching of the ancients. Now the former Yüan officials who have been captured and those who have surrendered should be moved within the empire so that they may submit to the teachings of our sages, gradually learn our rites and etiquette and change their old customs.

His policy was successful, and the Mongols who had been assimilated caused little trouble.

To the south-west the Chinese had to establish relationships with the aboriginal peoples, especially in Szechwan, Yünnan, which was not conquered until 1382, and Kweichow, which did not become a province until 1413. In these areas the Ming founder confirmed in their positions the tribal chieftains who had been recognized by the Yüan. These chieftains were referred to as 'aboriginal officials' and were given Chinese official titles, but on the whole they were allowed to govern in their own traditional ways. Acceptance of Chinese suzerainty meant that the rulers had to accept investiture by the Ming emperor, adopt the Ming calendar, and acquire some cursory knowledge of the Confucian proprieties. The tribes were required to send tribute at stated intervals, and at the beginning of the period the chieftains were expected to present themselves at the capital in person. The object of this exercise was not to milk the tribes, but to impress them with the majesty and glory of court and empire: the sumptuous gifts and the opportunities of lucrative trade bestowed on the tribesmen meant that the tributary relationship even brought economic advantages and prestige to the The chieftains were expected to have troops available to fight of a privilege than a humiliation. There were snags, of course. The chieftains were expected to have troops available to fight alongside Chinese in campaigns against other tribes. Trouble could also be caused by the fact that the Chinese administrators appointed to these remote and unattractive parts of the empire were sometimes of an inferior breed and thus inclined to treat the natives with contempt. On the whole, however, the policy adopted towards these tribal chieftains was one of appeasement, which had the support of hallowed Confucian writ because the ancient sages from the dawn of Chinese history had similarly had to appease the barbarian tribes by which they were surrounded. Moreover it was the only feasible policy to adopt in these remote areas with difficult terrain. Nevertheless it was hoped that this system would simply be the first step towards full integration into the Chinese empire. The native chiefs generally had Chinese advisers, and there was much political and cultural pressure towards assimilation, but many of these aboriginal peoples have succeeded in retaining their own independent culture right up to the present time.

To cope with these various frontier problems, and consolidate the dynasty, the creation of a strong army was a matter of paramount importance. There was a high degree of continuity between Yüan and Ming institutions, and it was natural that the Ming military organization in particular should be under heavy influence from so militarily powerful a people as the Mongols. A most important aspect of this influence was that the Ming adopted the Yüan practice of registering families by hereditary occupation, one of the categories being that of 'soldier'. The scheme was not so detailed as it had been under the Mongols, and the great majority of commoners, who were engaged in agriculture, commerce, trade and many other occupations, were merely classified as *min* ('people'), so that in fact much freedom to change occupation was open to this large group. In addition there were a number of important hereditary occupations which involved relatively few people, such as medical practice and postal work, together with the major categories of artisan, soldier and salt producer. The purpose of this system of registration of families by occupation was to ensure a continuous supply of personnel in certain vital jobs, so in view of the importance of national defence, especially strict regulations were devised to control the military families, which were required to provide army personnel in return for certain exemptions from taxation and labour service. By 1392 the strength of the army was about 1,200,000 men, and it continued to increase thereafter. The men were assigned to garrisons throughout the empire for training, but there was a particularly heavy concentration of troops in the metropolitan area. Army officers were also recruited on a hereditary basis. The lower-ranking offices were apparently transmitted from father to son without the son having to be content with a lower rank than his father, but higher-ranking commissions were filled by selection from among the holders of hereditary offices.

To supply such an enormous army was not easy, and special measures had to be taken to secure provisions for the units stationed on the frontier. As far as possible, garrisons were intended to be self-supporting by means of the institution known as the military agricultural colony: at these establishments seventy or eighty per cent of the soldiers, generally the older and less fit, were occupied with farming, each independently operating his small area of land just like a peasant, while only the remaining twenty or thirty per cent were actually kept on garrison duty. But along the frontiers, and particularly the heavily defended northern frontier, it proved impossible for the garrisons to be self-sufficient; so that various methods of making up the deficit were employed, such as the use of convicts to transport grain, or the award of honours to those who delivered supplies to the army. But the most important expedient devised during the Hung-wu period involved a link-up between military supplies and the salt monopoly. It was decided that merchants who transported grain to the frontier areas would be entitled to receive certificates which would enable them to obtain salt and so take part in the lucrative trade in that commodity. Soon these merchants saw the advantage of bringing new land under cultivation in the border areas to save transporting grain from far away, and there developed a new system of 'merchant colonization' which proved very beneficial, not only to the merchants and to the military garrisons, but also to the destitute vagrants who thus found employment.

The Ming founder also appreciated the value of a strong navy. Very early in his career, before he became emperor, he had used fleets effectively on the Yangtze and he had later employed them in the conquest of the coastal provinces and in the supply of his northern armies. He soon instituted annual patrols which cruised far out to sea to take vigorous measures against Japanese pirates. No ruler in Chinese history was better equipped by early privations to appreciate the evils of economic injustice, and we have seen how the Hung-wu emperor soon curbed the influence of rich families by wholesale deportations to Nanking. He also tried to make burdens fall more equitably on the mass of the people by a thorough registration of the population. Through what were commonly called the Yellow Registers, because the copy held by the Board of Revenue was bound in yellow covers, the government had at its disposal a more satisfactory record of population than was to become available again before the late eighteenth century; and details of the age, sex and occupation and property owned was included in the census returns. At the same time an ambitious project to compile land-survey maps and land-tax handbooks, entitled the Fish-Scale Maps and Books (so described because the configurations of the maps looked like fishes' scales) was undertaken. Although such surveys were compiled for most provinces in the early Ming, the labour involved in making them thorough and accurate was obviously enormous, and it appears that the work was only carried out with the requisite thoroughness in Chekiang and Southern Kiangsu, the richest parts of China, where there had been much resort to illegal practices which had served to make the rich richer and the poor poorer. Nevertheless the material obtained from these two remarkable projects did provide some basis for the extremely complex fiscal structure of the period.

The Hung-wu emperor also set up a new grass-roots organization to try to secure adequate machinery for future registrations of the population, for collecting taxes, and for distributing the burden of labour services fairly. His method was to divide the population into 'communities' of 110 families. Heads of the ten most prosperous households were appointed community chiefs, and it was their task to serve a year each in turn to represent the community in its dealings with the local government officials. Similarly the hundred households which did not provide a community chief were divided into groups of ten, each of which in turn had the responsibility throughout a whole year for supplying the labour services required from the community, such as work on roads, waterways, irrigation systems and public buildings, or employment in various humble capacities (as lictors, couriers, bearers, etc.) for the local government and local military authorities. Communities were also expected to manage their own affairs by settling disputes among themselves and to preserve good order by acting as guarantors of the good conduct of all their members. Apart from serving in this way as self-policing organizations and a means of preserving law and order without expense to the government, they were also a useful instrument for the dissemination of the conventional morality. Community assemblies were held every month, and all the members recited an oath that they would observe propriety, maintain the law, care for the needy and assist one another in the expense of weddings and funerals; and the community was expected to maintain a school, a religious altar and a granary for charitable purposes. So this was a system of local self-government which at the same time gave the imperial authorities a powerful means of mass control. For the sake of security it was clearly better that the people should be organized for community purposes within the state machine rather than that they should seek to organize themselves in the kind of secret societies which the Hung-wu emperor had suppressed.

This poor peasant's son had come far. When he was in his teens famine, epidemics and family bereavements had meant appalling privations, and his only means of survival had been to become a Buddhist novice. Later he had led a group of rebels from the same humble origins as himself and eventually his political skill had enabled him to broaden the basis of his revolution and win the support of many talented officials, scholars, landlords and generals and finally enjoy for thirty years the great prestige of being Son of Heaven. Dynastic founders were always far freer to introduce new ideas than their successors, whose own conduct was bound to be guided by the precedent set by the revered Grand Progenitor, so his decisions and his style of government profoundly influenced the course of the Ming Dynasty. His achievement was not unblemished, for the harsh experiences of his youth had left their mark and made him suspicious, intolerant and vindictive, so that many men of ability were too scared to serve at his court. The weight of Yüan precedent and his own mistrust of others meant that he was more autocratic, particularly after 1380, than fits the Confucian ideal. But he made the country secure by his skill in military organization, and prosperous since his peasant virtue of frugality allied itself to the Confucian abhorrence of luxury. He had none of the love of extravagance which marred the reigns of some emperors, and publicly regretted the old wasteful practice of the burial of valuable objects with the dead. He also rigorously insisted that eunuchs should be few and well controlled so that they did not interfere in government. He was careful in his choice of ministers and his very harshness also ensured probity in public affairs. Although he had made some big mistakes, he had laid the foundations for a strong and prosperous dynasty.

2

Nevertheless, at his death in 1398, the Hung-wu emperor left a legacy of trouble for the dynasty by not making sensible provision for the succession. On the death of his eldest son in 1392, instead of picking out one of his numerous other sons to be crown prince, he chose a son of his recently deceased heir. This was a very dangerous policy, especially as the imperial princes, who had been given military power in the interest of state security, had taken every opportunity to increase their armed strength in defiance of imperial regulations. The ageing emperor had professed to his grandson his intention of bequeathing him the empire free of the danger of internal strife, and the sceptical and anxious prince was also persuaded by his chief adviser that the central government forces would be strong enough to contain any threat of rebellion from his uncles. When the old sovereign passed away after a short illness, his dying proclamation forbade his sons to come to the capital for his funeral, but the Prince of Yen, one of the most powerful of the imperial princes, believed that this was a forgery concocted by the new emperor's advisers. He accordingly proceeded towards Nanking until halted by an order from his recently enthroned nephew, backed with the persuasive presence of an army. The Prince of Yen deeply resented this action, although it was in fact mandatory that the princes should mourn the emperor's death in their own principalities and remain guarding the frontiers at a time when a new emperor was establishing himself on the throne.

The new emperor's reign-title, Chien-wen ('Establishing Culture'), in contrast with his predecessor's 'Boundless Valour', gave promise that his epoch would be more renowned for civil than for military virtues. The Chien-wen emperor was indeed a studious young man, in whom the scholar-bureaucrats reposed hopes for a more liberal administration in which they could play a more secure part. His main ambition seems to have been to reconstitute the idealized system of government described in the ancient work *Chou Ritual*, but he also showed early evidence of a more practical skill in government. He gave notice of his intention to keep eunuchs firmly in their place by issuing orders that they should be punished by local officials for the slightest misdemeanour committed while fulfilling missions outside the capital. He also set about the very difficult task of reducing his uncles' power. Several of them were soon deprived of their titles and privileges, and in the spring of 1399 two ministers were sent out with a staff to spy on the remaining princes with the intention of bringing charges against them. This policy soon goaded the Prince of Yen into revolt. The fourth son of the Hung-wu emperor, he had been entrusted with special responsibilities by his father in the defence of the northern frontier and must have seemed the natural successor after the death of the sovereign's eldest son. An energetic and experienced general now nearing forty, it was inevitable that he did not sit back and let himself be dispossessed of everything by this callow youth of twenty-one. During the rebellion the Prince of Yen made much use of eunuchs, who were only too eager to escape from the firm control of the new emperor and place at their new master's disposal intelligence on conditions at the capital to help him in his campaign, hoping that they would fare better under the intending usurper than under his two predecessors. Their expectations were fulfilled, and the cancer of eunuch influence was soon at work again on the body politic.

The rebellion was finally successful in 1402. Though a corpse, supposedly that of the Chien-wen emperor, was taken from the ruins of the burnt palace and buried, there were persistent rumours that he had escaped, perhaps disguised as a Buddhist monk, and he was sought long afterwards by the Prince of Yen, who now came to the throne, adopting the reign-title of Yung-lo ('Eternal Contentment').

Not content with stealing the throne from his nephew, the new emperor ushered in the period of Eternal Contentment by wreaking a terrible punishment on the young man's chief supporters, wiping out whole clans in the process. In the case of his principal adviser, not only was the whole clan obliterated, but also many of his pupils, so that in all 870 people are said to have perished because of their adherence to him; and there were many other cases of officials loyal to the Chien-wen régime who were wiped out together with their whole clans, the majority of them coming from Chekiang and Kiangsi. At the same time the Yung-lo emperor naturally took steps to ensure that no other princely rebel would succeed as he had done, and with the powerful and victorious army he had got together he was in a strong position to enforce his will. In future the only military forces permitted to the imperial princes was to be a small personal bodyguard, and they were not to be allowed to play any part in government. Imperial approval would be necessary before they could leave their provincial residences or get married; and permission would not be granted for unions with women of imperial descent. The Yung-lo emperor was successful in weakening the imperial princes: only two princely rebellions took place later in the dynasty, and neither was a serious threat to the throne.

The major political changes which took place during the Yung-lo period were rather predictable in view of what had happened under the Ming founder. The abolition of the Secretariat in 1380 left a gap which was bound to be filled sooner or later. The Hung-wu emperor had soon found himself in need of a body of assistants and advisers, and in 1382 he had already expanded the Hanlin Academy, so that it could provide the kind of high-grade secretarial assistance he needed. Under the Yung-lo emperor these grand secretaries from the Hanlin Academy began to play an increasingly positive role in government. They were already being informally described as the Grand Secretariat (*nei-ko*), although the existence of this body was not formally acknowledged until the middle of the sixteenth century. The position of these grand secretaries was to become even stronger in the reign of the Yung-lo emperor's short-lived successor, when they were given nominal posts as high-ranking officials and also loaded with grandiose traditional titles, their Hanlin posts now being treated merely as concurrent appointments. But although they now took precedence over other members of the bureaucracy, they were not trusted by the civil service as a whole because, instead of having enjoyed the wide experience of other senior civil servants, their career had been confined to the Hanlin Academy. For the same reason they came to be regarded as creatures of the emperor and instruments of his autocratic power rather than as representatives and spokesmen of the bureaucracy.

There was a similar reaction against the Ming founder's fragmentation of local government authority, which was bound to give way to a more unified control of provincial affairs. The work of the three autonomous agencies responsible for provincial government obviously needed to be co-ordinated, and for this purpose the Yung-lo emperor started a practice of sending metropolitan dignitaries out to tour and inspect various parts of the country: these were the fore-runners of resident co-ordinating officials, who in turn foreshadowed the institution of the provincial governors who, in the Ch'ing Dynasty, administered provinces which enjoyed a great deal of independence.

The Yung-lo emperor also departed from his father's style of government by giving increasing scope to eunuchs. These now began to throng the palace, staffing agencies concerned with all kinds of domestic matters which had previously been in the hands of the palace women, who now only retained control of the Bureau of Apparel. Apart from the task of servicing the palace, more important and more sinister responsibilities also came into their hands. They were even given charge of the palace treasury, and in 1420 a eunuch agency known as the Eastern Depot was established as a kind of secret service headquarters, which was later to develop into an organ of terrorism. The most powerful eunuch was the head of the directorate of ceremonial, and the occupant of this post normally also controlled the Eastern Depot at the same time.

Eunuchs were also given important responsibilities outside the capital during the Yung-lo period. The most famous of these was the admiral Cheng Ho, who led a number of voyages as far afield as the East Indies, Southern India, the Persian Gulf, the Red Sea and the coast of East Africa as far south as Kenya. These voyages were undertaken in large 'treasure-ships' which carried a complement of about 500 men, and in the first voyage, undertaken in 1403, there were as many as sixty-two of these ships. These fleets, using Malacca, whose sultanate was established under the aegis of Chinese naval power, as an overseas base, were accompanied by diplomatic missions. They served to demonstrate China's wealth and strength throughout the known world, and assured her position as the greatest power in the East. Political protection and material rewards were vouchsafed to those states which accepted suzerainty, and representatives of more than thirty realms, including seven kings, came bearing tribute to the Ming emperor during this period, while the king of Ceylon and two Sumatran chieftains who had been so rash as to defy the Ming power were captured and brought as prisoners to China.

It has been suggested that one reason for embarking on this unique series of voyages was that the threat of attack by Tamerlane made China anxious to win goodwill on her southern flank so that she could concentrate on the defence of her north-western frontier. But this great conqueror, who had already achieved victories in eastern Europe and western Asia in pursuit of his ambition to restore the Mongol empire to its former glories, died in 1405 on the eve of an assault on China; so considerations of defence against this new scourge could not have been responsible for the continuance of the series of voyages, nor could they explain why the fleets went so far afield. The reason for the expeditions must simply be the natural desire of a vigorous emperor, whose career had been largely occupied with warfare, to assert the greatness of China at this early stage in the dynasty and to pursue glory by the expansion of Chinese frontiers and interests. After all it must have seemed that what the Mongols had achieved by martial vigour unallied to the natural superiority of the Chinese would be nothing to what the Chinese could achieve if they added military zeal and adventurousness to their cultural appeal.

Parallel with these maritime expeditions were overland missions to distant Central Asian cities, the official object of which was the emperor's desire that 'none of the ten thousand countries in distant lands should not be his subject'. Notable among these contacts were those with Tamerlane and his son and successor, Shahrukh Bahadur, initiated when the Hung-wu emperor had sent a diplomatic mission to Tamerlane. As usual, the trade stimulated by these missions was officially treated by the Chinese as tribute from vassal states. But Yung-lo's attempts to patronize Shahrukh Bahadur met with a haughty response, and eventually he was constrained to address him as an equal. But although this was a blow to the self-esteem of the Son of Heaven, which showed a striking disparity between the myth and the reality, there was no need to record the true state of affairs in official documents. In the official Ming view these proud independent sovereigns of Central Asia would continue to be regarded as vassals and tributaries of the Chinese.

The Yung-lo emperor was also well aware of the material benefits of overseas trade with the tributary states. Many of the imported goods, such as horses, copper, timber, hides, drugs, spices, gold, silver and rice were much needed by China and to some extent she could get away with sending in return goods which were prized more for reasons of prestige than for their intrinsic value, although silk, ceramics and tea were, as always, much in demand in the overseas countries. The Yung-lo emperor sent forty-eight missions to South-east Asia during a period of twenty-two years. The great majority were under the supervision of his trusted eunuchs, which emphasized the personal nature of this relationship between sovereigns far more clearly than if the embassies had been headed by bureaucrats.

The Ming navy was also in action against Japanese freebooters and played an important part in the conquest of Annam, where Chinese intervention, originally the result of provocative behaviour on the part of the Annamese, led to the country being organized as a province of the Middle Kingdom from 1407 to

1428. A further sign of the growth of Chinese influence in the south was the creation for the first time of the province of Kweichow in 1413. By this time the Chinese had more energy for activities in the south since the northern frontier seemed relatively secure. The situation had become more stable, with the territory north of the Great Wall now being largely left to the Mongols while the Chinese firmly occupied the land to the south of the Wall, and the Yung-lo emperor put much effort into con-solidating this defensive line. The Mongols were still weakened by internal troubles, and many came over to the Chinese in 1409 because they refused to accept the newly elected Great Khan. There were repeated small-scale clashes on the frontier, but the only incident which caused the Chinese serious loss took place in 1409 when a whole Chinese army was lured into a trap and destroyed. The Yung-lo emperor energetically pursued his father's policies for supplying and feeding the army, and he also estab-lished a special government department for horse-breeding so that the country should not be dependent on the import of horses from the northern grasslands for military purposes.

The importance attached to the security of the northern frontier was also reflected in the change of capital city which took place during the Yung-lo period. Right at the beginning of his reign the emperor had elevated Peking, which happened to be the city on which his own principality was based, to the status of auxiliary capital; and in 1421 he made it the chief city of the empire, relegating Nanking to the position of auxiliary capital. The Yung-lo emperor did not inherit his father's frugality. On the contrary he had a love of grandeur. One of his main concerns was to expand and improve the new city laid out by Khubilai at Peking and make it fit to be the capital of a great empire, and it was during his reign that the Forbidden City as we know it today began to take shape. The imposing ceremonial buildings with their yellow-tiled roofs and vermilion colonnades, each raised upon its own marble terrace, must have struck awe into the hearts of the many foreign visitors who came to Peking at this time as members of tribute missions.

After Peking had been elevated to the status of auxiliary capital, the reopening of the Grand Canal route, which had fallen into disuse, was obviously a matter of priority, and work on this was completed in the first few years of the Yung-lo period. But improvement in the inland waterway system meant, as we have seen before, a decline in the importance of the sea-route for grain transportation. Indeed it was not long before this route came to be abandoned, with the result that government need for big sea-going ships suffered a decline which created a depression in the shipbuilding industry.

The Yung-lo emperor also went down in history as a patron of learning, but in this connection, as in the building of Peking, he favoured the grandiose scheme : his name is especially associated with the enormous encyclopaedic work known as the *Yung-lo Ta-tien*, which was compiled in the years 1403–7 and contained over eleven thousand manuscript volumes. The work provided harmless employment for over two thousand scholars and doubtless some reputation for scholarly patronage at a time when the emperor needed to woo the intellectuals to cause them to forget their enthusiasm for his predecessor. Of this enormous compendium of human knowledge, of which only three copies were ever made, only about 370 volumes are now known to exist, although other individual items which were separately printed at a later date have also survived. This big co-operative effort was also a sign of the expansion of learning since the titans of the Sung Dynasty, such as Ou-yang Hsiu and Chu Hsi, had produced their great individual works. The development of printing was making individual mastery of a wide range of knowledge more difficult. By this time as many as a third of the works in the imperial palace library were printed.

The end of the Yung-lo reign was marked by signs of decline. Even the run of naval successes came to an end when a Ming fleet was defeated at the mouth of the Red River in the Gulf of Tonkin in 1420. The economic situation deteriorated. The transfer of the capital to Peking and the building of palaces and public works had proved very expensive, and the cost of warfare in the north became increasingly high, especially when the emperor, ignoring the warnings of his ministers, personally conducted a series of campaigns against the Mongols. The graft and profiteering almost inseparable from great public enterprises was also growing and one contemporary maintained that political corruption set in during the last year of the Yung-lo period, when the emperor was either ill or absent from the capital.

Whatever their failings, at least during the reigns of the Hung-wu and Yung-lo emperors China was given strong and vigorous rule by men in their mature forties and fifties. On the death of the latter another mature and experienced man in his forties came to the throne to inaugurate the period of Boundless Splendour (Hung-hsi). One advantage of the more autocratic rule of the early Ming was that the heir was not kept secluded in the imperial palace, but was allowed to acquire experience of empire; so, although the Yung-lo emperor had found it politic to deprive the other imperial princes of influence, his eldest son and destined successor had had a long training for his future role going back to the days when he had served as a military commander during his father's bid for the throne. More recently he had often served as regent when his father had been campaigning against the Mongols. Much was hoped of his rule and, although he inherited a quick temper from his father and grandfather, he had obtained a reputation for benevolence and for concern for the public interest which caused the Ming official history to liken him to model emperors of antiquity.

If he had survived to give his mature years to the service of the state and had fulfilled the promise of his earlier life, it is possible that the dynasty's fortunes might have ridden high for longer, but unfortunately he died within a year, to be succeeded by his eldest son, whose reign-period was called Hsüan-te ('Radiant Virtue'). He also was considered to be of great promise and had had early experience of responsibility, having served his father as imperial deputy at Nanking. He shared his father's concern for the welfare of the people. He acquired a reputation for lenience and mercy, and for granting pardons and reductions in penalties and for the introduction of a system of redeeming crimes by making payments of grain. His concern for the people was also evidenced by his frequent tours of the countryside to inspect conditions for himself, following the regular practice of the sage emperors of antiquity. On one of his inspection tours of the northern frontier he is said to have led a force of picked troops to inflict a crushing defeat on some Mongol tribesmen who had been raiding nearby. This was also the period of the 'three Yangs', exemplary officials in the best Confucian tradition and elder statesmen of unrivalled prestige who were entrusted with much responsibility by the Hsüan-te emperor, so that the 'three Yangs' in later times became a byword for good ministers.

Nevertheless, although this was in some respects a brief interlude of government in accordance with Confucian ideals, we must not ignore the fact that this was the period in which the tide of Ming power began to ebb. After a series of defeats at the hands of a local chieftain the Chinese had to relinquish their uneasy hold on Annam in 1428. The final overwhelming defeat made it easy for one of the three Yangs to mouth Confucian platitudes about the superior man not fighting with the inferior man and to laud the retreat as a sign of great virtue. Annam was never again made part of the Ming empire, and it was obviously wise to abandon it, especially as Chinese forces were kept constantly on the alert, both in the south-western provinces of Kwangsi, Kweichow and Szechwan, where there were repeated aboriginal uprisings, and on the northern frontier, where the Oirats were becoming an increasing danger because they were gaining dominance over other Mongol tribes. Moreover, at this time there seems to have been a sharp decline in the morale and efficiency of the army. So many men deserted that in 1428 it became necessary for the government to order a fresh registration of hereditary army families. The men deserted in large numbers because they were exploited by their officers, who used them as domestic servants or manual workers, or appropriated army rations and supplies so that the soldiers could not live without taking on part-time jobs. At the same time the status of the military occupation, which had carried some prestige because of the Mongol influence, steadily declined, especially because of the practice of putting convicts into the army. Steps were taken to try to remedy the military weakness, particularly after the Annam fiasco, and censors were sent off on 'troop-purifying' commissions. On the northern frontier, starting in 1432, two censors were regularly commissioned to serve one-year terms as inspectors of the frontier passes, and they were required to report on the general state of the defences in this area. But the measures taken seemed unable to check the general deterioration. Discipline was not improved by the fact that the Hsüan-te emperor was notoriously lenient towards military men because they were often illiterate and unversed in Confucian niceties and therefore not so morally responsible for their misdemeanours as their civilian counterparts.

The navy too was in decline. The Hung-hsi emperor had put a stop to Cheng Ho's expeditions when he came to the throne and, although another treasure ship voyage was undertaken in 1431–3, this was the last. It has been suggested that they were abandoned because they were too costly to mount or because the civil service regarded them as trivial attempts by the eunuchs to pander to the emperor's whims by bringing back rare or precious objects like giraffes for the imperial zoo; but it is clear that these expeditions had had the far more serious object of profitable trade and political prestige, and that one powerful reason why they were dropped was that the decline in Ming standing after the retreat from Annam meant that it would now be necessary to provide goods of real value instead of unloading prestige commodities on overawed vassals. There was also a loss of confidence in the Ming currency both at home and abroad, and it became impossible to compel foreign envoys to sell goods at arbitrarily low prices. Consequently foreign trade no longer proved so profitable as to justify these great expeditions. At the same time the government was proving unable to enforce its ban on private trade overseas, so this gradually supplanted the official tributary trade. It seems likely, therefore, that powerful private interests helped to influence official circles and make sure that there was no resumption of the naval expeditions. After this time the Ming court gradually gave up its active international role.

At the same time there was a general decline in the morale of naval personnel, which may be attributed mainly to the abandonment of the grain transport fleet after the reopening of the Grand Canal. Many men from this fleet and from the coastal patrols which had vigorously pursued the Japanese pirates earlier in the dynasty were now transferred to work on the Canal, and were reduced in status from fighting men to labourers. Shipbuilding also consequently suffered a decline as compared with the Hung-wu and Yung-lo periods, when huge fleets had been built and the shipwrights had been well paid and well treated.

Under the moderate rule of the Hsüan-te emperor, who relied heavily on such advisers as the three Yangs, the Grand Secretariat began to play a full part in the administration of the state, although it was still not formally recognized. Similarly there was a further move towards centralization in the provinces when the metropolitan dignitaries sent out to perform co-ordinating functions began to be given long-term responsibilities in provinces or places of special strategic importance. When the area of their jurisdiction covered a whole province, these Grand Co-ordinators in effect fulfilled the function of provincial governors; and such appointments were made for most of the provinces as well as for many vital strategic areas along the northern frontier. Nevertheless these officials were theoretically still individual delegates from the central government and were merely considered to be serving in an acting capacity in their roles as Grand Co-ordinators.

In spite of the high reputation of the administration at this time, it is clear that the power of the eunuchs was steadily growing as a result of the influence they had won during the Yung-lo period. The admiral, Cheng Ho, retained the great prestige he had enjoyed under that emperor, and now it became a commonplace for eunuchs to hold high military positions, as well as to serve on special assignments of all kinds. They were not restricted to commissions which would spring naturally from their service roles within the palace, such as the requisitioning of supplies, but also acted as envoys to foreign states following the precedent established in the Yung-lo period. The emperor directly contravened the Ming founder's charge that eunuchs should be kept illiterate, by establishing a school at which young eunuchs could learn to read and write, thus clearing the way for a further strengthening of the eunuch position.

At the outset of his reign the Hsüan-te emperor had been threatened by an uprising led by an uncle, but instead of the harsh measures the Yung-lo emperor had employed to suppress opposition at the beginning of his reign, the rebellious uncle was subjected to a rather lenient house arrest at the capital for his misdemeanour. The ruthlessness of the Yung-lo emperor had made it possible for the Hsüan-te emperor to govern mildly; and the young man, who was a considerable painter and a person of sensitive disposition, lacked the vigour and aggressiveness which his job required.

3

The Hsüan-te emperor's death early in 1435, while still in his thirties, meant that the throne passed to his eldest son, a boy of only seven, whose reign period was entitled Cheng-t'ung ('Correct Government'). The situation was ready-made for the rise to power of Wang Chen, the first of the notorious Ming eunuch dictators. For the next decade-and-a-half the state's affairs deteriorated alarmingly. At the beginning of the reign there was severe retrenchment in the production of armaments, and all naval units were seriously reduced in size. Yet at the same time huge sums of money were appropriated for the construction of the deceased emperor's mausoleum, and large resources were also being employed for the maintenance of the imperial princes, who now no longer served any useful purpose to the state.

Although the government's apparatus for army inspection was improved, there was no improvement in army morale, but ever larger funds from the national treasury had to be expended on it. Moreover, among the ordinary population the community system introduced by the Ming founder was breaking down and there was much oppression of the common people by the gentry, who could easily revert to their old habit of exploitation now that there was no longer a strong central government in power. The misery of the people began to show itself in rebellion and banditry, the worst outbreaks taking place in Chekiang and Fukien in 1448 at a time when the country was facing the threat of invasion from the Oirats in the north and was also involved in warfare on the Yünnan borders. In the same year the Yellow River overflowed its banks and millions were rendered homeless. Taxes constantly rose, but so did the skill of the powerful families at evading them, and so the burden fell more and more upon the ordinary people.

And in the following year there was an even more serious crisis.

The Mongol Great Khans were still regarding themselves as successors of the Yüan Dynasty and using Chinese reign-titles, but at this time, owing to the rise of the Oirats, the nominal Great Khan had little power, and the Oirat chieftain Esen-tayisi was the most powerful figure north of the frontier. For some years before this time the Oirats had pressed the Ming to open up markets on the frontier, where they could sell their horses to the Chinese. The Ming had agreed to do this in 1438, but had refused to sell weapons, copper or iron to the Mongols. In 1449, provoked by the low prices which were being offered for their horses, the Oirats under the leadership of Esen launched a major invasion across the frontier and soon reached the vicinity of Peking, and even succeeded in capturing the Cheng-t'ung emperor, who had foolishly taken the field on the advice of Wang Chen. The Oirats roamed freely over North China with their captive, plundering as they went, and Esen-tayisi made himself Great Khan and styled himself the Great Khan T'ien-sheng of the Great Yüan, T'ien-sheng meaning Heavenly and Holy. This humiliation at least meant the end of the powerful eunuch Wang Chen, who had been so foolish as to take the young emperor, ignorant of the world and totally unskilled in the military arts, with him on this campaign; and now the chief power passed into the hands of Yü Ch'ien, the Minister of War, who had succeeded in beating off a Mongol attack on the capital. The succession, in other hands, might have gone to the captured emperor's baby son, to usher in another period in which an infant ruler was used by powerful forces behind the scenes, but General Yü placed the previous emperor's brother on the throne. The Mongols had hoped to get a large ransom for the return of the Cheng-t'ung emperor, but decided in the end that there was more to be gained through embarrassing the Chinese by returning this unfortunate man free of charge. But his younger brother continued to reign for another seven years until he fell ill and was replaced in a coup d'état by the former emperor.

For the next decade after this humiliating defeat by the Mongols intermittent fighting went on all along the Great Wall, placing a heavy strain on the Chinese, whose morale had been deeply affected by the events of 1449. The Oirat invasion had severely damaged the already creaking machinery for supplying the huge number of soldiers in this area. The system of military agricultural colonies had long since ceased to work effectively because of the corruption in its administration and the dissatisfaction and desertion of the soldiers. The system of merchant colonization was also in a decline which was speeded up by the disruption caused by the Mongol invasions. The emphasis therefore shifted back to the salt exchange system, but the interest of the merchants in this arrangement also declined because the government, deprived of other means of supplying the troops with grain, insisted on increasing the amount of grain to be paid in return for salt certificates, which made it very difficult for the merchants to net a profit. Moreover, to make good the severe shortage of food, during the critical period after the Mongol invasions both military personnel and civil officials had been allowed to take part in the salt exchange system, so that the long-term advantage of the tightly organized government monopoly system, in which only a few merchants were allowed to handle the salt, had been sacrificed to meet a temporary crisis. At the same time there was an increase in the traffic in 'private salt', which undercut the official government monopoly prices, and so further undermined the system.

Another emergency measure taken by the government at this time was the award of honours to commoners who contributed grain or money for famine relief or defence purposes. Such people were called 'philanthropic commoners' and were entitled to exemption from corvée labour and to the privilege of wearing a minor official's cap and dress. Imperial Academy studentships were also awarded for such services. In earlier periods the state had sold monk certificates in times of crisis, but this was clearly a more prestigious type of reward for services to the state.

The decline from the enterprising and expansive days of the Yung-lo period was quite remarkable, and it seems clear that a really strong and united power north of the frontier at this time could have completed the conquest of North China. But the Mongols had been seriously weakened by the fact that many of their own people had stayed behind in China after the fall of the

Yüan. China also continued to be a magnet to them in difficult times and a refuge from oppression in their own country, and in 1457 famine in Northern Mongolia drove many hundreds of its people to take refuge in Ming territory. Conditions among the Mongol tribes continued to be unsettled for the next few decades, so that they posed no powerful threat to the Chinese, although there were occasional invasions whose seriousness cannot be accurately gauged because of the lack of truthful reports to the central government. Although the Oirats had come to terms with the Chinese and a large mission had been feasted in Peking and given lavish gifts and allowed to sell horses, relations were strained and there was no resumption of regular tribute missions and horse-markets.

The decline in power and prestige suffered by the Ming within the space of a single generation serves to underline once again how precarious was the hold of imperial Chinese governments over their vast territories in an age of primitive communications. The founder emperor of a dynasty, whose success marked him out as a man of superior talent and energies and whose position was strengthened by the prestige of having received the Mandate of Heaven, could impose firm government and hand over a position of strength to his immediate successor. But the machinery of power required very skilful handling. The emperor had to ensure that there were strong armies on the frontiers without allowing any military leader to secure enough support to become a menace to the centre. Failure to achieve this had been the ruin of the T'ang, and the Ming founder also made a big mistake by giving military power to the imperial princes, although it was a generation before his error bore fruit in the uprising of the Prince of Yen. He had to ensure that there was a strong and efficient navy to protect the coasts from pirates, to transport grain, and to secure the benefits of overseas trade. But here the restoration of peace and the consequent reopening of the Grand Canal itself sowed the seed of naval decline, which now entered its final phase since the humiliating defeats which had been suffered on the northern frontier meant that all available resources were concentrated on preventing their recurrence. On the frontier one defeat, with the damage it caused to both morale and prestige, could undo the work of countless victories; and once a local leader had been able to organize determined and spirited resistance, as happened in Annam, there was no alternative for the Chinese but to extricate themselves as gracefully as possible. Despite the ingenious methods which were devised to govern this vast country, the machinery could easily be thrown out of gear by disasters, either natural or man-made, just as the ordinary peasant's life was only a short step from famine, starvation and beggary.

As we have noticed in the case of other dynasties there was an inbuilt tendency for the economy to get into difficulties because the pauperization of the peasants led to a decline in the number of tax-payers. But the matter was made more serious if the state monetary policy was also a failure. Unfortunately the Ming governments, despite the experience gained under the Yüan, handled this matter very badly. Paper money was re-introduced in 1374 and people were forbidden to use gold or silver as media of exchange. Some copper cash were minted, but not in sufficient numbers because of the shortage of the metal, so they were soon driven off the market because they were of real value, whereas the paper notes were issued in increasing numbers and were inconvertible, so that they rapidly declined in value. Although all kinds of devices were used to try to maintain the exchange value of notes, they failed completely, and most business was being conducted in silver in spite of the fact that this was illegal. The officials suffered because, although under the Hung-wu emperor their salaries were generally paid in rice, under the Yung-lo emperor only the nobility were paid entirely in rice and officials were paid partly in rice and partly in paper money. Thereafter the proportion of paper money in the salary increased, while the value of the notes also declined, so that this deterioration in the real value of their salaries inevitably had an adverse effect on the honesty of the bureaucracy. Although the manufacture of paper money stopped in 1450, it was still in circulation over a hundred years later. But in the late Ming much silver poured into the country as a result of foreign trade and throughout the seventeenth and eighteenth centuries paper money never recovered its former importance, silver ingots and copper cash serving as the main forms of currency during this period.

When the emperor died in 1464 he was still only in his thirties, and his eldest son, a boy of seventeen, came to the throne with the reign-title Ch'eng-hua ('Complete Transformation'). Unfortunately he was not equipped to give the dramatic new impetus that the dynasty now needed. Afflicted by an embarrassing stammer, he hated to make public appearances and avoided his officials as much as possible. As had happened in his father's childhood, the real power fell into the hands of a eunuch dictator, and the country had to suffer further disruption of normal processes of government. The eunuchs' dominance brought about a further decline in the military services because they were able to take control of those units which were stationed at the metropolis, which were undoubtedly exploited even more ruthlessly than were the frontier armies at the hands of their generals and officers.

There continued to be little pressure on the frontiers to keep the armed forces in good trim. Because of their internal troubles the Mongol threat was not serious, and the Japanese also were concerned with their own civil wars, so that there were no raids on the coast for a period of fifty years from 1466. This meant a further deterioration in naval efficiency : the men were now almost entirely concerned with the building and repair of ships, payment was constantly in arrears, and they were forced to accept a new arrangement whereby they were renumerated for only six months in the year when they were actually on duty. The status of the hereditary officer class also continued to decline. In the 1430s military academies had been introduced, but since they offered a watered-down version of civilian education, this would not have done very much to boost their self-esteem. In 1478 a system of military examinations parallel with the civil examinations was introduced to serve as an additional means of officer recruitment. This arrangement remained in force throughout the Ming and Ch'ing Dynasties, but it cannot have made very much difference to the quality of the officers since the 'examinations' were merely tests in practical subjects like shooting and riding.

Such tests did, however, ensure that prospective officers kept up their military skills and did provide opportunities in the army for younger sons of military officers who would not have had the opportunity to inherit their fathers' ranks. The examinees probably came almost entirely from such families.

The civil examinations became increasingly stereotyped. The sheer memorization of the prescribed Neo-Confucian commentaries on the Classics had had a profoundly dulling effect on the intellectual life of the country, and matters became worse in the Ch'eng-hua period, when the notorious 'eight-legged' essays became the method by which examination questions were to be answered. These essays were so called because they were rigidly divided into eight sections, corresponding to various stages in the exposition of the theme, which would be a tag from one or other of the Confucian Classics. The style and even the number of characters in the essay was rigidly controlled. This type of essay later became a byword for formalism and sterility, and was satirized and castigated by writers who regarded it as even more harmful for Chinese intellectual history than the reviled burning of the books by the despotic first emperor of the Ch'in Dynasty in antiquity.

Meanwhile the inevitable process of social change had eroded the Ming founder's attempt at forcing people to pursue their hereditary occupations. It was recognized that people should be freer to change their status. Thus at the beginning of the dynasty there had been two main categories of artisan families: some were required to live permanently at the capital to be available for government work, and others were required to report at the capital for a limited period, often as rarely as once in four or five years, on the basis of one month out of every twelve. The full-time government artisans numbered about twelve thousand at the beginning of the dynasty, and the part-time ones totalled about twenty times as many. The system gradually broke down because artisan families did not necessarily keep up their traditional skills and did their best to evade their responsibilities, while at the capital more and more construction work was being done by naval and military personnel. Moreover the government had long recognized the wisdom of permitting ambitious and talented people from the hereditary crafts and professions to compete for the civil service. It was recognized, too, that it would be sensible to permit part-time artisans who had to come from great distances to make a money payment in lieu of service; so from 1485 onwards it became possible for artisans in remote provinces to commute in this way if they wished.

Like his father the Ch'eng-hua emperor was dead before his fortieth birthday. He was succeeded in 1488 by his third son who, like the Ch'eng-hua emperor, was only seventeen at the time of his accession. There, however, the resemblance ends, for the new emperor, reigning under the title Hung-chih ('Mighty Government'), acquired a reputation for being a model ruler of benevolent disposition who paid proper regard to the advice of his officials, being the only Ming ruler apart from the Hsüan-te emperor and his very short-lived predecessor who enjoyed such a reputation. But again the pattern repeated itself. The emperor died in his thirties and was succeeded in 1506 by his son, whose reign-title was Cheng-te ('Upright Virtue'). The new emperor this time was only thirteen at his father's death. An adventurous spirit, he would wander about the capital in disguise in search of thrills with a group of sycophantic companions. A spirited young man might well react thus to the cloistered life of the palace, but he went too far when, acquiring a taste for military adventures, he would stage campaigns simply to give himself the pleasure of leading troops in the field, and would then mark his purely imaginary victories by heaping upon himself increasingly grandiose military titles. Court officials who protested at his conduct were flogged or otherwise humiliated.

With such a young man on the throne a further spell of eunuch domination was inevitable: this time the new eunuch dictator, Liu Chin, succeeded in getting rid of rival cliques and in filling the highest posts in the state with his own supporters. He encouraged the emperor to devote himself to his pleasures while he himself went about the actual business of government. He even had the effrontery to extract a special tax for his own benefit, and thus amassed an enormous fortune. Fortunately for the state his downfall came about in 1510, but the young emperor's extravagance imposed a further strain on the state's resources.

Large sums of money were levied as extra taxes for palace construction, for which soldiers stationed in the capital were increasingly roped in as unskilled labourers. During this period there was an abortive revolt under the leadership of one of the imperial princes, and this was the only occasion between 1425 and the end of the Ming when an imperial prince rose against the state.

The general who was responsible for crushing this rebellion and who also had charge of important pacification campaigns in the south-west was Wang Yang-ming, who was not only the most prominent military leader of the age, but also has the reputation of being the outstanding thinker of the Ming period. Wang was a strong critic of Chu Hsi, and thus let some daylight into the intellectual world of early sixteenth-century China at a time when it was much needed. A man of action himself, he reacted against Chu Hsi's vast accumulation of knowledge, and envisaged morality in action as the Confucian ideal. He steered the intellectual history of his time on a less contemplative course with his famous theory of the unity of knowledge and action ('Knowledge is the beginning of action and action is the completion of knowledge'). His belief in man's instinctive moral sense was based on Mencius' famous doctrine of the goodness of human nature, and he sought a return to the practical wisdom of the ancient sages. His influence throughout the rest of the dynasty was extremely powerful.

4

At the same time as Wang Yang-ming was trying to change the intellectual climate of his age, there appeared off the coasts of China visitors from a continent which in course of time would have a profoundly greater impact on the minds of the Chinese. The Portuguese pioneers in India had heard of the Chinese and had also taken back to Lisbon samples of the porcelains and silks they produced, which had stimulated King Manoel I to seek further information about them. After the Portuguese capture of Malacca in 1511, the routes to South China were explored and the advantages of trade with that country began to be seriously considered. They obtained help and advice from Chinese merchants and sailors who were in Malacca against the law of the Chinese state which forbade people to go overseas, and as early as 1514 Alvarez, the first recorded Portuguese visitor to the Middle Kingdom, was already dealing in more lowly commodities than silk and porcelain, such as tung-oil. The first official Portuguese embassy to China reached Canton from Malacca in 1517, but it was not till 1520 that the envoy, Pires, was allowed to proceed to Peking, a delay which must have been extremely frustrating to people who were not conversant with the Peking view that it was a high privilege to be permitted to enter into a tributary relationship with the Chinese. When Pires eventually arrived in Peking, he found that the emperor had travelled south on a tour of inspection. Meanwhile unfavourable reports of the behaviour of foreign sailors and traders along the south coast had reached Peking, and when the emperor died in May 1521, a few months after his return to the capital, he still had not accorded Pires the privilege of an audience, so the unfortunate envoy was packed off back to Canton. Continued allegations of Portuguese crimes, such as carrying children off into slavery, caused the Chinese to ban trade with the Europeans; and soon Pires and his staff were thrown into prison in Canton, where they were to spend the remainder of their lives. Letters smuggled out by two of the prisoners in 1524 were the first detailed eyewitness accounts of life in China to reach Europe as a result of the age of seaborne expansion and discovery. In spite of the Chinese ban clandestine trade continued, based on islands off the coast of Kwangtung, Fukien and Chekiang. The imperial navy was now so run down that it was no longer capable of checking this activity, which was, in any case, carried on with the connivance of the local officials.

The premature death of yet another ruler, for the Cheng-te emperor was the sixth in succession to die before reaching the age of forty, brought to the throne one who is not surprisingly best known for his interest in the quest for longevity. This emperor was a grandson of the Ch'eng-hua emperor, and his reign-title was Chia-ching ('Prosperous Tranquillity'). He had better luck than some other rulers who sought to prolong their lives by taking immortality drugs, and survived to reign for forty-five years. He did, however, like his predecessor, come to the throne as a malleable thirteen-year-old and the government was once again at the mercy of whatever clique could exercise dominance. More concerned with personal immortality than with the survival of the state, the emperor himself was prepared to withdraw almost entirely from the cares of government for long periods, leaving decisions to an unpopular Grand Secretary, named Yen Sung. It was under the Chia-ching emperor that the existence of the *nei-ko* (Grand Secretariat) was at last formally recognized.

During this reign the defences and the economy of the country continued to drift into a worse condition than ever. The entire Chinese coast was now being harassed again by Japanese pirates, but an inspection of the state of coastal garrisons revealed that, owing to widespread desertion, they were, on average, manned at only about one-third of their proper strength. The forces on the northern frontier were an increasingly serious drain on the state's resources, and between the beginning and the end of the reign there was a four-fold increase in the annual amount of silver which had to be appropriated for the purchase of food for the garrisons in that area.

The chief cause of this extra expenditure was the resurgence of Mongol power. The frequency of Mongol attacks on the frontier increased, and there were particularly serious invasions of Shansi in 1541 and 1542, when it was reported that as many as two or three hundred thousand Chinese men and women were either killed or captured, together with a very large number of animals. There were also a number of Chinese fugitives and deserters in Mongolia, and as the north Chinese peasants suffered more and more from oppression and over-taxation and the generally depressed state of this area of the country, there was increasing migration north of the Great Wall, especially in the two decades after 1550. In the 1540s the Board of War had offered rewards for the rescue or return of Chinese from Mongolia, as well as inducements to the Chinese to return home, so clearly this flow of people into Mongolia was beginning to be viewed seriously by the authorities. The Mongol invasions were stimulated by repeated Chinese refusals to consider their requests for a tributary relationship to be established. On two occasions in the 1540s the Chinese had been so foolish as to put Mongol emissaries to death. Finally in 1550 the Mongol chief Altan Khan, who had been very keen to establish trade relations with the Chinese and who also wanted their help against a rival in his own country, gave up hope of receiving a favourable response to his requests and launched a major invasion. The commanding general on the frontier at Tatung, facing the Mongols, managed to divert the attack by bribery and promises of trade; so Altan swept eastward, broke through the Great Wall near Peking, plundered cities in this part of China and laid siege to the capital for three days before withdrawing.

The morale of the Chinese soldiers on the frontier could not have been lower. They were mainly concerned to make life tolerable by keeping on good terms with their enemies across the border by fraternizing with them and indulging in illicit trade, and even by acting as guides for them in their forays into Chinese territory to plunder the goods which they repeatedly requested the Chinese government they might be permitted to obtain by open and legal commerce. At the same time on the Mongol side of the frontier there were many Chinese, deserters, fugitives and immigrants; and some of these were specialists and craftsmen who gave excellent service to the Mongols, notably in military technology and in the building of an elaborate palace for Altan. On the Chinese side, on the other hand, there were still many Mongol soldiers who were particularly loyal and effective defenders of the frontier.

A further request from Altan Khan for the opening of markets was acceded to in 1551, but they did not work amicably. Many Chinese were hostile to the arrangement because they thought that this fraternization with the Mongols would weaken their defences. They also thought that the grain requested by the Mongols must be needed for the Chinese traitors on their side, since it was not appreciated that the Mongols now used grain themselves. The Mongols, on the other hand, were displeased because they had hoped that their poorer people would be able to trade with cattle and sheep, but the Chinese insisted that they only wanted horses, which only the rich Mongols could afford to trade with. The Chinese also accused the Mongols of unruly behaviour at the markets, and the Mongols, when they became aware that they were not going to get all that they wanted out of the arrangement, did not give up their plundering expeditions across the frontier. In the following year the whole arrangement was abandoned by the Chinese and the frontier markets were closed. But the power of Altan Khan continued to grow and he repeatedly besieged the Ming government with requests for consumer goods of various kinds. The invasions continued, generally inflicting much heavier losses on the Chinese than the Mongols themselves suffered. At the same time large numbers of troops were being used to deal with aboriginal uprisings in the south.

At a time when huge funds were needed for the military forces the revenue position was weak because of large-scale evasion of the land-tax on the part of the gentry. Village chiefs, local government clerks and others were often bullied, bribed and cajoled to falsify the records; and another serious weakness was that land registers were out of date, so that in some parts of the country the area of land brought under cultivation had increased many times without any corresponding change in the tax assessment. Tax evasion could also be practised by officials, for they were legally entitled to exemptions on certain amounts of property, so if they acquired estates in various parts of the country they could obtain exemptions far in excess of their entitlement, and they could resort to other means, such as temporary transfer of ownership, to the same end. At the same time there was much high-handed encroachment on the land of the ordinary people by, for example, imperial relatives, members of powerful local families and high officials of the government. This had resulted in the area of taxed land being halved during the course of the fifteenth century instead of being greatly increased because much land had newly been brought under cultivation. The loss of government revenue was so serious that in the first half of the Chia-ching period a nationwide land reassessment was embarked upon.

At the same time the arrangement whereby local labour

services were provided by the local families on a decennial rota no longer worked smoothly. Such a system was far too rigid to operate in the normal conditions of social and economic change, and could only collapse completely once families were driven by poverty to flee their obligations, leaving their burdens to be shouldered by others in the community. Moreover the system was more open to abuse than the land tax, if only because the land was there to be seen and checked on, while the labour requirements were much more left to the discretion of the officials.

Another great fault of the Ming taxation system was its complexity, and in the mid-sixteenth century there was a gradual process of simplification and rationalization, which depended largely on local conditions and local initiatives rather than on any nationwide plan. The first thing that generally happened was the simplification of the complicated labour service requirements and the substitution of money payment in lieu of labour. Such substitution had already been practised to some extent by the wealthier people, and this further development was in keeping with the growth of the money economy, which was particularly noticeable in the south-east, where the growth of trade with the Europeans brought increasing quantities of silver into the country. In many localities also there was a tendency for the commuted labour service payment to be merged with the land tax. As the taxation system became less complicated, it was possible to rationalize arrangements for collection and the burden was taken from the private individuals who had been charged with the task of tax collection in their locality and made the responsibility of the authorities. Similarly the hiring of substitutes to perform the labour service became the responsibility of the government. This was a great relief to the private tax collectors, who had suffered severe hardships through having to make up deficits out of their own pockets and had been subjected to all kinds of irregular government demands. An example of this comes in a story of the Hsüan-te period. The emperor was fond of cricket-fighting, and sent out emissaries to obtain crickets, which caused prices to rocket. A tax collector was ordered by the local authorities to obtain crickets, and for a particularly fine one he had to exchange a horse. His wife and concubine decided to steal a look at this marvellous and valuable insect, and unfortunately allowed it to escape. The wife thereupon committed suicide, followed shortly afterwards by her husband.

All these processes of simplification were described as the 'method of combining into one', which, since the words 'combine' and 'whip' have the same pronunciation in Chinese, was soon converted by peasant humour into 'single-whip method'. These reforms undoubtedly helped to arrest the process of dynastic decline. At the same time the country's basic resources had been expanding quite rapidly owing to improvements in agricultural productivity. Big advances had been made in rice cultivation. In ancient and medieval times it had taken about six months to grow rice, but during the Sung Dynasty a hundred-day strain of rice had been introduced from Champa, and by the twelfth century Chinese farmers had improved on this by developing strains which matured in a mere sixty days. This meant that rice could now be used as a fill-in crop which had more food-value than other auxiliary crops, and that the double-cropping which is so familiar a feature of modern Chinese agriculture could be used on a large scale. Further increases in production were due to the fact that these early-ripening varieties also needed less water than the older types, so that they could be grown on higher land which had previously been considered unsuitable. During the Sung these improvements had been confined to the Lower Yangtze area, and had obviously contributed to the flourishing economy of that part of the country; but during the Ming they gradually became common throughout the whole of the rice-growing area, notably Hupei and Hunan, which have since become the country's most important centres of rice cultivation. The new rice could be grown on terraced paddies on the hillsides, so the landscape of the Lower Yangtze area and Fukien began to take on its modern appearance.

At the same time as rice cultivation was spreading to land which had previously been unsuitable for it, inferior land in the south was also being increasingly used for the dissemination of various crops from North China, such as wheat, barley and millet. The cultivation of these crops in the south had been much encouraged by some of the Sung emperors, with rent-exemption as an incentive, and they continued to spread during the Ming period. In areas where climatic conditions were not unsuitable, they provided a means of putting marginal land to good use and made a valuable contribution to the nation's food supply.

Another change in land utilization was caused by the introduction of American food plants, which dates from the Chia-ching period. Before the middle of the sixteenth century peanuts were being grown in the Shanghai area and maize was being cultivated fairly extensively in the south-west of the country, while the sweet potato was to be found in Yünnan in the 1560s. The peanut had been introduced by sea, probably by Portuguese traders, and the other two crops both by sea and via the Burma–Yünnan overland route. Although it was not till later that these new plants were cultivated on a very large scale, their appearance is a further reminder of how food production was continually being improved and China's still adequate supplies of undeveloped land were continually being brought into use.

Another healthy development during the sixteenth century was a certain growth of intellectual vitality. Although education during the early Ming had been a somewhat stifling process, it remains true that owing to the stimulus provided by the Ming founder, great numbers of people were educated by the state, and education was much more widely available than in Europe at that time. The development had at least stimulated advances in the technique of printing and publication. Movable type was a comparatively recent introduction compared with block-printing, and a Wuhsi family pioneered the use of copper movable type, and other printers made reputations for the outstanding quality of the books they produced. The growing demand for supplies of basic texts was met by large-scale reproduction of important works, such as the Thirteen Classics and the Twenty-one Dynastic Histories. The civil service examinations continued to provide a stimulus to the acquisition of books, and a notable development of this period was the publication of successful examination essays, which were always in heavy demand.

The increase in the availability of books not only resulted in a wider spread of education and educational opportunity, but also broadened scholars' horizons, since many rare early works were reproduced. At the same time the teachings of Wang Yang-ming had provided a stimulus to greater intellectual freedom as well as to a less rigid attitude to the class structure of society. His theory of the unity of knowledge and action constituted a powerful challenge to the bookishness of Chu Hsi, and an inspiration to fresh and uncluttered thinking. At the same time he put forward a theory of innate knowledge latent within everybody, which amounted to a revival of the ancient Confucian concept that everyone was capable of attaining sagehood. This doctrine had an egalitarian influence on society, and many of Wang's followers and disciples established private academies in which all men, of whatever class, were welcome to attend the public lectures, in line with the Confucian doctrine that 'in education there should be no class distinctions'. Many of the men who attended these lectures and chanted the Classics later became famous, and as in the early days of the dynasty there were still liberal opportunities to cross the class barriers. In earlier history private academies, generally sited, like monasteries, in remote and attractive retreats, had been havens for scholars in difficult times. During the early Ming they had served as venues for philosophical conferences, and some private tutoring of candidates for the civil service examinations had also been undertaken at them. But now they began to play a more public role, for not only did they provide platforms for exponents of unorthodox philosophies, but they also developed into meeting-places for people of similar political persuasions. This could not be tolerated by the government, which proscribed private academies in 1537. But this was not a relentless persecution and in some parts of the country private academies continued to flourish, and Wang Yang-ming's following was so large and influential that his impact on society survived this attempt to stifle it.

During this period an important change took place in the cult of Confucius. In 1530 it was proposed that there should be a reduction in the veneration paid to him, which had gone far beyond what Confucius himself would have approved, for he had been very hostile to the usurpation of titles and honours. The main changes approved by the emperor were that Confucius should no longer have the title of *wang* (prince), that the building used in the ceremonies conducted in his honour should be called a hall, rather than a temple, and that the images should be destroyed and replaced by tablets. The abandonment of images in the worship of Confucius was to prove especially important in the history of relations between China and Europe since it enabled the Jesuit missionaries who reached China at the end of the sixteenth century to regard the Confucian ceremonies with tolerance instead of condemning them as idolatrous.

The relative longevity of the Chia-ching emperor was not inherited by his son, whose reign-title was Lung-ch'ing ('Abundant Blessings'). His short reign (1567–73) was marked by the establishment of relations with Altan Khan, which relieved the tension on the northern frontier for a considerable period. Early in the Lung-ch'ing period the Mongol chieftain had been able to conquer large areas of Shansi, plundering as he went, but fortunately at this moment one of his grandsons, who nursed a resentment against the old man, surrendered to the Chinese with a small group of followers; so the Chinese were able to work out a policy of using the grandson as a pawn in negotiations with Altan Khan. Eventually an agreement was reached, which involved the restoration of the grandson to the Mongols and the resumption of tributary and trading relations between Altan Khan and the Chinese. Altan Khan swore not to invade China again, and in 1571 the title of Submit-to-Righteousness Prince was conferred on him by imperial edict, and he was presented with the gift of a dragon robe and some bolts of coloured silk. Arrangements were made for the opening of regular markets and for periodic tribute journeys to China, and it was understood by the Chinese that money saved from the heavy cost of defence could be expended on gifts to Mongol emissaries to keep them happy with the situation. Altan Khan was now an old man, and he kept peace with China and is said to have embraced Buddhism in his declining years. Good relations continued after his death ten years later, both under his son and grandson, and finally under his great-great-grandson, who received the Ming investiture in 1613.

The death of the Lung-ch'ing emperor meant that yet another child emperor occupied the dragon throne. The reign of the

Wan-li emperor, who was only nine when his father died, lasted for forty-seven years and was the longest of the Ming Dynasty. It has some reputation as a period of cultural brilliance, but this had nothing to do with the emperor's own qualities. Fortunately the dominant figure in the government during his boyhood was an able and strong-willed Grand Secretary called Chang Chü-cheng. He had already played an important part in the discussions leading to peace with the Mongols, and he was now able to bring about a thorough overhaul of the frontier defences under two very distinguished generals. The process of tax reform continued, and the economy was developing rapidly, with silver now confirmed as the basic unit of exchange and of taxation. Officials were now paid entirely in silver, and at long last the circulation of paper money came to an end. Under Chang's firm hand the country flourished, and the new *modus vivendi* with the Mongols proved especially beneficial.

Chang's strong government was bound to make enemies. He suppressed what he considered to be irresponsible censorial criticism, and in 1577, when his father died, he caused grave offence by not going into retirement to observe the customary mourning period of twenty-seven months. Instead he was merely excused attendance at court audiences, but continued to perform his duties as Grand Secretary. Four officials who protested were beaten at court and eventually banished to military service on the frontier. Resentment at Chang's high-handed methods had to be bottled up until after his death in 1582. Within a year he was posthumously disgraced and his closest adherents fell from power, while those who had been exiled because of their criticism of Chang were restored. With no strong man capable of filling the gap left by Chang's death, officialdom broke up into factions, each concerned to see that no representative of a rival group should step into Chang's shoes.

At the same time a serious split developed between the emperor and the civil service over the investiture of the heir apparent, which the emperor repeatedly delayed because he hoped to be able to persuade his ministers to accept the eldest son of his favourite concubine instead of his legitimate heir. This battle dragged on for fifteen years before the emperor, who had had many officials degraded or banished for criticizing him, finally gave way in 1601 and bestowed the title of crown prince upon his eldest son. Finding his advisers more and more frustrating and tiresome, the Wan-li emperor had increasingly withdrawn from contact with his ministers, and soon even the Grand Secretaries had only seen him on very rare occasions. For the last half of his reign he ceased to have any personal contact with the bureaucracy, so that memorials remained unanswered, urgent business remained undealt with and appointments remained unfilled. When he did bestir himself to play a part in affairs, he was entirely dependent on the palace eunuchs as his channel of communication with his ministers; so the Grand Secretaries were forced to connive with these minions of the emperor in order to get essential business done. In the long run the integrity of the civil service was gravely weakened because the more unprincipled members curried favour with powerful eunuchs by means of bribery and flattery, while the stronger and more independent were cowed and terrorized by the eunuch-run secret service agency within the palace.

Unfortunately too the healthy financial situation was now deteriorating fast. The surplus of the 1570s turned into deficits in the 1580s, which became catastrophic in the 1590s when the huge accumulated cash reserves which had existed in some provinces were finally exhausted. Court extravagance was now a very heavy burden on the state. Enormous sums were spent on the investiture of imperial princes and on the repair of palace buildings, especially as the result of great conflagrations which took place in 1596 and 1597. At this time there were 70,000 palace eunuchs and 9000 palace women and the emperor would think nothing of diverting money collected for water control purposes to the manufacture of fine silks for his own establishment. The 1590s was also a decade of renewed military activity. In 1592 there was a fresh outbreak of war in Mongolia. At the same time there was much fighting against aboriginal tribesmen in the south-west, and the Japanese pirates were again proving troublesome; but, more importantly, an entirely new military commitment was undertaken when the Chinese went to the support of the Koreans when they were invaded by the famous Japanese warlord Hideyoshi.

This was a considerable policy departure since for many years the Chinese had allowed themselves no military involvement except in the defence of their own frontiers. But Hideyoshi's activities represented a very serious threat to the Chinese. Indeed many years before this he had declared his intention of conquering China as soon as he had settled affairs at home to his liking, and he was so wildly optimistic about the success of his plans that in the summer of 1592, soon after mounting the invasion of Korea, he wrote to his mother telling her that in the autumn of the same year he would be able to receive her presents in the capital of China.

The Japanese forces had carried all before them at the beginning of the invasion, and the first small contingent sent by the Chinese was soon trapped and cut to pieces by the enemy. Later a larger force arrived and arranged a fifty-day truce with the Japanese while terms were discussed in Peking. The Japanese were ready to call a halt since they had been seriously harassed by guerrillas and were also worried at the size of the force the Chinese had now sent against them. Early the following year, after the armistice had expired, the Japanese were driven back to Pyongyang and then Seoul. Faced with a great Chinese army, they now concentrated on the defence of Seoul, but eventually agreed to terms whereby they evacuated the city.

Among the terms agreed by the Japanese general was that Hideyoshi should be named King of Japan by the Ming emperor, but when Ming envoys arrived in Japan later in the year Hideyoshi insisted on recognition of Japan's ownership of the southern provinces of Korea. Finally after many delays and much misunderstanding a further embassy from China reached Kyoto at the end of 1596 for the investiture, but when Hideyoshi found that the message from the Chinese court was patronizing and that the members of the mission were not even aware of the peace terms which he had proposed, he flew into a rage and ordered the resumption of hostilities against China. In the spring of 1597 a new invasion was mounted, and by January of the following year another Chinese force had crossed the Yalu and was already making its way south from Seoul. The Japanese general was pessimistic about the outcome, but his indomitable warriors, having withstood repeated onslaughts from the Chinese and Koreans throughout the summer, eventually fought back and routed their attackers. But Hideyoshi's death in the autumn brought the whole war to an end, for there had been much opposition in Japan to this second Korean venture.

These Korean campaigns cost the country an unprecedented sum of money and a heavy increase in taxation was necessary, so trusted eunuchs were appointed by the emperor to supervise and expedite the payment of a whole new range of emergency taxes, which were so oppressive that revolts began to break out in various parts of the country. By the end of the century military expenditure and court extravagance had cancelled out the very considerable commercial and industrial expansion which had been taking place, with the effect that the economy, which could have been extremely healthy, was once again in a critical situation.

The development of the economy can be seen in the growth of new industries and crafts during the late Ming period, in the increasing diversification and regional specialization in crops, and in the stimulus to economic development brought about by the influx of silver. Old industries like the ceramics industry thrived with the growing demand from the palace for large quantities of high-quality porcelain, and the cotton industry was already beginning to make rapid progress. The great quantity of domestic trade was to make a deep impression on the Jesuits by comparison with conditions in Europe, and the late Ming period witnessed the rise of merchants of great wealth, especially among the salt monopolists of Yangchow. The Yangtze valley was the centre of the country's economic strength. Soochow had a population of well over two million, and Nanking also far exceeded Peking in size and splendour. But the basic weakness in the economy was still the fact that the government tax administration never succeeded in penetrating the rural areas and distributing the tax burden effectively; so that in times of weak central authority the local gentry could arrange matters to their own advantage.

5

Meanwhile another threat to Chinese security was growing in the north-east with the rise to power of a petty Manchu chieftain called Nurhaci, who had inherited the leadership of a small tribe in 1583. The Manchus were related to the Jürched, the people who had founded the Chin Dynasty in North China in the twelfth century. Early in the Ming Dynasty when the Chinese had used their system of regional military guards to try to absorb some of the frontier Mongols into their administration, they had adopted the same method in dealing with the Jürched. By this means they made the succession to chieftainships dependent on their own confirmation and investiture, and it was also their policy to try to attach the tribes-people to a definite territory so as to increase their control over them and improve the stability of the area. To achieve this end they encouraged the development of agriculture. The Jürched readily adopted this way of life and evolved small states which were dependent on agriculture as well as on hunting, and which had walled towns. The luxury trade with China permitted by the emperor in accordance with the tributary relationship helped to strengthen the financial position of the Jürched leaders and to increase their knowledge of Chinese culture.

The cradle of Manchu power was the petty frontier state which had developed out of the Chienchow guard, the first Jürched guard to be established by the Chinese. At the beginning of his career Nurhaci's position was weak and precarious and he only grew in strength by having to fight for survival against powerful enemies. Gradually he improved his position and obtained the favour of the Ming. In 1590 he took part in a tribute mission to Peking, and in 1595 was awarded the high title of General of the Dragon and Tiger for maintaining order among the Chienchow tribes. By the end of the century he had amassed a great deal of wealth and had set out to subdue his neighbours and enlarge his state. He had made his fortune by mining, by operating trade monopolies, and by pillaging weaker tribes.

In order to gear himself for the creation of a strong and inde-

pendent Jürched state he introduced a new military organization
in which the basic unit was the *niru*, of 300 men; and the whole
army was divided into four, and after 1615 eight, divisions known
as banners. Each *niru*, or company, also included the families of
the warriors, so it was an all-embracing organization designed for
peace as well as war, reminiscent of the system introduced by
Genghis Khan. The new state organization also reflected the
transition from feudalism to bureaucracy which was natural
when the Jürched no longer operated as isolated units separated
off by the river valleys, but proceeded to occupy the large plains,
where collaboration for the purposes of defence, agriculture and
flood prevention was very important. Nurhaci gradually became
more independent of the Ming. He sent tribute for the last time
in 1609, having the previous year reached a boundary agreement
with the Chinese. The development of a bureaucratic state continued and, while the banners formed the units of local government, in 1616 a rudimentary central government apparatus was
created, and in the same year Nurhaci inaugurated a new dynasty
after the Chinese pattern. He named it the Chin after his Jürched
predecessors, and adopting the reign-title of T'ien-ming ('Heaven-
ordered'), his own full title being 'Brilliant Emperor who Benefits
all Nations'. In 1618 Nurhaci made his first invasion of China,
when he led ten thousand men against the town of Fushun,
which he captured along with several other towns. Wavering
Chinese officials on the frontier began to ally themselves with
the Manchu cause, and as more and more Chinese went over to
the Manchu state and were able to assist in the administration,
so its bureautic nature developed. But although many Chinese
became incorporated into the Jürched state with the capture of
Fushun, Nurhaci wisely allowed merchants from other parts of
China who happened to be there to go to their homes, spreading
news of the Manchus' generosity and of their political aims. This
new threat meant an additional burden to the Chinese people,
and to meet the defence requirements the basic land-tax rate
was increased this same year. But although defence expenditure
rose enormously, the Wan-li emperor was deaf to all pleas to
release the abundant funds which were still at his own disposal
although the state's coffers were empty. Army morale was as low

as ever, for the dwindling numbers of the hereditary military class were supplemented by mercenaries raised to meet the emergency, who were mainly peasants pauperized by the recent rises in taxation. At the capital the army was a joke, and to make ends meet the rank and file occupied themselves as part-time pedlars or craftsmen, while the palace was manned by eunuch forces.

At the same time, in the latter part of the Wan-li emperor's reign, factional controversies had continued to rage, and they developed a new bitterness after the re-establishment of the Eastern Grove academy in 1604. This was a revival of an old Sung academy which had long fallen into ruins. It was set up by a group of local scholar-officials, presently out of favour, at Wuhsi in the Lower Yangtze valley. After the half-hearted attempt at suppression of the private academies in the Chia-ching era, a more bitter attack had been made on them by Chang Chü-cheng, who loathed fashionable philosophical discussion and thought that scholars should devote themselves to the practical problems of government. But the effect of his hostility was not long-lasting, and after his death new establishments were founded and old ones revived. Among these the Eastern Grove concerned itself not only with philosophy but also with the controversies of the times. Its founder, Ku Hsien-ch'eng, attributed the political immorality of the age to a relaxation of Confucian standards by Wang Yang-ming's followers, and started a moral crusade to try to get control of the government into the hands of 'upright men' instead of the sycophants and time-servers who then held the reins of power. Ku's views obtained considerable support and in 1611, when Eastern Grove men held some key positions in the government, they tried to get leaders of opposing factions removed from office, but met with such resistance that most Eastern Grove men went into voluntary retirement. Ku himself died in 1612, and a serious incident in 1615 put the few remaining Eastern Grove partisans into the emperor's bad graces. An attack on some eunuchs in the crown prince's residence had been interpreted by the judicial authorities as the act of a madman, but the Eastern Grove people had insisted that it was another attempt to do away with the crown prince so that the emperor's favourite son could succeed him after all. The consequent disgrace of the remainder of the Eastern Grove faction meant that for the last few years of the Wan-li reign the government was in the hands of people who were not disposed to interfere with the emperor's inclination to let things drift, and it was at that low point in domestic politics that the country had to face the first Manchu invasion.

By the time of the Wan-li emperor's death in 1620, it is doubtful whether even a most able and vigorous sovereign could have restored the fortunes of the dynasty, but what prospect was there of kingly qualities being nurtured in such an environment? In fact the new emperor fell ill within a week of his accession, and was dead within a month. The malicious hinted that his illness was induced by a congratulatory present of eight beautiful maidens from the late emperor's favourite, Madam Cheng, who had vainly hoped that her own son would succeed to the throne, and had now taken cunning advantage of the new emperor's known reputation for lechery. Finally the emperor died after taking some red pills made for him by a minor functionary, and afterwards there was much factional dispute about the responsibility for his death. The crisis continued when Madam Li, the favourite consort of this brief occupant of the dragon throne, refused to move out of the palace and expressed her intention of dealing with official business since the new emperor, his eldest son, was a boy of only fifteen. But officialdom was horrified that a female usurpation might now be piled upon all the dynasty's other troubles and their vigorous protests finally persuaded her to withdraw. The crisis thus came to an end, but the events of the past month had increased the acrimony between court factions.

Unfortunately the new emperor, whose reign-name was T'ien-ch'i ('Heaven-ordered'), was totally lacking in the qualities needed by the holder of the Mandate of Heaven. The deaths in rapid succession of his grandfather and father meant that he himself had not been prepared for the throne with the lofty Confucian indoctrination which was customarily inflicted upon heirs apparent by distinguished scholar-officials. Indeed he is reputed to have been illiterate. Certainly his absorbing interest was carpentry, and he very soon wearied of the demands of state. On the other hand he became obstinate and high-handed when dealing with the suggestions of officials who hoped they could mould the young man to a proper sense of his responsibilities. He was urged to improve his education, but during the winter months he insisted on abandoning work with his tutors. He was deaf to the appeals of the Board of Revenue to limit expenditure on his wedding ceremony and to other attempts to curb his extravagance at a time when there was much distress among the populace and a serious shortage of resources to meet increasing military commitments. He scandalized his officials by making arbitrary appointments of his own without waiting for their nominations, thus challenging one of the time-honoured checks on imperial absolutism; and he did violence to the Confucian ideals of sovereignty by following his grandfather's practice of dealing out harsh treatment to censorial officials and others who criticized him.

Deaf to the appeals of tradition, patriotism and humanistic Confucianism, the young emperor was only too ready to heed promptings of a far less worthy sort. The first place in his heart was occupied by his former nursemaid Mistress K'o, who in turn became passionately attached to a ruthless schemer called Wei Chung-hsien, in spite of the fact that he was one of that numerous fraternity within the palace who were not properly equipped for the consummation of such a relationship. Through this bizarre liaison Wei soon became the trusted adviser of the Son of Heaven. It is said that this sinister pair introduced the young emperor to a life of debauchery. Certainly, out of gratitude for their great services, numerous honours were heaped upon them, and at the end of 1623 Wei achieved a conspicuous goal of eunuch ambition when he was put in charge of the Eastern Depot, the notorious palace secret-service headquarters. At the beginning of the T'ien-ch'i era a swing of the pendulum had brought the Eastern Grove party back into power, and by late 1624 they held all the key posts in the government. But their attempts to clean up the administration ensured that Wei did not lack allies among those whose dismissal they had secured.

It was not long before a head-on clash between the Eastern Grove party and the supporters of Wei Chung-hsien took place.

Yang Lien, who had played a prominent part in steering the ship of state through the hazards of the 1620 crisis, chose to submit a denunciation of what he described as 'the twenty-four great crimes' of Wei Chung-hsien, a passionately indignant document which is perhaps the most famous memorial submitted by a censor in the whole of Chinese history. Reminding the emperor of the Ming founder's decision to limit the role of the eunuchs, he produced a long list of crimes of which murder was almost the most innocent. The memorial reached its climax in a warning that Wei Chung-hsien had designs on the throne itself, and taunted the emperor with being a nonentity beside the eunuch, for 'whether in the palace or in the government, whether in great matters or in small matters, there is nothing that is not decided solely by Chung-hsien'. At the time Yang was merely rebuked and his friends remained firm in his support. But Wei soon found himself strong enough to initiate a great purge of Eastern Grove partisans, and in 1625 he had Yang Lien and others arrested on trumped-up charges that they had accepted bribes from a disgraced general who was then awaiting execution. They were thrown into prison and cruelly tortured, and did not long survive the ordeal.

By ruthless terrorism Wei Chung-hsien now succeeded in reducing the entire civil service to abject servility. Censors who at the beginning of the reign had complained vociferously about court extravagance now made every effort to secure increased revenue for the splendid buildings whose construction had become the eunuch's special whim. (According to Yang Lien's memorial, he had already built himself a tomb comparable with an imperial sepulchre.) Officials vied with each other to think of new means of flattery. All memorials began to include unstinting praise of this new master of the Chinese world, and imperial rescripts commenced with the formula 'We and the Palace Minister'. Titles and honours were heaped upon him, his forebears and his relatives, and in the provinces temples were erected in his honour, and prayers offered for his longevity. One of his nephews substituted for the emperor at a sacrifice in the imperial temple, and Wei himself was even ranked on a par with Confucius in ritual observances, while a unicorn, symbol of the appearance of a great sage, was reported to have been seen in Shantung.

Meanwhile as the fortunes of this great and ancient state rested in such unworthy and degenerate hands, only a short distance away to the north-east the skilful and vigorous Nurhaci had been making further advances. In 1621 the important cities of Liaoyang and Shenyang (which in modern times has been called Mukden) were captured, and the whole of the territory east of the Liao fell into the control of the Manchus. Fortunately for Peking Nurhaci was not yet in a position to exploit to the full the weakness and poor morale of the Ming forces. For the present he was occupied in establishing himself firmly in his recently acquired Chinese territories. For a while he made Liaoyang his capital, and then in 1625 he moved to Shenyang, which was to remain the Manchu capital right through to the end of the Ming Dynasty. In the following year he was ready for a further advance, but when he attacked Ningyüan he met with unexpectedly strong Chinese resistance and suffered his greatest defeat. A few months later he died of wounds suffered in this engagement.

At the time of Nurhaci's death eight members of his family (six sons, a nephew and a grandson) each controlled one of the eight Manchu banners, and their positions were to remain hereditary. These eight also formed a grand council of state, and since 1621 the four most senior of them had taken monthly turns to act as chief minister. They also had the responsibility of electing the ruler after Nurhaci's death, and their choice fell on Nurhaci's eighth son, Abahai, who continued to probe the Chinese defences.

Throughout the T'ien-ch'i period there were also serious disturbances in the south-west and government forces met with many setbacks in their attempts to quell the aboriginal rebels. In Shantung too there was a serious rebellion of a secret society of Buddhist inspiration known as the White Lotus Society, which at one time severed the Grand Canal transport route. Meanwhile the Fukien coast was harassed by the Dutch, who had established themselves in the Pescadores but had failed to negotiate a trade agreement with the Chinese and so were foiled in their attempt to get a share of the China trade like the Portuguese, who had been established at Macao since the middle of the previous century. The burdens of taxation borne by the people were increasingly heavy and administration in some parts of the country was beginning to disintegrate. Large-scale banditry and rebellion would soon follow, and faced with external pressure and internal disorder the dynasty would surely die an inglorious death.

But at least the Ming were soon relieved of Wei Chung-hsien's reign of terror. When the young emperor died suddenly in 1627, the throne passed smoothly to a seventeen-year-old brother who, although somewhat limited in ability, proved to be a conscientious and hard-working monarch. After a few months he plucked up the courage to banish the evil and notorious eunuch, who later, fearing a worse fate which his own monstrous crimes made him particularly well qualified to imagine, committed suicide. Mistress K'o was beaten to death and his various henchmen punished, while those of his opponents who had survived the reign of terror were recalled to power. But unfortunately this did not mean a recrudescence of Eastern Grove influence. This party had suffered severely from deaths and suicides at the time of Wei Chung-hsien's dominance, and the T'ien-ch'i emperor had actually ordered the destruction of the Eastern Grove and other academies because they were in effect the breeding grounds of political parties, which the traditional Chinese conception of the state, based on the idea of government by a supreme emperor acting on the advice of *individual* ministers and subjects, could not tolerate or find room for. Although the Academy was restored early in the next reign, the Eastern Grove party never achieved any kind of ascendancy because the new emperor soon grew weary of factionalism, from however worthy a source, and the disputes at court tended not to be stimulated by rival concepts of what was best in the interests of the state, but by backward-looking wrangling over blame for the events of the Wei Chung-hsien era. In future the private academies were much more carefully supervised by the government and were in effect incorporated into the state educational system.

The new reign (called Ch'ung-cheng, which means 'Respect for pillars of the state') was marked by the continued growth of Manchu power and a steady disintegration of internal order.

Abahai made vast increases in his domains. He made some raids into China, and in 1629 even attacked Peking and briefly held some Chinese cities west of Shanhaikuan, but these were largely pillaging operations and his main conquests were in non-Chinese territory. By 1635 he had completely subjugated the Chahar Mongols, the strongest of the Inner Mongolian tribes. The Inner Mongolians were then organized into companies and banners and were to remain largely loyal to the Manchus throughout the dynasty they founded. As the Manchus acquired Chinese subjects, they also were incorporated in banners, and by 1644 there were eight Mongol and eight Chinese banners which, with the addition of the eight Manchu banners, made twenty-four in all. Soon after he became ruler of the Jürched Abahai had failed in an attempt to subjugate Korea, but at the end of 1638 he took personal command of an army which soon completed the conquest, the King of Korea being forced to send annual tribute and surrender his sons as hostages. In the north Abahai mounted several expeditions, which had succeeded in bringing the whole Amur region under Manchu rule by the time of his death in 1643, and by the same time the brilliant Manchu leader had extended his southern territories to the vicinity of Shanhaikuan. He did not survive quite long enough to see the conquest of China, for which he had skilfully prepared the way.

It was not only by increase of territory, wealth and power that Abahai had laid the foundations of empire, but also by a further development within his domains of the type of bureaucratic government which was needed to administer this great country. In this he was much assisted by the increasing numbers of Chinese officials that came over to him as his power grew, for in a frontier situation, in which a strong process of acculturation between the Chinese and the Manchus had long been taking place, the border Chinese could easily be attracted into the Manchu service by a combination of threats and promises, especially when the Ming government was so weak and corrupt. The transformation of all the diverse elements at his disposal into a dynamic new political organization was an achievement which even outshone Abahai's military conquests.

Abahai was first faced with the problem of strengthening his own position as ruler, for Nurhaci had intended that after his death authority should revert to the clan in the form of the grand council consisting of the leaders of the eight banners, and it was much more difficult for Abahai to assert himself than it had been for Nurhaci since all except one of these leaders were of his own generation. Abahai's position of *primus inter pares* was made clear in the oath inaugurating his rule, for he and the clan members vowed loyalty to each other. However, he gradually succeeded in weakening the power of the princes and asserting monarchical government. He was able to do this largely because the increasing administrative needs of the state demanded a greater measure of bureaucracy, so that the administration of the banners came more and more into the hands of a staff of officials. In 1629 Abahai further strengthened his position by handing over the rotating premiership to the junior princes. The senior princes soon found themselves in disgrace and before long there was no further effective limitation on Abahai's power from his clan coevals. His military successes had brought him enormous prestige, and in 1631 an administrative reform had put the whole governmental apparatus under his rule, and the six ministries and other features of the Chinese system had been introduced.

In 1635 the word Manchu, which is of uncertain origin, was adopted for the first time to replace the name Jürched which carried the stigma of Chinese suzerainty; and in the following year Abahai proclaimed himself emperor, adopting the new dynastic name of Ch'ing, meaning Pure, and hence making the Manchu policy of gaining the Chinese throne open and unmistakable. The Manchus had fully adopted the Confucian ideology and the Chinese idea of a world state, which comprised the only sophisticated political philosophy available to them; so if they were right in their claim that their virtues were superior to those of the decadent Ming, it followed that the people of China would flock to them and that the Mandate of Heaven would pass to them. To instil this philosophy into their people the Manchu rulers had promoted the translation of Confucian books in their new writing system, which was an adaptation of the Mongolian alphabet. In their attempt to bring down the Ming house the Manchus had an overwhelming advantage over internal rebels, for in his early days Nurhaci had been allowed and even encouraged to build up state power, since vassal states could be invaluable defenders of the frontier, and if they were imbued with Confucian ideology, so much the better.

Nevertheless, in the numerous peasant uprisings which racked the late Ming, there were two rebels who did succeed in gaining sufficient power to enable them to entertain serious dynastic ambitions. These were Chang Hsien-chung and Li Tz'u-cheng. Chang was a soldier who, having been severely beaten and dismissed from the army for committing crimes of violence, set up as a bandit raiding villages in northern Shensi, which by this time had suffered bitterly not only because of the general deterioration in administration, but more specifically because of a serious famine in 1628. In the early days many of the rebels were ex-servicemen like Chang, most of them being deserters. In 1629, when the government, for reasons of economy, made a big reduction in the imperial post-station system, many of the dismissed post-station attendants joined their ranks, and Li Tz'u-cheng was one of these. This post-station system was, incidentally, a long-established and essential implement of imperial rule which had been developed to a high level of efficiency and complexity in Yüan and Ming times, so that a serious reduction in the number of post-stations servicing a network of land and water transport throughout the country provides a striking example of the disintegration of institutions which characterized the decline of the dynasty.

In the early days of the rebellion Chang and Li and countless other bandit leaders carried out unco-ordinated and isolated raids in search of plunder. Although they were vastly inferior in military capability to the government forces, it was very difficult for the authorities to deal effectively with these outlaws, for they could seek safety in difficult mountain country, and make raids as opportunity permitted. In the early stages they made a point of seizing horses and draft animals, so that rapid movement became an important feature of their success. As opportunity offered, rebel activity spread into other provinces, and eventually became particularly strong in the whole area between the Yangtze and the Yellow River, from Szechwan and Shensi in the west to the Southern Metropolitan Area in the east. The rebels were naturally slow to develop the capacity to seize and hold walled towns, although the capture of Fengyang in the Southern Metropolitan Area in 1635 was a serious blow to Ming prestige since it was the ancestral home of the imperial family. At the same time, even when rebels were forced to surrender, the government was inclined to deal leniently with them, partly because there was still enough sense of Confucian humanism abroad to suggest that the suffering must be won over by kindness, and partly, no doubt, because there was no real alternative except mass extermination. Thus in 1638, when the government had the upper hand, Chang was forced to surrender, but, although he was by now recognized to be the most powerful rebel leader, he was even allowed to retain his forces and was given a position in the Chinese army. Sure enough, he merely used this respite to recoup his strength, and he resumed his rebellion in the following year.

A major weakness of the rebels' position was that they almost entirely failed to attract gentry support. Consequently it was a long time before their intellectual horizons broadened so that they were able to contemplate something more ambitious than mere raiding for the purposes of plunder. But powerful government attempts to suppress the rebels in the late 1630s had the ironic effect of leaving Chang and Li in a much stronger position to pursue new and more sophisticated aims. The government had succeeded in wiping out many of the lesser bandit chiefs, so there was a greater concentration of rebel support for them, as the most prominent of the survivors. Soon the concept of establishing more permanent régimes began to influence their actions. As far as Chang was concerned, the period of recuperation after his surrender in 1638 gave unprecedented opportunity for making contact with the gentry, whose ideas and support were essential to the development of dynastic ambitions. By 1643 he was strong enough to capture major cities, but after short-lived attempts to set up administrations based on Wuchang and then Changsha, he withdrew to the Szechwan basin to try to establish a power base there, as others had done before in this relatively isolated part of China. But it was not until after the Ming emperor's suicide,

which signalled the end of the dynasty in the summer of 1644,
that he captured Chungking. Later in the year he occupied
Chengtu and was enthroned as King of the Great Western Kingdom. He established a government on traditional lines, with a
Grand Secretariat and six ministries, and was able to induce some
of the local gentry to serve in it, although the President of the
Board of Punishments was a Taoist priest and his opposite number at the works ministry was an arrow-maker. He occupied the
palace of the local imperial prince, held civil examinations, minted
money, introduced a local community system and reorganized
the army preparatory to a conquest of the rest of China, and
much impressed Jesuit missionaries who came into contact with
him. But the whole edifice soon collapsed like a pack of cards. He
never succeeded in controlling the whole of the Szechwan area,
so resistance was built up by Ming loyalist ex-officials in remote
parts of the province, and by the spring of 1645 one of these had
even managed to recapture Chungking. As opposition mounted,
his only recourse was a reign of terror. He never really trusted
the gentry, especially after the interception of a secret message
from some prominent Chengtu citizens inviting Li Tz'u-cheng to
invade Szechwan, and on one occasion he had several thousands
of them massacred in Chengtu, having enticed them there by
announcing the holding of a civil service examination. Chang
also used harsh methods to try to stamp out conflicts in the army
between the newly recruited Szechwanese and the older elements.
Soon his reign of terror was turned against the population at
large. By 1646 his government had completely disintegrated. He
abandoned Chengtu and headed for Shensi, but was killed at the
beginning of the following year on the Shensi–Szechwan border
by Manchu troops. Szechwan had suffered serious depopulation
as a result of the slaughter and havoc caused there, although the
true extent of the damage is not easy to estimate because of the
wild exaggeration of the sources, which convict Chang of mas-
sacring six hundred million people, which was about two hundred
times the population of the province at that time !

In heading for remote Szechwan Chang had effectively re-
nounced all hope of replacing the Ming. To do this it would be
necessary to seize an area of vital importance, and it was Li

Tz'u-cheng who did in the end come nearer to establishing a new dynasty. Late in 1640, after a period of relative inaction, he moved into Honan and began to attract a large following as a result of the famine conditions in that area. Before long he was strong enough to capture the great city of Loyang. At about this time he was joined by a member of the gentry called Li Yen, who helped to give his movement the sense of direction it had previously lacked. The year 1642 was notorious for the siege of Kaifeng, which was terminated when the rebels cut the Yellow River dike so that the city was completely inundated. The loss of life was appalling : probably several hundred thousand people met their deaths, either from drowning or from starvation earlier during the siege. Later Li tried to extend his sphere of influence and at the end of 1643 he was attempting to establish a new dynasty at Sian, whose name he changed back to Changan to stir memories of the city's ancient glories. On the first day of 1644 he proclaimed the establishment of a new dynasty called the great Shun, and at last began the march on Peking for which he had waited so long.

In the doomed capital the court waited, powerless to stem the advancing rebel tide, but rejecting the idea of a flight to Nanking since this would prove to be a fatal blow to the dynasty's prestige. Desperate attempts were made to raise money to continue the struggle, but the final blow to the emperor was that military commanders failed to heed the general order to come to the defence of the capital. Among these the most powerful was Wu San-kuei on the Manchurian frontier, who was already thinking that his best hope for the future lay in an accommodation with the foreign contender for the succession rather than in a vain patriotic gesture. With a breakdown in the channels of information, the court was only dimly aware of rebel movements, so the end came rapidly and ingloriously. On the very day Li arrived at the outskirts of the capital, the military units stationed outside the walls promptly surrendered, and on the following day the eunuch responsible for the internal defence of the city opened one of the gates and allowed the rebel troops to come in. At a final family meeting at the palace the empress embraced her children and retired to hang herself. The emperor, having ordered his sons to escape, attempted to kill his daughter with a sword, but failed even in this and left her severely wounded in the arm. He then wandered about the palace grounds before hanging himself on Coal Hill, which overlooks the splendid pavilions and palaces of the Imperial City, bitterly lamenting that he had been fated to preside over the ruin of a dynasty.

It is a sign of the resilience of Chinese political institutions that the Ming state was able to survive for so long in spite of the poor quality of most of the occupants of the dragon throne. Even in the declining years of the last great native Chinese dynasty, the Middle Kingdom was still a most impressive country in the eyes of European visitors. Matteo Ricci, the first Jesuit to establish himself in China, sent back to Europe favourable reports of the country in spite of the fact that he had a hard struggle to make any progress in his evangelizing activities. Although he arrived in 1583 he was not given permission to establish himself in Peking until the beginning of the seventeenth century. Having at first mistakenly adopted the apparel of a Buddhist monk, he came to appreciate that he could not expect to gain serious attention unless he made himself acceptable to the scholars by becoming conversant with their own Confucian tradition, which to them represented a system of universal validity. Immersing himself in Chinese learning, he was able to send back enthusiastic reports about China as a country 'governed by philosophers' (although occasional hints of the true condition of the government during the decade which he spent in Peking, not the most noble period in Chinese history, do emerge, particularly in his references to eunuch power). But he made few converts, and he and his successors in the Jesuit mission had slight influence on the course of Chinese affairs as compared with their impact on European intellectual history through the reports they sent back home, which deeply impressed such important figures as Leibnitz and Voltaire.

Europeans also gained an impression of the high quality of Ming culture from the very fine porcelains which were produced during this period. Great improvements in the technique of painting under the glaze meant that Ming porcelains were very different from those of the Sung, which relied largely on incised or moulded decoration of monochrome wares. Particularly famous products of the Ming period were the blue and white wares, which were copied in Japan, Indo-China and Persia, and inspired European potters at Delft and elsewhere. Many of these wares were made at Ching-te-chen, to satisfy the almost insatiable demands of the court, but in the last century of the dynasty cruder types were being made for export; and after 1600 blue and white reached Europe in great quantities and was imitated, although the secret of true porcelain was not discovered until 1708, almost a thousand years after the technique was perfected in China. Of equal appeal in Europe were the beautifully modelled figurines in white porcelain made at Te-hua in Fukien, which came to be known in Europe as *blanc-de-Chine*, and the five-colour wares of white porcelain painted in enamel colours. By the end of the dynasty Chinese factories were already making porcelain on order for European customers.

In literature and scholarship the Ming has generally been considered as a period in which the old traditions were restored after the rude interruption of the Mongols, leaving little energy for fresh developments. Certainly there was a strong streak of antiquarianism in Ming intellectual life, and much effort was put into works of traditional scholarship. Among the many valuable compilations of scholarly material that were produced, fifteen hundred multi-volume local histories were already available by the end of the Ming period, and there were also several important encyclopaedic works completed under imperial sponsorship. The epoch's outstanding contributions to practical knowledge are exemplified by the famous *materia medica* (*Pen-ts'ao kang-mu*) of 1578, which reveals the advanced state of medical knowledge at that time, inoculation against smallpox being one of the most striking items included. Although the orthodoxy imposed by the examination system may have inhibited the development of new political and philosophical ideas, with the growth of scholarly interest in this period it is becoming increasingly clear that there were a number of truly original thinkers, of whom Wang Yang-ming was merely the most famous. Certainly learning became more widespread, not only because of the egalitarian influence of Wang Yang-ming's ideas, but also because economic development meant that a larger proportion of the population could take part in cultural activities. Merchants and artisans joined literary societies, and composed poetry in the classical style. An even wider readership was reached by literature of a practical kind, such as popular encyclopaedias and books of morality which purveyed a kind of plebeian Confucianism with a strong admixture of Taoism and Buddhism, a kind of syncretism which is paralleled in the work of philosophers of the period who attempted syntheses of the three religions.

Intellectuals continued to show an interest in the vernacular literature, although this was still not accorded the prestige of work written in the classical language. The novel continued to develop, and three of the few that are especially highly regarded by the Chinese and have also become known in the West through translation were produced. *Shui-hu chuan* (*Water Margin*) was based on legends about a Sung Dynasty band of outlaws who championed victims of oppression, rather like Robin Hood and his merry men. *Hsi-yu-chi* (*Monkey*) tells amusingly of the exploits of a monkey who makes liberal use of magic powers to overcome all kinds of difficulties when escorting the monk Hsüan-tsang on a journey to the Western Paradise. *Chin P'ing Mei* (*Golden Lotus*) is a rich feast of urban social life with pornographic trimmings, its hero being a businessman who dabbles in politics in the corrupt world of the late Ming period. The two former were based on existing story-cycles, but the latter is an original composition, which for the first time in the history of the Chinese novel fully succeeds both in portraying the development of characters and in showing in rich detail the texture of the society in which they lived. It was not until the sixteenth century that original novels began to be written. The greatest of these is *Hung-lou Meng* (*Dream of the Red Chamber*), which is the story of a great house in decline after the loss of imperial patronage. But this was not written until the Ch'ing Dynasty, which is the subject of the following chapter.

6

The Ch'ing Dynasty

1

When Abahai died in 1643, the succession was a cause of contention. By the old clan rules the princes of Abahai's own generation should have elected someone from the next generation, so there was a strong candidate in the person of Haoge, the deceased ruler's eldest son. He was already in his thirties and had considerable military and political experience, and he stood out as the logical successor even more clearly because his next living brother was less than sixteen. But he had a powerful and ambitious rival in his uncle Dorgon, the fourteenth son of Nurhaci. Although he was of an older generation, he was three years younger than Haoge, but he had proved himself so successful a soldier that he had been entrusted with the command of one of the two armies invading China. But, although he and the princes of his generation saw that they would lose all influence if Haoge became emperor, Dorgon himself was reluctant to accept the throne and thus show disregard for clan precedence and disloyalty to Abahai, who had brought him up. Since many generals who had fought under Abahai were in favour of one of his sons succeeding, it was finally settled that the throne should go to the five-year-old Fu-lin, with Dorgon and Jirgalang acting as regents. In the following year, after Dorgon's army had entered Peking, Fu-lin was proclaimed emperor of China with the reign-title Shun-chih.

Soon after becoming regent Dorgon had struck a further blow at clan power by decreeing that the clan nobility should have no further control over the six ministries, and once established in China he accelerated the process of centralization and departure from the old clan traditions. Before the end of 1644 Jirgalang had already been reduced to the position of assistant regent, and for the first seven years of his young nephew's reign Dorgon exercised supreme power and laid the firm foundations of the dynasty. Within two years of entering Peking, his generals had succeeded in conquering the whole country apart from the south-western provinces, and a temporary revival of Ming fortunes in 1648 was soon crushed.

In domestic affairs Dorgon showed much political wisdom in attracting Ming officials to work for him and in confirming local functionaries in their posts, so that the transition to Manchu rule could take place as smoothly as possible. In many respects Ming institutions and practices were retained, but he took steps to remedy some of the worst abuses of the recent dynasty, by reducing taxation and by keeping the eunuchs firmly under control. He continued to build up his own power and dealt ruthlessly with any of the princes who ventured to stand in his way. Jirgalang was removed from his post in 1647 on charges of having usurped imperial privileges, and was sent off to put down a rebellion in the south-west. In 1648 the unfortunate Haoge returned from a successful mission to conquer and consolidate control of Shensi and Szechwan, but in less than a month he was seized and thrown into prison, where he committed suicide. Several other princes were harshly treated. Dorgon also took control of three banners, whereas the emperor only had charge of two, and at the same time he adopted the latest and grandest in a series of grand titles, that of Imperial Father Regent. Power seems to have gone to his head, for he ordered the King of Korea to send princesses to be his concubines and planned to build a great palace in Jehol, where he could give himself up to the pursuit of pleasure, doubtless appreciating that the days of his regency could not last for ever, now that the young emperor was growing up. But in fact he did not survive to enjoy his retirement, for he died at the end of 1650 while on a hunting trip, aged only thirty-eight.

The vacuum left by the death of Dorgon was rapidly filled by a group of those many princes and high officials whom he had antagonized during his supremacy. Dorgon himself was posthumously disgraced and several of his supporters put to death. The regency was formally abolished, and the young Shun-chih emperor himself ruled with the support of men such as Jirgalang, Wu Liang-fu, the leading eunuch of the time, and Oboi, who had been one of Dorgon's trusty lieutenants but had played a leading role in destroying the Dorgon faction. The Shun-chih emperor was a conscientious youth, and he studied hard to master the Chinese language so that he could deal with official papers. Despite his very busy official life, he found time to develop an interest in Chinese novels and drama. He was also of a religious disposition and during his teens he came under the influence of the Jesuit missionary, Adam Schall, whom Dorgon had appointed to head the Imperial Board of Astronomy, and who had rendered further useful service to the Manchu royal house by curing the young emperor's mother of a serious illness. Schall was frequently summoned to the palace to counsel his imperial master not only on ethical and religious matters but also on affairs of state, and the young man even took to calling him grandpa and visiting his church. But unhappily for the missionary effort Schall did not secure a conversion, and for the last few years of his short life the emperor turned increasingly to Buddhism. Persuaded that in a previous incarnation he had been a Buddhist monk, he associated much with clerics, and became profoundly interested in the Zen sect; and in grief at the death of his favourite consort in 1660, he tonsured his hair and was with difficulty dissuaded from entering the priesthood. But his own poor health did not permit him to survive for long. He is thought to have suffered from tuberculosis, and early the following year he contracted smallpox and died.

During the Shun-chih reign period, which occupied the first seventeen years of the Ch'ing Dynasty's rule over China, the government's most urgent tasks were, firstly, to wipe out the remnants of the Ming forces and secure control over the Chinese territories and, secondly, to integrate Manchu and Chinese society and avoid stirring up too much hostility among the Chinese people by their actions. The former task was not too difficult. When the news of the Ch'ung-cheng emperor's suicide reached Nanking, a dissipated character named Chu Yu-sung, who was a grandson of the Wan-li emperor, was installed as emperor there. Dorgon had been prepared to leave his court unmolested if he gave up all claim to the empire and accepted the status of a dependent kingdom, but although the offer was rejected, the Nanking court was so torn by internal dissension that in the following year it was possible for the Manchus to capture the city without meeting any resistance. Chu Yu-sung was taken to the capital, where he soon died. Others tried briefly to keep Ming hopes alive, including the Prince of T'ang who ruled for thirteen months at Foochow in Fukien, and his brother, who succeeded to his princely title, but survived only a month after establishing an imperial court at Canton. Another member of the imperial family, Chu Yu-lang, prince of Kuei, also a grandson of the Wan-li emperor, assumed the task of continuing the Ming court. He showed more spirited resistance, and after being hounded from place to place by the enemy, he succeeded in recovering a large part of south-west China, so that by the end of 1648 he was enjoying relative tranquillity, and even fostering some hope of a restoration of the Ming régime. But heavy attacks were made on him in 1650, which destroyed any hope of his building up a suffi-cient base for the re-conquest of the country. Nevertheless he was able to continue to hold some sort of court in the remote and mountainous country of Kweichow and Yünnan, until Ch'ing pressure finally forced him to take refuge in Burma. Three years later he was restored by the Burmese to the Ch'ing authorities and put to death together with his young son, and thus the dynasty was finally extinguished.

The main thorn in the Manchu flesh during this period was, however, the romantic character known to Europeans as Koxinga. His real name was Cheng Ch'eng-kung, and his father had been an adventurer and pirate based on Taiwan, preying on Dutch and Chinese trade. From this he graduated to a position of re-spectability, wealth and influence by giving himself up to the Ming authorities and taking part in defending the coast against pirates, a task at which he proved to be very proficient. Owing to his father's influence the young Cheng became a favourite at the short-lived Foochow court, and was even granted the imperial surname, for Koxinga is in fact a corruption of the Chinese words for 'Lord of the Imperial Surname'. After the downfall of this régime Koxinga continued to fight for the Ming cause and presented the Ch'ing forces with a great deal of trouble in the Fukien coastal area. By 1655 he had built up a strong military and civil organization, and was carrying out raids all along the coast from Kwangtung to Shantung and up the Yangtze River. In 1658 he was strong enough to capture a number of cities on the Chekiang coast, and in the following year he invaded Kiangsu and, after capturing Chinkiang, rashly fought a full-scale battle before Nanking, from which he retired with heavy losses. Back in his base at Amoy he was able to beat off a strong Ch'ing attack in 1660 and had still survived when the Shun-chih reign came to an end.

Unlike Koxinga, his father, who had earlier in his career made a very profitable change of sides by deserting piracy for employment under the Ming, soon saw the wisdom of going over to the Ch'ing. Clearly there were many others who soon decided that the Ming cause was hopeless and accepted the inevitable, so that the military problem facing the Manchus and the many Chinese who had been on their side since long before the conquest was not nearly so severe as that which had faced the Mongol invaders. Nevertheless the problem of social adjustment between the two peoples would not be easy to solve.

The Mongols had made use of many foreigners to run the country, but the Manchus, as has already been suggested, relied as much as possible on Chinese administrators. With their poor knowledge of the language and customs of the Chinese Manchus might stir up resentment if appointed to the chief civil offices in the provinces, so they had to be content with the major military posts instead. There were now eighteen provinces, as compared with thirteen under the Ming, and by this time the institution of provincial governor was fully fledged, and above them there were governors-general, who were normally in charge of two provinces. The overwhelming majority of governors and governors-general, both in this and the succeeding reign, were Chinese bannermen, while at a lower level it was the general rule, both in the six boards at the capital and in provincial posts, that a ratio of one Manchu to one Chinese was observed, so that the latter's expertise could be used but could be kept firmly in the right path. Very few non-banner Chinese could be entrusted with very senior posts in spite of Manchu attempts to win their support, and this meant that much distinguished Chinese talent was wasted and there was a great deal of frustration among the intellectuals. Typical of the patriots who refused to co-operate with the invaders was the distinguished philosopher and classical scholar Wang Fu-chih, who as a young man of twenty-four when Peking fell to the invaders abandoned all thought of advancement and gave himself up to private study for the next four years. Then he emerged briefly to form an army and throw in his lot with the Prince of Kuei, but in 1650, appreciating the hopelessness of the Ming military resistance, he withdrew to his native place and devoted himself to study for the next forty years, producing an enormous output in spite of the fact that he could hope for no recognition during his lifetime because his books could not be published under the Manchu régime.

The early Ch'ing period was, then, an exceptionally prosperous time for the Chinese bannermen, for they had the requisite knowledge of the Chinese language and institutions and had also proved their loyalty to the Manchus, so that they were more suitable for office than either the ordinary Chinese or the Manchus. The bannermen, Manchus and Mongols as well as Chinese, were feather-bedded by the state, for much of the best land in the Peking area was handed over to them in lavish allotments. Although the process started with the distribution of the large areas of land which had become ownerless because of the hostilities, great distress was eventually caused to the peasant families which were uprooted to make way for the Manchus, for the land they were given in compensation was generally inferior to what had been confiscated from them, and was often in very distant places, so that they suffered severe hardship through not having the wherewithal to make the journey. Even more upheaval was caused by the attempt to segregate Manchus and Chinese to avoid friction, which was another reason why many Chinese peasants had to move their homes. Similarly, continuous friction in Peking had caused Dorgon to order a massive movement of population in 1648, so that the main part of the city was henceforward occupied exclusively by bannermen, while the Chinese had to move outside the main walls to the south to live in what came to be called the Chinese city. Later the Manchus appreciated that, since they were less experienced in agriculture than the Chinese, it would be much more satisfactory to give some of the land back to the native peasants and give their own people rations and subsistence money instead.

It was not easy for the Manchus, with their totally different way of life, to become absorbed into the Chinese population. They exchanged a homeland of vast open spaces for an increasingly heavily populated country in which the best use had to be made of every available piece of cultivable land, and it was no longer possible for them to supplement their agriculture by hunting, as they did in their own country; for the future they must stifle their old instinct to make war for economic gain and turn to the responsible task of fighting for the pacification of a great empire; and they must also cope with a land in which economic conditions were more complicated and the money economy more advanced than in their own. They could only withstand the rude shock of this dramatic change by insulating themselves from the Chinese community, so they were forbidden to intermarry with the Chinese or adopt Chinese customs such as foot-binding. Indeed throughout the Ch'ing they were never to become completely absorbed, always remaining a privileged group of conquerors, retaining their military and feudal traditions.

Another source of friction was the breakdown of the old Manchu slavery system, which could not survive the transition from the small tribal state to the great empire, but which the Manchus were slow to relinquish although it was no longer an essential part of their way of life. Prisoners of war were now no longer enslaved, although they had formed the majority of slaves before the conquest of China; and it became much easier for Chinese slaves to desert once the Manchu conquering forces had passed within the Great Wall. The Manchus tried to make conditions easier by giving the slaves leave to visit their homes and by permitting members of their family to join them, in an attempt to cut down the rate of desertion. Harsh penalties were inflicted on those who did flee, and it is estimated that several thousands of Chinese families perished, for not only the fugitives but also those who harboured them were liable to the death penalty. Further distress was caused by the fact that fugitives from slavery often made themselves out to be famine victims, so that local authorities became reluctant to assist genuine refugees from natural disasters for fear of implicating themselves in charges of harbouring runaways. The Manchu government seems to have been slow to appreciate that, now there were plenty of Chinese tenants paying rent to Manchu landlords, slavery was no longer a necessity to them; but the harshness of the law did gradually begin to soften, and in 1649 the death penalty for harbourers was replaced by exile, and soon it was possible for relatives of fugitives to redeem them by paying a ransom. But although the harshness of the dynasty's first few years gave way to more enlightened policies, much cause for dissatisfaction survived because of the privileged status of the bannermen, who, being outside the control of the ordinary law, could indulge in oppressive practices with impunity and shelter any of their hangers-on who did likewise. Another apparently minor cause of stress which did lead to serious friction was the compulsion to braid the hair and shave the forehead in Manchu style, which was later to be regarded by Europeans as an essential Chinese characteristic. But in the long run the worst excesses of the bannermen were curbed by legislation, the status of slavery was gradually transformed into tenantry, the cultivation of the land came back into the hands of the Chinese, and the Manchus adapted themselves to Chinese culture, so that the two peoples began to live relatively peacefully with one another.

Nevertheless the Manchus preserved their banner organization as the chief sign of their separateness as a people. Moreover they did not merge their country into China, but instead kept it as a separate homeland, which would serve as a permanent power base and a reminder of their past, just as the emperors tried to preserve the glorious military traditions of their people. Separate ministries were maintained at the capital, Mukden, as branches of the new ministries which had been established in Peking, and these branch ministries were destined to remain in existence until 1907.

It is clear that in these early days of the dynasty much work was being done towards the economic rehabilitation of the country, which laid the foundations of the prosperity which was to be enjoyed in the eighteenth century. The government gave encouragement to the people by abolishing all the late Ming surtaxes and granting liberal tax exemptions to war-torn areas. The general expansion of inter-regional trade and increase in the growth of specialized crops, which had characterized the late Ming period, developed further under government encouragement once conditions had returned to normal. Industry too was put back on its feet: for example, the important textile factories at Soochow and Hangchow, which had fallen into utter decay in the last years of the Ming, were most energetically restored to efficiency by a Chinese official, given surprising freedom to use his own initiative; and such careful rehabilitation must have been going on in enterprises all over the country, often at the hands of Chinese who were willing to work for a foreign master, provided things went smoothly. New settlement was encouraged in places like Szechwan, which had suffered terribly from the depredations of Chang Hsien-chung. Under a national plan for granaries fixed in 1660 great care was taken to see that rice prices were stabilized.

In the 1650s foreign contacts showed that the Manchus were already firmly in the saddle. In 1652 the Dalai Lama travelled in person all the way from Tibet to Peking to acknowledge the suzerainty of the new dynasty, and in the following year the King of the Ryukyu Islands, which had first had official relations with the Chinese in 1372, began to pay tribute. Within a few years all the khans of Mongolia had vowed allegiance. Relations with European powers were also developing. The Portuguese, who had been established at Macao since the middle of the previous century, were allowed to continue to monopolize foreign trade there, and in 1653 they were granted direct access to Canton; while two years later a Dutch embassy came to Peking and secured for its country the privilege of trading in China once every eight years. For the first time, too, relations with Russia were developing. It was in the late sixteenth and early seventeenth centuries that the Russians, who had been under the Mongol yoke until 1480, crossed the Ural Mountains and moved in a relentless tide across Northern Asia, the motive force being the adventurousness of the Cossacks and the merchant enterprise of the age. By 1620 the Yenisei had been reached and a fur-trading centre established at Yeniseysk, and only twelve years later they were establishing a fortified post at Yakutsk, twelve hundred miles further east. At the time when the Manchus were moving into China the Russians reached the Amur River, a mere stone's throw of a few hundred miles from Mukden and Peking as compared with the many thousands of miles from Moscow. During the early years of the Ch'ing Dynasty the Manchus had their hands full and the Amur tribesmen had to suffer unaided at the hands of the Russians, who came down from the inhospitable Yakutsk area in search of food and tribute, but by 1652 the Manchus had got the situation in China sufficiently under control to send a force there, and this resulted in the first conflict between China and Russia. In 1657 it was considered necessary to establish a permanent frontier post to guard against the Russian menace, but by the end of the decade Chinese victories had compelled the Russians to abandon the Amur region completely, although they were later to return in greater strength when the Chinese relaxed their vigilance. At the same time the Russians had been attempting to establish diplomatic relations with the Chinese. The Baikoff mission of 1655 failed, ostensibly because of the difference between Russian and Chinese court etiquette and the Russians' refusal to perform the kowtow, but basically because the Russians were at the time behaving in hostile fashion in the Amur region, while the Manchus themselves were not secure enough in the south of China to afford to be at all conciliatory. In 1660, however, when the Russian threat had momentarily been removed from the Amur region, Russian envoys were received as tribute-bearers in Peking.

2

Before the death of the Shun-chih emperor at the tender age of twenty-two, his third son out of the fourteen children he had already begotten had been designated as his heir. This son, whose reign-title was K'ang-hsi, was destined to be one of the greatest and longest-lived of Chinese sovereigns. He was chosen to be emperor for the simple reason that he had survived an attack of smallpox and so was less likely to die young. Four Manchu nobles had been appointed regents, and their first act was to destroy the late emperor's will and produce another one in which he allegedly blamed himself for preferring Chinese to Manchu officials, for the extravagant funeral he had accorded his favourite consort, and for the restoration of eunuch-controlled offices; and it was not long before the late emperor's favourite eunuch, Wu Liang-fu, was executed. The most dominant figure among the regents was Oboi, who proceeded to get rid of his opponents in ruthless fashion. He also exacerbated the difficulties caused by the settling of bannermen on land near Peking by securing a geographical rearrangement of the banner lands, which seems to have been primarily aimed at securing the best for his own banner. The young emperor, then only thirteen, stepped in and took power into his own hands, but since Oboi still proved strong enough to secure the summary execution, against the imperial will, of one of his fellow-regents together with several members of his family, he had him arrested for insolence. Oboi died in prison shortly afterwards, and several members of his faction were put to death.

While still in his teens the young emperor had to deal with another very serious crisis in the south. Four leading Chinese generals who had fought for the Ch'ing in its battles to conquer the south of the country had by now worked themselves into positions of considerable independence. The most powerful was Wu San-kuei, who had helped smooth the Manchu path to power and had since consolidated his strength and prestige in campaigns to destroy the last remnants of the Ming. These had taken him to the furthest frontiers of the south-west, and beyond them into Burma where he had secured the surrender of Chu Yu-lang. These conquests, together with victories over local aboriginal tribes, gave him successive promotions and accretions of power until he was strong and independent enough to resist government attempts at disbanding his forces, to establish trade monopolies for himself, to increase taxes, to build palaces and even to usurp the right to appoint his own officials. Eventually he was virtually in control of Hunan, Szechwan, Shensi and Kansu, as well as of the south-western provinces of Kweichow and Yünnan. Kwangtung province had similarly been under the control of Shang K'o-hsi ever since 1660, while Keng Ching-chung was dictator in Fukien. In 1673, on reaching the age of seventy, Shang asked permission to retire. The emperor, despite contrary advice from his ministers, decided not only to grant permission, but also to make arrangements for Kwangtung to be fully restored to the jurisdiction of the central government. Seeing this as a danger signal, Wu and Keng both rebelled. Wu set up a new dynasty called Chou, and ordered the restoration of Ming customs and ceremonies. He informed the emperor of his intention of restoring the Ming régime and promised him Korea as a reward if he would agree to lead the Manchus back to their homelands. If Wu had advanced speedily he might have succeeded in his attempt, but although the north-western provinces declared their support, the Manchus had time to concentrate troops on the north bank of the Yangtze to halt his progress. Wu died at the end of 1678 and was succeeded by his son, and it was not until the end of 1681 that the rebellion was finally stamped out. The episode is known as the Rebellion of the Three Feudatories, after Wu, Keng, and the son of Shang K'o-hsi, who also took part in the rebellion although his father had remained loyal to the Manchus.

Two years after this rebellion had been crushed the Manchu pacification of South China may be regarded as complete with the conquest of Taiwan, nearly forty years after the Shun-chih emperor had been placed on the throne. For the past two decades the island had been in the hands of Koxinga's family, since Koxinga himself, conscious of the weakness of the Dutch position on the island, had decided to make his base there soon after his disastrous defeat at Nanking. He landed in 1661 with a force of nine hundred ships and 25,000 marines. The Dutch garrison withdrew to Castle Zeelandia and after a siege of nine months they were forced to capitulate and withdrew to Batavia. Koxinga established a régime, which was continued by his son Cheng Ching after his death in 1662. In the meantime the Ch'ing government had caused great distress by removing inland all the inhabitants from a large stretch of coastline, as a means of avoiding depredations from Taiwan and cutting off supplies. But for a time Cheng Ching was successful in maintaining proper trading links with other countries, so that the Fukien coast opposite Taiwan became peaceful and the local people gradually drifted back to their former homes.

In 1674, however, Cheng Ching had become involved in the Rebellion of the Three Feudatories, attracted by promises of reward made by Keng Ching-chung; but after much fighting in Fukien and Chekiang he was finally forced out of his last stronghold near Amoy and had to return to Taiwan, where he died in 1681. A son of his took control of the island, but in 1683, after extensive preparations and training, the government dispatched a force of three hundred warships and 20,000 crack troops, which soon succeeded in securing the surrender of Taiwan and the Pescadores. After this there was little further serious internal threat to the government during the K'ang-hsi era, although the only surviving son of the last legitimate Ming emperor was working under an assumed name as a teacher in Shantung, and small uprisings occurred as late as 1708 in support of his claim to the throne. Nevertheless the young emperor, now approaching thirty, could afford to turn his attention to other military problems.

On the northern frontier the Russians had infiltrated back into the Amur region during the period of the Oboi regency, and local tribespeople were again forced to pay them tribute, and the K'ang-hsi emperor was not in a strong position to do anything about a major invasion of the area which took place in 1669. The Russians at the same time continued to attempt to establish diplomatic relations and a mission to Peking proposed that the K'ang-hsi emperor accept Russian suzerainty. This not surprisingly failed, so a further embassy in 1676 was content with trying to establish that the Czar and the Emperor should be regarded as on an equal footing. As this was again totally foreign to Chinese ideas, this mission also was doomed to failure, especially as the Ch'ing government resented the hostile actions of the Russians on the border and would in the long run be in a strong position to deal with them.

Tension grew in the succeeding years as the Russians interfered with Chinese hunters and traders, harboured Chinese criminals, and weaned tributaries from their allegiance in spite of Chinese protests. So immediately after the rebellion of the Three Feudatories had been put down the K'ang-hsi emperor started large-scale preparations for war on the Amur. Much attention was paid to problems of communication and supply, and special transports were built for use on the Manchurian rivers. A canal was excavated to connect the Liao with the Sungari. After a last warning from the K'ang-hsi emperor, which the Russians ignored, the Ch'ing forces advanced, and by the end of 1683 all Russian settlements on the Lower Amur and its tributaries had been destroyed, and only the garrison at Fort Albazin remained. In 1685 and 1686 the Ch'ing forces laid siege to this stronghold, and in the latter year the Russians were in very sore straits when diplomatic approaches from their side persuaded the emperor to reach a peaceful settlement of the border dispute, and the siege was raised. Finally, in 1689 a meeting of representatives of both sides at Nerchinsk produced the treaty of that name, which was China's first equal treaty with a foreign state, and indeed the first treaty between China and a Western power. This was the first time a European nation had succeeded in getting the Chinese to make some attempt to fit in with European conceptions of international relations instead of sticking rigidly to their old attitude of regarding all other nations as tributary. For this much credit must go to the two Jesuit missionaries, Gerbillon and Pereira, who were attached to the mission as interpreters. They were much respected by the K'ang-hsi emperor, so they undoubtedly had an influential voice with the members of the delegation and were able to instruct them in the Law of Nations. The terms of the treaty included the destruction of Albazin and withdrawal of the garrison, and the careful demarcation of the frontier. While the Chinese were mainly concerned with fixing the frontier, and in this respect drove a good bargain because of the Russians' ignorance of the Far East and their basic military weakness there, the Russians were still primarily interested in trade. By means of the treaty and supplementary arrangements made later they secured satisfactory trading arrangements, and soon Russian caravans began to arrive in Peking at the rate of one a year.

A strong reason why the emperor chose the path of conciliation at this stage was that the north-west was seriously threatened by Galdan, khan of the Sungars, a tribe of the Western Mongols. His father had established his seat of power in the region of the Tarbagatai Mountains and Urumchi, and in 1678–9 he himself subjugated many of the Muslim peoples of Eastern Turkestan. Later he was able to take advantage of dissension among the Khalkas of Outer Mongolia, which the K'ang-hsi emperor had vainly tried to patch up in order that they might act as a strong buffer on his frontier, to sweep right across Outer Mongolia to the Kerulun River, causing thousands of Khalka refugees to pour across into Inner Mongolia, where the emperor had to relieve their distress. This had happened in 1688 and had been influential in causing the emperor to make peace with Russia, for he feared the possibility of a concerted move by the Russians and the Western Mongols, with whom they had long-standing trade and diplomatic relations. In 1690 a further advance by Galdan into the same region met with little resistance, so he turned south, apparently with Peking itself as his objective, but was halted by a force under the command of a half-brother of the emperor at the Ulan-butung hills near Chihfeng in Jehol, only two hundred miles from the capital. This engagement, although far from resulting in a decisive victory for the Ch'ing army, forced Galdan to retreat and stiffened the morale of the Khalkas, and in the following year the K'ang-hsi emperor went to Mongolia and received in person the homage of all their chiefs. For the rest of the dynasty the Khalkas never rebelled, and Outer Mongolia was secured for the Ch'ing. The next time Galdan invaded the Khalka territories, the emperor, determined to be rid of this menace, personally led a force of eighty thousand men which inflicted a decisive defeat upon him in 1696, so that he was left deserted by all but a handful of followers. In the following year Galdan committed suicide and the war was over. A large army was now established for defensive purposes near Kyakhta, which is the centre of the present northern frontier of Outer Mongolia, and the Buriats of the Yenisei region also accepted Chinese suzerainty.

The solution of his various military problems left the emperor free for more agreeable journeyings. He kept in close personal touch with the south by means of six grand tours undertaken at intervals between 1684 and 1707. He also made five western tours, but the southern ones are of greater interest and importance. In the Chinese records these expeditions are represented primarily as tours of inspection to visit river conservancy projects, while to the emperor's foreign admirers they were 'meet-the-people' tours, supreme manifestations of a benevolent sovereign's concern for the well-being of the poorest of his subjects. Certainly there was a huge turn-out of the populace wherever he went, but these were not voluntary exhibitions of enthusiasm, and indeed officials who lived within about fifteen miles of the route but failed to show their faces might be required to forfeit a whole year's salary.

Each tour had its special flavour. On the first occasion the emperor was cautiously sizing up the attitude of the central provinces towards the Manchu régime. He carefully avoided some of the former Ming-loyalist strongholds, and when he did go to Nanking he was most punctilious in his attention to local susceptibilities, and was careful to stay in the Manchu area and not venture into the city proper. As opportunity occurred he urged officials to deal benevolently with their people, made much of the diligence with which he was studying Chinese literature, and in all respects gave as conciliatory an impression as possible. The second tour was more informal and the retinue was much smaller, and more serious attention was paid to the business of inspecting river conservancy works; but by the third tour the emperor had gained the confidence to abandon his references to the Confucian Classics and the image of aesthetic sensibility which he had cultivated on the previous occasions, and appear more as a typical Manchu, even treating his audience at one place to a memorable exhibition of his skill in mounted archery. The fourth tour was less important since it was interrupted by the illness of the heir apparent. The final tours, in 1705 and 1707, were made entirely by water, but otherwise followed the precedents set on earlier occasions, with the emperor receiving officials and discussing the local situation with them, inspecting conservancy work, talking to local worthies, holding examinations, pardoning criminals, remitting taxes and submitting to popular requests that he increased the length of time in which he honoured the people by his presence. As he travelled on his leisurely way, visiting temples, holding archery contests or poetry meetings, admiring the scenery and attending banquets and operatic performances, temporary palaces would be prepared en route and eunuchs would go ahead to inspect the places where it was intended that the imperial retinue should stay. They would give instruction on the proper etiquette to those who were to receive the emperor, so that despite his efforts to prevent it, his progresses clearly did impose a burden on the communities through which he passed. But, as he travelled, he was able to by-pass the usual bureaucratic channels and take a close personal look at how the empire was being administered.

Another of the emperor's methods of playing his own highly personal part in affairs was his conversion of the Imperial Household into a kind of private bureaucracy responsible only to himself. The Shun-chih emperor had instituted a division between the upper three banners controlled by the emperor and the lower five banners controlled by the princes, and the descendants of men who had been made bondservants in the upper three banners became household servants of the emperor. As members of the Imperial Household, they were doing the kind of work that had been done by eunuchs in previous dynasties. Although most of them were occupied in clerical capacities or on maintenance duties or in any of the routine tasks of running a great establishment, and not many were employed in military guard duties, they were given military ranks and were subject to military law. Bond-servants were occasionally given posts in the provincial bureaucracy and some even had distinguished careers in this field, but the normal route to power and influence for such men was as textile commissioner or occupant of some other such important post which the emperor could manage to keep under his own control. Through the agency of such bondservant officials substantial sums of money flowed directly into the Imperial Household, and organizations like the great porcelain and textile factories, whose task was to supply the court with the finest quality table-ware and robes, were inseparably linked with the Imperial Household, which might better be termed the emperor's personal bureaucracy.

Despite their bondservant status such functionaries of the

Imperial Household could acquire considerable prestige and wealth through their appointment to these lucrative posts. One such person was Ts'ao Yin, the grandfather of the author of the most famous Chinese novel, *The Dream of the Red Chamber*, who enjoyed a long career in the emperor's confidence, being employed in turn as textile commissioner and salt censor. Both his father and grandfather had been favoured with similar appointments, so a considerable fortune had been built up by the family. Having had a good education, he mingled with scholars and literary men and wrote poetry, and because of the wealth amassed by his family, he was able to live in considerable style.

Having established his trusted bondservants in these lucrative and responsible posts in the provinces, it was also the K'ang-hsi emperor's policy to use them for other tasks not connected with their official duties, such as the stabilization of rice prices, the procuring of rare objects for the imperial palace, and the management of the purchase of copper for the imperial mints. More importantly, in the latter part of his reign he began to use them as confidential informants. It was impossible for secrecy to be observed by using the ordinary bureaucratic channels, so he developed a system of secret 'palace memorials', which went direct to him and were seen by him alone. The K'ang-hsi emperor's successor was to expand this practice into an important device of autocratic rule, but he himself only used it in an experimental and flexible way, and only employed people like Ts'ao Yin, in whom he had great trust. Now that the emperor was getting too old to undertake tiring southern tours, the information supplied by such people provided a valuable check on the regular bureaucracy, for he went so far as to discuss high provincial officials in the frankest possible terms with his bondservant informants.

The K'ang-hsi emperor's exchanges with Ts'ao Yin and others reveal that he was an extremely practical and conscientious emperor, who took a close personal interest in the welfare of his officials and paid a surprising amount of attention to matters of detail, such as monthly variations in the rice prices. He completed the elimination of the power of the imperial clan by excluding its members from all offices of importance. As to the ordinary

Chinese officials, he continued the policy of trying to attract the best talent, but the shortage of senior posts available was a disincentive to a political career, for many Chinese with the highest qualifications found themselves confined to junior posts. During his reign the pointlessly large quota of *chin-shih* ('Presented Scholar') degrees awarded earlier in the dynasty in order to attract the Chinese was realistically reduced, since there was no point in having the degree if there were no suitable jobs to follow. Another measure of far-reaching importance was introduced in 1702. Important cultural centres had produced consistently high numbers of *chin-shih* graduates, but some parts of the country often produced none at all. This situation had been partly remedied in the Ming Dynasty by the introduction of broad regional quotas, forty per cent of degrees being allotted to the North and sixty per cent to the South, but the 1702 plan went further by establishing a separate quota for each province, so that it became necessary to reach a much higher standard to pass in a culturally advanced province than in a place like Kansu. But adjustments of this kind could not hide the fact that it was much harder to make progress in an official career than it had been during the Ming Dynasty.

In order to provide another outlet for talent the emperor patronized various literary activities. In 1679 various distinguished scholars were invited to take a special examination, and successful candidates were employed in the compilation of the official history of the Ming Dynasty. Many other famous compilations were commissioned by him, including the *K'ang-hsi Dictionary*, which became the standard Chinese dictionary for more than two hundred years, a comprehensive collection of T'ang poetry containing nearly fifty thousand poems, and various important encyclopaedias and dictionaries. Other learned men served as his personal secretaries in the Imperial Study. He was also a great patron of the arts, and a studio and repair shop was established in the palace, where the painters, architects and mechanics who were in his service worked. These included some of the Catholic missionaries, who worked at painting, engraving, and the repair of clocks and other mechanical devices which had come from Europe as gifts for the emperor. The art of printing also attained a high level under his patronage, and porcelain of the very finest quality was manufactured during his reign. The emperor was extremely interested in scientific matters, which had come to his attention at the time when, still a boy, he had just got rid of the tyrannical regent, Oboi. At this time serious controversies had been raging over calendrical methods, for the great German Jesuit Schall, who had been entrusted with the directorship of the Imperial Board of Astronomy, was now dead, having finally lost favour after constant attacks from Chinese who were hostile to the missionaries and from disgruntled Muslims who regarded the control of the calendar as one of their perquisites. Suspecting that his own advisers were not in a very strong position to judge the merits of the rival systems of calculation, the emperor made a personal study of the problem. The Jesuits won his confidence in this matter and were restored to the control of the Astronomy board, which they held right through until the early nineteenth century. They were also required to instruct the emperor in Western sciences.

For most of his reign the missionaries succeeded in retaining the emperor's favour, and they were often used as interpreters or advisers on foreign affairs, as on the occasion of the treaty of Nerchinsk. A major undertaking which they persuaded the emperor to embark on and played the leading part in was a complete survey of the empire. But in religious matters it was not easy for the Jesuits to hold their position. We have seen how Schall's promising attempts to convert the emperor's father had petered out when the boy's interest had switched to Buddhism. Now, after a period in which Catholic missionaries had suffered some persecution in the provinces, the K'ang-hsi emperor was persuaded in 1692 to issue a decree legalizing and protecting missionary work throughout the empire. Later, when the missionaries cured him of malaria with the use of quinine, his favour increased and they were granted permission to erect a church within the Forbidden City. But in 1705 a Papal Legate came to Peking to forbid Chinese converts to practise ancestor worship and other traditional rites, which the Jesuits had not considered to be in conflict with the Christian religion. The K'ang-hsi emperor was naturally indignant and unwilling that his subjects should take orders from Rome, and thereafter his attitude towards the missions hardened. The Rites Controversy, as this episode was called, also increased the animosity between the Jesuits and members of rival orders who were jealous of their success and attributed it to an excessive tolerance of heathen practices.

It is clear that the K'ang-hsi emperor was more interested in the Jesuits' science than in their religion. He was, however, deeply concerned with the morality of the people and in 1670, soon after he began to rule independently, he issued the famous *Sacred Edict*, consisting of sixteen moral maxims designed to stress such virtues as filial piety, frugality and diligence, and to encourage the people to abide by the law, pay their taxes, venerate scholarship and disregard false doctrine. It was to gain a wide influence in the eighteenth century when it was issued in a colloquial version, and there were compulsory public readings of it twice a month. On the other hand, he did not neglect the martial traditions of his people, for he went on regular hunting trips, and was himself a very fine horseman and archer as well as a successful general. His reign of over sixty years showed that, although he was a foreigner, he possessed many of the qualities which went to make a successful emperor of China, and could provide suitable leadership in the political, military and cultural fields.

The last decades of his long reign, after the recovery of Taiwan, were a period of internal peace and growing prosperity rare in China's history. Once extra revenue was no longer needed to pay for the various military activities of the early part of the reign it was possible to cut taxes, and the population, which had dropped appallingly as a result of the late Ming catastrophes, began to recover and grow at an increasing rate. Contemporary descriptions of conditions in China during the first two decades of the eighteenth century testify to a remarkable improvement in the standard of living among the peasants, derived both from the internal peace of the country, improvements in agricultural techniques and further spread of the new crops introduced during the Ming period. The frontiers were quiet except for further troubles with the Western Mongols after 1715. They were to be a nuisance on and off for the next forty years, and in 1717 they conquered Tibet, but the Ch'ing government forces succeeded in recovering that country in 1720 and retained suzerainty over it for the future.

The commander-in-chief of the Ch'ing forces in this theatre was Yin-t'i, the fourteenth son of the emperor, who seemed most likely to inherit the throne, although the ageing sovereign would not accede to his advisers' requests that he designate an heir. He had had twenty sons and eight daughters who had reached maturity, but only one of these, his second son Yin-jeng, had been born of an empress; and he had been designated as heir while still a baby. He had been appointed regent to look after affairs in Peking in 1696 and 1697 when the emperor went off on his distant campaigns against the Western Mongols, but on his return it was reported to him that his heir had been mixing with undesirable characters and indulging in immoral practices. After this Yin-jeng gradually fell into disfavour and eventually he was deprived of his position and put into confinement. In the meantime factions had been forming in support of the claims of various other sons of the emperor, but despite this poisoning of the political atmosphere he firmly refused to designate another heir, and dealt extremely harshly with officials who urged him to do so, thinking that they were attempting to push their own candidates. The last years of the reign were consequently marred by this indecisiveness. But the honours accorded to Yin-t'i on his departure for the western front in 1719 inclined people to anticipate that he would be the emperor's choice, especially if he could bring this important military campaign to a triumphant conclusion.

Unfortunately for Yin-t'i, he was at the front when the K'ang-hsi emperor died late in 1722. The prince who was in the strongest position to profit from the situation was Yin-chen, the emperor's fourth son, who was a full brother of Yin-t'i and ten years his senior, and so would have been in a very exposed position if he had not acted to safeguard his own interests. His principal asset was the support of Lungkodo, who was both a cousin and a brother-in-law of the dying emperor, and even more importantly, was general commandant of the Peking gendarmerie. The emperor died at a garden palace four miles west of Peking, and official accounts say that Lungkodo and several princes were at bedside to hear that he wished Yin-chen to succeed him; but there is much evidence to support unofficial stories that the succession was contrived by Lungkodo, who was able to preserve calm in Peking with the aid of his gendarmerie while Yin-chen escorted his father's remains back to the capital, attended by an escort of soldiers with drawn swords; and none of the other princes was in any position to dispute the succession. Some accounts assert that Yin-chen murdered his father.

3

The reign of Yin-chen, the Yung-chen emperor, was marred by the aftermath of the bitter struggle between rival claimants to the throne. The new emperor could not feel secure while the other contenders remained as a threat to his position, especially when there was a suspicion that he had usurped the succession. The people's doubts were so serious that in 1730 he seized the opportunity presented by the trial of a rebel to proclaim that he had not murdered his father, his pronouncement being printed and distributed throughout the empire. The rival contenders for the throne suffered severely : they soon found themselves under the surveillance of reliable friends of the emperor, and eventually false charges and degradation would be their lot. Two of the sovereign's brothers died miserably in prison in the year 1726, and thus he avoided the scandal of having condemned his own brothers to death. Yin-t'i was more fortunate, for he survived to be released by the next emperor and restored to his princely honours. Some of the Yung-cheng emperor's supporters suffered as severely as his rivals. Even Lungkodo, although heaped with honours in the first years of the new reign, fell from favour in 1725 and died three years later after being condemned to life imprisonment on numerous charges. Yet another brother, who had been associated with several Chinese scholars in the editing of the *Synthesis of Books and Illustrations of Ancient and Modern Times*, a very important encyclopaedic work in many volumes, died in prison in 1732. In order to deprive an opponent of any share in the glory of taking part in this monumental project the

Yung-cheng emperor confiscated the manuscripts as soon as he came to the throne, and when the work was finally published, it contained no mention of his brother's name. He also suppressed many official records dating from the previous reign which showed him in an unfavourable light or reflected credit on his brothers, with the result that little is known about some important events, such as Yin-t'i's Tibetan campaign. Not surprisingly the editor of the official account of the K'ang-hsi period received the accolade of having his name celebrated in the Imperial Ancestral Hall, the only civil official to share this honour with several generals who had helped to found the dynasty.

Other brothers who seemed to pose less of a threat were showered with honours and employed by the emperor, but it was his general policy to cut down the power of the princes, particularly by depriving them of the control of the bannermen who were allotted to them as retainers. To ensure that imperial princes would in future be subservient to the throne he had the young ones attend a special school within the palace where they were submitted to a course of instruction by tutors who could be trusted to instil the virtues of obedience and loyalty; and this policy, helpful to the stability of the dynasty, was the one good thing to emerge from the bitter factionalism which had clouded the end of a great reign and spoilt the Yung-cheng era, which otherwise saw considerable progress.

To combat factionalism, which he felt had been the ruin of the Ming, the emperor wrote an uncompromisingly authoritarian essay on the subject, commencing with the words 'Just as Heaven is exalted and Earth is low, so are the roles of prince and minister fixed', and going on to speak of the minister 'sharing his prince's likes and dislikes'. He attacked Ou-yang Hsiu's famous essay on factions (written over 600 years before!), and even went so far as to hold himself up as an example of one who, before he ascended the throne, did not form factions. That was why his father had chosen him as his successor! The emperor regarded his essay as of fundamental ideological importance and he had it distributed to all schools throughout the empire, together with copies of his father's *Sacred Edict* with his own comments attached. It had to be read aloud twice a month, a practice which was destined to continue for several generations.

There is no doubt that firm and able rule was necessary after the lax final years of the previous reign, when some corruption and deterioration of standards had crept into the administration. The Yung-cheng emperor did supply this need. In his latter years his father had been inclined to take a lax attitude towards peculation among officials who had served him well, but the Yung-cheng emperor took a very stern view of dishonesty. Because he knew that much corruption was due to the inadequacy of official salaries he introduced a system of extra stipends as rewards for incorruptibility. His rescripts show his extreme diligence and deep knowledge of administrative matters, and he was very wise in his appointments, so that in the view of one authority, 'through close surveillance of officialdom he achieved a level of administrative honesty and efficiency unsurpassed by any other Manchu ruler'. He introduced financial reforms which benefited the country greatly, and among the ordinary people the general prosperity continued. A great blessing was that, unlike formerly, the people no longer had to do military service or compulsory labour, since workers were hired by the authorities for public construction projects.

But the price of efficiency was an increase in autocracy. One manifestation of this trend was the development of the palace memorial system, which the Yung-cheng emperor turned into a very efficient network of secret communication. Many quite junior officials were granted permission to send palace memorials containing reports on their colleagues, and those who were permitted to send palace memorials but failed to do so were reprimanded.

Another important change came in 1729 with the establishment of the Grand Council, which was to become the most important organ of government. The occasion of its creation was an attempt to inject more speed, efficiency and confidentiality into coping with problems raised by military operations then taking place in Shensi and Kansu. Thus the Grand Council started as an emergency body, with a borrowed staff and a poorly equipped office; but when the military emergency passed it was kept on because it had developed a role in government which was most useful to a strong emperor who liked to keep things in his own hands. Now it was no longer necessary for him to discuss important issues with a large body of officials outside the palace, but instead he could thrash matters out with a small group of five or six men, whom he could appoint or dismiss at will. Depending on the imperial pleasure for their tenure of office, their terms ranged from less than a year to more than thirty-eight years. During the eighteenth century the Manchus were in a majority on this body, but in the Yung-cheng era no princes were allowed to become members, although they did later. The function of the Grand Secretariat was now reduced to dealing with ordinary routine memorials, while the Grand Council handled those of special importance. The Grand Councillors were summoned to audience with the emperor at least once a day, and had to attend the palace at a very early hour to await his summons. They also accompanied him on all his trips away from the capital.

The creation of this body had very far-reaching effects both on the central and on the provincial governments. In the first place it took over responsibility for all major matters which had previously been under the jurisdiction of the various boards, so that the Board of Civil Office no longer had anything to do with the appointment of the most important officials, and the Board of War was no longer concerned with the formulation of military policies, but dealt only with routine business; and the Grand Council was also expected to deal with some important matters which were really within the purview of the other government departments. In fact it served at one and the same time as an inner cabinet for dealing with the business of civil government, a general staff for dealing with military matters, and a secretariat for the purpose of drafting and dispatching some of the more important imperial edicts. Thus the emperor was able to achieve a very considerable measure of personal control over the government. Outside the capital, too, the emperor's hand was strengthened, not only because he received secret information through the medium of the palace memorials, but also because, with the assistance of the Grand Council, he made it his business to deal with important civil and military matters in the provinces, to review provincial budgets, and to keep a check on the records of high-ranking provisional officials. It also became the practice for Grand Councillors to be sent out to trouble spots in the provinces and to make on-the-spot decisions to rectify the situation.

The military campaigns which had prompted the organization of the Grand Council were against the Western Mongols. The death of their ruler, who was a nephew of Galdan, had been taken by the emperor as an opportune moment for mounting a new assault upon them, since they were still a threat to the Khalka territories, which they had raided so devastatingly in Galdan's time. But a rash advance by the commanding general of the Ch'ing forces led to his falling into a trap and losing four-fifths of his men, so that the raids on Khalka territory were immediately resumed. Fortunately the Western Mongols also overstretched themselves, and suffered a crushing defeat in the following year. In 1734 peace negotiations began in an attempt to reach a boundary settlement, but by the end of the Yung-cheng period they still had not succeeded.

The Yung cheng emperor's military achievements did not match his political ones. The other major campaign of the era was an attempt to break the hold of the hereditary chieftains over the south-western aborigines in order to bring them properly into the provincial administrative system. As governor-general of Yünnan and Kweichow, O-erh-t'ai pursued this policy energetically for a period of six years, confiscating where possible the land belonging to the hereditary chieftains and thus greatly extending the taxable lands of the state and helping to improve the provincial finances. But it was a rather ruthless policy, not in keeping with previous Chinese practice, and further rebellions broke out after O-erh-t'ai left. But for the most part the country continued to prosper. The population was now growing rapidly and people were living longer, so that in 1726 there were nearly a million-and-a-half people over the age of seventy. The growth in population could still be comfortably absorbed, as people were urged by the government to grow new crops, and there was much movement to areas where there was virgin land still to be exploited.

Before he came to the throne the Yung-chen emperor had become thoroughly acquainted with Chinese literature and had also developed an interest in Buddhism, which he continued to pursue after his accession. He transformed the palace in Peking in which he had lived as a prince into a lama temple, and as such it is one of the sights of present-day Peking; but his main interest was in Zen Buddhism, and during his last years he ran a study group on this sect, and was also responsible for some publications on the subject. There are many stories about the manner of his death, some saying that his health suffered from doses of Taoist longevity drugs, and others that he was murdered by a relative of someone he had executed, but the official accounts say that he died peacefully. Despite his ruthlessness he had been an able ruler and had been responsible for many reforms which contributed to the greatness of the succeeding era.

The Yung-cheng emperor had not openly designated an heir, for his way of coping with the problem which had bedevilled his father's reign was to place the name of his chosen successor in a box which was to be opened only at his death. This was to set a precedent which future emperors adopted. The emperor thus chosen was the late monarch's fourth son, a young man of twenty-five, who bore the reign-title of Ch'ien-lung. As a boy he is said to have deeply impressed his grandfather, but it is inevitable that legend should link these two great monarchs, and the story that the K'ang-hsi emperor left the throne to the Yung-cheng emperor in order that his favourite grandson might eventually succeed is too far-fetched, especially in view of the dubious means whereby Yung-cheng succeeded to the throne.

The Yung-cheng emperor's favourite officials were O-erh-t'ai and Chang T'ing-yü, who was one of the founder members of the Grand Council and was to retain membership of it until his retirement. Before he died the emperor had ordered these two together with two princes to assist his successor in the conduct of affairs, and for the early years of the Ch'ien-lung emperor's reign they had a very considerable influence on policy. Although the rivalry between these two men and their factions grew and was a cause of some dissension, on the whole it was a quiet and prosperous period, and it was only after the death of O-erh-t'ai in 1745 and the retirement of Chang in 1749 that the Ch'ien-lung emperor really began to dominate the government and make his mark on Chinese history.

The middle period of his reign may be regarded as the high-water mark of the traditional Chinese state, with the country more prosperous, its administration more stable, its level of culture higher and its frontiers more secure than they had ever been before. Inspired by the example of his grandfather, the Ch'ien-lung emperor was a very conscientious sovereign who lived a frugal life and devoted long hours to the intensely demanding routine of autocratic government. At the same time, like his grandfather, he appreciated the importance of appearing not only as the administrative head of the country but also as its cultural leader : only thus could he, a foreigner, commend himself to the Chinese intellectuals as fit to preside over the universal culture which had its seat in the Middle Kingdom. But not only was he a patron of scholarship and literary endeavour : he also painted and wrote verse, and was credited with an enormous poetic output.

During this middle period of his reign he also emulated his grandfather in making a series of six southern tours. Despite his own personal frugality, these imperial progresses seem to have caused considerable economic dislocation, since local officials vied with each other to show loyalty to the emperor by making the most elaborate preparations to receive the imperial retinue, and temporary palaces had to be constructed, food supplies diverted, and the embankments of the Grand Canal repaired so that they would stand the weight of the vast crowds thronging to watch the progress of the royal barges. The cost of receiving the emperor and his entourage was also ruinous for those private individuals upon whom the duty of entertainment fell, but fortunately wealth made through commerce was no longer considered socially inferior, and the emperor stayed at the residences of several salt-merchants during his journeys. Their wealth was so enormous that they were used to expending it on conspicuous consumption of the most frivolous kinds and could even survive the cost of a royal visit.

But although these grand progresses apparently did have some inflationary effect and there was also heavy military expenditure at about this time, the general prosperity of the country continued to grow, and there was an enormous increase both in population and in the area of land under cultivation. This happened because there was much peasant migration into the more mountainous country of southern China, resulting in the land being deforested and turned over to new crops, such as maize and sweet potatoes, the cultivation of which was encouraged by the government. The principal area affected was the whole of the vast stretches of hilly and mountainous terrain which comprised the drainages of the Yangtze and Han Rivers. Much of this land had been covered with virgin forest until about 1700, and even so central an area of China as south-western Hupei was at this time still under the administration of tribal chieftains. The large-scale immigration of Chinese peasants into territory which had formerly been inhabited sparsely by aboriginal peoples not only produced an enormous revolution in land-utilization, but also sparked off outbreaks of rebellion among the dispossessed tribes-people, particularly the Miao who lived in western Hunan. These rebellions, which broke out periodically in the latter half of the eighteenth century, were ruthlessly suppressed by government forces. Unfortunately the boom in agricultural production was only a short-term one, since the migrant farmers had no attachment to their new land and were merely concerned to exploit it and get the maximum return from it. Not being used to hill-farming, they ignored the dangers of soil erosion, so that after a few successful years the topsoil would all be washed away by the heavy rains. Soil erosion became a serious problem in the latter part of the eighteenth century, not only because large areas of land had been rendered infertile and had to be abandoned, but also because waterways in the low-lying land tended to silt up with the displaced soil and cause serious inundations. The long-term effect of this spread of the Chinese farmers into the uplands was therefore disastrous because of their lack of technique in dealing with these new agricultural problems. But at the same time the lowland farmers were continuing to develop their tradtional skills, and much quicker-maturing strains of rice, taking as little as forty days, were developed during the eighteenth century. In the middle of the century the country still flourished. The great cities of the Yangtze area became centres of luxurious and extravagant living, and the population of China more than doubled in less than a hundred years to reach over three hundred millions by the end of the eighteenth century. This huge increase would result in a sharp decline in living standards at the beginning of the nineteenth century.

From the military point of view the Ch'ien-lung era was very successful, particularly in the far west. The continuing menace of the Western Mongols was wiped out in the 1750s, and the Ili River region, which had been the centre of Sungar power, was occupied from 1757. Shortly afterwards firm Ch'ing control was established over the Tarim basin right up to the Pamir mountains. Chinese suzerainty over this area, which had only previously existed during relatively brief periods of military greatness, was to survive for a whole century after this. During the same decade a protectorate was firmly established over Tibet, which was to become virtually an integral part of the Chinese empire after 1792, when an expedition, sent there to expel a force of Gurkha invaders from Nepal, won remarkable victories over these warlike people in this very unfamiliar and distant territory. During this reign Ch'ing armies were also on active service in Taiwan, Burma and Annam, and were busy crushing rebels in Szechwan; and the emperor made much of his martial exploits, although the Central Asian campaigns were the only ones which had much long-term importance. All these military activities imposed a heavy burden on the treasury, but the economy was so buoyant that they were easily borne.

As patron of scholarship the Ch'ien-lung emperor commissioned the most ambitious of all collections of Chinese literature, entitled the *Complete Library of the Four Treasuries* (referring to classics, philosophy, history and belles lettres, the four branches into which the Chinese traditionally classified their writings). This contained over 36,000 volumes, and many thousands of copyists were employed in producing the seven manuscript sets that were made. The practice of assembling rare books and manuscripts and saving them for posterity in this way was an honourable tradition, but unfortunately the Ch'ien-lung emperor, in addition to having a genuine interest in the preservation of Chinese literature, was also concerned to ensure that works which he thought inimical to dynastic interests should not survive. Indeed the same officials who were required to select texts for this project were also expected to report to the throne any items which merited censorship. A special Bureau of Book Censorship was soon established, and several different criteria were consulted in order to determine whether or not a book was fit to exist. If it contained material which was anti-Ch'ing or seditious or was insulting to previous non-Chinese dynasties, or gave an anti-Manchu account of the Sino–Manchu conflict preceding the establishment of the dynasty, it should be destroyed; and works on frontiers and defence were also carefully scrutinized for dangerous material. The works of certain authors who were out of favour with the emperor were completely obliterated, and heterodox opinion on the Confucian Classics was also liable to destruction. Books could even be condemned merely for being unliterary. About 2300 works were totally suppressed, so the literary inquisition proved to be an enormous loss to scholarship. The authors and their families were treated with the brutality which was characteristic of the Chinese law. Nevertheless at the same time the Ch'ien-lung emperor was giving employment to scholars by commissioning massive encyclopaedic works, notably on a variety of subjects relating to government. He was indeed resolved to dominate and control literature, for this he would have regarded as a legitimate concern of an autocratic ruler whose duty was not only to govern but also to give moral guidance to his subjects.

The literary inquisition did not start until the emperor had been on the throne for thirty-six years, and if there had been a retiring age of sixty for emperors to compensate for the arduous nature of their duties, the Ch'ien-lung era would have been outstandingly successful. But when he ascended the throne the emperor had prayed that he would live long enough to enjoy a reign of almost equal duration to that of his grandfather, a tall order from one who was already twenty-five when he succeeded. However, his wish was granted and it was necessary for him to abdicate so as not to exceed the sixty-year length of the K'ang-hsi era, although such deference did not prevent him from continuing to exercise supreme power behind the scenes until his death in 1799. Unfortunately the literary inquisition was not the only blot on the last decades of his reign. For the last twenty-four years of his life he came under the influence of an unprincipled courtier named Ho-shen. Handsome, clever and self-possessed, he made a meteoric rise in the emperor's favour, and while still in his twenties he was honoured by being allowed to ride a horse in the Forbidden City, a privilege normally only granted to senior statesmen who were too infirm to walk. In the same year he was also given the vital position of general commandant of the Peking gendarmerie. Two years later he consummated his relationship with the throne by securing the betrothal of his nine-year-old son to the emperor's youngest daughter. He amassed innumerable offices, at one time concurrently holding as many as twenty, and by the age of thirty-six he was already a Grand Secretary and controlled the two most important ministries, the boards of Revenue and Civil Office. As he grew older, the Ch'ien-lung emperor, who was very anxious to believe in his greatness as a sovereign, became increasingly resentful of criticism. Hence it was possible for Ho-shen to pack the bureaucracy with his henchmen; and the more he did so, the more impregnable his position became, for criticism of Ho-shen and any members of his faction could only be interpreted as criticism of the emperor for having placed so much faith in his favourite. Before long all kinds of corruption began to clog the machinery of empire, affecting not only the civil government, but also the army, whose campaigns were now prolonged so that the increased funds appropriated for military purposes could be used to line the generals' pockets. So at last, when all the other major hazards which confronted Chinese emperors, such as giving excessive power to imperial princes, ambitious frontier generals, empresses and eunuchs, had been avoided, and when successful campaigns had made the frontier safer than at almost any time in Chinese history, the Ch'ien-lung emperor proved vulnerable in the Achilles' heel of his own vanity, which proved an easy target for Ho-shen's flatteries.

It was not until after his sovereign's death that Ho-shen was arrested and permitted to take his own life, and the enormous wealth he had acquired at the state's expense was at last confiscated. His success may be traced ultimately to the Manchu emperors' suspicion of factionalism. They had always posed as reformers of the decadent Chinese state, which they maintained had been ruined by the factional struggles of the last decades of the Ming period. The Yung-cheng emperor had been especially sensitive about factions and had attacked them in an important essay. In the early years of the Ch'ien-lung era factions had begun to form round the elder statesmen, and this had made the emperor discontented at not being his own master, to whom all subjects addressed their loyalty as individuals without forming coteries. Ironically the only way for an ageing emperor to ensure the continuance of autocracy and stop a fresh growth of factionalism was to rely on one young and vigorous adviser.

The military corruption quickly resulted in the demoralization of the banner forces, so that in 1795, when a rebellion of the White Lotus sect broke out in the Han River area, the very place where soil erosion was bringing diminishing agricultural returns and consequent poverty, the banner armies were unable to suppress it until it had lasted for eight whole years. Here was the real point of no return in the fortunes of this proud military people. By this time the Manchus, although they struggled to maintain their separate identity, found themselves submerged in a sea of Chinese culture, as the Mongols had done before. At first they had attempted to make the Ch'ing régime bilingual, but this effort was doomed to failure since the Manchus quickly learnt Chinese, and it soon became unnecessary for the state to encourage Chinese civil servants to learn Manchu. Although the formality of producing government documents in both languages and having inscriptions on coins in Manchu as well as Chinese continued throughout the dynasty, at the local government level Chinese had been the sole language in use all the time. A severe blow to the possibility of developing a Manchu literature was struck when the Ch'ien-lung emperor banned translations of Chinese novels and plays, so that in future these could only be read by Manchus in the original Chinese. Towards the end of his life the eighteenth-century poet, Yüan Mei, who had been required to take a course in Manchu as a young man and became friendly with some of the most cultivated Manchus of his day, went so far as to say that 'nowadays the Manchus are much more cultivated than the Chinese. Even their military men all write poetry.'

Nevertheless there was no question at this time of the Manchu dynasty being removed from power. Right from the start the Ch'ing régime had been a collaboration between Manchus, Chinese and Mongols; and by mastering Chinese culture and methods of government the Manchus themselves had become legitimate contenders for the rule of what was not simply a one nation state, but the centre of civilization. The apparatus of government was spread thinly on the surface, and it mattered little in the villages and small towns up and down the country whether the icing consisted of Chinese or Manchus, for the mixture inside the cake was very much the same as it always had been. Although there was some frustration among Chinese intellectuals, and much suffering under the literary inquisition, a great number of the literati were absorbed into the administration at the lower levels and perhaps ninety per cent of civil servants were now Chinese, while much opportunity for scholarly work was provided by the government. A change of dynasty could only have been brought about through massive peasant revolt, but order was carefully maintained in the villages by means of the same type of family mutual responsibility groupings as existed during earlier dynasties. Designed to ensure public order and morality and mutual assistance in the local communities, they at the same time constituted a powerful means of state control with the minimum of obvious interference from above. There was also little danger of a military coup, since the banner armies were garrisoned in small groups of about four thousand men up and down the country, and the remnant of the Ming forces had been turned into a kind of gendarmerie to maintain local order and suppress bandits. Command was carefully divided, with every precaution being taken to ensure that no individual could build up independent military power.

Thus the Manchus had proved themselves to be excellent inheritors of the traditional civilization and in no sense a force for innovation or revolution in Chinese society. The old patterns continued very much as before, with a huge mass of peasantry being exploited by the landlords, whose families were largely the source from which the administrators were chosen by the familiar process of examination in the now rigid curriculum of the Confucian Classics. As a result of these contests there was an élite of privileged degree-holders, many of whom were employed either in government or in education, but all of whom had such prestige that academic success was the goal of all who could afford to study (except for those who still refused to take part under this alien régime). Within this system there was scope for a family to go from rags to riches in a short time as a result of scholarly success and to revert to rags again almost as quickly, since there was no effective means of hanging on to privilege, and wealth could rapidly diminish when split up between sons and squandered in extravagant living. In fact a regular cycle of fortune (reminiscent of dynastic cycles) can be discerned in the histories of successful clans: the virtue of frugality would provide opportunities for study, which would lead to examination success and then to office, but the wealth brought by office would lead to a decline from Confucian morality and a love of luxury and display which would bring a rapid decline in the clan's fortunes. By this time, of course, the classical social categories of scholar, peasant, artisan and merchant had lost all vestige of validity, and men would plough or engage in trade while they studied, and the aim of wealthy merchant families would be to attain the prestige of scholarly success. By rewarding the socially ambitious in this way the civil service examination system clearly helped to ensure the stability of traditional Chinese society.

In the field of scholarship the Ch'ing Dynasty saw no revolutionary trend, for most of the effort went into working over and evaluating centuries of tradition. The most notable achievements were those of the School of Han Learning, which sought to approach the wisdom of the ancient classics more closely by discarding the work of the Sung Neo-Confucianists and resorting to the commentaries of the Han Dynasty scholars. This school made great advances in scholarly method and the use of evidence, so that important discoveries were made in philology and textual criticism and genuine progress was possible in dealing with problems of the authenticity of ancient texts. Their work developed a kind of scientific method as applied to literary studies.

There was unfortunately no comparable development of scientific method in the fields of natural science and technology, such as was enabling Europe to leap ahead of this ancient civilization which had long been its superior. At the same time conditions in Chinese society militated against the growth of capitalism, which was another cause of European advance. The salt merchants, in particular, made immense fortunes, but social pressures were all hostile to the retention and accumulation of capital. Their business was more in the nature of tax-farming than of capitalistic enterprises of a European type, and opportunities of investing their money in other enterprises were limited. In any case it was only by spending their fortunes on libraries, art collections and other things prized by the scholars that they could hope to become members of the true élite. Moreover the merchant's wealth was extremely insecure, not only because natural disasters happened frequently in China, but also because he was always likely to be milked by the government, so there was more incentive to spend rather than accumulate than there is in modern Western societies.

At the end of the eighteenth century China appeared to be entering into another phase of dynastic decline, following earlier patterns, and to contain within itself no radical impetus towards the development of an entirely new form of society. The country's contribution to the history of human society had been enormous. The Chinese had succeeded in developing a political system which for long periods had brought relative peace to a large proportion of the world's population. This was no small achievement even by contemporary standards, and an incomparable accomplishment in a vast country covered by relatively primitive communications; and although the methods used had often been harsh and autocratic by the standards of the most civilized states of our own times, even as early as the eleventh century they had worked out remarkably sophisticated procedures for the selection and promotion of officials, of a kind not paralleled in the rest of the world until modern times. In the field of science and technology they had made many discoveries at a very early period and had presented the rest of the world with such valuable gifts as paper and printing, the magnetic compass and many other devices and techniques which did not appear in Europe until after a delay of many centuries. They had also proved to be the most superb craftsmen that the world has ever known, showing their genius in remote antiquity with the magnificent bronze sacrificial vessels of the Shang period, and later with the development of fine porcelain more than a thousand years before the secret of its manufacture was discovered in Europe. Throughout this millennium their factories had continued to turn out wares of supreme beauty which were the envy of the world, from the delicate monochromes of the Sung to the Ming blue and white and the more ornate and colourful wares of the Ch'ing period, which were exported to Europe and set off a craze for chinoiserie. Jade-carving was another supreme expression of Chinese craftsmanship, whose origins dated back to neolithic times. This beautiful stone was so hard that it required infinite patience and skill and a variety of specialized techniques to work the material, but objects of a miraculous delicacy and apparent fragility which belied the years of hard work put into their manufacture have been achieved. In the fine arts they had shown themselves to be a people of unusual sensitivity: their very writing, done with the brush, had much in common with painting, so that calligraphy was esteemed as the purest and noblest of arts; and their paintings are regarded as not the least worthy products of their genius, although it was long before their different techniques and conceptions were appreciated in the West, especially since they placed refinement within a tradition above the originality which Europeans prize so highly. Chinese literature also boasted incomparable achievements: in a work of this kind no attempt can be made to convey the unique quality of Chinese poetry, but from the little which has been said in this volume it can be appreciated that no other people cultivated the art of historical writing in so sophisticated a way at such an early stage of their history as the Chinese. And finally the Chinese ideal man, who combined aesthetic sensitivity with practical wisdom, the scholar-official, who conscientiously practised his role as 'father and mother' of the people under his charge and in his spare time wrote poetry, painted, collected antiques and enjoyed his jar of wine, an ideal which even in this imperfect world was sometimes translated into reality, was no bad model of the civilized man.

This is not to say that the problem of securing contentment and an adequate livelihood for the vast mass of ordinary people was ever solved for long. Barbarian invasions and natural disasters would have prevented this, even if the Chinese had succeeded, where the most sophisticated modern states fail, in implementing a system for running the economy based on just taxation and optimum use of the natural resources in this vast country. Certainly by the end of the eighteenth century the Ch'ing had no new contribution to make to the betterment of the lot of the ordinary people of China, which the great increase in population and the corruption of the last years of the Ch'ien-lung era had already sent into rapid decline. It would take the impact of the West to bring any change in this now rather stagnant civilization.

The Western impact was to come principally from the desire to expand trade rather than from missionary endeavour, for the Catholic Church in China, which had suffered a severe blow because of the Rites Controversy, went into decline during the Ch'ien-lung era, especially after the dissolution of the Society of Jesus in 1773. Commerce, on the other hand, had increased briskly, and the British had gradually become the dominant European traders in the ports of South China. However in 1757 the Ch'ien-lung emperor had decreed that all foreign trade, except Russian, should be restricted to the single port of Canton. Soon a corporation of nine merchants, which came to be known as the Co-hong, was established to monopolize trade with the European powers; and it was to protest against these restrictions and get better trading facilities that an embassy was sent out to China under Lord Macartney. It arrived in August 1793 and was granted two audiences by the Manchu sovereign at his summer palace in Jehol, the second taking place on his eighty-third birthday. Much pomp and ceremony attended the embassy's reception, but Macartney achieved nothing. The emperor issued an edict thanking the King for his 'tribute presents', but rejecting the British requests in the flowery and condescending language which was appropriate when the Son of Heaven addressed the ruler of a small tributary power. For his own part Macartney stoutly refused to kowtow before the emperor, and his opinion of the country's prospects was that

China was an old, crazy, first-rate man-of-war, which a fortunate succession of able and vigilant officers has contrived to keep afloat for these one hundred and fifty years past, and to overawe their neighbours merely by her bulk and appearance, but whenever an insufficient man happens to have the command upon deck, adieu to the discipline and safety of the ship. She may perhaps not sink outright; she may drift some time as a wreck, and will then be dashed to pieces on the shore; but she can never be rebuilt on the old bottom.

The story of the shipwreck of imperial China must be left to the third and final volume of this trilogy, and we must abandon this ancient civilization under the sovereignty of an aged monarch whose self-delusion about his own qualities as emperor and about the status of his own country gives warning of the great shock to its self-esteem that China will suffer during the nineteenth century, the reaction from which is still being felt in our own times.

Chronological table

The dates of emperors are given in the index. For the periods when there are different régimes in the north and south of the country, the northern régimes are given to the left of the page and the southern régimes to the right.

SHANG ?1523–?1027

CHOU ?1027–256

CH'IN 221–206
(*having annihilated CHOU in 256 and other rival states afterwards*)

FORMER HAN 206 BC–AD 9

HSIN AD 9–23

LATER HAN 25–220

THREE KINGDOMS

WEI 220–265   SHU 221–263   WU 222–280

WESTERN CHIN 265–316

SIXTEEN KINGDOMS 304–439   EASTERN CHIN 317–420

NORTHERN WEI 386–581   LIU SUNG 420–479

| WESTERN WEI 537–557 | EASTERN WEI 534–550 | SOUTHERN CH'I 479–502 |
| NORTHERN CHOU 557–581 | NORTHERN CH'I 550–577 | LIANG 502–557 / CH'EN 557–589 |

SUI 581–618
T'ANG 618–907

FIVE DYNASTIES 906–960	TEN KINGDOMS 907–979
(LIANG 907–923	(WU 902–937
LATER T'ANG 923–936	SOUTHERN T'ANG 937–975
LATER CHIN 936–947	SOUTHERN P'ING 907–963
LATER HAN 947–951	SOUTHERN HAN 907–971
LATER CHOU 952–960)	EARLIER SHU 907–925
	LATER SHU 934–965
NORTHERN HAN 951–979	WU-YUEH 907–978
(*reckoned as one of the Ten Kingdoms*)	MIN 909–944
	CH'U 927–951)

SUNG 960–1126
(*the extreme north of China being ruled by the* LIAO 947–1125)

CHIN 1126–1234
SOUTHERN SUNG 1127–1279

YUAN 1279–1368
(*having succeeded the* CHIN *in North China in* 1234)

MING 1368–1644
CH'ING 1644–1912

Maps

1 Map of China showing places mentioned in this book. The boundary is that of the People's Republic of China.

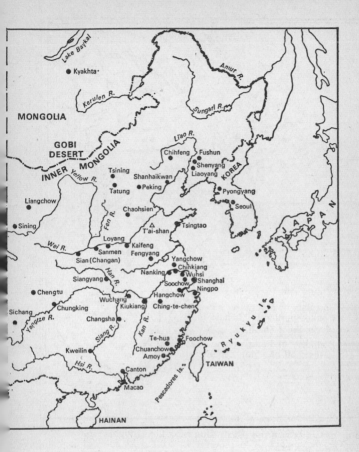

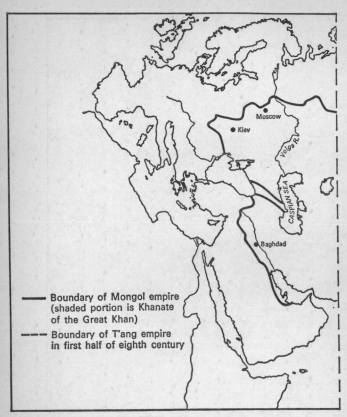

Boundary of Mongol empire
(shaded portion is Khanate
of the Great Khan)

Boundary of T'ang empire
in first half of eighth century

2 Map of Asia and Europe illustrating extent of Mongol empire at end of thirteenth century.

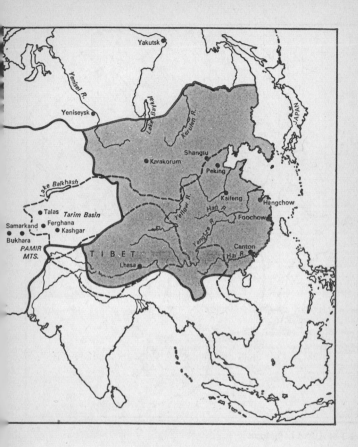

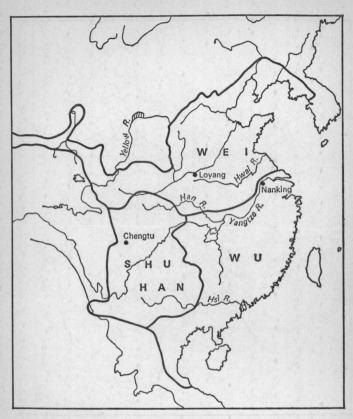

3 The Three Kingdoms.

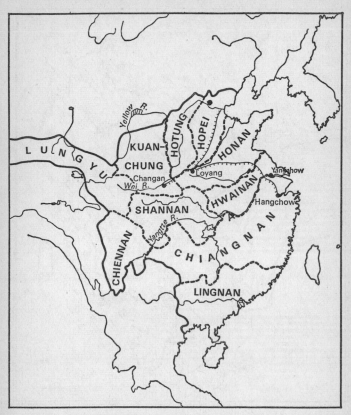

4 *Administrative divisions* [circuits] *at the end of the seventh century.*

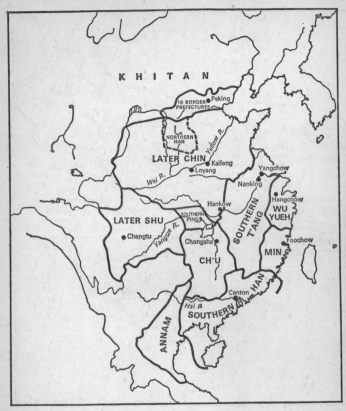

5 *China during the period of the Five Dynasties and Ten Kingdoms.
This is the situation in the time of the later Chin Dynasty (937–46),
except that Northern Han did not exist until 950.*

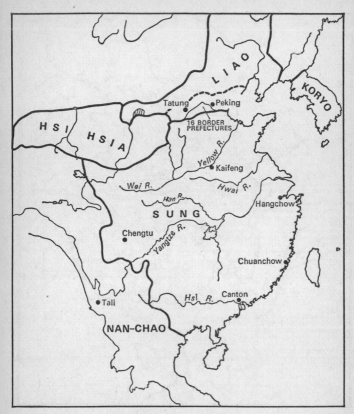

6 *China in the middle of the eleventh century.*

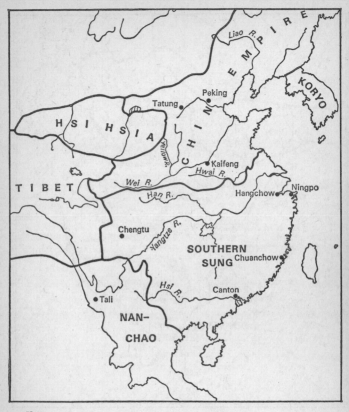

7 *China early in the Southern Sung period.*

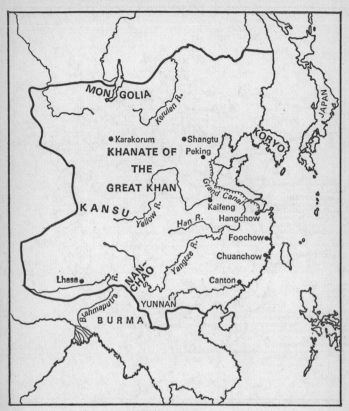

8 China under the Mongols.

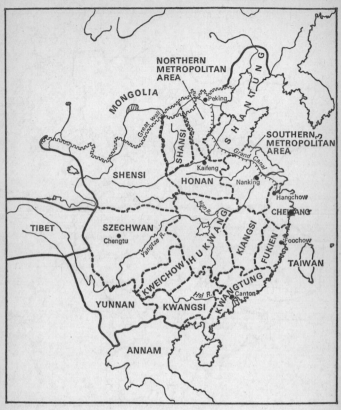

9 *China under the Ming.*

10 China in the eighteenth century.

Index

365

More about Penguins and Pelicans

Penguinews, which appears every month, contains details of all the new books issued by Penguins as they are published. From time to time it is supplemented by *Penguins in Print*, which is our complete list of almost 5,000 titles.

A specimen copy of *Penguinews* will be sent to you free on request. Please write to Dept EP, Penguin Books Ltd, Harmondsworth, Middlesex, for your copy.

In the U.S.A.: For a complete list of books available from Penguins in the United States write to Dept CS, Penguin Books, 625 Madison Avenue, New York, New York 10022.

In Canada: For a complete list of books available from Penguins in Canada write to Penguin Books Canada Ltd, 41 Steelcase Road West, Markham, Ontario.

Some Books on China published in Penguins

China's Long Revolution

Edgar Snow

Edgar Snow knew Mao Tse-tung, Chou En-lai and the other Chinese leaders in the 'days of bitterness' and the Long March, a time which he described in *Red Star over China*.

In *China's Long Revolution* the story is brought up to date. The author describes the arcane lore of 'Chinese medicine', the intricacies of the Cultural Revolution, life on the Communes and in the May Seventh schools of political reorientation. Most interesting of all, he describes conversations with Mao Tse-tung and Chou En-lai which throw new light on the recent rapprochement between China and the United States.

'A unique and invaluable glimpse of the men who run the world's most populous nation' – U.S. Senator George McGovern

'No-one can understand today's China unless he has read and studied Ed Snow' – Harrison Salisbury

800,000,000: The Real China

Ross Terrill

In 1971, as the Nixon ping-pong diplomatic initiatives got under way, Ross Terrill, journalist, scholar and author of *Flowers on an Iron Tree*, returned to China after seven years' absence. Fluent in Chinese, he was able to get behind the official hand-outs and speak to the people face-to-face. At the same time he took part in high-level discussions with Chinese officials, including Chou En-lai.

The result is a fascinating account of China as it is today, which encompasses both the principles of her foreign policy, and the realities which have to be faced by the ordinary people of China.

'Perception is the greatest quality of the book. Mr Terrill managed to notice and find out things that so often get missed.' – *The Times Literary Supplement a Peregrine Book*

Emperor of China

Jonathan Spence

This book is a portrait of a remarkable emperor, K'ang-hsi, whose reign from 1661 until 1722 was one of the longest in Chinese history. It was a time when the Manchu dynasty was at its height, when contact with the West had not been soured. Throughout his reign, K'ang-hsi was possessed of an insatiable curiosity, inquiring into classic Chinese literature, medicine, astronomy, disputing with the Jesuits and speculating on the problems of government. Gathering material from an immense variety of sources, Jonathan Spence has penetrated the ritual facade of imperial life, weaving together K'ang-hsi's own words to reveal the personality of this splendid emperor through his thoughts on hunting, religion, government, growing old, and on the tragedy of his son, Yin-jen, whose immorality and bitter feuding led to his father's ruin.

'Dr Spence obliges us to share his interest in a man who questioned everything, thought for himself and wrote freshly' – Hugh Porteus in the *Observer*